The Afterlives of Georges Perec

Rowan Wilken:
For Karen, who understands

Justin Clemens:
To my family

The Afterlives of Georges Perec

Edited by Rowan Wilken and Justin Clemens

EDINBURGH
University Press

Edinburgh University Press is one of the leading university presses in the UK. We publish academic books and journals in our selected subject areas across the humanities and social sciences, combining cutting-edge scholarship with high editorial and production values to produce academic works of lasting importance. For more information visit our website: edinburghuniversitypress.com

© editorial matter and organisation Rowan Wilken and Justin Clemens, 2017, 2018
© the chapters their several authors, 2017, 2018

Edinburgh University Press Ltd
The Tun – Holyrood Road, 12(2f) Jackson's Entry, Edinburgh EH8 8PJ

First published in hardback by Edinburgh University Press 2017

Typeset in Monotype Ehrhardt by
Servis Filmsetting Ltd, Stockport, Cheshire,
and printed and bound in Great Britain by
CPI Group (UK) Ltd, Croydon CR0 4YY

A CIP record for this book is available from the British Library

ISBN 978 1 4744 0124 1 (hardback)
ISBN 978 1 4744 3741 7 (paperback)
ISBN 978 1 4744 0125 8 (webready PDF)
ISBN 978 1 4744 0489 1 (epub)

The right of Rowan Wilken and Justin Clemens to be identified as the editors of this work has been asserted in accordance with the Copyright, Designs and Patents Act 1988, and the Copyright and Related Rights Regulations 2003 (SI No. 2498).

Contents

List of Figures   vii
Acknowledgements   ix
Notes on Contributors   xi

1. Posthumous News: The Afterlives of Georges Perec   1
   Justin Clemens and Rowan Wilken

PART I: Art of the (Un)realisable

2. Georges Perec's Enduring Presence in the Visual Arts   23
   Mireille Ribière

3. Apoetic Life: Perec, Poetry, Pneumatology   45
   Justin Clemens

4. UnSearching for Rue Simon-Crubellier: Perec Out-of-Sync   69
   Darren Tofts

5. Invoking the Oracle: Perec, Algorithms and Conceptual Writing   85
   Mark Wolff

PART II: The Poetics of the Quotidian and Urban Space

6. Georges Perec and the Significance of the Insignificant   105
   Ben Highmore

7 What Perec Was Looking For: Notes on Automation, the Everyday and Ethical Writing   120
Caroline Bassett

8 'Things That Should Be Short': Perec, Sei Shōnagon, Twitter and the Uses of Banality   136
Anthony McCosker and Rowan Wilken

PART III: Ludic Intensities and Creative Constraints

9 Perec and the Politics of Constraint   157
Alison James

10 The Architecture of Constraint and Forgetting   171
Sandra Kaji-O'Grady

11 Georges Perec: A Player's Manual   189
Thomas Apperley

PART IV: Productive Problems of Description and Transcription

12 'An Attempt at Exhausting an Augmented Place in Paris': Georges Perec, Observer-Writer of Urban Life, as a Mobile Locative Media User   205
Christian Licoppe

13 The Quick Brown Fox Jumps Over the Lazy Dog: Perec, Description and the Scene of Everyday Computer Use   225
Rowan Wilken

Afterword

14 The Afterlives of a Writer   245
David Bellos

Index   257

List of Figures

2.1 Daniel de Paula, *Pieces and Other Species of Spaces* (extract). Courtesy of the artist. 33
2.2 Christl Lidl, *La Polygraphie du cavalier*, a performance given at Galerie du CROUS (10–12 rue de l'Abbaye, 75006 Paris) on 13 December 2014, with Christl Lidl as The Performer and Maxime Mikolajczak as The Narrator. (Photograph: M. Ribière.) 34
4.1 Introduction card of M. Gaspard Winckler. (Source: Georges Perec, *Life A User's Manual*, London: Harvill, p. 54.) 70
4.2 Mike Leggett filming *UNWORD 4*, Swansea University, Wales, 30 January, 1970. (Source: *UNWORD*, © Ian Breakwell Estate and Mike Leggett, 1970, http://legart.drupalgardens.com/projects/unword-ian-breakwell.) 80
10.1 Student Lluis Alexandre Casanovas Blanco's work from Enrique Walker's Spring 2012 Advanced Architecture Studio IV The Dictionary of Received Ideas, at the GSAPP. (Source: Enrique Walker; reproduced with permission.) 179
10.2 Students Emanuel Admassu, Lluis Alexandre Casanovas Blanco, Idan Naor and Eduardo Rega Calvo's work from Enrique Walker's Spring 2012 Advanced Architecture Studio IV The Dictionary of Received Ideas, at the GSAPP. (Source: Enrique Walker; reproduced with permission.) 180
10.3 Students Laura Buck, Myung Shin Kim, Alejandro Stein and Rui Wang's work from Enrique Walker's Spring 2014 Advanced Architecture Studio IV The Dictionary of Received Ideas, at the GSAPP. (Source: Enrique Walker; reproduced with permission.) 181

viii LIST OF FIGURES

12.1 (*left*) and 12.2 (*right*)   These figures are scans from parts of the list of places which became visible on screen in 2013 when one connected to Foursquare from the same cafe terrace used by Perec. The places in Figure 12.1 are in the top part of the list and those in Figure 12.2 appear after some amount of scrolling down. Of note are the locations in nearby streets in both figures, and the highly indexical-relational formulation '*soeur*' ('sister') in Figure 12.2. (Source: © Christian Licoppe.)   210

12.3 One 'mayor' of 'Place Saint-Sulpice' at the time of our study, as she appeared when we clicked first on this 'place' on the Foursquare list, and then on the 'mayor' active link. (Source: © Christian Licoppe.)   213

12.4 A typical screen which would appear after checking in in Place Saint-Sulpice. (Source: © Christian Licoppe.)   218

12.5 Clicking on the icon of one of the users present 'here' unveils further personal information. (Source: © Christian Licoppe.)   218

13.1 Diagram illustrating the use of 'critical path analysis' and which depicts 'a schedule chart and critical path for the example sentence for a 60-gwpm typist with an initial motor operator estimate of 230 msec'. (Source: Bonnie E. John [1996], 'TYPIST: A Theory of Performance in Skilled Typing', *Human–Computer Interaction*, no. 11, p. 331.)   231

13.2 Diagram illustrating 'assumed movement of the left, middle, and index fingers when striking keys on a QWERTY keyboard'. (Source: Bonnie E. John [1996], 'TYPIST: A Theory of Performance in Skilled Typing', *Human–Computer Interaction*, no. 11, p. 348.)   231

Acknowledgements

Edited collections are, by definition, a collaborative enterprise, and many people contribute to their successful completion. We would like to thank Julian Thomas, and, at Swinburne University of Technology, Anthony McCosker, Esther Milne, Darren Tofts, Grace Lee and Teresa Calabria for their intellectual input, assistance and support. Rowan would also like to thank Suneel Jethani for crucial research assistance early on in this project. At the University of Melbourne, we would like to thank Professors Rachel Fensham and Ken Gelder for their support. Justin would also like to thank Ali Alizadeh, A. J. Bartlett, Christian Gelder, Joseph Hughes and Claire Smith for their intellectual advice, encouragement and help with references. Justin's contribution to this volume has been made possible by an Australian Research Council Grant.

A very special mention and debt of gratitude goes to Emily van der Nagel for all her hard work, done with such efficiency and good humor, in helping pull this collection together.

Justin and I are especially grateful to Pierre Getzler for giving us permission to use his wonderful photograph of his friend Georges Perec at Rue Vilin as the cover image for this book.

We also wish to express our gratitude to Carol Macdonald at Edinburgh University Press for supporting and helping realise this collection. And, of course, to all the excellent contributors to this collection for their interest and faith in this project, their willingness to contribute their work, and for the patience and good humor with which they have responded to our requests, promptings and questions, often within very tight timeframes.

Finally, closer to home, Rowan would like to thank Karen, Lazarus, Maxim and Sunday, for their love, support and encouragement. And Justin would like to thank Helen and Una for theirs.

Rowan Wilken, RMIT University
Justin Clemens, The University of Melbourne
January 2017

Notes on Contributors

Tom Apperley, PhD, is a researcher of digital media technologies. His previous writing has covered digital games, mobile phones, digital literacies and pedagogies, and the digital divide. Tom is currently a Senior Lecturer at UNSW, Australia. He is the editor of the peer-reviewed journal, *Digital Culture and Education*, his book *Gaming Rhythms: Play and Counterplay from the Situated to the Global* was published by the Institute of Network Cultures in September 2010.

Caroline Bassett is Reader in Digital Media and Director of the Centre for Material Digital Culture at the University of Sussex. She has written about Perec in a series of pieces considering the phenomenology of everyday life, memory and digital culture. She researches digital transformation and cultural form and critical theories of new media, and has published widely on new media and narrative, the social imaginary, questions of gender and technology, and the digital humanities. Recent work includes projects exploring science fiction and innovation design and on cultural transformations and (digital) expertise.

David Bellos is Professor of French and Comparative Literature at Princeton, where he also directs the Program in Translation and Intercultural Communication. He is the translator of many of Georges Perec's works, notably *Life A User's Manual*, and the author of the principal biography of the writer, *Georges Perec. A Life in Words* (1993), which was awarded the Goncourt Prize for Biography in its French translation. His most recent book, *Is That a Fish in Your Ear? The Amazing Adventure of Translation* (2011) was shortlisted for the LA Times Book Prize and the National Book Critics Circle Award. He recently completed an English translation of Georges Perec's earliest known novel, *Le Condottière*, which he discovered.

Justin Clemens is Associate Professor in English and Theatre Studies at the University of Melbourne. He is the author of many books, most recently *Lacan Deleuze Badiou* (2014), with A. J. Bartlett and Jon Roffe, and *Psychoanalysis Is an Antiphilosophy* (2013). He is also co-editor of *The Jacqueline Rose Reader* (2011), *The Work of Giorgio Agamben: Law, Literature and Life* (2008), co-translator of Alain Badiou's *Infinite Thought* (2003) and co-editor of a number of collections on Badiou. He is currently an ARC Future Fellow, working on contemporary Australian poetry.

Ben Highmore is Reader in Media and Cultural Studies at the University of Sussex. His research is broadly concerned with the culture of everyday life: investigating what is extraordinary in ordinary life (for instance habit) and in looking at the ordinariness of what might be thought of as extraordinary or exotic or esoteric or elite. His particular interests at the moment congregate around cultural feelings, domestic life and postwar British art, craft and architecture (specifically the cultural movement New Brutalism). His most recent books are *A Passion for Cultural Studies* (2009), the edited collection *The Design Culture Reader* (2009) and *Ordinary Lives: Studies in the Everyday* (2010).

Alison James is Associate Professor of French at the University of Chicago, where she teaches twentieth- and twenty-first-century French literature. Her research focuses on postwar experimental writing, the Oulipo group, representations of everyday life and the connections between literature and philosophy. She is the author of *Constraining Chance: Georges Perec and the Oulipo* (Northwestern University Press, 2009), which demonstrates that Perec uses formal and semantic constraints both as a spur to literary inspiration and as a means of exploring the tension between chance and determinism, fate and human agency. She has also edited a special issue of *L'Esprit créateur* on 'Forms of Formalism' (Summer 2008), and has published articles on Oulipo writers (Jacques Roubaud, Harry Mathews), on the American reception of Oulipo, on the contemporary French novel and on philosophical approaches to literature (Clément Rosset, Jacques Rancière).

Sandra Kaji-O'Grady is Professor of Architecture and Head of School at the University of Queensland where she teaches design, history and theory. She has held academic positions at the University of Melbourne and Deakin University. Sandra's research is in the transfer of techniques and knowledge from other disciplines, such as art, music and medicine, to architecture. Her particular focus is on the 1960s and 1970s. Sandra writes regularly for professional journals. Additionally, Sandra has investigated seriality, colour and coding through her own work, exhibited in Sydney and Singapore. Sandra's partner, John de Manincor, is a director of DRAW architects and they juggle their mutual architectural obsessions with two children, Marita and Xavier.

Christian Licoppe trained in history and sociology of science and technology. He is Professor of Sociology and currently the head of the Social Science department at Telecom Paristech, after a stretch in industrial research where he managed social science research at Orange R&D. Among other things he has worked in the field of mobility and communication studies for several years. He has used mobile geolocation and communication data to analyse mobility and sociability patterns of mobile phone users. He has studied various phenomena related to the proliferation of mediated communication events and 'connected presence'. He has also studied extensively one of the first location-aware communities (the Mogi players in Japan 2003–8) and the rich configurations of augmented encounters its evolving culture supports. He is also interested from a social and juridical perspective in the way systems based on Bluetooth recognition of proximate mobile terminals may provide serendipitous opportunities for spurious and enriched encounters. He has also developed ethnographic approaches to complex activity systems relying on innovative use of communication technologies at the intersection of the sociology of work, organisation studies and the anthropology of activity, such as call centres (in the telecommunications and banking sectors) or the introduction of videoconferencing in French courtrooms.

Anthony McCosker is a Senior Lecturer in Media and Communication and is Media Course Coordinator at Swinburne University of Technology, Melbourne. His research explores media affect and intensity, new media technologies, digital and visual cultures, digital health and social media platforms, publics and practices. He is author of the book *Intensive Media: Aversive Affect and Visual Culture* (2013), along with numerous book chapters and journal articles, and is co-editor of the edited collection *Rethinking Digital Citizenship* (2016).

Mireille Ribière gained her PhD on Georges Perec (Birkbeck College, London) in 1985 and since then has published extensively in the fields of Perec studies, French literature and the visual arts. She is the author of *Barthes* (2002, 2010) and co-author of *Les Poèmes hétérogrammatiques de Georges Perec* with Bernard Magné (1992). She edited *Parcours Perec* (1990) and *Perec – Aujourd'hui* (2002), and co-edited Georges Perec, *Entretiens et conférences* (2 vols, 2003), *De Perec etc., derechef* (2005), *Georges Perec: inventivité, postérité* (2006) and Georges Perec, *En dialogue avec l'époque* (2011). She also edited a special issue of *History of Photography* on 'Photonarrative' (1995) and co-edited *Time, Narrative and the Fixed Image* (2001). Her first book of photographs *Columbus Day* was exhibited in the US as a winning entry to Photobook 2013, and her artist's book *Catching the Light* was shortlisted for Kaleid 2015. She works and lives in the UK.

Darren Tofts is Professor of Media and Communications, Swinburne University of Technology. His publications include *Memory Trade. A Prehistory of Cyberculture* (with artist Murray McKeich, 1998); *Parallax. Essays on Art, Culture and Technology* (1999); *Prefiguring Cyberculture: An Intellectual History* (edited with Annemarie Jonson and Alessio Cavallaro, 2003); *Interzone: Media Arts in Australia* (2005); and *Illogic of Sense: The Gregory L. Ulmer Remix* (edited with Lisa Gye, 2007).

Rowan Wilken is Principal Research Fellow at RMIT University. He is the author of *Cultural Economies of Locative Media* (Oxford University Press, forthcoming) and *Teletechnologies, Place, and Community* (Routledge, 2011), and is co-editor (with Gerard Goggin and Heather Horst) of *Location Technologies in International Context* (Routledge, forthcoming) and (with Gerard Goggin) of *Locative Media* (Routledge, 2015) and *Mobile Technology and Place* (Routledge, 2012).

Mark Wolff is Associate Professor of French at Hartwick College in Oneonta, New York, USA. His research interests include the Oulipo, computer code studies in the humanities, canon formation and the nineteenth-century French novel.

CHAPTER I

Posthumous News: The Afterlives of Georges Perec

Justin Clemens and Rowan Wilken

Georges Perec's writings not only provide a rare pleasure, they can also sometimes offer an even rarer gift: a sort of light, yet tenacious fever from which the only means of recovery – is to take up a pen.[1]

The fetters [Perec] selected, then, were never senseless, never were perverted pretence. These fetters were seeds.[2]

Georges Perec is today considered one of the most significant twentieth-century writers worldwide. He is perhaps best known for his first novel *Les Choses* (*Things*),[3] which won the Renaudot prize in France, his monumental *La Vie mode d'emploi* (*Life A User's Manual*),[4] as well as for his involvement in the Oulipo group. In addition to these achievements, over the course of his writing career Perec produced, in Alison James's words, 'a body of work that is astonishing in its breadth and originality',[5] including the release of a new book nearly every year. Perec's stated ambition was to 'write every kind of thing that it is possible for a man to write',[6] from acrostics and palindromes to crosswords and revealing parodies of academic journal articles. The sheer polymathy of Perec's own literary output, not to mention the richness and insight of many of his non-fiction essays, have provided scholars, writers and artists with a veritable toolbox of ideas for adaptation and wider application. It is precisely this situation – the posthumous re-uptake of Perec's work in an astonishing range of disciplines and contexts – that this collection examines, and which provides its titular orientation as *afterlives*, at once posthumous, multiple and contemporary. The contributions to this volume thus show Perec's ongoing impact upon the fields of architecture, art history and art practice, cultural studies, new media, games studies, poetry and more. If such a collection necessarily runs a certain risk of hagiography – its very focus upon a celebrated individual producer perhaps entailing inadvertent prejudicial affirmations – such a risk seems to us worth taking. This is not least because, as several of the contributors here are at pains to point out, a focus on Perec's difference also enables certain new takes on the present that might otherwise go unmade.

This introduction sets the scene with a brief account of Perec's life and extraordinary literary output, before developing the argument that Perec was, in key respects, ahead of his time, and that many of his literary experiments were prescient in the way that they speak to and shed significant light on a range of contemporary issues and debates. These include his explorations in computational logic, his construction of archival systems and his embrace of collage techniques. Yet we will also interrogate such terms as 'prescience', 'adaptation' and 'application' here, for any familiar, general terms we might like to deploy regarding the nature of *afterlives* are themselves put under pressure by the peculiar nature of our current era, as well as by Perec himself, who precisely foregrounded the insuperable contemporary difficulties of *life-* and *thing-*management, as well as some of the unintended consequences upon life itself of such abstract managerial systems. These consequences are implicated with epistemological and temporal paradoxes. As we shall shortly see, aspects of Perec's contemporaneity are due to his being out-of-step, even backwards, blind or behind, with respect to his times and our own.

PEREC'S LIFE

The facts of Perec's life are by now well established.[7] Georges Perec, the only child of Jewish immigrants from Poland, was born in Paris on 7 March 1936 and died of cancer on 3 March 1982 at the age of 45. Perec's father, Icek Judko Perec, died in 1940 of wounds received while defending France against German invasion. During the German occupation, Perec was evacuated by the Red Cross to Villard-de-Lans, where his aunt and uncle (his father's sister, Esther Bienenfeld, and her husband) cared for him. His mother, Cyrla Szulewicz Perec, remained in Paris, where she was arrested and deported and killed at Auschwitz in 1943.

Perec was educated at day schools in Paris, and as a boarder at Collège d'Etampes, south of Paris, where he met sociology professor, Jean Duvignaud, 'who became a lifelong mentor and friend'.[8] Paul Schwartz notes that, after receiving his *baccalauréat* in 1954, Perec spent six years (interrupted by military service as a parachutist between 1958 and 1959) writing, 'attending courses at the Sorbonne' and supporting himself with occasional work.[9] During this period, Perec completed two book manuscripts, *L'Attentat de Sarajevo* and

Le Condottière, the first unpublished, the second published posthumously in English as *Portrait of a Man*.[10]

Following a shorter than anticipated stay in Sfax, Tunisia (cut short due to the Algerian War and rising Arab–French tensions), Perec returned to Paris and took up a lowly paid position in 1961 as an archivist-librarian (a *documentaliste*) at a neurophysiology research unit, CNRS Laboratoire Associé 38, or LA 38 for short.[11] Perec was to retain this job for a further seventeen years, finally giving it away following the success of *Life*. As Schwartz notes, he 'also published weekly crossword puzzles in *Le Point* and *Télérama*, which supplemented his income'.[12]

In 1965, Perec achieved his literary breakthrough with the publication of *Things*, a book which 'propelled Perec onto the French literary scene' and gained him worldwide recognition.[13] Perec's propensity for formal experimentation was evident very early on, with his first three published novels – *Les Choses* (*Things*), *Quel petit vélo* (*Which Moped . . . ?*)[14] and *Un Homme qui dort* (*A Man Asleep*)[15] – all markedly different in style and subject.[16]

In 1967, Perec's friend Jacques Roubaud introduced him to the *Ouvroir de Littérature Potentielle* (Oulipo), a group interested in exploring the possibilities of formal constraint- or rule-based writing, and which was founded in 1960 by the writer Raymond Queneau and the mathematician François Le Lionnais. Perec was to become their shining light, publishing a significant body of work that integrated writing constraints of one form or another, mostly famously in *Life*, and in the lipogrammatic novels *La Disparition* (*A Void*)[17] and *Les Revenentes* (*The Exeter Text*).[18]

In addition to his heavy investment in Oulipo, Perec also became actively involved with *Cause commune*, a publication founded by his mentor, Jean Duvignaud, in 1972, with Duvignaud's two key collaborators being Perec and Paul Virilio. One of the stated aims of the new journal was 'to undertake an investigation of everyday life at every level, right down to the recesses and basements that are normally ignored or suppressed'.[19] In terms of published books, Perec's interest in these questions of the 'infra-ordinary' and the 'endotic' (that which is the opposite of the 'exotic'), which *Cause commune* promoted, is perhaps most clearly represented by his *Penser/Classer* and *L'Infraordinaire*, both of which were published posthumously, as well as his *Espèces d'espaces* (*Species of Spaces*) and *Tentative d'épuisement d'un lieu parisien* (*An Attempt at Exhausting a Place in Paris*).

Throughout the 1970s, Perec also produced a remarkable body of autobiographically inflected work, including *W ou le souvenir d'enfance* (*W or The Memory of Childhood*), *La Boutique obscure* and *Je me souviens*. Central themes – not just of this work, but also across Perec's *oeuvre* – are the issues of grief, loss and tragedy.[20] In a 2001 interview, Paul Virilio reflects back on this period and points out that the past that Perec was responding to in his writing (the Second World War and its implications for his immediate family) was 'monstrous', and that, consequently, 'we cannot understand Perec without the tragic'.[21]

It was also over the last decade of his life that Perec's polymathic qualities and voracious appetite for writing were most clearly in evidence, with the production of works for film and television, radio, theatre (such as *Théâtre I*, which included two major works, *L'Augmentation* and *La Poche Parmentier*), poetry (with two collections, *Alphabets* and *La Clôture*) and much more.

Tragically, 'what had promised to be a long and brilliant literary career' was 'abruptly truncated'.[22] Having become unwell towards the end of 1981, following a trip to Australia 'to write a book in fifty-three days'[23] while writer-in-residence at the University of Queensland, Perec succumbed to cancer and died four days short of his forty-sixth birthday on 3 March 1982.

PEREC'S *OEUVRE*

Perec's work, as captured above, is noted for its range and virtuosity, spanning everything from fat encyclopaedic novels, thin novellas, radio plays, screenplays, librettos, crosswords, acrostics, poetry, lipograms, palindromes, detective fiction, mock scientific papers, descriptive pieces, lists and so on. In his short essay, 'Statement of Intent', Perec compares himself to a farmer tending 'many fields'.[24] He writes:

> The books I have written belong to four different fields, four different modes of questioning, which, in the last analysis, perhaps address the same problem, but approach it from different perspectives, each of which corresponds [. . .] to a specific kind of literary work.[25]

These 'four fields', or 'modes', as he describes them, comprise the 'sociological' ('it has to do with looking at the ordinary and the everyday'); the 'autobiographical' (*W or The Memory of Childhood*, *La Boutique obscure*, et cetera); the 'ludic' ('which relates to my liking for constraints, exploits and "exercises", and gives rise to all the work based on the notions and devices gleaned from the Oulipo's experiments'); and the 'novelistic' (which 'grows from my love of stories and adventures, from my wish to write books to be read at a gallop').[26] David Bellos cautions against taking these categorisations too literally, suggesting that 'Perec's apparent helpfulness to the reader looking for a map or guide is a characteristically gentle and effective trap, forcing us to find our own path through his universe of words, every part of which is different, and yet a constituent of an elusive whole'.[27] While admitting that there 'are many aspects of Perec's writing that are best approached with little regard for chronological development', Bellos does just that, eschewing the 'ill-fenced "fields" of [Perec's] literary farm' for a more straightforwardly chronological periodisation of Perec's *oeuvre*.[28] In his introductory essay setting out the contents of an updated 2009 Perec-themed issue of *The Review of Contemporary Fiction*, Bellos categorises Perec's writing according to four phases of literary production that broadly follow the trajectory of his life. This remains a productive approach, especially in introducing Perec's work for those who are less familiar with it and with the sheer breadth and extent of his output. These four 'phases' are as follows:

1. 'Perec before *Things*', which includes 'the essays on literature that Perec wrote around 1960 for the left-wing review *Partisans*', as well as the aforementioned manuscripts, *L'Attentat de Sarajevo* and *Le Condottière*.
2. Perec in the mid-1960s – the 'short era of *Things* and *A Man Asleep*', 'stories and novels which attempt to grasp the self as well as a social reality'.
3. Perec in the period which began in 1967, 'when he was co-opted by Oulipo' and which 'could be said to culminate in the completion of *Life A User's Manual*'.
4. Perec post-1978, 'the regrettably brief phase of Perec's career', between the publication of *Life* and the end of his life, which 'had no clear dynamic', but was driven by his insatiable appetite for tackling all sorts of writing, 'from travel pieces for the Air France in-flight magazine to essays, detective fiction [including the unfinished "*53 Days*"], and pastiche',[29] as well as his last published book, released in 1979, *Un Cabinet d'amateur* (*A Gallery Portrait*).

This book is concerned with staking out and surveying the contours of a *fifth phase* of literary and creative production: what we are calling the 'afterlives' of Georges Perec. This fifth phase is not simply concerned with Perec himself as much as it is with the wider dissemination and uptake of his ideas and work in a variety of fields and areas of creative production and critical inquiry. Interest in Perec's work, it seems fair to say, has traditionally been concentrated within literature and French studies. But, like the circulation of Perec's spoof scientific paper on the study of the yelling reflex in female opera singers who are pelted with tomatoes,[30] which, 'for many years', 'circulated from hand-to-hand' in 'ever-fainter photocopies',[31] Perec's writing, ideas and influence have spread steadily across various fields of creative and critical endeavour, finding root in media and communication (and its various subfields of inquiry), architecture, the arts and beyond.

During his almost two decades as an 'archivist cum secretary'[32] in the neurophysiology lab, LA 38, Perec invented a revolutionary information-storage-and-retrieval system, called Peekaboo, that pre-empted (and was ultimately replaced by) computer database software.[33] Peekaboo consisted of 'a system of cards with number-coded locations around all four sides that could be hole-punched using a mechanical, number-driven device'.[34] It worked as follows:

> Each hole position would indicate the presence (punched) or absence (not punched) of a key word in the article indexed by the card. The user operated the system by placing a stack of cards in front of a light source and shuffling them until all the required key positions showed light shining through.[35]

The Peekaboo system presents a useful frame for approaching the growing, posthumous influence of Perec's own work. His body of work is a substantial and diverse archive that can be assessed, if you like, via the 'number-coded' filing system of his 'four fields' (among other possible criteria). Held up to the light source of different disciplinary contexts, and shuffled and recalibrated according to specific critical interests, and Perec's own *oeuvre* becomes a textual archive rich with possibilities and potential. There is, it would seem, something for almost everyone. And, part of this expanding diversity of interest in Perec's work is due to the growing availability to Anglophone readers of increasing amounts of his *oeuvre* (see Bellos, this volume).

The result is that the afterlives of Georges Perec take many forms. Bellos notes how 'the set of keys that open doors to the house of his writing [. . .] is remarkably large' and ever-expanding.[36] And, in Perecian list style, Bellos provides an inventory of the varied work that has appeared to date, which includes:

> Perec and the Algerian War Perec and Antelme Perec and Autobiography Perec and the Avant-Garde Perec and Balzac Perec and François Bon Perec and Borges Perec and Calvino Perec and Crosswords Perec and the Everyday Perec and Fantasy Perec and Foucault Perec and Forgery Perec and Hide-and-Seek Perec and the Holocaust Perec's Left-Handedness Perec and the Lipogram Perec and Marx Perec and Melancholy Perec and Memory Perec and Memory [sic] Perec and the Missing One Perec's Mistakes Perec and Mourning Perec and Nabokov Perec and the Oulipo Perec and Perspective Perec and Photography Perec and the Post-Nouveau Roman Perec and Proust Perec and Psychoanalysis Perec and Puzzles Perec and Social Description Perec and Sport Perec and Translation Perec and Trauma Perec and Utopia Perec and Vichy Perec and the Visual Perec and W.[37]

In this collection, we gather key examples of this expanded interest in Perec's ideas and writing, that span architecture, digital humanities, human–computer interaction, media arts and visual arts, mobile media, social media, poetry and more (contributor chapter summaries follow below). There is, evidently, much contained in and inspired by Perec's work that could not, for reasons of space, be included here. For instance, Michael Sheringham examines a number of examples within France where 'Perec's interweavings – of space and memory, the modest proposal and the spiritual exercise, the logbook and the inventory – have provided enduring inspiration for innumerable later explorers of the everyday'.[38] The Association Georges Perec continues to produce Les Cahiers Georges Perec on a semi-regular basis: these assemble scriptural, scholarly, and sometimes sardonic texts on or about their eponymous subject.[39] In the Francophone world, highly detailed academic work continues to be done on the influences, the rhetoric and the politics of Perec, as on the Oulipo more generally, as well as their impact upon the entire range of the arts, such as dance and cinema.[40] Indeed, many major Oulipians are themselves still alive and well and writing (if these terms remain meaningful in the ambit of a group for which death does not mean the end of belonging), along with a number of newer members and fellow-travellers: Marcel Bénabou, Jacques Roubaud, Anne Garréta and so on. Yet, as Bellos' extraordinary inventory suggests, scholarship has still barely scraped the complex surfaces of Perec's writing and its implications.

If, as we are arguing here, the questions raised so intensely and urgently by Perec's *oeuvre* are marked by a singular contemporaneity, this is also partially because they induce an unprecedentedly detailed reinvestigation of some of the most ancient traits of writing itself – not least in regard to the boundaries between life and death, constraint and chance, creation and destruction, aesthetics and anaesthetics. Recent scholarly work across a number of fields, from new media to philosophy, has often returned to these questions in new ways, under rubrics such as 'biopolitics', which signifies, in the canonical impetus given the term by Michel Foucault, a form of 'government that takes into account the lives of people as a systematic calculation, utilising scientific knowledge'.[41] This biopolitical context includes other now familiar themes, including such disparate critiques as 'the death of the author', 'control society' and 'the gamification of everyday life'. Perec clearly speaks to these themes and others in important ways that this collection seeks to track – not least in his intimate contestation of biopolitical constraints.

It is worth noting that, if Perec's relationship with the work of Henri Lefebvre and his epigones is well-known and well-documented, the emphasis has often been placed on the problematic of the *everyday* of 'everyday life'. In a way, this is not surprising: the second volume of Lefebvre's magisterial *Critique of Everyday Life* was released in 1961, bearing the subtitle *Fondements d'une sociologie de la quotidienneté*, the repetition seeking to make certain nobody misses the crucial links between academic knowledge and quotidian experience. Yet the 1960s also witnessed a significant efflorescence of philosophical, psychoanalytic and scientific studies of the status of 'life' itself, which reconsidered the changing relationship of sense and functions of the biological substrate in different *epistemes*, to use Foucault's famous coinage in *The Order of Things*.

Lefebvre was of course himself instrumental in this efflorescence. As he writes in a brief section titled 'Lived and Living':

> The traditional theory of consciousness, which congeals it by reducing it to the 'I' (thus to a congealed form of the lived) disregards this conflict. The 'living' has no precise frontiers, either on the dark side (nature and spontaneity), or on its social horizon.[42]

Although Lefebvre's 'dialectical' approach works strenuously to decentre the practical aspects of consciousness, it is still 'consciousness' that functions as one of the key polarities of his research, even as its privileges are displaced. As Perec's *Things* itself famously describes, contemporary capitalism separates and subjugates life to commodities:

> For a modern, rigorous literary version of the Marxist theme of alienation – especially the prevalence of things over existence – and therefore of the subjective consequences of the fact that *le mort saisit le vif*, one might read or re-read Georges Perec's book *Things: A Story of the Sixties* (1965).[43]

In stressing the 'life' of everyday life, then, it immediately becomes necessary to reintroduce certain other factors over which Perec himself famously obsesses: the activity of the irrevocably absent, the obliterated, trauma and death. These factors immediately introduce the possibility of a non-discernible rift into all forms of presentation, such that – from description, through analysis, to invocation – it thereafter becomes absolutely impossible to know whether the most fervently pursued demonstration is nonetheless still lacking the real that it seeks. Moreover, at the same time as these non- or anti-themes of the non-living routines of life are expressly thematised by Perec, he also sets out to analyse and produce a kind of 'afterlife' for himself.

In this, Perec gives a new twist to the near-universal trait of human beings to try to survive their own death. One of the most ancient and popular means for achieving this ambivalent ambition has been the making of artworks. If doing so is of course a risky business – one not only without any guarantees of success, but where whatever success there may be will be forever unknown to its biological maker – this has never stopped people from making the attempt. Art is an attempt at a material afterlife. Perec himself certainly confessed to this desire: 'To write: to try meticulously to retain something, to cause something to survive: to wrest a few precise scraps from the void as it grows, to leave somewhere a furrow, a trace, a mark or a few signs'.[44] The vicissitudes of such an afterlife are thus also of extreme interest. How and why has this or that writer, this or that text not only survived but flourished, perhaps even under extremely unpropitious conditions?

In a now-famous essay, the German Jewish critic Walter Benjamin cites the celebrated Latin tag by Terence: *Habent sua fata libelli*. Benjamin immediately continues:

> These words may have been intended as a general statement about books. So books like *The Divine Comedy*, Spinoza's *Ethics*, and *The Origin of the Species* have their fates. A collector, however, interprets this Latin saying differently. For him, not only books but also copies of books have their fates. And in this sense, the most important fate of a copy is its encounter with him, with his own collection. I am not exaggerating when I say that to a true collector the acquisition of an old book is its rebirth.[45]

Benjamin's remark draws attention to a number of peculiarities pertaining to the afterlife of books. First, a book is not, perhaps never, simply an idea or a disposition of words: it is a material object, most likely attaining its codex form through the concerted interventions of many persons who are not the book's 'author'. Second, as a printed object, it is a multiple, a copy without an original. It is a *particular* book. As such, third, this particular copy is impelled upon its own hazardous trajectory, threated by fire and floods and pestilence, scuffed and scarred by carelessness, at the mercy of dishonest borrowers or a change in taste. Fourth, its very survival in the face of such vagaries renders it materially unique in its scarred resistance to time. And, fifth, this uniqueness is what excites the collector. For such a personage, the encounter is tantamount to a quasi-mystical, even weakly messianic moment – that of the 'rebirth' of the book in the present. Yet, finally, the very uniqueness of the material object communicates, in a complex and singular fashion, with conceptual materials that go far beyond its own objecthood.

Benjamin's use of the metaphor of rebirth is not an accidental one. It goes back to a set of ancient rhetorical figures which model the productions of *poiesis* upon natural cycles of birth, growth and death, as they simultaneously acknowledge the artificial, unnatural character of works of art. So, artworks at once acquire a character of life, one that outlives the life of their makers, although this life is not really reducible to biological 'life' at all. As the great seventeenth-century English poet John Milton figured it in his important anti-censorship tract, *Areopagitica* (1645):

> Books are not absolutely dead things, but do contain a progeny of life in them to be as active as that soul was whose progeny they are; nay, they do preserve as in a vial the purest efficacy and extraction of that living

intellect that bred them. I know they are as lively, and as vigorously productive, as those fabulous dragon's teeth; and being sown up and down, may chance to spring up armed men. And yet on the other hand, unless wariness be used, as good almost kill a man as kill a good book: who kills a man kills a reasonable creature, God's image; but he who destroys a good book, kills reason itself, kills the image of God, as it were in the eye. Many a man lives a burden to the earth; but a good book is the precious lifeblood of a master spirit, imbalmed and treasured up on purpose to a life beyond life.[46]

'Life beyond life' – this phrase, despite Milton's overtly Christian language, designates not so much the possibility of an other-worldly destiny for the souls of humans, but an entirely material *afterlife*. The name *afterlife* would then denominate the abiding activity, the *liveliness*, of the particularities of books, which, if material, multiple and mimetic in several of the aforementioned senses of these words, is also abidingly productive in ways that the life itself may never have envisaged. Yet, in accordance with the invocation of biopolitics above, the afterlife of texts needs also to be considered according to its contemporaneous management by various actants and agencies.

The current collection thus offers a range of studies of the continuing *material activities* of Perec's diverse writings. It does not primarily concern itself with the original locales, motivations, constructions, nor with the *potentiality* of Perec's writings – although these are necessarily discussed – but with what we might call Perec's *actualités*, with his currency, his current affairs. In other words, we are interested in the continuing *news-worthiness* of Perec's work. Yet, this status of *posthumous news* is self-evidently a paradoxical one. If the very name of the Oulipo, the Workshop of Potential Literature, notoriously places the stress upon *potentiality* – that is, upon potential-without-or-beyond-any-necessary-or-possible-actualisation – Perec's own work, as many essays in this volume explicitly argue, was directed from the first towards *actualities* and *actualisation*.

For Mireille Ribière, Perec's actuality is legible in his rejection of the French avant-garde and its theoretical dogmas, as he essayed to find a way to extend those aspects of modernism that asserted constructed intentionality against authorial domination. Picking up on one of Perec's own intra-artistic oppositions between Pablo Picasso and Paul Klee – the first supposedly only varying a single painting, the latter constantly finding different solutions to different problems – Ribière shows how Perec found models for his own practice in two different periods of artistic experiment, the early modernist avant-garde and 1960s postmodernism. Perec and his friends were reacting against Sartrean 'committed literature' for its pamphleteering qualities, as well as against 'human interest' for its reactionary obsolescence. One of the problems for Perec was thus to situate himself against these tendencies, while refusing the problem of the self-negating or purely self-referential artwork. In offering his extraordinary 'solutions', Perec becomes a privileged muse for subsequent work in contemporary art by, as Ribière puts it, 'providing material and procedures that can be reused, recreated and transformed; then, as a brotherly or tutelary figure; and, finally, as a "plagiarist by anticipation"'. Ribière discusses some of these effects with respect to a variety of works by artists such as Christl Lidl, Anne Deguelle and Ignasi Aballí, among many others.

Like Ribière and other contributors to this collection, Justin Clemens affirms the double nature of Perec's work to attend simultaneously to rigorous formal techniques and to the presentation of the real. He shows how Perec's notoriously stringent uptake of poetry at a particularly fraught and significant moment of his life enabled a kind of compressed intensification of Perec's already-existing practices. In a minor yet decisive way, poetry became a privileged laboratory for Perec, enabling him to focus in an unprecedentedly micrological fashion on the relationships between constraint and chance, convention and content, in the innovative production, disposition and circulation of texts. Clemens shows how this inventive quadruple address to constraint, chance, convention and content is continually interwoven in Perec's writing in such a way that the force of affect and the patency of the absent are simultaneously placed in irreducible tension with each other, yet cannot be separated. Some important developments in contemporary poetry and poetics – including flarf, spoetry, conceptual poetry and bot-poetry – therefore owe much to Perec's experiments, if, in their explicit extraction and externalisation of sets of techniques and attitudes, they thereby also vitiate, divide or occlude part of their predecessor's force. Perec, moreover, can induce us to rethink not only the futurity of afterlives, but their prehistory: just as the Oulipo proposed an 'analytic' study of their antecedents, culminating in the paradox of anticipated plagiarism, we find that, under pressure of Perec's proposals, even Shakespeare turns out at times to be a self-reflexive lipogrammarian as well as a stager of generic undesirabilities.

Darren Tofts further radicalises this fundamental problematic of address in Perec's writings which, as he notes, is often literally – even diagrammatically – limned by borders suggesting mortification or death. Something is always missing in Perec, 'the aporia of an absent detail', which the palimpsest of letters and the worldly pressure of things indicate to be a glitch of non-existence. Tofts discusses the project of the Australian artists, Norie Neumark and Maria Miranda, collectively known as 'Out-of-Sync', who decided to search for Rue Simon-Crubellier, mentioned in *Life A User's Manual*, as if it were real. Their 'forensic vigour' partakes of 'a detective aesthetic' that sees the artists visiting 'the reassuringly non-fictive offices of civic officials, mapmakers, and bureaucrats, the Town Council offices of the 17th arrondissement and even the Office of Town Planning responsible for the naming of streets in Paris'. This singular project is what Miranda herself names the 'unsitely', the usually negative prefix instead functioning here as the unleashing of potential rather than an excision from reality. For Tofts, Perec – along with his stablemate Italo Calvino – thus becomes one of the 'tutelary deities of media and undecidable art in the 21st century'.

It is here that Mark Wolff returns to the relationships between Perec, algorithms and conceptual writing, to argue that – as this collection incontrovertibly demonstrates – that part of Perec's genius was to push beyond the potentiality of constraint, such that he serves as one of the indispensable conditions for the recent work of conceptual writers such as Craig Dworkin and Kenneth Goldsmith. Taking up the crucial Oulipian dialectic of constraint and chance again, Wolff points to Perec's perhaps-surprising disinterest in computational media. Yet, as Wolff shows, this disinterest – most likely due to Perec's abhorrence of the exclusion of error – links Perec directly to Alan Turing's theories of computation regarding aspects of the decision problem and the universal machine. Here, Turing's Oracle Machine, that is a model of an agency that can perform non-computational operations, offers an analogon to a number of Perec's ambitions, as can be seen from the latter's collaborations with Marcel Bénabou on PALF, with Eugen Helmlé on the radio play *The Machine*, or Perec's own celebrated flowchart, *The Art and Craft of Approaching Your Head of Department to Submit a Request for a Raise*. For both Perec and Turing, then, the incalculability of imagination is irreducible in the ambit of the computational.

Despite the famously 'experimental' nature of much of Perec's writings, Ben Highmore underlines that Perec was, above all, attempting to register actuality: the current, the existent, the present. This makes Perec a realist writer: that is, an heir to Balzac, Flaubert and Zola, rather than to Joyce or Robbe-Grillet. Yet, in pursuing his extraordinary form of realism, Perec attended to what had withdrawn from, or was otherwise inaccessible to, prevailing received forms of realism. He drilled down into sites in order to 'reveal the significance of the insignificant'. In doing so, however, this micrological attentiveness opened further questions regarding the principles of such selection – not only of the sites themselves, but of the status of the optic with which they might be approached. Realism involves a politics because its claims concern the contestation of reality, but it also integrally involves the life of the observer, according to a host of factors at once subjective and objective. Observing one thing means missing another, whereas boredom, exhaustion, perceptual uncertainties and intellectual capacities are also at stake. Furthermore, and along the lines of inquiry opened by Henri Lefebvre's work, the question of the social whole is inscribed within the tiny events of the everyday. Highmore shows how Perec's attention to the insignificant simultaneously leads him to the reconstruction of a totality that was not presupposed in advance.

Like Highmore, Caroline Bassett also underlines Perec's commitment to the insignificant. Noting Perec's binding together of the tiny and the automated, the intimate and the computational, she draws a distinction between what he was looking *at* and what he was looking *for*. Such a distinction further problematises the targets of Perec's writings, as well as their means. Algorithms can select, sort, permute, grid or otherwise display information, thereby rendering, in this extraction, previously invisible things, as well as their unexpected relations. Can even imperceptible elements of the everyday be made perceptible by the use of more rigorous means? Or does such a focus bring out that certain elements must remain below or beyond any threshold of possible perception? Or is it even that much of the everyday is itself lacking – is fully absent from – the everyday itself? Bassett also notes how 'the everyday' is not necessarily a good in itself: indeed, it is more intolerable than the mediatised public events of disaster and trauma which can function as distractions. Here, one wonders if Perec's realism was calibrated to make visible an unfigurable loss, one which his writings cannot describe or even show directly, but nonetheless make palpable in their delineations of an irretrievable absence.

In '"Things That Should Be Short"', Anthony McCosker and Rowan Wilken turn their attention to the relation between brevity and banality in Perec and the social networking platform of Twitter. In the intense public debates surrounding the uses and import of the platform, it is precisely 'banality' for which both users and designers are blamed. Taking up Perec's analysis of Sei Shōnagon's *The Pillow Book* – which notes her attention to the infraordinary production of the everyday, and the decisive role played by the constant remaking of unsorted lists – McCosker and Wilken deploy this doublet as a conceptual pincer for grasping and extracting aspects of social media that would otherwise be missed. Part of the paradox is that everyday life, almost by definition, escapes notice; by the very fact of attending to its banality, one runs the risk of further distorting its practice and sense. In regard to Twitter, these matters have tended to tie the platform's developers, users and commentators in knots. Partially this is due to the problem of big-data style monetisation: if all you can register from Twitter is vacuous babble, then you're not selling; to do so, it's time to up the excitement of the trending topic or the big events; hence, the everyday disappears once more beneath the veil of the banal. But, if we bind a practice of recurrent disjointed listing with an attention to the manners of the everyday, a method for researching contemporary social media can be developed that avoids the pitfalls of banality. In this sense, Perec's literary rereading of Shōnagon's ancient literary readings becomes in turn a mode of social scientific investigation that circumvents common critical and cognitive blindnesses towards the everyday.

Like many of the other contributors, Alison James highlights the politics of Perec's use of constraints. Such a politics is, as she notes, hardly representational, whether in the sense of representational democracy, or in the sense of representing its structure or operations. Nor is it a politics of recognition, in the strong philosophical sense of recognition that a certain line of modern liberalism has given to this term. On the contrary, Perec's work can even appear anti-democratic in its common acceptation. Hence, James cites contemporary writers such as Christian Bök and Kenneth Goldsmith, who both tar Perec with such a brush. Moreover, Perec's very genius has tended to function as a kind of blocking-agent for his own enthusiastic inheritors, such as the surviving Oulipians: in this context, he appears 'as both exception and exemplar', inimitable yet a model – that is, a classic great author. Yet, as James continues, Perec can therefore be read as offering a kind of open communal and participatory politics. After all, 'the Oulipo's achievement lies precisely in the collective creation of shared constraints' and, as for Perec personally, he is democratic in the sense of appealing to wildly different cadres of readers who he invites to participate in the ongoing complexes of his literary games.

From the first to the last, Perec is also a writer of spaces, from the minimal to the maximal, from the real to the fantastic. He can attempt to exhaust the space of a desk at the moment that he is using it; he can generate impossible spaces that nonetheless have the sense of an easy verisimilitude about them. Perec is also, along the lines of his already mentioned non-standard 'realism', an exemplary writer of Paris, of the city, of cities. It is thus somewhat puzzling that, as Sandra Kaji-O'Grady notes, Perec is unlikely to be graced any time soon with a laudatory architectural application along the lines of Jacques Derrida or Gilles Deleuze. Perhaps, Kaji-O'Grady speculates, this is partially due to his presentation as a literary mnemonist, shuttling between inscription and disintegration. If it is also the case that Perec's systems fail by design rather than necessity, his 'engagement with compositional constraints has obvious synergies and attractions for architecture'. Finally, for Kaji-O'Grady, Perec's modes of registering urban spaces anticipate Google Street View.

The omnipresent, if elusive, melancholy that marks so much of Perec's writings rejoins his justly famous enthusiasm for games of all kinds. Thomas Apperley returns to this fundamental aspect of Perec in order to bring it forward to our 'gamified' present, according to which almost all aspects of life are consciously integrated into the routines of various kinds of enforced games. From language-learning apps on a mobile phone through precarious reskilling to corporate team-building exercises, they are now impossible to avoid. Apperley shows how Perec himself deployed games in his life at every scale: he used them to procrastinate, as well as to accelerate his writing, refining his own processes by forging new links with Lefebvrian everydayness, as well as with Oulipian formal constraints. What Apperley shows is that Perec's experiments were destined to at once ramify the formalisms as well as to multiply breaches of form across sites and situations, according to the powers of Chance.

It is in the field of new media that Christian Licoppe presents an *Auseinandersetzung* between Perec's mode of 'exhausting a place in Paris' and 'a high-tech reincarnation of Perec equipped with a smartphone and himself an active user of mobile locative media', including the application Foursquare. The confrontation turns out to be an illuminating one: the city space today could not be exhausted, by design and in principle. Perec and other contemporaneous observers of city life, such as William H. Whyte and Erving Goffman, still owe something to the nineteenth-century situation of Charles Baudelaire's *flâneur*. This *flâneur* was a quasi-anonymous 'man of the crowd', who participated in the turbulent and hazardous spectacle offered by the great metropolis, whose public places were openly available for present participant onlookers. This is a space of distances, gazes, strangers and perambulations, of physical happenstances and encounters. Perec's 'Attempt' itself presumes a host of anonymous strangers, all of whom have access to essentially the same human sensorium, shared generic terms and institutional powers. As Perec sits and sees and scribbles, he is just as much an object of observation by others as they are for him. With applications such as Foursquare, the situation is entirely different. The medium now, first, places selective representations onscreen in a pre-organised fashion (e.g. through ranked lists); second, makes the conditions of appearing not simply physical visibility, but by subordinating it to in-app geolocation; third, presents places in a 'textual and iconographic fashion', enabling the personalisation of things or localisation of events. Foursquare does not only 'gamify' spaces, but subordinates their apparition and import to its own operations, thereby also seeking to encourage its users to participate in an entirely app-based competition to take virtual possession of those spaces. Licoppe therefore tracks a shift from the presumed generic anonymity of public urban modernity to the ranked privatised virtual formattings of technical devices, which divide places and persons from themselves in entirely new ways.

Licoppe's thought experiment has the further benefit of suggesting that subsequent developments in technology have rendered essential aspects of Perec's work out of date, possibly irrelevant, perhaps even obsolete. To this extent, Licoppe suggests that a too-enthusiastic or un-nuanced affirmation of the continuing activity of Perec's work will falsify both Perec's contribution and the current situation. Perec's extraordinary literary act, for instance, of co-presence, hyper-attentive observation in real-time and minute description might once have paradoxically shown its inability to exhaust a place by means of its very exhaustiveness – but today that inability is patent from the start. The facts of machine observation, virtual proliferation and app-specificity combine to reveal that *there is now neither practised places nor participant observers*; rather, any possible 'place' and 'participant' has been shattered into a kind of irreducibly plural event significantly unavailable to phenomenological description, yet which is nonetheless subject to unprecedented levels of specific interactions through hyper-differentiated technical means. If this is indeed the case, then we would also need to speak of Perec's 'afterdeaths' as well as of his afterlives; in doing so, we would also have to worry about whether Perec's nominal afterlives are themselves only derisory wisps rather than active spectres.

But this afterdeath of one of Perec's most famous innovations might then present us with a further paradox: that an essential part of his contemporaneity is his non-contemporaneity. It is here that the problem of the bonds between time and life enters the picture in another way. Resistance to the present is possible only insofar as a gap between the present and itself might be exposed – even if it is in its *exhaustion*, that is as a kind of impossibility.[47] In an essay titled precisely 'The Exhausted', Gilles Deleuze remarks that 'the combinatorial is the art or science of exhausting the possible through inclusive disjunctions. But only an exhausted person can exhaust the possible, because he has renounced all need, preference, goal, or signification. Only the exhausted person is sufficiently disinterested, sufficiently scrupulous.'[48] If Deleuze is writing here about Samuel Beckett, one can immediately see that Perec's various attempts 'to exhaust' spaces bear not only on places but on persons, including on his own person. Moreover, as Dominic Pettman also notes, exhaustion is a sign of life or, as we can now add, a sign of afterlife.[49]

It is here that Rowan Wilken's attention to so-called 'residual media' – which now perhaps include even desktop and laptop personal computers – comes into its own. For the alleged becoming-obsolescent of such pervasive devices, declared so by persons who were once among their most enthusiastic and influential purveyors, can serve to illuminate the daily practices that concretised around them – but whose essence remained hidden while they were operating at full force. To this end, Wilken concentrates upon their (literally) *key* medium, the history of the inculcation, study and management of the hands/eye/posture/keyboard relation through skilled typing. Wilken shows how both Perec and human–computer interaction (HCI) investigators project as their exemplary cognitive mode highly particularised, even obsessive micro-level descriptions, whether of the state of a study desk or of the most minimal twitching of a typist's hands. These modes have extraordinary consequences for the use of time and space, their management and modification, for, on the one hand (so to speak), an avant-garde writer such as Perec and, on the other hand, for work management consultants whose interests go far beyond the gross physical movements of classical Taylorist disciplining towards the micro-detailed quantifications of contemporary 'immaterial' labour. Whereas the typing studies are naturally focused on cognitive command and control processes under extremely restricted conditions, Perec's descriptions direct our understanding of the quotidian into environmental situations that exceed the narrow band of HCI quantification. If Licoppe may be right regarding the difficulties posed to Perecian description by locative media, Wilken shows that the routines of the *interface* between app and user may yet be best presented and cognised by means of Perecian-style descriptions.

The collection concludes with a bravura summation by David Bellos of the peculiarities of Perec's reputation, both dead and alive. As Bellos notes in his Afterword, while the smart money would have been on Perec's death killing his reputation, quite the contrary transpired. Perec died intestate, without children, a legal spouse, literary agent or a single publisher behind him; his friends and relations, the Oulipo and a small group of enthusiastic fans were the circles most affected by his death. Alive, he had never really been a bestselling author and, despite the relative critical success in France of *Things* and *Life A User's Manual*, many of his other works had been almost entirely ignored. So, the work done by Perec's cousin Ela Bienenfeld was indispensable, including her definitive role in helping to establish 'The Friends of Georges Perec', with its archive, its conferences, its publications and republications of manuscripts and often difficult-to-acquire materials. Associated kinds of aid not only came from old friends like Harry Mathews and Jacques Roubaud, but also from Philippe Lejeune, the well-known scholar of auto-life-writings, as well as the highly successful theatricalisation by the actor Sami Frey of *Je me souviens*. The English translation of *Life A User's Manual* – by Bellos himself – gave the Perecian corpus another boost, opening Perec's masterpiece to vast and (perhaps unexpectedly) variegated readerships, ranging from aficionados of the native British tradition of the comic novel to sociologists and maths geeks. Because Anglophones are oddly more enthusiastic than almost anyone else about the desirability of biographies, it was also Bellos who became Perec's first biographer: we have already quoted extensively from his magisterial *Georges Perec: A Life in Words*. Further serendipities aside, Bellos also makes the absolutely fundamental point that, whatever Perec's genius, he did not set himself up as an inimitable stylist. On the contrary, he proffers himself as a kind of exemplar of the 'inherently learnable', what Bellos calls here 'a pedagogy of writing'. To read Perec is also to be inspired to write back to and beyond Perec, cutting across inherited divisions and hierarchies of literature, to commit, create and communicate with constraints transmuted into eminently *partageable* play (to momentarily speak Franglais).

It is perhaps, then, in his relentless expansion and intensification of the problematics of constraint, description, commitment and invention that Perec became the greatest and most successful Oulipian, pushing its programme to the limit at which it was no longer *potential* but *exhausted*, overturning and fulfilling the programme by saturating it and, in this saturation, opening up new vistas for ongoing invention. The essays in this collection testify to the continuing afterlives of such an exhaustion.

NOTES

1. Marcel Bénabou (2001), 'The Lumber-Room Revisited', *AA Files*, trans. Ian Monk, no. 45–6, p. 100.
2. Ian Monk (2005), 'Perec's Letterless Texts', quoted in Harry Mathews and Alastair Brotchie (eds), *Oulipo Compendium*, London: Atlas Press, p. 150.
3. Georges Perec (1991), *Things: A Story of the Sixties* with *A Man Asleep*, trans. David Bellos and Andrew Leak, London: Harvill.
4. Georges Perec (1992), *Life A User's Manual*, trans. David Bellos, London: Harvill.
5. Alison James (2009), *Constraining Chance: Georges Perec and the Oulipo*, Evanston: Northwestern University Press, p. 4.
6. Georges Perec (2009), 'Statement of Intent', in *Thoughts of Sorts*, trans. David Bellos, Boston: Verba Mundi, p. 4.
7. The definitive account is most certainly David Bellos (1999), *Georges Perec: A Life in Words*, London: Harvill; see also Paul Schwartz (1988), *Georges Perec: Traces of His Passage*, Birmingham, AL: Summa Publications.
8. Schwartz, *Georges Perec*, p. 1.
9. Schwartz, *Georges Perec*, p. 2.
10. Georges Perec (2014), *Portrait of a Man*, trans. David Bellos, London: MacLehose Press.
11. Bellos, *Georges Perec*, p. 251.
12. Schwartz, *Georges Perec*, p. 3.
13. Schwartz, *Georges Perec*, p. 3.
14. Georges Perec (2004), 'Which Moped With Chrome-plated Handlebars at the Back of the Yard?', in *Three By Perec*, trans. Ian Monk, Boston: Verba Mundi, pp. 3–52.
15. Georges Perec (1991), *Things: A Story of the Sixties* with *A Man Asleep*, trans. David Bellos and Andrew Leak, London: Harvill.
16. Schwartz, *Georges Perec*, p. 3.
17. Georges Perec (1995), *A Void*, trans. Gilbert Adair, London: Harvill.
18. Georges Perec (2004), 'The Exeter Text: Jewels, Secrets, Sex', in *Three By Perec*, trans. Ian Monk, Boston: Verba Mundi, pp. 55–120.
19. Bellos, *Georges Perec*, p. 492.
20. These issues are central, for example, to his collaborative exploration in film and text with filmmaker Robert Bober of Ellis Island, which was, from 1894 to 1954, the port of entry into the United States for immigrants arriving by boat. See Georges Perec with Robert Bober (1995), *Ellis Island*, trans. Harry Mathews and Jessica Blatt, New York: New Press.
21. Enrique Walker and Paul Virilio (2001), 'Paul Virilio on Georges Perec', *AA Files*, no. 45–6, p. 18.
22. Warren F. Motte (1984), 'Georges Perec on the Grid', *French Review*, vol. LVII, no. 6, p. 820.
23. Bellos, *Georges Perec*, p. 686.
24. Perec, 'Statement of Intent', p. 3.
25. Perec, 'Statement of Intent', p. 3.
26. Perec, 'Statement of Intent', pp. 3–4.
27. David Bellos, 'The Old and the New: An Introduction to Georges Perec', *The Review of Contemporary Fiction*, vol. xxix, no. 1, p. 17.
28. Bellos, 'The Old and the New', p. 17.
29. Bellos, 'The Old and the New', pp. 13–16. On his 'parodic' writings, see Georges Perec, with Harry Mathews (2008), *Cantratrix Sopranica L.: Scientific Papers*, trans. Anthony

Melville, Ian Monk and John Sturrock, London: Atlas Press. Stephanie Sobelle suggests that 'Perec's scientific writings remind readers that all languages', including those as apparently dry and unappealing as scientific and other academic scholarship, 'contain poetry and possibility'. Stephanie Sobelle (2009), '[Review] Georges Perec, *Cantatrix Sopranica L.: Scientific Papers*', *The Review of Contemporary Fiction*, no. XXIX: 1, p. 230.
30. Georges Perec (2008), 'Experimental Demonstration of the Tomatotopic Organisation in the Soprano (*Cantatrix sopranica L.*)', in *Cantatrix Sopranica L.: Scientific Papers*, London: Atlas, pp. 11–28.
31. Bellos, *Georges Perec*, p. 264.
32. Bellos, *Georges Perec*, p. 251.
33. As Jacques Jouet notes, a 'tireless anticipator of modern technologies, Perec just missed out on the world wide web'. Jacques Jouet (2004), 'In Brief', in *Yale French Studies*, trans. Alyson Waters, no. 105, p. 7.
34. Bellos, *Georges Perec*, pp. 257–8.
35. Bellos, *Georges Perec*, p. 258.
36. Bellos, 'The Old and the New', p. 13.
37. Bellos, 'The Old and the New', p. 13.
38. Michael Sheringham (2006), *Everyday Life: Theories and Practices from Surrealism to the Present*, Oxford: Oxford University Press, p. 291. In particular, see Chapter 8 (pp. 292–359) of Sheringham's book, 'After Perec: Dissemination and Diversification'.
39. See their website http://associationgeorgesperec.fr/les-cahiers-georges-perec/ for further details of their publications and events.
40. See, for example, Christophe Reig (2011), 'Oulipo-litiques', in *Poésie et politique au XXe siècle*, Paris: Hermann; the ongoing work of Christelle Reggiani, including her 1999 monograph, *Rhétoriques de la contrainte: Georges Perec – l'Oulipo*, Saint-Pierre-du-Mont: Éditions InterUniversitaires; or indeed the work of Mireille Ribière, one of the contributors to the present volume.
41. See Mark Kelly (2015), *Biopolitical Imperialism*, Winchester: Zone Books, p. 13.
42. Henri Lefebvre (2002), *Critique of Everyday Life, Volume II: Foundations for a Sociology of the Everyday*, trans. John Moore, preface Michel Trebitsch, London: Verso, p. 217.
43. Alain Badiou (2012), *The Rebirth of History: Times of Riots and Uprisings*, trans. Gregory Elliot, London: Verso, p. 20, n.1.
44. Georges Perec (1997), 'Species of Spaces', in Georges Perec, *Species of Spaces and Other Pieces*, ed. and trans. John Sturrock, Harmondsworth: Penguin, p. 91.
45. Walter Benjamin (1992), 'Unpacking My Library', in *Illuminations*, trans. Harry Zohn, intro. Hannah Arendt, London: Fontana, pp. 62–3.
46. John Milton (1959), *Collected Prose Works, Vol. II. 1643–1648*, New Haven, CT: Yale University Press, pp. 492–3.
47. The metaphor of 'exhaustion' is widely deployed in Perec studies, undoubtedly in homage to his own attempt to 'exhaust' the description of places; however, it is rarely given the properly conceptual rigour we believe it requires. See, for example, Lauren Elkin and Scott Esposito (2013), *The End of Oulipo? An Attempt to Exhaust a Movement*, Winchester: Zero Books.
48. Gilles Deleuze (1997), *Essays Critical and Clinical*, trans. Daniel W. Smith and Michael A. Greco, Minneapolis: University of Minnesota Press, p. 154.
49. See Dominic Pettman (2002), *After the Orgy: Toward a Politics of Exhaustion*, Albany, NY: SUNY.

PART I

Art of the (Un)realisable

CHAPTER 2

Georges Perec's Enduring Presence in the Visual Arts

Mireille Ribière

Despite his use of diverse techniques, Picasso's work is always the same, like a variation on a single painting. Conversely, each painting by Klee is the solution to a different problem. I am [more] like Klee.[1]

Far from waning, Georges Perec's reputation worldwide is still gathering momentum more than three decades after his untimely death. While his work is often cited as inspirational by established writers, his legacy in the field of literature – with a few exceptions – seldom goes beyond allusions or derivative writing.[2] In the visual arts, however, the resonance of his work appears to be more profound and wide-ranging. Christelle Reggiani suggests that this may be due to the fact that Perec does not have a distinctive discursive style that readily lends itself to literary appropriation or emulation, and that his multi-faceted contribution to literature is based on formal inventiveness rather than idiosyncratic discursive practices centred on the sentence. Furthermore, it is as if he has exhausted the possibilities inherent in each of the various and varied work-specific writing strategies he adopted, leaving his potential followers limited creative options. While Reggiani's analysis goes some way to explain why few writers have been able to simultaneously espouse Perec's aesthetic principles and emulate his practice, it does not altogether account for the strong convergence between his creative concerns and those of visual artists.

Although Perec's early ambition was to become a painter and he did make a number of gouache abstract paintings in the late 1960s, he was only moderately interested in the visual arts, with the exception of cinema. Nevertheless, art played an important role as subject matter and fictional generator in his work – more often than not, as a metaphor for writing[3] – and he collaborated with a number of painters and photographers on catalogues and artists' books.[4]

While there is inevitably some correlation between these aspects of his work and his current status on the art scene, it would be an oversimplification to simply posit a causal relationship between them. It would seem, rather, that the issues tackled by Perec are closely related to those raised in other art forms in the 1960s and 1970s, and the creative strategies he developed in answer to those questions have become increasingly relevant to successive generations of visual artists.

To understand Perec's aesthetics, and how they relate to some of the main trends and concerns in twentieth-century art as well as contemporary art, one needs, first, to briefly go back to the 1950s and 1960s – his formative years as a writer. These were essentially marked by the *Ligne générale* project, his attendance at Roland Barthes's seminars at the École des hautes études en sciences sociales from 1963 to 1965 and his membership of Oulipo from 1967.

MODERNISM AS MODEL AND COUNTERMODEL

In the late 1950s, Perec and a few friends formed a group intent on producing a Lukács-inspired Marxist critique of literary and artistic production.[5] It was named *La Ligne générale*, after Sergei Eisenstein's 1929 film, *The General Line*, which, significantly, included his pioneering montage technique. Perec's ambitions for the group – to produce a literary review[6] – never came to fruition. However, in the 1960s Perec published several articles that were later edited under the title *L.G.* by Claude Burgelin.[7]

As explained by Burgelin in his introduction, *La Ligne générale* was born out of the anger and frustration felt by Perec and his friends at the state of literature, and the arts in general, in the late 1950s: by then, Sartrian or communist-inspired 'committed literature', which had dominated the French literary scene since the end of the Second World War, had ceased to treat the novel as a specific genre distinct from political pamphleteering, and thus was in something of a rut. As for the novels praised at the time for their 'human interest' or their 'emotional freshness', the *L.G.* group judged them to be facile, even downright reactionary, for they put forward, Perec wrote, a 'falsified image of the world and mankind', using 'obsolete language' that referred to an 'outdated reality'.[8] True, the Nouveau Roman and the theatre of the Absurd, cherished at the time by French intellectuals, offered alternatives. But Perec and his friends found them wanting: the former, embodied by Robbe-Grillet, because it was altogether removed from the real in its social and historical dimensions, despite its claim to a new form of realism; and the latter because it was equally, albeit differently, putting forward the vision of a world without meaning. For these young *L.G.* idealists, some of whom had been orphaned as a result of the German invasion of France and were now facing the prospect of military service to fight in France's protracted colonial war in Algeria, passive acceptance was not an option:

> Literature creates a work of art because it orders the world, because it makes it appear as a coherent whole, because it reveals it beyond day-to-day anarchy by integrating and prevailing over the contingencies that make up the immediate fabric of it [. . .]. This ordering of the world is what we call realism [. . .], realism is describing reality but describing reality means delving into it, bringing out the essence of the world: its movement, its history.[9]

In their search for renewal and potential models, Perec and his friends turned to the political and cultural upheavals of the early twentieth century, that is to the time of the birth of modern art as exemplified by the works of Eisenstein, Joyce, Kafka, Klee and Thomas Mann. It was clear that there was still much to learn from Modernism. One important lesson was that when a work of art sets out to destroy the stifling conventions from which it issues, it is at risk of destroying itself and of becoming merely the expression of the destruction it has enacted. In one article, Perec and his co-writer Jacques Lederer are at pains to point out that, unlike *Ulysses*, Joyce's *Finnegans Wake* came to express the absolute impossibility of language to refer to anything other than language itself. Similarly, non-figurative painting ended up destroying itself as painting, only to survive as testimony of the *act* of painting and the impossibility of the latter to refer to anything other than itself.

These self-same issues were being faced by other artists in the 1950s and 1960s. In France, the novel as a genre reached a state of near implosion in the wake of the Nouveau Roman.[10] In the US, painters, largely unaware of the achievements of the early twentieth-century Russian avant-garde, repeated the experiments of Malevich, with works such as Frank Stella's *Black Paintings* or Ad Reinhardt's *Abstract Painting* series, which were said to herald the end of painting itself. But Perec did not revisit those issues in the light of this new formalist avant-garde; his interest in the mid-1960s lay somewhere else, as we shall later see.

For *L.G.*, and Perec in particular, the countermodels to self-devouring forms of experimental art were the works of artists like Klee, who managed to rise above the 'false' conflict between figurative and non-figurative painting by integrating the conventions they sought to destroy within a wider and more open framework. Klee would remain for Perec a primary point of reference and a model. As early as 1959, in 'Défense de Klee', Perec argued that Klee's work demonstrated that art could be rooted in the real without necessarily being figurative in the traditional sense. In this article, he established a distinction between naturalism, which claims to mirror reality, and realism proper, which attempts to 'enrich' the real and make it more 'significant' – adding that art is all about 'the relationship between man and the world'.[11] In 1978, he would use a quotation from Paul Klee's *Pädagogisches Skizzenbuch* as the epigraph to *La Vie mode d'emploi* to illustrate the relationship between reader and writer: 'The eye follows the paths that have been laid down for it in the work.'[12] In fact, at the time of his death, Perec's personal library included no less than fifteen books by and about Paul Klee, including his *Theory of Modern Art* and two different editions of Will Grohmann's seminal monograph.

ART IN THE MAKING

As it became obvious to his generation that the marketplace had made consumers of them all, Perec's militant stance tended to shift. However, he never abandoned his concern about establishing a relationship between art and the real while retaining critical distance. The need to produce an interpretative grid, a mediation system that efficiently addressed the real, continued to be the cornerstone of his approach to writing. *Les Choses*[13] was the first published demonstration of this. The novel reflected the development of language studies and sociology and owed much to Barthes's *Mythologies*:

> Originally the intention of the book was twofold: first an exercise on Barthes's *Mythologies*, that is to say on advertising language and how it is reflected in our attitudes; then a barely exaggerated description of a particular social milieu, which happens to be mine.
> [I mentioned] Barthes – I should have added *Madame Express* [. . .] that is to say I wrote *Things* with a stack of *Madame Express* at hand and, as a mouthwash after having read slightly too many *Madame Expresses*, I would read some Barthes, and that gave me some respite.[14]

Barthes's early writings as well as Perec's attendance at the latter's seminars at the École des hautes études en sciences sociales in Paris – notably 'Sociology of Signs, Symbols and Representations: Inventory of Contemporary Systems of Meaning' and the study of rhetoric – were to have a lasting influence on Perec's writing and his views on art.[15]

In October 1967, Perec was invited to give a paper at a conference entitled 'Mass media et création imaginaire'. His contribution, 'Écriture et mass media', examined the potential impact of mass media on the act of writing.[16] He was convinced that mass media could function both as a challenge and an opportunity for renewal in the way it had transformed the language and structures of works by 'mixed media' artists associated with both Pop Art and Performance Art, such as Andy Warhol, George Segal, Claes Oldenburg and Tom Wesselmann. Literature had attempted to involve the reader at various times in its history, most notably in the eighteenth century, but the techniques used by mass media questioned anew the relationship between audience and artist, helped undermine the distinction between highbrow and popular cultures and, in the process, opened new avenues for experimentation. Perec identified audience participation, 'simultaneity' and 'discontinuity' as key components in contemporary sensibility as defined by mass media. He then went on to explore how these features could be adapted to writing so as to create 'open' works that would involve their readers as co-producers of meaning. He had already tackled these issues in his Warwick lecture,[17] placing emphasis on: 'quotational' practices that create a sense of cultural complicity, objectivity and ironic distance that leaves the reader some freedom to interpret, and tension between continuity and discontinuity, between coherence and disparity, that also demands interpretative solutions. Significantly, in 'Écriture et mass media' he cited as examples works by Raymond Queneau: notably his seminal Oulipian work, *Cent mille milliards de poèmes*, which plays *systematically* on simultaneity and disruption, on constraint and subversion.

OULIPO AND THE DUCHAMP CONNECTION

In March 1967, Perec had become a member of Oulipo,[18] then a discreet and marginal literary group devoted to the search for new forms and structures in literature. He later described his joining Oulipo as a 'key moment' in his development as a writer.[19] Yet, rather than a radical departure, it seems to have been a natural progression: since the early 1960s, Perec had become increasingly focused on experimenting with structure, form and technique, reaffirming in the process his essentially modernist rejection of conventional mimesis and the romantic view of artistic endeavour.

Raymond Queneau, the co-founder of Oulipo in 1960 with mathematician François Le Lionnais, had been a surrealist under André Breton from 1924 to 1929 and was particularly suspicious of the Surrealists' 'exaltation of subjectivity', which he saw as a resuscitation of the romantic vision of the messianic artist. Surrealism thus served as a countermodel for Oulipo. Perec embraced wholeheartedly Queneau's claim that

> inspiration which consists in blind obedience to every impulse is in reality a sort of slavery. The classical playwright who writes his tragedy observing a certain number of familiar rules is freer than the poet who writes that which comes into his head and who is the slave of other rules of which he is ignorant.[20]

As Perec put it in his 'History of the Lipogram', 'exclusively preoccupied with its great capitals (Work, Style, Inspiration, World-Vision, Fundamental Options, Genius, Creation, etc.) literary history seems deliberately to ignore writing as practice, as work, as play'.[21] It is, among other things, this conception of writing as praxis, as craft, on the one hand, and of literature as constructed intentionality, as the result of a process of pre-planned moves, on the other, that makes Perec's approach to literature relevant to the arts in general, and particularly to those artists who took their inspiration from Minimalism and the Conceptual Art of the 1960s and 1970s. Marcel Duchamp's essentially passive and largely overlooked membership of Oulipo from March 1962 onwards, at a time when he was being 'discovered' by a new generation of American artists seeking alternatives to Abstract Expressionism, is particularly relevant in this respect. As Marcel Bénabou pointed out:

> Several decades before the official birth of Oulipo, '[Duchamp] had himself anticipated, even outlined, some of its basic principles', most notably 'the breaking down of barriers between disciplines, the solidarity between the poetic and the scientific, his unrestrained boldness in experimentation, his ironic and distanced view of established art forms'.[22]

One might add that Duchamp's membership of Oulipo prefigured the current blurring of lines between Formalism and Conceptualism in their various manifestations.

A NEW DEAL

In the context of the present chapter, it is particularly significant that Perec should have sought and found models in two periods of intense experimentation that came to be seen as turning points in the history of the visual arts: on the one hand, the Avant-garde and Modernism of the early twentieth century, and, on the other, the (post)modernism of the 1960s, which itself was revisiting the art of the early twentieth century. This, together with his readiness to experiment with a variety of styles, forms and practices, which he attributes to the influence of Klee on his work, may help us understand why he was somewhat at odds with the French literary scene between 1965 and 1978, and instead shared the same 'mental space' as that of his contemporaries in the visual arts.[23] It may also explain, as we shall later see, the congruence between Perec's work and that of the next generation of visual artists who in turn were to revisit these two key periods in the history of art.

It has now become customary[24] to discuss Perec's invigorating contribution to the current art scene in the light of his 'Statement of Intent' of 1978:

As I see it, I would rather compare myself to a farmer with several fields: in one field he grows beets, in another wheat, in a third alfafa, and so on. In like manner, the books I have written belong to four different fields, four different modes of questioning, which in the last analysis, perhaps address the same problem, but approach it from different perspectives, each of which corresponds, for me, to a specific kind of literary work.

The first of these modes could be called sociological: it has to do with looking at the ordinary and the everyday. [. . .] The second mode is of an autobiographical kind [. . .] The third is the ludic mode, which relates to my liking for constraints [. . .] The fourth and last is the novelistic mode, and it grows from my love of stories and adventures [. . .]

This is a rather arbitrary distribution, and it could be greatly refined. Almost none of my books is entirely devoid of autobiographical traces [. . .]; likewise, almost none is assembled without recourse to one or another Oulipian structure or constraint, even if only symbolically.[25]

The four modes outlined by Perec are indeed strands that run through many contemporary works with varying emphases, as we shall later see, but their coexistence within the same works may be regarded as equally important, for it questions received ideas of what literature is, just as contemporary artists question the nature of art.

In this respect, Perec's appropriation of hyperrealism for his own ends is quite instructive. It has been argued[26] that hyperrealism, which Perec often mentioned in connection with *Life A User's Manual*, was a convenient label that encapsulated his concern with the everyday rather than a reference to actual works by the artists known as hyperrealists or photorealists. Yet, by 1978, when Perec first used the term,[27] hyperrealism was well established and the two fictional paintings described in *Life A User's Manual* are far from being unrepresentative of that trend:

[. . .] a large hyperrealist canvas portraying a steaming plate of spaghetti and packet of Van Houten cocoa.

[. . .] a work by the American artist Organ Trapp [. . .] It shows a gas station at Sheridan, Wyoming, in full detail: a green garbage can, very black, very whitewalled tyres for sale, bright cans of motor oil, a red icebox with assorted drinks.[28]

They illustrate the subject matter favoured by the hyperrealists, who generally extended the consumer culture and mass media iconography of Pop Art by embracing everyday banality in its many manifestations. They are also representative of two of the compositional techniques associated with hyperrealism: on the one hand, the close-up, perhaps best illustrated by Ralph Goings's work;[29] on the other, the cramming of details often associated with Richard Estes's 'urban landscapes', such as *The Candy Store* and *Bus Reflections*.[30]

Most interestingly, the commonality between Perec's approach to representation and that of the hyperrealists lies in the process of mediation enacted by both. Just as the hyperrealists painted from photographs rather than direct observation, Perec borrowed the surname 'Trapp' and the description of the gas station from Nabokov's *Lolita*,[31] thus interposing, between the real and his rendition of it, the 'relay'[32] of a ready-made linguistic description. True, the media used to access reality are different, language being symbolic and photography indexical, but the processes and results are comparable. They explore and problematise the notion of realism: the 'reality' produced is a simulated reality, a distanced mixture of fact and fiction that is both vivid and dreamlike.

This is quite different from the *tableaux-pièges* or 'trap pictures' conceived by 'Nouveau Réaliste' Daniel Spoerri, to whom Perec is sometimes compared.[33] These were leftovers of actual meals – plates, cutlery, debris – glued onto wooden table tops and then hung vertically like conventional pictures; the 'trap' consists in fixing in time mundane objects meant to be discarded or washed, and confronting the viewer with their tangible reality. Conversely, Perec's hyperrealist 'Trap[p]' has to do with simulation and the relationship between the readers and the represented reality they are invited to view in their mind's eye. Hence the parallel between *trompe l'œil* painting and hyperreality, which Perec establishes in 'This is Not a Wall . . .', his introductory essay to *L'Œil ébloui* ['The Dazzled Eye'].[34] For Perec, *trompe l'œil* has nothing to do with aesthetics and everything to do with how we view and relate to reality. It stops us in our tracks – and momentarily creates a disturbing sense of uncertainty – by letting fictional space intrude into the reality that we take for granted. As such, it refers to the way 'we look at – and occupy – space'.[35] Perec's view of production as reproduction when it came to representing the real and the space we inhabit thus coexisted with a questioning of space as experience, which coincided with similar concerns in the visual/plastic arts and provided the subject matter of *Species of Spaces*.[36]

From the moment of its publication in 1974, Perec's book about space struck a note with architects and town planners, and since then has become a standard textbook in the field, despite the fact that, as a non-architect, Perec had the 'mistaken view [that] a building is a pure product of imagination'.[37] The interest aroused by his fascinating musings on space tended to overshadow the fact that *Species of Spaces* is first and foremost a work of literature by a man who defined himself as a 'man of letters', that is a man whose primary material is the alphabet.[38] The nearest we have to an image in *Species of Spaces* is a blank square – the 'Map of the Ocean' from Lewis Carroll's *Hunting of the Snark* – on the first page of the book. It is followed by a foreword explaining that, 'To start with, then there isn't very much: nothingness, the impalpable'. The first space addressed in the book is the page: the first chapter, entitled 'The page', begins with the words 'I write' repeated over several lines; and the book ends with:

> Space melts like sand running through one's fingers. Time bears it away and leaves me only shapeless shreds:
> To write: to try meticulously to retain something, to cause something to survive, to wrest a few precise scraps from the void as it grows, to leave somewhere a furrow, a trace, a mark or a few signs.[39]

In his attempt to retain something, it is as though Perec has set out to say about space 'everything that it is possible for one person to say, and in every manner possible',[40] since the book explodes the notion of genre and includes a remarkably large range of discourses – playscript, autobiography, fiction, draft love letter, poetic lists, schedules, etc. It includes, in particular, practical tasks to be carried out by readers and precise descriptions of some of his then current projects. One such is *Lieux*:

> In 1969, I chose, in Paris, twelve places (streets, squares, circuses, an arcade), where I had either lived or else was attached to by particular memories.
> I have undertaken to write a description of two of these places each month. One of these descriptions is written on the spot and is meant to be as neutral as possible. [. . .] The other description is written somewhere other than the place itself. I then do my best to describe it from memory [. . .]. Once these descriptions are finished, I slip them into an envelope that I seal with wax. [. . .] I have also had occasion to slip into these envelopes various items capable later on of serving as evidence: Métro tickets, for example [. . .]. I begin these descriptions over again each year, taking care, thanks to an algorithm [. . .], first, to describe each of these places in a different month of the year, second, never to describe the same pair of places in the same month.
> This undertaking, not so dissimilar in principle from a 'time capsule', will thus last for twelve years, until all places have been described twice twelve times.[41]

It is clear that *Lieux* has great affinities with conceptual art. Thus we find ourselves with the apparent paradox of an author who demonstrated in his writing both a degree of self-referentiality worthy of Clement Greenberg's High Modernism and the fluidity of approach of artists associated with Postmodernism, notably Conceptualism and its legacy.

AFTERLIFE

When examining Perec's 'afterlife', one is faced with a clear choice: either offer a general thematic survey of the ever-widening ripples his work continues to make in the visual arts, an undertaking that would necessarily be superficial within the context of a single chapter; or, alternatively, focus on a limited number of works from the 1980s onwards with the aim of showing how his texts still act as a powerful stimulus to the creative imagination and how those aesthetics we tend to associate with him play out. Personally I find the latter approach more useful. The enduring presence of Perec and his work in contemporary art will therefore be discussed here from three distinct points of view: first as providing material and procedures that can be reused, recreated and transformed; then as a brotherly or tutelary figure; and finally as a 'plagiarist by anticipation'.[42]

Literal store and tool box

A number of artists from different countries are currently using Perec's books, not as models, but literally as source material (be it in French or in translation), suggesting, thereby, that his texts are now part of our common cultural heritage and belong to us all. The diversity of approaches and media manifest in these works is, in itself, remarkable, but one is also struck by both the close understanding of the particular aspects of the works quoted and the artists' ability to extrapolate and use them for their own purposes. In that sense, one is reminded of the way Perec himself collaborated with artists on various projects, trying to achieve the equivalent in language of what they did in their own medium.[43]

Brazilian artist Daniel de Paula (1987–) takes an actual book, a copy of the Penguin edition of *Species of Spaces and Other Pieces*, as his starting point. The book has been cut vertically into eight pieces or slices, which have then been rearranged so as to obtain a new version carrying on the front a sliced-up portrait of the author and the title, *Pieces and Other Species of Spaces* (see Figure 2.1).

It is a site-specific work of sorts since it was designed for and included in *Cahiers Georges Perec* no. 12, where it is deployed in stages. Each complete slice is first featured on its own at the beginning of each of the eight sections of the *Cahier* – the front being reproduced on one side of the page and the back on the reverse of the same page – and then they all appear pieced together at the very end of the *Cahier*, where the whole of the new front cover shows on one side of the last page, and the new back cover on the reverse. Not only is this work remarkable for its playful and self-reflexive simplicity, it is also clearly reminiscent of key aspects of Perec's practices, such as his play with quotations, fragments, collage and permutations.[44]

PEREC'S ENDURING PRESENCE IN THE VISUAL ARTS 33

Figure 2.1 Daniel de Paula, *Pieces and Other Species of Spaces* (extract).

La Polygraphie du cavalier ['The Knight's Tour'], a performance piece by Belgian artist Christl Lidl (1970–), illustrates a different type of tension with her reading of *Life A User's Manual*, by contrasting the tabular overall construction of the book and the linear development of the narrative in time (see Figure 2.2).

The starting point of the performance she gave in December 2014 is the description of the overall structure of the novel, given by Perec himself in the journal *L'Arc* in 1979:

> It would have been tedious to describe the building floor by floor and apartment by apartment; but that was no reason to leave the chapter sequence to chance. So I decided to use a principle derived from an old problem well known to chess enthusiasts and known as the Knight's Tour; it requires moving a knight around the 64 squares of a chess-board without its ever landing more than once on the same square. [. . .] For the special case of *Life A User's Manual*, a solution for a 10 × 10 chess-board had to be found [. . .] The division of the book into six parts was derived from the same principle: each time the knight has finished touching all four sides of the square, a new section begins.[45]

Figure 2.2 Christl Lidl, *La Polygraphie du cavalier*, a performance given at Galerie du CROUS (10–12 rue de l'Abbaye, 75006 Paris) on 13 December 2014, with Christl Lidl as The Performer and Maxime Mikolajczak as The Narrator.

Lidl's performance consists in reconstituting *Life A User's Manual* by placing one by one on the floor the 99 chapters of the novel, while an actor reads in chronological order passages from the book that mention jigsaw puzzles. At the beginning of the performance, the actor stands in a room that is empty, except for a small trolley carrying 594 laminated pages photocopied from the original edition (six pages for each chapter). The actor begins reading. Then the performer starts to place the pages, one by one and face up, inside each of the squares of the 10 × 10 grid that has been lightly traced on the floor beforehand. The performer's gestures and moves are carefully synchronised with the actor's reading of the various extracts. The performer stays inside the space of the book/grid, while the actor walks along the edge; at times their paths meet. It takes 90 minutes to reconstitute the whole book, which covers 20 square metres at the end of the performance. As the actor reads the passage from the last chapter of the book that describes the death of the central character who is still holding in his hand a piece that is the wrong shape for the sole empty space left in the jigsaw puzzle before him, the performer puts down the last pages from the trolley, thereby revealing that there is an empty square at the bottom left-hand corner of the grid.

The effect of this performance is complex and paradoxical, since it is both a reflection of the book as well as an extension of it. Although it does not render, in any way, either the amount of time that it took Perec to write the book (nine years from 1969 to 1978), or the time required to read it, it gives a physical reality to those two processes. Once completed, the carefully choreographed performance makes the whole book, or at least the structure that can only be perceived through analysis, 'instantly and simultaneously visible',[46] thus offering a visual equivalent of that single moment, just before 8 p.m. on 23 June 1975, when the action of the entire novel takes place. Yet, the empty square in the grid, as well as the reading of mere fragments from the narrative, deny closure.

Anne Deguelle (1943–) also deals with issues of openness, as well as coherence and disparity, in *Monument à Georges Perec – la disparition*, a collective project that is both a homage to Perec and a celebration of handwriting, whose 'demise now seems foreseeable'.[47] The '*disparition*' of the title – no capitals – refers to this potential loss while evoking the title of Perec's lipogrammatic novel, *La Disparition*. Anne Deguelle invited a group of students, apprentices, teachers, artists and other volunteers to transcribe by hand the entirety of Perec's novel, each of them copying one or more of the 300 pages of the novel on A3 paper, without omission or correction, but with a free rein as to the style. The resulting 300 pages of handwritten, calligraphed and/or illustrated texts were exhibited over 90 linear metres of exhibition space at the Gallery Dix9 in Paris in September 2014. Commenting on the result, Anne Deguelle pointed out that, in spite of the diverse approaches and levels of skill of the contributors, this hybrid collection was remarkably homogeneous. The constraint imposed on the contributors was, like the omission of the letter e in the novel, simple and straightforward – it only concerned the size of each sheet of paper and the amount of text contained therein. Yet, it had far-reaching creative results.

The project's *raison d'être* is quite removed from Perec's avowed desire to reinvent narrative. Yet, it is faithful to the spirit of *La Disparition*. *Monument à Georges Perec – la disparition* is both a single uninterrupted quotation and a collage. It is a joyous, collective, non-hierarchical project, as was *La Disparition*, which itself included not only literary quotations but also an essay by a schoolgirl and texts by friends and acquaintances. Furthermore, *Monument à Georges Perec* is reminiscent of the appearance of some of Perec's manuscripts, particularly the 'Cahier des charges de *La Vie mode d'emploi*', where inks and highlighters of different colours are used and drawings and doodles proliferate.[48] More generally, like Perec's *I Remember*, which ends with a number of blank pages to be completed by the reader, Anne Deguelle's project is not finite, and can be re-made by others in different contexts and different languages. It is an open invitation to creativity.

Verbatim quotations from Perec are also present in the titles of several works by Spanish artist Ignasi Aballí (1958–) and constitute the material of one of them. *Tentative d'épuisement I/II*[49] are framed photographs, in reverse order, of two unnumbered pages from the Christian Bourgois 1982 edition of Perec's *Tentative d'épuisement d'un lieu parisien*: the last (blank) page, and the previous page where the text, having exhausted its subject, ends halfway down. This particular piece is relevant here because of the stark contrast in terms of scale and medium with Deguelle's *Monument*, and because its self-referential quality recalls that of Daniel de Paula's *Pieces*. However, it might more appropriately appear in the next category given that Aballí's work as a whole is permeated by recurrent themes of absence and silence, and is clearly informed by his reading of Perec.

Tutelary presence

The name Georges Perec has become a byword for idiosyncratic innovative art, often in relation to works that have to do with the everyday as a subject matter or the use of self-imposed rules, in which case it functions as little more than a convenient peg. There are, however, artists who claim their kinship with Perec because they recognise something of themselves in his work, and develop particular aspects of it within their own *oeuvre*.

In 2002, Ignasi Aballí realised Perec's project of creating a cinematographic equivalent of the lipogrammatic constraint used in *La Disparition*: that is, a visual narrative in which the faces of the characters would never be seen.

Perec's project was entitled 'Signe particulier: NÉANT' ('Distinguishing Features: NIL');[50] Aballí's video is called *Desaparició*, after *La Disparition*.[51] The same year, he also designed and showed under the title *Desapariciònes*,[52] a series of twenty-four cinema posters in which Perec's name is credited in various capacities – some were for films that Perec actually made (*Les Lieux d'une fugue*) or adaptations of his books that actually existed (*Un homme qui dort*); others were for film projects that never saw the light of day (*Les Choses, Dites-le avec des fleurs*).[53] In the catalogue of his 2005 Birmingham exhibition, Aballí acknowledged his empathy with Perec's work by quoting in full 'Brief Notes on the Fine Art of Arranging One's Books',[54] which concludes: 'we fluctuate between the illusion of completeness and a head-swimming sense of the elusive'. Without oversimplifying, one could say that Aballí's work as a whole illustrates the Perecian pull between, on the one hand, presence, totality and exhaustiveness, manifest in his compilations of names, numbers and images, and, on the other, absence, elusiveness, manifest, for example, in blurred, blank or white spaces.

Christian Boltanski (1944–) also acknowledges his kinship with Perec with explicit references to his work. He chooses quotations from *W or The Memory of Childhood*, *I Remember* and *An Attempt at Exhausting a Parisian Site*,[55] thus placing the emphasis on memory and documentation. Much has been said and written about the 'congruence' between Perec and Boltanski,[56] their formal use of lists and inventories, their focus on the minute details that make up one's everyday life, and their concern with biography and autobiography. Among the many projects that could be examined in the light of Perec's work, Boltanski's *What They Remember* is especially revealing. Although he omits the phrase 'I remember' throughout the work, the title of the work is obviously an allusion to *I Remember* – that Perec had, in turn, modelled on the eponymous book by American artist Joe Brainard. For the version of *What They Remember 1990*,[57] Boltanski quotes one hundred brief memories about himself from relations and acquaintances. Like many of his projects, the emphasis is on the person as subject, be it the author or other people through their names, personal belongings or photographed faces. Given that collective acts of remembrance on a large scale tend to take place after the death of those remembered, undertakings of this kind take on funereal overtones, particularly when they are staged as dramatic installations in darkened rooms. In 1997, Boltanski explained that affect – 'to touch people' as he puts it – is important to him;[58] one might add that, despite protestations that there is something positive, even optimistic, about memories living on,[59] the effect of some of his installations is disturbing, even overwhelming. While Boltanski shares Perec's concerns with immediacy, his approach is closer to that of contemporary Indian artist Suboh Gupta (1964–), whose accumulations of domestic objects tend to create alternatively effects of overwhelming abundance or deep pathos,[60] than to Perec's compelling lightness of touch and his often repeated ambition to *engage* his readers in play.

Sophie Calle (1953–) is another conceptual French artist with an international reach for whom Perec can be said to represent a tutelary figure. Among the many aspects that relate her work to Perec's,[61] the most important one came to prominence through a third party. In his book *Leviathan*, American novelist Paul Auster modelled one of his characters, Maria, on Sophie Calle and some of her works, and also attributed to her projects that they were inspired by *Life A User's Manual* and Perec's poetic practices. In *Double Game*, and most notably the sections entitled *Chromatic Diet* and *Days Under the Sign of B, C, & W*,[62] Sophie Calle became an artist born out of both Auster's and Perec's writings. This highlights one of the major differences between some of her work and that of Cindy Sherman[63] with whom, oddly, she and Perec have also been associated. It is not so much that Calle uses herself as a subject to construct fictional identities. She is primarily a writer,[64] who often turns fiction, a pre-defined programme or a set of self-imposed constraints into life, in order to document the experience and turn it into a work of art that often takes the form of a narrative sequence – be it verbal, visual or both. Calle's approach to narrative highlights, in turn, two overlapping aspects of Perec's work that are often now taken for granted: on the one hand, his recourse to formal constraints and his drawing on the conventions of adventure and detective novels to revitalise the novel; on the other, the way he used biographical data to inform his writing[65] and devised for himself projects based on constraints that required a particular type of behaviour, even shaped his life, such as *Lieux*. Calle explores simultaneously the novelistic and the autobiographical along similar lines, and has done so since the very beginning of her career in the late 1970s, although there is no evidence that she was particularly aware of Perec's work at the time.

Plagiarism by anticipation

The playful Oulipian notion of plagiarism by anticipation will be used here to refer to those aspects of Perec's practice that were considered idiosyncratic, even marginal, before the acclaimed publication of *Life A User's Manual*, but have turned out to be of central concern for subsequent generations of artists; so much so that when we view their works, we have a sense of familiarity: our understanding and appreciation of them has already been shaped through our reading of Perec. This section, however, could include scores of examples, particularly since certain forms favoured by Perec, such as serial works playing on repetition and variation, as well as the manipulation of archival material, have become so ubiquitous in contemporary art that they almost constitute a genre of their own. One must resist the temptation to associate Perec with all such manifestations. For the sake of clarity and brevity, I shall comment on the work of just one artist that illustrates issues not directly addressed so far in the present study.

Joachim Schmid (1955–) lives and works in Berlin. He began collecting found photographs in 1982, which happened to be the year that Perec died. He did not know about the latter's existence until 2008, yet there is much overlapping between their respective works.[66] While they are not of the same generation, both show an acute awareness of their place in twentieth-century European history and society: most of the thousands of photographs bought at flea markets that are included in Schmid's *Archiv* (1986–99) date from the 1920s to the 1970s, as do the many stories told in *Life A User's Manual* – not to mention *W or The Memory of Childhood* and some of the entries in *I Remember*. Another congruence between Schmid and Perec's work is their common sociological – some might say anthropological – concern for the ordinary, the commonplace. This is coupled with a keen awareness of the nature of their respective media, as well as their use of comparable techniques and procedures. The latter is best illustrated by the way the photographs that make up *Archiv* were sifted, sorted, compiled and arranged into 726 panels (40 cm × 50 cm each):

> I emptied the biggest room in our apartment and I threw all the photographs on the ground and I sat there for weeks and started making piles ... and when a pile got too big I started making smaller piles out of it ... just discovering patterns and how they repeat and after a while I started arranging them on pages.[67]

This three-stage procedure – collecting, editing, arranging in patterns – is commonplace enough, but it is seldom done on such a scale, and, as such, is prefigured in Perec's *Attempt at a Description of Things Seen at Mabillon Junction on 19 May 1978*, which consisted initially of a six-hour audio recording of what Perec saw at that particular place on that day, then an edited version of Perec's description whittled down to two hours, and finally a formal poeticised inventory of the items described. The two-hour edited version, overlaid with a reading of the inventory by an actor, was broadcast on French Radio (France Culture, 25 February 1979).[68]

Perec's experiment at Mabillon Junction also foreshadows *Bilder von der Straße* ['Images of the Street'], which includes all the photographs or sets of photographs Schmid found in the street between 1982 and 2012 – one thousand altogether. Although not originally intended as such, *Bilder von der Straße* charts in real time, over three decades (as opposed to the six hours of *Mabillon Junction*), the demise of analogue photography, manifest in the increasing rarity of found photographic prints. Schmid now tends to find his source material on the Internet and uses digital technology to self-publish photobooks, his medium of choice.

CONCLUSION

The fundamental questions raised by Perec's work, the conversations he initiated and the various methodologies he proposed, are undoubtedly relevant to many contemporary artists, and his blurring of the lines between what were once distinct aesthetic stances is now common currency. One might therefore assume that artistic references to his work would have become more general and allusive as time goes by. Yet, judging by the artworks mentioned here to illustrate his afterlife, this is not the case: far from including loose references to his *oeuvre*, works produced in the last few years have chosen to appropriate some of Perec's most well-known texts verbatim, using widely differing creative approaches, while simultaneously demonstrating a thorough understanding of the original. Perhaps not surprisingly given their emphasis on primary sources – but in stark contrast with the immensity of scale, and technological, logistical and financial excess displayed in some contemporary art[69] – these recent projects are often centred on the modest format of the book, which, as handwritten or printed object, has lately become the focus of renewed interest.[70]

Thus, in all respects, whether as provider of source material, tutelary figure, or plagiarist by anticipation, Perec's work clearly continues to resonate as a vital and dynamic force in the visual arts today.

NOTES

1. Georges Perec (2003), *Entretiens et conférences*, ed. Dominique Bertelli and Mireille Ribière, Vol. 1, Nantes: Joseph K., p. 186 (author's translation).
2. See Christelle Reggiani (2006), 'La lettre et l'image: paradoxes de la réception posthume de Georges Perec', in Mireille Ribière and Yvonne Goga (eds), *Georges Perec: inventivité, postérité*, Actes du colloque de Cluj-Napoca, 14–16 mai 2004, Casa Cartii de Stiinta. For an overview of Perec's legacy in the field of literature, see also Maryline Heck (ed.) (2011), *Cahiers Georges Perec*, no. 11: *Filiations perecquiennes*, Bordeaux: Le Castor Astral, 2011.
3. Bernard Magné (1989), 'Peinturecriture', *Perecollages 1981–1988*, Presses Universitaires de Toulouse-Le Mirail, pp. 207–17.
4. Several exhibition catalogues, most notably *Jacques Poli: Peintures entomologiques* (Galerie Maeght, 1979) and *Peter Stampfli: œuvres récentes* (Centre Georges Pompidou, 1980), include texts by Georges Perec. He collaborated on several limited edition artists' books: *La Clôture* with Christine Lipinska (self-published, 1976), *Trompe l'œil* with Cuchi White (self-published, 1978), *Métaux* with Paolo Boni (posthumous edition, Dutrou, 1985), and

    Un peu plus de quatre mille poèmes en prose/dessins fantastiques with Fabrizio Clerici (posthumous edition, Impressions nouvelles, 1996). Perec died before new collaborative projects with Jacques Poli bore fruit; for further details see *Jacques Poli, rétrospective 1966–2002*, exhibition catalogue, La Nerthe Éditeur/Villa Tamaris, 2012.
5. See Manet van Montfrans (1999), *Georges Perec – La Contrainte du réel*, Amsterdam: Rodopi, pp. 17–48.
6. For further details see Georges Perec and Jacques Lederer (1997), « *Cher, très cher, admirable et charmant ami . . .* ». *Correspondance 1956–1961*, Paris: Flammarion; as well as Georges Perec and Roger Kleman (2011), *56 lettres à un ami*, Le Haillan: Le bleu du ciel.
7. Georges Perec (1992), *L.G. Une aventure des années soixante*, Paris: Seuil.
8. Perec, *L.G.*, Ibid., p. 26 (author's translation).
9. Perec, *L.G.*, p. 51 (author's translation).
10. See, for instance, the novels of Claude Simon and Robert Pinget in the late 1960s, which experimented with increasingly complex narrative strategies.
11. Georges Perec (1996), 'Défense de Klee' [dated 19 August 1959], in *Cahiers Georges Perec*, no. 6: *L'Œil d'abord . . . Georges Perec et la peinture*, Paris: Seuil, p. 22 (author's translation).
12. Georges Perec (1987), *Life A User's Manual*, trans. David Bellos, London: Collins Harvill.
13. Georges Perec (1990), *Things*, trans. Andrew Leak and David Bellos, London: Harvill Press.
14. Perec, *Entretiens et conférences*, vol. 1, p. 48, p. 83 (author's translation).
15. For a detailed analysis of the relationship between their respective works, see Mireille Ribière (2005), 'Georges Perec, Roland Barthes: l'élève et le maître' in Eric Beaumatin and Mireille Ribière (eds), *De Perec etc., derechef. Textes, lettres, règles & sens*, Nantes: Joseph K., pp. 336–51.
16. Perec, *Entretiens et conférences*, vol. 1, pp. 96–103.
17. 'Pouvoirs et limites du romancier français contemporain', 5 May 1967; Perec, *Entretiens et conférences*, pp. 76–88.
18. Marcel Bénabou (1989), *Cahiers Georges Perec*, no. 3: *Presbytère et Prolétaires. Le dossier P.A.L.F.*, Éditions du Limon.
19. Perec, *Entretiens et conférences*, vol. 2, pp. 148–9.
20. Raymond Queneau, *Le Voyage en Grèce*, quoted in Marcel Bénabou, 'Rule and Constraint', in Warren F. Motte Jr (ed. and trans.), *Oulipo: A Primer of Potential Literature*, Lincoln: University of Nebraska Press, 1986, p. 41.
21. Georges Perec (1986), 'History of the Lipogram', in *Oulipo: A Primer of Potential Literature*, p. 98.
22. Marcel Bénabou (2008), 'Duchamp à l'Oulipo ou un secret trop bien gardé', in « *regarde de tous tes yeux regarde* », – *l'art contemporain de Georges Perec*, exhibition catalogue, Nantes: Joseph K., pp. 74 and 76.
23. See Jean-Pierre Salgas (2008), 'Le Centre Georges Perec', in « *regarde de tous tes yeux regarde* » – *l'art contemporain de Georges Perec*, pp. 9–25. 'Art contemporain' in the title of this catalogue refers to post-1960s art and not specifically, as is the case in the present article, to works that correspond roughly to Perec's 'afterlife', that is art of the mid-1980s onwards.
24. Salgas, 'Le Centre Georges Perec', and Olivier Rolin's essay in Christine Macel, Yves-Alain Blois and Olivier Rolin (eds) (2004), *Sophie Calle: Did You See Me?*, New York: Prestel.
25. Georges Perec (2011), *Thoughts of sorts*, trans. David Bellos, London: Notting Hill Editions, pp. 1–2.

26. Cécile de Bary (2010), 'L'hyperréalisme n'est qu'un mot', in Jean-Luc Joly (ed.), *Cahiers Georges Perec*, no. 10: *Perec et l'art contemporain*, Bordeaux: Le Castor Astral, pp. 83–90.
27. 'I take inspiration from so-called 'hyperrealism' in painting, which purports to be a neutral, objective description of reality, but in fact offers such an insane accumulation of details that it pulls you away from reality.' Perec, *Entretiens et conférences*, vol. 1, p. 219 (author's translation).
28. Perec, *Life A User's Manual*, Chapter LXII, Altamont 3, p. 295 and Chapter LXIX, Altamont 4, p. 330, respectively.
29. See the Ralph Goings's 1970s diner and pick-up series exhibited at the Butler Institute of American Art in 2004, available at: http://ralphlgoings.com/downloads/goings_catalog-butler.pdf. The steaming spaghetti is also reminiscent of Pop artist James Rosenquist's numerous paintings including, or simply consisting of, close-ups of cooked spaghetti (*I Love You with My Ford*, 1961; *Spaghetti*, 1964).
30. *Richard Estes: The Urban Landscape*, essay by John Canaday, catalogue and interview by John Arthur, Museum of Fine Arts, Boston, 1978. Some of Richard Estes's paintings are also held by the Whitney Museum of American Art, which Perec visited (see *Entretiens et Conférences*, vol. 1, p. 248).
31. Vladimir Nabokov (2000), *Lolita*, Part II, Chapter 16, London: Penguin Classics, p. 211 *et seq.*
32. *Entretiens et conférences*, vol. 1, p. 102.
33. See Tania Ørum (2006), 'Georges Perec and the avant-garde in the visual arts', *Textual Practice*, vol. 20, no. 2, pp. 319–32.
34. Georges Perec and Cuchi White (1981), *L'Œil ébloui*, Vanves: Chêne/Hachette, no page numbers.
35. Perec and White, *L'Œil ébloui*, author's translation.
36. Georges Perec (1997), *Species of Spaces*, in *Species of Spaces and Other Pieces*, trans. John Sturrock, London: Penguin.
37. Guillemette Morel Journel and Vincent Corny (2015), 'Dessine de tous tes yeux, dessine! Apprendre l'architecture avec Georges Perec' in Danielle Constantin, Jean-Luc Joly and Christelle Reggiani (eds), *Cahiers Georges* Perec, no. 12: *Espèces d'espaces perecquiens*, Bordeaux: Le Castor Astral, p. 83 (author's translation).
38. Perec, *Entretiens et conférences*, vol. 1, p. 266.
39. Perec, *Species of Spaces*, pp. 91–2.
40. Perec, *Entretiens et conférences*, vol. 2, p. 252 (author's translation).
41. *Species of Spaces*, pp. 55–6. *Lieux* was never completed.
42. See François Le Lionnais, 'Second manifesto', in *A Primer of Potential Literature*, p. 31.
43. See, for example, *Trompe l'œil* with Cuchi White and *Un peu plus de quatre mille poèmes en prose pour Fabrizio Clerici*.
44. By contrast, Simon Morris's 'Pigeon Reader' (IAM Publications, 2012) merely consists of an integral facsimile of the Penguin edition of *Species of Spaces and Other Pieces*, in which the appearance of a passage comparing the act of reading to that of pigeons pecking for food has been electronically distorted, and superimposed with photographs of pigeons.
45. Harry Mathews, Alastair Brotchie and Raymond Queneau (eds) (1998), *Oulipo Compendium*, London: Atlas Press, p. 172. For a detailed explanation of the chess problem known as the Knight's Tour, see Georges Perec's 10 ×10 Knight's Tour, available at: http://www.borderschess.org/Perec.htm.
46. From Perec's description of the drawing by Saul Steinberg that partly inspired this novel (see *Species of Spaces*, p. 40).

47. For further details see Anne Deguelle (2014), 'Monument à Georges Perec – la disparition', Galerie Dix9, available at: http://www.galeriedix9.com/fr/expositions/presentation/79/monument-a-georges-perec-la-disparition, and http://www.galeriedix9.com/cspdocs/press/files/anne_deguelle_qda-2014_09_19.pdf.
48. See the facsimile of the manuscript of *Life A User's Manual* in Georges Perec (1993), *Cahier des charges de* La Vie mode d'emploi, ed. Hans Hartje, Bernard Magné and Jacques Neefs, Paris: CNRS éditions. For an analysis of the visuals, see Mireille Ribière (2015), 'En deçà de l'écriture: statut de l'iconique dans le *Cahier des charges de* La Vie mode d'emploi', in *Cahiers Georges Perec*, no. 12, pp. 269–80.
49. See Ignasi Aballí, 'Tentative d'épuisement', available at: http://www.ignasiaballi.net/index.php?/projects/tentative-depuisement/. I wish to thank Cristina Hidalgo Jaén for drawing my attention to Aballí's work.
50. See the manuscript of 'Signe particulier: NÉANT', in *Vertigo*, no. 11–12, 1994, pp. 61–6.
51. Documented in *Ignasi Aballí, 0–24 h* (2005), Museu d'Art Contemporani de Barcelona/Museu de Arte Contemporânea de Serralves/Ikon Gallery, pp. 170–3.
52. Ibid., pp. 162–6 and p. 167.
53. For an overview of Perec and the cinema see Cécile de Bary (ed.) (2006), *Cahiers Georges Perec*, no. 9: *Le Cinématographe*, Bordeaux: Le Castor Astral; and for unfinished projects, see Mireille Ribière (2006), 'Cinéma: les projets inaboutis de Georges Perec', in *Cahiers Georges Perec*, no. 9, pp. 151–71.
54. Georges Perec (2005), 'Brief Notes on the Fine Art of Arranging One's Books', trans. John Tittensor, in *Ignasi Aballí, 0–24 h*, Museu d'Art Contemporani de Barcelona/Museu de Arte Contemporânea de Serralves/Ikon Gallery, pp. 211–19.
55. Christian Boltanski (1997), 'Artist's Choice', in Didier Semin, Tahar Garb and Donald Kuspit (eds), *Christian Boltanski*, London: Phaidon, pp. 112–23. Quotations are from Georges Perec (1989), *W or The Memory of childhood*, trans. David Bellos, London: Harvill Press; Georges Perec's *I Remember*, which is quoted in an uncredited faulty translation, is now available as a book (trans. Philip Terry, Boston: David R. Godine, 2014); the same applies to *An Attempt at Exhausting a Parisian Site*, now available under the title *An Attempt at Exhausting a Place in Paris* (trans. Marc Lowenthal, Cambridge, MA: Wakefield Press, 2010).
56. See 'Signalement' [Christian Boltanski interviewed by Jean-Pierre Salgas], video cassette ('Les revues parlées'), Centre Georges Pompidou, 1997; 'Ensembles, [dialogue Christian Boltanski/Jacques Roubaud], in Jean-Luc Joly (ed.), *L'Œuvre de Georges Perec: réception et mythisation*, Publications de la Faculté des lettres et sciences humaines de l'université Mohammed-V (Rabat), 2002, pp. 13–31; and Jean-Luc Joly in 'Compter/Créer: Boltanski/Closky/Kawara/Opalka//Perec', *Cahiers Georges Perec*, no. 10, pp. 374–86.
57. *Christian Boltanski*, pp. 130–43.
58. See 'Tamar Garb in conversation with Christian Boltanski', ibid., pp. 37–40.
59. See 'Ensembles' in *L'Œuvre de Georges Perec: réception et mythisation*, p. 22; and 'Compter/Créer', in *Cahiers Georges Perec*, no. 10, p. 380.
60. See Subodh Gupta (2014), *Everything Is Inside*, London: Penguin.
61. See Véronique Montémont's article, 'Portrait de Sophie Calle en héroïne perecquienne' (*Cahiers Georges Perec*, no. 10, pp. 273–86), notably her comments on the themes of memory and absence manifest in Calle's *Disparitions* and *Fantômes* (both included in *Fantômes*, Actes Sud, English Edition, 2013).
62. Sophie Calle and Paul Auster (2007), *Double Game*, London: Violette.
63. See Eva Respini and Johanna Burton (2012), *Cindy Sherman*, New York: Museum of Modern Art.

64. 'I will rewrite my texts one hundred, two hundred times. I don't do that for a picture. [. . .] The written is never finished. [. . .] I can delegate photography. [. . .] But no-one ever wrote even a line for me.' *Sophie Calle: The Reader* (2009), exhibition catalogue, Whitechapel Gallery/Louisiana Museum of Modern Art, p. 136.
65. For a detailed analysis of the way biographical data shapes Perec's writing, see Bernard Magné, *Georges Perec*, Paris: Nathan, 1999.
66. For further details, see Mireille Ribière, 'Georges Perec/Joachim Schmid – Tentative de description d'un projet de livre d'artistes', followed by 'Entretien avec Joachim Schmid', in *Cahiers Georges Perec*, no. 10, pp. 227–52.
67. From the original English version of my interview with Joachim Schmid, published in *Cahiers Georges Perec*, no. 10.
68. 'Tentative de description de choses vues au carrefour Mabillon le 19 mai 1978 Mabillon' (1997), CDs 3 and 4, in *Georges Perec*, box set including four CDs and two booklets, Marseille: André Dimanche Éditeur.
69. For multiple examples, see *Art Now. Vol. 4* (2013), Köln, London: Taschen.
70. At a time when the very existence of the book in its traditional form is under threat, artistic interest in the book as a specific artefact with still unexplored potential is thriving, and international competitions and exhibitions of artists' books and photobooks are increasingly becoming important events in the art world calendar.

CHAPTER 3

Apoetic Life: Perec, Poetry, Pneumatology

Justin Clemens

> ... To be worst,
> The lowest and most dejected thing of fortune,
> Stands still in experience, lives not in fear.
> The lamentable change is from the best,
> The worst returns to laughter.
> William Shakespeare, *The History of King Lear* (1608), 4.1.2–6

> ... To be worst,
> The lowest and most dejected thing of fortune,
> Stands still in esperance, lives not in fear.
> The lamentable change is from the best,
> The worst returns to laughter.
> William Shakespeare, *The Tragedy of King Lear* (1623), 4.1.2–6

PREPOTENTIAL CONSTRAINT: EXPRESSION AT A STANDSTILL

Once 'constraint' has become a fundamental theme, it is almost impossible to know where it begins or ends. If, in regard to composition, the term has now perhaps acquired a primarily technical signification, it should not be forgotten that it derives from the Latin for binding together, tied, inhibited or compressed. The *Oxford English Dictionary* gives such meanings as 'the exercise of force to determine or confine action; coercion, compulsion'; 'compulsion of circumstances, necessity of the case'; 'confinement, bound or fettered condition; restriction of liberty or of free action'; 'pressure of trouble or misfortune; oppression, affliction, distress'. *Constraint* implies pain, coercion and incarceration, with political, theological and even ontological overtones.

In the two major independent extant printed play texts of Shakespeare's *King Lear*, the first a 1608 quarto version, the second appearing in the 1623 First Folio – which make *Lear* a work with at least two different titles, each denominating a different genre[1] – there are also a large number of other variations: missing, extra or different words, lines and punctuation. If the scholarly wrangling over the provenance and significance of these divergences is unlikely to find happy resolution in any foreseeable circumstances, following their vicissitudes returns us to the volatile and violent problematic of constraint.[2]

Indeed, once one starts to ask such questions, it is difficult to stop: not only because we are lacking essential historical details, but because the principles which might enable a decision regarding these ever-differentiating differences are themselves lacking. Take, for instance, the single nominal difference between 'experience' and 'esperance' in the epigraphs reproduced above, spoken by the character of Edgar: what difference might this difference make to our interpretation of the passage, let alone the play more generally? The words are, after all, quite different in meaning. 'Experience' in early seventeenth-century English could refer to a test or trial, facts or events, observation, an experiment, knowledge or skills drawn from what had been personally undergone. Etymologically, it has the sense of an emergence-from or passing-through danger, a coming-out-of-peril. The now-obsolete 'esperance', on the other hand, means expectation or hope. Whereas experience by definition derives from the particularity of a body's encounter with past events ('what happened'), esperance designates a particular kind of attitude taken towards the unknown future ('what will happen?').[3] And, while experience is a common word in Shakespeare, esperance turns up only a handful of times. In addition to its single appearance in *King Lear*, it turns up twice in *Henry IV, Part I*, as the battle-cry of the Percy family, uttered from the mouth of Hotspur (2.3.44 and 5.2.96), and once in *Troilus and Cressida*, where Troilus himself speaks of 'an esperance so obstinately strong' (5.2.117).

Yet, it is also worth noting the near-homophony of the two terms. One can hear how they might easily enough be confused in performance, whether by the enunciation of the actor or the ear of the auditor. Although the relation between iambic pentameter and prose in *King Lear* is itself often quite uncertain, one further notes that 'experience' might have to be pronounced something like 'ex-peer-ance', with the stress on the first and third syllables, in order to meet the rhythmic expectations of the line. If it is indeed true that actors spoke much faster in Elizabethan and Jacobean drama, and with a wider range of accents, anyone then or now could be forgiven for confusing the sounds corresponding to 'x' and 's' or, indeed, to 'ie' and 'a'.[4] If *experience* and *esperance* clearly have divergent signifieds, they seem tempted to converge at the level of their vocalised material presentation: in the current context, it is at least amusing to note that they both anagrammatically contain the name 'Perec'.

To interpret the differences in the context of Edgar's declarations suggests that they are by no means as semantically irreconcilable as the dictionary would have it. If I have briefly invoked the diverging temporalities, quantities and modalities projected by the words, here it appears that 'to be worst' means that, whether we are speaking of experience or esperance, either or both must stand still, must be forced to a standstill. Whoever you are, whatever you have experienced or whatever you might believe – or whatever you might know, do or hope for in Immanuel Kant's famous trinity – makes no difference at all in the ambit of 'the worst'.[5] Part of what is worst about the worst is precisely that all such differences are literally stopped in their tracks, giving onto – or as at least Edgar here asserts that they give onto – the asemantic biophysical spasm that is laughter. It is presumably for reasons of such language-incapacitating laughter that Edgar later adds: 'The worst is not / As long as we can say "This is the worst"' (4.1.25–6 (1608); 4.1.27–8 (1623)). The worst is perhaps not death but life at a standstill – aporetic life. The reality of the worst creates a void in expression which is filled by the constrained rhythmic contractions of the respiratory system. Aporetic life is an apoetic life.

Putting laughter momentarily aside, is this minimal difference to be considered continuous with the other differences between the printed texts? Perhaps the various differences between the two texts are not all due to the same causes? Is *this* particular difference a question of an intentional authorial change, an actor's slip, an auditor's ear, a transcriber's error, an editorial decision, several of these, or even more than these? Such questions regarding the emergence, nature and implications of multiple, extra-intentional *constraints* – and not simply their operative presence – can be read as already inhering in, as they necessarily disrupt, the very emblem of imaginative authority that founds the modern literary canon. 'Shakespeare' turns out to be less an ur-figure of polyphiloprogenitive literary power than an impossibly complicated compaction of un-known constraints and their mutation-in-transmission, which both induces and undermines the history of interpretations under pressure of literality itself.

SOME EFFECTS OF CONSIDERING CONSTRAINT AS SUBSTRUCTURE

Such an attention to the priority of constraints – here considered in their widest acceptation, including biographical, biological, historical, ecological, media and linguistic factors – enables a shift from what we might call a *special* to a *general* economy of literariness. This shift not only disseminates any particular agency that might serve as a putative unifying force, including authorial intent and genre distinctions, but enables a new kind of micrological attention to be paid to previously infravisible elements. Weird combinatory and operatory substructures start to emerge from the cracked shells of formal writing assemblages. Moreover, the ancient orders of modality – necessity, possibility, impossibility and contingency – start to appear clumsy and untenable in the dark light cast by the emergence of such orders. To attend to constraints is to prioritise the articulation of expressions which, as we have briefly seen, start to multiply to the point that they unground the received principles of creation and interpretation that they reveal in and by this very ungrounding.[6]

The above remarks about *King Lear* might be seen as a brief exercise in what the Oulipo referred to as an 'analytic' investigation into the use of constraints, as distinguished from the 'synthetic' (or 'experimental') programme that the group established for itself. That is, in starting with the axiom that *there are always constraints*, we can not only present an in-principle indefinite number of varying models of constraint, but expose or flush out constraints we didn't know about, or knew about but didn't know were constraints, or knew were constraints but didn't know how they were functioning, and so on. The attention to constraints enables the isolation and identification of components that were previously fused, as well as the disposition of conditions that could not otherwise be thematised, let alone even recognised. As Daniel Levin Becker puts it:

> The line, in effect, is this: writers are constrained whether or not they acknowledge it – not just by the strictures of poetic forms like the sonnet or haiku, but also by the conventions of their chosen genre, the format in which they publish, even the grammar and lexicon of their native (or adopted) language. Embracing a set of carefully chosen rules is meant to focus the mind so narrowly that those obscure pressures and preoccupations fade, revealing paths and passageways that one would never notice without the blinders.[7]

Hence, we find that there are always already constraints; that the formalisation of the role of constraints transforms the status of authorship; that constraints are always necessarily contingent without for all that being arbitrary; that the reason for a choice of constraint is not always able to be rationally grounded; that constraint has an emancipatory potential for both knowledge and action. Such a programme illuminates, separates and rebinds levels of discourse into functions of materials and techniques, such as punctuation, letters, numbers and words; syntax and semantics; narrative and character; etc. In doing so, however, the status of constraint itself comes to be radically complicated.

THE MORALITY OF CONSTRAINT

So, though it seems everybody is agreed that one of the crucial lessons from the work of the Oulipo, including that of its most famous member Georges Perec, has something to do with this something called 'constraint', this something – this 'transcendental object = X', to speak like Immanuel Kant, or 'the Central Object', to speak like Alain Badiou[8] – proves at once a goad and an obstacle to comprehension. Constraint is simultaneously a condition of possibility and an object of dissent. *That* constraint is not only foundational for Perec, but continues to make an important claim upon us today, is universally agreed upon – yet *what* it means and *how* it works remains surprisingly controversial. Such terms as 'experimental', 'the everyday', 'constraint' and 'play' – whether *despite* or *because of* their near-ubiquity in the scholarship on Perec and the Oulipo more generally – can remain obscure, if not obscurantist, if their sense and reference are not very carefully re-examined.

Take a recent epistolary exchange in the *London Review of Books*, initiated not by the nominal focus of Adam Mars-Jones's review of Anne Garréta's novel *Pas un jour*, but by one of that reviewer's passing remarks. Garréta's work, Mars-Jones comments, 'may qualify as a piece of self-disciplined formal choosing (*ascèse* is the word used), but it isn't a constraint in the Oulipo sense, lacking . . . the necessary element of arbitrariness'.[9] Well! Just over a month later, Lauren Elkin responded to this provocation with a correction of her own. It is worth quoting her letter at length:

> I would quibble with the assertion that Oulipian constraint is necessarily arbitrary. On the contrary, one of the most important and debated concepts within the group is the relationship between constraint and subject matter; Jacques Roubaud declared that the one must follow from the other, a notion summed up in the two principles set out in his *Atlas de littérature potentielle*:
>
> A text written according to a constraint
> must speak of this constraint.
>
> A text written according to
> a mathematisable constraint
> must contain the consequences of the
> mathematical theory it illustrates.
>
> Thus the missing 'e' in Perec's *La Disparition* is not an arbitrarily missing vowel, but a homonym for *eux*, or 'them', in a novel about a detective who is trying to find some people who have gone missing – a reference to those who died in the Holocaust, including Perec's own mother (his

father was killed in the phoney war). It has been noted that without 'e' you can't spell *père, mère* or, for that matter, Georges Perec.[10]

Elkin's attempts to clarify what she sees as a certain non-arbitrariness of constraint were immediately contested by Robin Durie, who, in the very next issue of the journal, fired off this broadside. 'For the Oulipians', Durie claims, 'the devising of the constraint consists in the creation of a function which has the potential to generate, or create, texts. The invention of the constraint is a purely formal exercise, and, as such, the constraint is necessarily arbitrary (i.e. without reason or sense, perspicuous or transmissible motivation, etc.). Indeed, from the outset, the Oulipians differentiated between inventors of constraints generative of potential literatures, and poets, whose application of the constraint consists in the writing of an actual text. The inventor always has priority over the poet, to the extent that the poet is forced to follow the rules of construction determined by the constraint.'[11] For Durie, Elkin's claims are merely matters of *interpretation*, having no bearing upon the *generation* and deployment of such constraints, which are chrono-logically prior to meaning.

If such disputes as these are hardly ever given such a long tail amid the letter pages of the *London Review of Books*, we find, just under a month later, Brian Reffin Smith explaining:

> As the only British member of Oupeinpo – Ouvroir de peinture potentielle, the art equivalent of Oulipo, also co-founded by François Le Lionnais, offering constraints that others might use to make art – I have to say that our problem is not whether the content relates to the constraint but rather trying to get rid of or neutralise the significance of the content altogether. We see ourselves as being perhaps a bit stricter than Oulipo, some of whose constraints are hardly that at all but rather methods: not the same thing. Oupeinpo does not make art, but invents constraints, which may inspire others to make art. But we have to illustrate the constraint, apply it to something; sometimes these illustrations of constraints are framed and hung in galleries. But they are not art, except by accident, to be avoided. How? We assert that all the work is in fact made by zombies, the philosophical or p-zombie, not the brain-eaters. Thus the work can have no emotional or any other real content, and if people see some, that's their problem. This is hugely liberating.[12]

I wish to underline some key aspects of this illuminating debate. First of all, its polite intensity: the correspondents clearly remain highly invested in the sense and implications of 'constraint', as, indeed, must be the journal's readers for such a recondite topic to be given such space over three months. Second, the necessity to discriminate 'constraint' from 'method', insofar as the former ought not be understood as just an updated or radicalised version of the latter, but different in kind. Third, the divergent clarity of the meta-positions regarding the sense of the 'arbitrariness' of constraint vis-à-vis its 'subject matter', namely (1) the constraint by which a text is constructed must be marked in and by this text itself; (2) the invention of constraint must be independent of and prior to the construction and deployment of any text using this constraint; and (3) that the invention of constraint must be expressly directed against any content in particular. Fourth, that a relation between constraint and its illustration is nonetheless irreducible. Fifth, that evidence for each of these positions (and, perhaps, even further ones) can be found in various explicit statements of Oulipo members themselves about constraint, as well as in their constraint-based works. Sixth, the promulgation of particular conceptual figures as the exemplification of the novelties introduced by such systems of constraint: the inventor as taking priority over the poet, for example, or the inventor-in-hand-with-a-zombie. Seventh, the sense of the crucial term 'potential' thereby becomes at once omnipresent and obscure.

FROM MORALS TO MATHEMATICS AND BACK AGAIN

My own thesis here will be the following: the most powerful deployments of constraint by the Oulipo are of an order in which, according to Elkin's terms above, constraint and subject matter are tied together in the presentation. Not only that, but there are at least two major different modes of this binding, which I will briefly exemplify here with respect to the work of Raymond Queneau and Georges Perec. The first radicalises *potentiality* and *inoperativity*, the second *actuality* and *passivity*, and in doing so, both pose new questions regarding the bonds – the constraints! – that link literal combinatories to the powers and passions of the body. Finally, Perec's singularity in this regard is due to a peculiar encounter with poetry.

Whatever the protestations to the contrary, an obscure kind of scriptural ethics remains at play in the 'must' of the constraint, both in its discussion and its deployment. The very concept of 'constraint' poses questions regarding its own generation, operation and evaluation. For constraint also turns what were previously usually considered – and indeed *de facto* functioned as – relatively autonomous divisions of human existence, such as literature and science, life and art, into an open environment of variegated constraints which, moreover, complicate the filiations of influence and reference. Yet, as they do so, another kind of ontological levelling occurs.

Take the much abused term 'experimental', which of course shares its roots with Shakespeare's word 'experience' discussed above. Although now definitively bifurcated in English, primarily due to certain decisive events dating back to the seventeenth-century,[13] the word retains a certain mobility in current French, at once designating experience in a personal – an 'everyday'? – sense, as well as a scientific experiment. If the syntagm 'experimental writing' is often still regularly invoked as a quasi-synonym for non-realist prose or difficult poetry, in the natural sciences 'experiment' clearly has a formal and foundational reference. Not only because the phrase 'experimental science' borders upon the tautological, but because experimental constraints are *never* unconscious in science, except as failure and oversight: on the contrary, scientific constraint must be explicit, formal, rigorous, quantifiable and repeatable. If experiment necessarily depends upon forms of observation (even in the 'mental' form taken by, say, Albert Einstein's famous 'thought experiments' or in cosmic telescopy), an experiment must nonetheless remain, precisely in order to meet such conditions as reproducibility, irreducible to empirical observation. Moreover, such constraints are directed, not towards proving or verifying general claims, but towards *not-dis-proving* specific hypotheses which themselves must be susceptible to being rendered in a propositional form, according to Karl Popper's famous principle of 'falsification': only denotative propositions whose negations are not contradictions are acceptable scientific statements insofar as they are susceptible to such falsification.[14] This doesn't necessarily mean that scientists always have such propositions to hand in advance; the point is that such propositions must be able to be reconstructed from the results in a formal manner in order to transform the observed data into knowledge.

Yet, there is also another condition of modern natural science that is not itself experimental, which constitutionally requires the full and explicit disclosure of constraint: it is mathematics. And, one of the early recognitions by the Oulipo – itself composed of several eminent writer-mathematicians – was that, once constraint becomes the crucial element of any structure, *the problematic of formalisation delivered by mathematics takes on a new and expanded role in the production and reception of literature itself.*[15] In an early essay that significantly predates the formation of the Oulipo, Queneau writes: 'The composite of logic and mathematics must not be seen merely as the appropriate and necessary language of science, nor as *one* of the sciences. In fact, it is Science itself.'[16] This conviction will later fuel a key programme of the Oulipo. As Christelle Reggiani notes: 'On the model of Bourbaki – a group of anonymous mathematicians, who, from the 1930s to the 1970s, accomplished a work of axiomatic refoundation of mathematics – Oulipo thinks of itself like a research team whose goal is to invent new creative "formulas" or make the forgotten reemerge'.[17] We see here the dismantling of received distinctions between mathematics and literature, writing and reading, between individual and group production, between human and machine.[18]

QUENEAU, POETRY, POTENTIAL

If this turn towards constraint necessarily undermines traditional genre distinctions (among much else) in the service of a kind of experimental mathematisation of the scriptural, where does this leave poetry? One of the most notorious early writings of the Oulipo was Queneau's *Cent mille milliards de poèmes*, glossed by Beverly Charles Rowe, one of his most inventive translators, as being:

> derived from a set of ten basic sonnets. In his book, published in 1961, they are printed on card with each line on a separated strip, like a heads-bodies-and-legs book. All ten sonnets have the same rhyme scheme and employ the same rhyme sounds. As a result, any line from a sonnet can be combined with any from the other nine, giving 10^{14} (= 100,000,000,000,000) different poems. Working twenty-four hours a day, it would take you some 140,000,000 years to read them all.[19]

In other words, Queneau has written an enormous number of poems that he did not write. Nor did he ever read them. The paradox of potential literature is exemplified here: a constraint, at once material and conceptual, has been implemented with empirical ease, which nonetheless unleashes vast numbers that beggar empirical life and literal comprehension. Yet, it is worth asking again: is this still *poetry*? As I've already suggested, hasn't the ancient distinction between 'poetry' and 'prose' shown to be a rather low-grade distinction in the light of constraint? Moreover, even if one wished to keep such a distinction, what sort of aesthetic and ethical evaluations might that imply? Surely using 'poetry' as a consistent nomination today is hardly justifiable, let alone as an honorific?

In fact, such questions would have already been familiar to Queneau himself from at least the 1930s, when he was attending – along with such luminaries as Raymond Aron, Georges Bataille, André Breton, Jacques Lacan and many others – the extremely influential lectures of Alexandre Kojève on G. W. F. Hegel's *Phenomenology of Spirit*.[20] Queneau's role in the transmission of the lectures is famous and determining: in addition to the lecture scripts and stenographed versions, he made his own notes and summaries, assembling and shaping a book that became one of the classics of twentieth-century philosophy, the *Introduction to the Reading of Hegel*.[21] Whatever else there is to say about Queneau's role in this publication, it has several features necessary to mark here.

First, the teleology ascribed to Hegel by Kojève's interpretation saw our own times configured as the 'end of history'. If Kojève famously nuances this position several times, what remains consistent throughout his doctrine is that, in aesthetic terms, the time of poetry is over, supplanted by the prose of the world. 'Prose' in the philosophical sense given it by Hegel is not simply opposed to poetry, but has incorporated its effective differences into its own elaboration. Here Queneau's own doctrines regarding the priority of formal languages – mathematics, logic and science – can be seen as a step beyond Hegel. Hegel himself famously contests the priority of mathematical knowledge in regard to philosophy;[22] Queneau, as I have briefly cited above, overturns this conviction while retaining Hegel's sense of an ending. Queneau's own writing practices are so diverse that they clearly exceed any received poetry/prose distinction, e.g. his editorial work, his group organisation, his *Exercises in Style*, *Zazie in the Metro* and the aforementioned sonnets, among much else.[23] This is to say that poetry no longer has any particular priority in Queneau's work, at the level of either doctrine or practice. Beneath the ancient opposition between poetry and prose are the mathemes of constraint.

Yet, this is not to say that Queneau's own obsession with formal concerns *simply* renders his work independent of its subject matter. On the contrary. For Queneau also signals a subjective and ontological question, around the two linked terms of 'potential' and 'inoperativity'. Regarding potential, as Jacques Roubaud and Marcel Bénabou put it, the *potentiel* signifies that literature can be produced in unlimited quantities until the end of the universe. But 'potential' can also mean: 'inactual' or 'not-actualised', perhaps even 'un-actualisable'. What could it mean to produce unlimited quantities of something that can't be? And, *where*, exactly, could such infinite potential take place? These questions go back beyond Hegel's famous meditations on the 'good' and 'bad' infinite in the *Science of Logic*, to the Aristotelian paradoxes regarding the problem of movement, potentiality and infinity in Book Gamma of the *Physics*. There, Aristotle proposes that 'there is no actual infinite, then, but there is an infinite potentially and by division. Still, the infinite is actual in the sense in which a day is actual or the games are actual.'[24] Aristotle's solution has historically pleased nobody. As Graham Priest notes: 'The potential infinite is neither potential nor infinite. It is not potential, at least in the way that most things are potential in Aristotle; for it (as opposed to parts of it) can never come into being. And it is not infinite, since at any stage it is finite.'[25] In other words, this potential is essentially unactualisable, a spectral infinite equivalent to the capacity to always go further, to continue – to not be fully exhausted in the act. This is one fundamental ideal for constraint.

For Queneau, then, at the end of history or, more precisely, in the *Sunday of Life* – a 1951 novel which has a quote from Hegel as an epigraph[26] – we find a profound link to the question of ethics, that is of how to live one's life. As Carlo Salzani notes, the word *désoeuvrement* (inoperativity) was itself first coined by Alexandre Kojève in the 1952 essay, 'Les Romans de la sagesse', a review of three novels by Raymond Queneau ... Kojève argues that the three protagonists of the novels, whom he calls *voyous désoeuvrés* (lazy rascals), embody, in a sense, the wisdom of man living after the end of history.[27]

In other words, for Queneau the compositional science of constraints, which emerges at the end of history and shows itself subjacent to received (historical) scriptural divisions, is integrally linked to the question of living under the new conditions, according to a kind of detachment of human beings from any form of natural or social compulsion. One now gives oneself constraints in clear consciousness and conscience according to the claims of contingency alone. Yet, the non-relation between the invention of a constraint and the subject matter of the models created from this constraint remains conditioned by a metaphysics of history. For Queneau, the seizure of *scriptural constraint* is correlated with the emergence of human freedom as *désoeuvrement*.

PEREC, POETRY, ACTUALITY

I do not believe that this is the case for Perec. Although he maintains a bond between constraint and action, it is of a different – if just as paradoxical – order from Queneau. Perec does not share the same doctrines of science as Queneau, nor the same philosophical references, nor the same relation to poetry.

According to the reconstruction offered by David Bellos, Perec

> came to poetry late in life, and by a singularly circuitous path. Like the question of Jewishness, poetry was not on his syllabus between the ages of twenty and forty, or thereabouts. His idea of it, acquired no doubt from French lessons at school, was at the antipodes of all his youthful aspirations: poetry, was sentiment, imagination, individuality, whereas what the young man valued was the epic, the real, and irony.[28]

Yet poetry is nonetheless already present, if in the mode of inversion and parody. Perec's very first work as an Oulipian is the collaborative *Hörspiel* or radio play, *Die Maschine* (1967), which Bellos calls 'an intentional derision of poetry', submitting a lyric of Goethe's, the *Wandrers Nachtlied*, to a barrage of distortion techniques, including the famous S+7 in which every substantive appearing in a text is replaced by the seventh noun after according to a standard dictionary.

On the one hand, this 'pseudo-computerized autopsy of Goethe's lyric'[29] is collaborative, mainly in German, written for a (fake) computer voice, for money, as a distorted parody and is, above all, *not* nominated as poetry. On the other hand, these very features exhibit a kind of plausible deniability, if not outright disavowal. Radio-performance-poetry-lucre-Germany: one doesn't have to be a psychoanalyst to discern that Perec, in working between languages, with multiple techniques, and inheritances, wreaking violence upon a famous lyric by one of greatest authors of the German language was, in addition to creating a brilliant piece, beginning to work through decisive relations with forms of writing and orphanage. (This period, incidentally, is close to the decisive psychoanalysis that Perec was undertaking.) Bellos himself suggests that 'deutschmarks must have seemed different when they were banked by a Frenchman of Jewish extraction whose father had died after defending the Marne and whose mother had been murdered at Auschwitz'.[30] As Bellos further comments: 'It was the first time since his teens that he had deigned or dared to confront poetry, and it was the first time that the theme of mortality . . . was allowed to enter his work.'[31] Judaism, Auschwitz, Babel: these emerge and return with the backdoor entry of poetry.

The following year, Perec published the e-less lipogrammatic text *La Disparition* (1969), followed by the 'Great Palindrome' (1970). The latter famously opens:

> Trace l'inégal palindrome. Neige. Bagatelle, dira Hercule. Le brut repentir, cet écrit né Perec. L'arc lu pèse trop, lis à vice-versa.[32]

> Trace the unequal palindrome. Snow. Bagatelle, says Hercules. Crude repenting, this writ born Perec. The read bow weighs too much, read vice-versa.[33]

It is necessary here to emphasise a number of this palindrome's features. First, its length. This is not simply a question of virtuosity (although it is certainly that): it is also that to do something of this magnitude requires extraordinary patience and work. Whereas Queneau's genius produces texts which he has never had to write, Perec struggles laboriously, letter by letter, from two ends at once. His body is literally bound to and divided by the painstaking production of letters. Second, the palindrome is explicitly reflexive, even meta-reflexive: it says what it is from its first moments, an unequal palindrome. It contains its author's name, as it consigns that name to that of its birth. It writes the Perec who writes it. It denotes itself as its own medium and material. It parodies the conditions of its own production: it is a tiny thing (a bagatelle), says Hercules, but he's so strong he may just be being honest or, again, engaging in a humility topos. A bagatelle, moreover, is not only a trifle, but also a light piece of verse or music, a bit of trumpery, and a game much like a form of billiards (according to the *Oxford English Dictionary*). It contains instructions for its own use: read backwards.³⁴ It alludes to a history of literary masters, including Mallarmé in the snow (*neige*) of the white page, as well as in the pun read/lily (*lis*). It forces out the relations – or non-relation – between letters and words in the French language, that is putting the relation between the *conditions* of sense (the letters and their physical disposition on a page) and *sense* (the words in (quasi-)grammatical order). The literal requires the oral it lacks and transforms in order to even have a sense it can no longer have but whose loss it exhibits *in extremis*.

Although Perec himself did not initially regard his palindrome as poetic, Harry Mathews came to convince Perec that poetry – far from being a humanistic practice of inspired affective effusions – shared something integrally with the Oulipo ideals: rigorous metre, constraints, games of reflexivity, that put the very distinction between contingency and necessity into question through literal permutations. From then on, Perec began to write – and destroy – enormous quantities of this 'poetry'. He began to give out around a hundred cyclostyled booklets of 'thematic puns' as new year's gifts to friends, *Voeux*, while other poems or poetic series include *Ulcérations* (Bibliotheque oulipenne), *La Clôture* (which had photos of Rue Vilin by Christine Lipinska) and *Metaux*, poems to accompany Paolo Boni's greaphisculptures. *Beaux presents, belles absentes* (1994), which is posthumous, is called by Bellos 'Perec's most exquisite formal poetry'.³⁵

In every instance, we see not only the choice of a singular constraint, but that this constraint is forced to reflect upon itself, while simultaneously being tied directly to features in the life of the writer or addressee (e.g. *W* has 37 chapters, Perec would be 37 on 7.3.73, there were 37 items on his bucket-list, etc.).³⁶ What Perec always does is suggest that, under the specific constraint that he is deploying, writing just won't make as much *sense* as it might have done, and not just semantically. The foreclosure of letters, for example, is also a loss of material and syntactic possibilities, that is possibilities of new articulations; yet, the loss of a letter also shows that new articulations are still possible, indeed, an entirely new articulation that would otherwise be impossible. But we must acknowledge the loss for the new articulations to have their real sense, which cannot be given within the lines themselves, being by definition what has been disappeared from them.³⁷ If constraint is chosen by Perec, it is not necessarily an index of freedom, as one may not know the constraints that constrain one's choice. Moreover, it is against this un-known constraint of constraint that one arrays chance or, at least, the clinamen:

> When you set up a system of constraints, you have to have anti-constraint in it. You must – and it's very important – you must destroy the system of constraints. It mustn't be rigid, it has to have some play, it has to creak a bit; the system mustn't be entirely coherent: the clinamen in Epicurus's

atomic theory; the world works because there was an imbalance at the start.[38]

So it is with the impact of 'poetry' that Perec starts to live and write consciously after the disappearance, but without being able to reinsert the disappeared. He therefore writes with the loss, writes the loss, and in such a way that it is not 'potential' nor 'inoperativity' that is at stake in his post-poetic work, but the woe of actuality and the labour of writing under the excised traces of compulsion. It is for such reasons that Bellos goes so far as to say that, 'from 1978 the reinvention of poetic form was at the centre of Perec's work', and, moreover, that 'His redefinition of the field of poetry . . . also has a retroactive implication for works that we have up to now treated just as prose'.[39] This is true, but it is also true that this is because a new kind of stopped breath comes to be inscribed in his work – in a way that, perhaps despite appearances, runs diagonally to Queneau and the other Oulipeans. It is the cancelled grain of the voice that is at stake in Perec's constraints, not a mathematical profusion of the unlimited.

PRELIVES AND AFTERLIVES OF CONSTRAINT

Along the lines that I have already broached with Shakespeare – that is, following the Oulipoesque suggestion of an analytic study of ancestral constraint, or that of what Queneau called 'prepotential literature' – we could re-examine literary, 'post-Shakespearean' modernity, not simply according to the passion for subjective expressionism, but by what seems to be its precise opposite: an obsession with impersonal or multiple creation through the rigours of constraint. The mad German poet Friedrich Hölderlin, who nobody could accuse of not being the very epitome of Romanticism, desired that poetry be elevated to a *mechanē* (craft), and complained of the contemporaneous lack of 'lawful calculation and other procedures through which beauty is brought out'.[40] Edgar Allan Poe famously explained his recipe for the writing of 'The Raven' in entirely technical terms.[41] In his own famous 1964 essay 'Potential Literature', Queneau notes the decisive role played by Stéphane Mallarmé: 'Mallarmé's sonnets are a privileged subject for us, as fruit flies are for geneticists.'[42] The point is not simply that there's an august lineage of experimentation with constraint in verse, but that our own epoch – through computerised algorithms – outsources, technicises and banalises the theme.[43] Here, the 'afterlife' of the Oulipo can perhaps today be seen most strongly in three modes: first, in the proliferation of conceptual interventions in poetics; second, in the enthusiastic thematic of contemporary scientific discoveries in and by poetry; and, third, in the electronic automation of constraint.

Regarding the first of these tendencies, we should mention the name of

Kenneth Goldsmith, the self-proclaimed 'ringleader' and publicist for so-called 'conceptual poetry' and 'uncreative writing'.[44] Goldsmith is notorious for various projects, including the *Printing Out the Internet* project (2013) which asked people to literally print out Internet pages, while, in 2015, he very controversially read out an altered version of the autopsy report on Michael Brown by the St Louis coroner's office.[45] For his part, Christian Bök has produced a stunning univocalic anthology titled *Eunoia* – the word is the shortest in English that contains all five vowels – and in which each chapter of the first section of the book contains words of only one vowel, A, E, I, O, U. The second section of the book is titled *Oiseau*, the shortest word in French to contain all the vowels, one of whose poems is titled 'W' and dedicated to Perec. Its first stanza runs:

> It is the V you double, not the U, as if to use
> two valleys in a valise is to savvy the vacuum
> of a vowel at a powwow in between sawteeth.[46]

Since then, Bök has pursued his incredible *The Xenotext Experiment*, which seeks to encode a poem into the extremophilic bacterium *Deinococcus radiodurans*.[47] Both with and against these conceptual poets, we also find a range of writers deliberately confounding identity politics with constraint-based routines, such as Juliana Spahr and Stephanie Young, who, under the heading of 'Foulipo', unleash homophonic distortions invoking 1970s feminist performance;[48] or, again, the young writers who contributed to the online journal *Anomalous*, as evidence of this ongoing volatile literary immixing of identity and constraint.[49]

In the second tendency, we can find a wide range of different kinds of writers, who nonetheless uptake various forms of contemporary science in their work. A recent *New Scientist* article titled 'Verse in the Universe: The Scientific Power of Poetry' even enumerated some major contemporary poets working with scientists, including the latest winner of the T. S. Eliot Prize, Sarah Howe, as well as Rebecca Elson and Simon Barraclough.[50] While many of their poems remain quite representational (in the sense of mingling received forms of realist description with lyric expressionism), we also find significant writers such as Rae Armantrout and Joan Retallack, who experiment with both contemporary science and formal procedures.[51]

Third, we find the exploitation of new computer languages and algorithms in the construction of poetry. The young Australian poet Oscar Schwartz has a website *bot or not* dedicated to the question of whether computers can write poetry.[52] Its front page explains:

> This website is a Turing test for poetry. You, the judge, have to guess whether the poem you're reading is written by a human or by a computer.

If you think a poem was written by a computer, choose 'bot'. If you think it was written by a human, choose 'not'.[53]

In its canonical form, the Turing Test – one of the founding documents of ongoing AI research, certainly much criticised and often modified – tests a machine's capacity to simulate human responses. The machine can be said to have passed the test when the human evaluator cannot discriminate the machine's answers from another human's.[54] For over two decades, the independent games developer Mez Breeze has been writing 'mezangelle', a form of hybrid poetry drawing on programming code and online environments.[55] Alongside the emergence of spoems, flarf and conceptual poetry, there's the attempt to write poetry that works simultaneously as poetry and as code.[56] As Roopika Risam puts it: 'In recent years, growing interest has emerged in the relationship between poetry and computer code. A higher brow version of ASCII art, code poems draw on programming languages like Java or C++ for their formal inspiration.'[57] While many of these projects are fascinating, the booster rhetoric that occasionally accompanies such attempts is disturbingly immodest and, indeed, often conceptually offensive: for instance, the claims that such works 'challenge the hegemony of natural languages' or 'break down old binaries' or 'are accelerating the post-human condition'. What, in a word, is missing from these post-Perec productions is the modality under which Perec himself binds together reflexivity, actuality and passivity throughout his work.

CONCLUSION

Perec's work thus attends simultaneously to rigorous formal techniques and to the presentation of the real, to the self-reflexivity of combinatorials on the one hand, and the dissimulating inscription of personal and political trauma on the other. Perec's notoriously stringent uptake of poetry comes at a particularly fraught and significant moment of his life, enabling a kind of compressed intensification of his already-existing practices. In a minor yet decisive way, poetry became a privileged laboratory for Perec, enabling him to focus in an unprecedentedly micrological fashion upon the relationships between constraint and chance, convention and content, in the innovative production, disposition and circulation of texts. This quadruple address is continually interwoven in Perec's writing in such a way that the force of affect and the patency of the absent are simultaneously in irreducible tension with each other, yet cannot be separated. Some important developments in contemporary poetry and poetics – including flarf, spoetry, conceptual poetry and bot poetry – therefore owe much to Perec's experiments, if, in their explicit extraction and externalisation of sets of techniques and attitudes, they thereby also vitiate, divide or occlude part of their predecessor's force.

This vitiation is in part due to the fact that these developments do not simultaneously tamper with the self-reflexivity of constraint, on the one hand, and the re-inscription of the trauma of the body, on the other. As Italo Calvino brilliantly puts it in 'Cybernetics and Ghosts':

> Literature is a combinatorial game that pursues the possibilities implicit in its own material, independent of the personality of the poet, but it is a game that at a certain point is invested with an unexpected meaning, a meaning that is not patent on the linguistic plane on which we were working but has slipped in from another level, activating something that on that second level is of great concern to the author or his society.[58]

For Perec, by contrast with so many of his inheritors, does not take the inexhaustibility of letters and literature for granted. Usually one just uses letters as if they were an infinite resource, endlessly available for use. But a little reflection will show that this cannot be the case: if letters are material things then they cannot not be limited. If they are material, then material is required for their inscription, whether through the ripples of modulated breath in air or by means of ink on paper. Resources are not inexhaustible. As I have tried to show, once Perec himself starts to take poetry seriously, he starts, too, to understand the environmental nature of writing's components differently: letters, breath, air. If one tampers with these at the most fundamental level, then combinatory is no longer simply a planar game but a self-reflexive one; moreover, it is also deictic, indicating a real of bodies which can nonetheless never be represented but whose violent absence exerts a terrifying pressure upon the writing of the text.

Whether surprisingly or not, in this he finds himself in a second-best bed with Shakespeare again. This is the case in the labour, the reflexivity, the puns and syntactic distortions, as well as in the short-circuiting of levels of writing and living. At one point in *King Lear*, Kent bellows at the unfortunate Oswald: 'Thou whoreson zed, thou unnecessary letter!' (2.2.58/2.2.60). This, it need not be said, makes the link between literality and life in the most aggressive way: Latin didn't have 'z', and its functions in English could also, some commentators held, be just as well given by 's'. But, it is just as much the case that Shakespeare recognised the short-circuiting of letters and numbers. As the Fool comments to Lear after the latter has foolishly divided and given away his kingdom: 'Now thou art an O without a figure' (1.4.180 (1603), 1.4.166 (1623)).[59] What is an O without a figure? The blank of a page, or the nothing of a human reduced to pure penury.

One used to use the phrase 'free as air', but now there's no way anybody today can consider that the air is free. As Marcel Duchamp, one of Perec's own inspirations (noting that the word 'inspiration' itself has a pneumatological etymology), wrote: 'Establish a society in which the individual has to pay for the air he breathes (air meters; imprisonment and rarefied air, in case of non-payment simple asphyxiation if necessary (cut off the air)).'[60] This pneumatological thanatopolitics perhaps takes us back to the φρένες of Ancient Greek, the diaphragm as the seat of consciousness,[61] through Shakespeare and his deadly airs, up to Perec's poetics of trauma, for which every constraint is also a choker or a gag.[62]

As Edgar puts it in 1623 (but not in 1608): 'Welcome then, / Thou unsubstantial air that I embrace: / The wretch that thou hast blown unto the worst / Owes nothing to thy blasts' (4.1.6–9). The unsubstantial air that we breath – or, more literally here, do not breathe but embrace – that appears nowhere on any page, but which is nonetheless the invisible environmental factor necessary to any human composition whatsoever, the anti-figural figure of the absolutely disappeared – this is also Perec's poetics of composition. The lipogram is only one of the names of this starvation programme for life and writing, whereby the fat of potential literature is sucked out through technically modified writing, and returned to the breathless terrors of actuality, that is 'the worst', where one can no longer even pronounce the letter 'e' – and, thus, can no longer speak experience nor esperance . . . nor Perec itself.

'The rest returns to laughter.'

NOTES

1. The full title page of the quarto reads: 'Mr. William Shakespeare: his true chronicle history of the life and death of King Lear and his three Daughters. With the unfortunate life of Edgar, son and heir to the Earl of Gloucester, and his sullen and assumed humour of Tom of Bedlam'. The edition upon which I rely here is William Shakespeare (1993), *King Lear: A Parallel Text Edition*, ed. René Weis, London: Longman. I would like to thank Ali Alizadeh and Joseph Hughes for their feedback on earlier versions of this chapter.
2. As René Weis notes in his introduction to his edition, 'The "real" Lear or Lears were not seen on the English stage between 1681 and 1823, when Edmund Kean restored the tragic ending of the play, and it was not till 1838 that William Charles Macready fully returned to Shakespeare's play' (p. 2). Until then, Tate's version had reigned, with the imprimatur of Doctor Johnson.
3. In this particular temporal sense, note that *experience*, corresponding to 'what happened?', and *esperance*, corresponding to 'what will happen?', are themselves correlates of a division repeatedly discussed by Gilles Deleuze according to the genres, respectively, of the novella and the tale, e.g. see Gilles Deleuze (1990), 'Tenth Series of the Ideal Game', in *The Logic of Sense*, trans. Mark Lester with Charles Stivale, ed. Constantin V. Boundas, New York:

Columbia University Press, and Plateau 8, '1874: Three novellas, or "What Happened?"' in Gilles Deleuze and Félix Guattari (1987), *A Thousand Plateaus: Capitalism and Schizophrenia*, trans. and foreword Brian Massumi, Minneapolis: University of Minnesota Press.

4. See David Crystal (2005), *Pronouncing Shakespeare: The Globe Experiment*, Cambridge: Cambridge University Press; also David Crystal (2013), 'Early Interest in Shakespearean Original Pronunciation', *Language and History*, vol. 56, no. 1, pp. 5–17.
5. 'All interest of my reason (the speculative as well as the practical)', Kant announces in the section titled 'On the Canon of Pure Reason, Second Section: On the ideal of the highest good, as a determining ground of the ultimate end of pure reason', 'is united in the following three questions: 1. What can I know? 2. What should I do? 3. What may I hope?' Immanuel Kant (1998), *Critique of Pure Reason*, trans. and ed. Paul Guyer and Allen W. Wood, Cambridge: Cambridge University Press, p. 677.
6. As one might expect, there is now an enormous secondary literature concerning the subtleties of constraint. In the current context, see, *inter alia*, Alison James (2009), *Constraining Chance: Georges Perec and the Oulipo*, Evanstown: Northwestern University Press; as well as selected pieces in Warren Motte (ed.) (1986), *Oulipo: A Primer of Potential Literature*, Lincoln: University of Nebraska Press, especially those by Bénabou, Calvino, Motte and Roubaud.
7. Daniel Levin Becker (2012), *Many Subtle Channels: In Praise of Potential Literature*, Cambridge, MA: Harvard University Press, pp. 12–13.
8. That is, that object that 'reduces the equivocity of similarity to the clarity of equality', Alain Badiou (2014), *Mathematics of the Transcendental*, trans. A. J. Bartlett and Alex Ling, London and New York: Bloomsbury, p. 73.
9. Adam Mars-Jones (2015), 'The Love Object', 30 July. As Mars-Jones (2015) further notes:

> American appropriations of Oulipo, Levin Becker's above all, with his perky choice of register ('badass', 'nerd', 'croak' used to mean 'die'), seek to put a democratizing spin on the elite caperings of a group of mavericks with mathematical as well as verbal obsessions. The risk is of turning Oulipo's speculative philosophy, the refusal to acknowledge the difference between a technical exercise and an aesthetic project, into a Zumba class for limbering up the writerly brain.

Note I have relied on the online *LRB* for these references, which lacks pagination.
10. Lauren Elkin (2015), 'Letter', *London Review of Books*, vol. 37, no. 17, 10 September.
11. Robin Durie (2015), 'Oulipian', *London Review of Books*, vol. 37, no. 18, 24 September.
12. Brian Reffin Smith (2015), 'Oulipian (not exactly)', *London Review of Books*, vol. 37, no. 20, 22 October.
13. One of the empirical reasons for the exceptional English bifurcation is undoubtedly due to its coupling of political and scientific revolutions, marked by the Restoration and the accompanying support by Charles II for the establishment of the Royal Society. See Marie Boas Hall (1991), *Promoting Experimental Learning 1660–1717*, Cambridge: Cambridge University Press, p. 9.
14. See Karl Popper (2002), *The Logic of Scientific Discovery*, London: Routledge. If there are undeniably many and perhaps irreconcilable theories and practices of what we might call (if anachronistically) 'modern scientific experiment', stemming from at least the seventeenth century, the key point of this minimal description here is at least triple: first, to suggest how *experiment* must be analytically separated from *formalisation* per se, in order

to enable a sense of the import of their peculiar re-articulation in the Oulipian context; second, to suggest how the necessary confusions of historical or empirical development do not thereby vitiate the attempt to extract and formalise a kind of 'matheme' (to speak like Jacques Lacan) of their functioning; third, to return 'experiment' to 'experience' à la the Shakespeare vacillation with which I began. In a French context, the interested reader might refer to the extraordinary work of J.-C. Milner (1995), especially *L'Oeuvre claire: Lacan, la science, la philosophie*, Paris: Seuil.

15. Drawing upon and extending the example of Bourbaki and French structuralism, a number of rival groups become involved in the mathematisation of literature in 1960s France. Exemplary would be the polemics between the *Tel Quel* collective and the Oulipo. As Julia Kristeva (1998) writes in 'Towards a Semiology of Paragrams' (originally 1967), the former sought 'the discovery of a formalism that corresponds isomorphically to literary productivity's thinking itself', for which 'only two methodologies could serve as a basis': 'mathematics and metamathematics – artificial languages that, due to the freedom of the signs they use, are more and more able to elude the constraints of a logic based on the Indo-European subject-predicate relation, and that as a consequence are better adapted to describing the poetic operations of language' (*The Tel Quel Reader*, ed. Patrick ffrench and Roland-François Lack, London and New York: Routledge, p. 25). See also the scathing responses by Jacques Roubaud and Pierre Lusson, 'Sur la "Sémiologie des paragrammes" de J. Kristeva', *Action poétique*, vol. 41–2 (1969), pp. 56–61, and vol. 45 (1970), pp. 31–6, as well as the commentary by Véronique Montémont (2004), *Jacques Roubaud: L'amour du nombre*, Pas-de-Calais: Presses Universitaires du Septentrion. I would like to thank Christian Gelder for alerting me to these articles, and providing me with photocopies. It is perhaps also worth mentioning that André Weil (Simone's brother) was not only a great mathematician and a member of Bourbaki, but a close friend of the great structural anthropologist Claude Lévi-Strauss, with whom he famously collaborated on Indigenous Australian kinship relations. Roubaud's own parents were friends of Simone Weil's at the ENS.

16. Raymond Queneau (2007), 'The Place of Mathematics in the Classification of the Sciences' (1943), in *Letters, Numbers, Forms: Essays, 1928–70*, Urbana and Chicago: University of Illinois Press, p. 100.

17. Christelle Reggiani (1999), *Rhétoriques de la contrainte: Georges Perec – L'oulipo*, Saint-Pierre-du-Mont: Editions InterUniversitaires, p. 7.

18. This dissolution of received distinctions of genre, etc., is expressly underlined by various members of the Oulipo, e.g. 'Several decades before the official birth of Oulipo, [Duchamp] had himself anticipated, even outlined, some of its basic principles', most notably 'the breaking down of barriers between disciplines, the solidarity between the poetic and the scientific, his unrestrained boldness in experimentation, his ironic and distanced view of established art forms' (Marcel Bénabou (2008), 'Duchamp à l'Oulipo ou un secret trop bien gardé', in *« regarde de tous tes yeux regarde »: l'art contemporain de Georges Perec*, Joseph K./Musée des beaux-arts de Nantes/Musée des beaux-arts de Dole), pp. 74 and 76. Cited in Chapter 2 by Ribière, this volume.

19. http://www.bevrowe.info/Queneau/QueneauHome_v2.html (accessed 20 August 2015). It is hard to recommend this site highly enough.

20. For the impact of Kojève's lectures, see Bruce Baugh (2003), *French Hegel: From Surrealism to Postmodernism*, New York and London: Routledge; Judith Butler (1987), *Subjects of Desire: Hegelian Reflections in Twentieth-Century France*, New York: Columbia University Press; Michael S. Roth (1988), *Knowing and History: Appropriations of Hegel in Twentieth-Century France*, Ithaca, NY: Cornell University Press. See also Italo Calvino's

(1999) chapter on Queneau in *Why Read the Classics?* trans. Martin McLaughlin, Boston: Mariner.
21. See Alexandre Kojève (1969), *Introduction to the Reading of Hegel*, assembled by Raymond Queneau, ed. Allan Bloom, trans. James H. Nichols, New York and London: Basic Books.
22. For his canonical view of mathematics, see Hegel's (1978) famous 'Preface' to *Phenomenology of Spirit*, trans. A. V. Miller, analysis and foreword J. N. Findlay, Oxford: Oxford University Press. For a recent account of Hegel's procedure here, see Alain Badiou (2005), *Being and Event*, trans. Oliver Feltham, London: Continuum, pp. 161–70; also, the essays collected in Antonio Calcagno and Jim Vernon (eds) (2015), *Badiou and Hegel*, Lanham, MD: Lexington.
23. See Raymond Queneau (2012), *Exercises in Style*, trans. Barbara Wright, with Chris Clarke, New York: New Directions; Raymond Queneau (1960), *Zazie in the Metro*, trans. Barbara Wright, London: John Calder.
24. Aristotle (1961), *Aristotle's Physics*, trans. Richard Hope, Lincoln: University of Nebraska Press, p. 54.
25. Graham Priest (1995), *Beyond the Limits of Thought*, Cambridge: Cambridge University Press, p. 28.
26. Raymond Queneau (1976), *The Sunday of Life*, trans. Barbara Wright, London: John Calder.
27. Carlo Salzani (2011), 'Inoperative/Deactivation', in Alex Murray and Jessica Whyte (eds), *The Agamben Dictionary*, Edinburgh: Edinburgh University Press, p. 106. See also Giorgio Agamben (1999), *Potentialities*, trans. and ed. Daniel Heller-Roazen, Stanford: Stanford University Press. It is no doubt pertinent that Agamben himself had at one time planned to establish a cultural journal with Italo Calvino and Claudio Rugafiori; see Giorgio Agamben (1999), *The End of the Poem: Studies in Poetics*, trans. Daniel Heller-Roazen, Stanford: Stanford University Press, p. xi.
28. David Bellos (1993), *Georges Perec: A Life in Words*, London: Harvill, p. 669.
29. Bellos, *Georges Perec*, p. 669.
30. Bellos, *Georges Perec*, p. 383.
31. Bellos, *Georges Perec*, p. 383.
32. Georges Perec (1980), *La Clôture et autres poems*, Paris: Hachette, p. 45.
33. Bellos' version reads: 'Trace the uneven palindrome. Snow. A trifle, says Hercules. Unadorned repentance, this piece born [of] Perec. [If] the bow of reading is too heavy, read back-to-front' (*Georges Perec*, p. 430). Although it is ridiculous to quibble with translations of palindromes, especially given that Bellos is attempting to give an English sense of the French non-sense, I do want to suggest that: (1) '*bagatelle*' works in English, and could remain 'untranslated'; (2) 'unadorned' is perhaps too fancy for '*brut*', which is raw, crude, monosyllabic; and (3) 'piece' for '*écrit*' loses the crucial scriptural reference. For his part, Mathews has: 'Trace the unequal palindrome. Snow. A trifle, Hercules would say. Rough penitence, this writing born as Perec. The read arch is too heavy: read vice-versa . . .'
34. The conceptual implications of palindromes are also, in my opinion, exceptionally interesting. On this, see my own essay: Justin Clemens (2014), 'Return to the Palindrome of the Real', in *Axon*, vol. 4, no. 2, http://www.axonjournal.com.au/issue-7/return-palindrome-real.
35. See David Bellos, 'The Afterlives of a Writer', Chapter 14, this volume.
36. See Bellos, *Georges Perec*, pp. 708–9.
37. As Warren Motte puts it (this is a position that Elkin repeats):

> The absence of a sign is always the sign of an absence, and the absence of the E in *A Void* announces a broader, cannily coded discourse on loss, catastrophe, and mourning. Perec cannot say the words *père, mère, parents, famille* in his novel, nor can he write the name *Georges Perec*. In short, each 'void' in the novel is abundantly furnished with meaning, and each points towards the existential void that Perec grappled with throughout his youth and early adulthood. A strange and compelling parable of survival becomes apparent in the novel, too, if one is willing to reflect on the struggles of a Holocaust orphan trying to make sense out of absence, and those of a young writer who has chosen to do without the letter that is the beginning and end of *écriture*. (Warren Motte (n.d.), 'Reading Georges Perec: Context No 11', http://www.dalkeyarchive.com/reading-georges-perec/ (accessed 2 February 2016))

38. Georges Perec (1983), 'Conversation in Warsaw with Ewa Pawlikowska', *Littératures*, no. 7, cited in Bernard Magné (2009), 'Transformations of Constraint', *Review of Contemporary Fiction*, vol. 29, no. 1, p. 197.
39. Bellos, *Georges Perec*, p. 670.
40. Friedrich Hölderlin (2003), 'Remarks on Oedipus', in J. M. Bernstein (ed.), *Classic and Romantic German Aesthetics*, Cambridge: Cambridge University Press, p. 194.
41. Edgar Allan Poe (1846), 'The Philosophy of Composition', *Graham's Magazine*, vol. XXVIII, no. 4, April, pp. 163–7.
42. Queneau, 'Potential Literature', in *Letters, Numbers, Forms*, p. 193. One could indeed track the continuing interest by contemporary philosophers in Mallarmé along lines that link them in lipogrammatic ways to Perec. As Jean-Claude Milner has pointed out:

> The 19th century French alphabet counts twenty-five letters: the allegedly foreign letter 'w' was not included (Brachet and Dussouchet, *Grammaire Française*, 1888, pp. 34–5). Mallarmé, trained in the linguistics of his time, knew this better than anyone. A conjecture: having excluded the 'w' like Brachet and Dussouchet, Mallarmé took a supplementary step by excluding the 'k' – a purely Greek or foreign letter (see Littré and, by contrast, the use made of it by Leconte de Lisle). It would be interesting to verify if Mallarmé uses the 'k' or 'w' in his *Poésies*, handwritten by him (aside from proper names, Whistler or Wagner). A first examination proves not . . . Mallarmé, or the hidden lipogram? ('Les constellations révélatrices', *Elucidation*, Vol. 8–9 (2003), p. 6)

See also the incredible interpretation by Quentin Meillassoux (2012), *The Number and the Siren*, trans. Robin Mackay, Falmouth: Urbanomic.
43. For an accessible survey of the history of the study of combinatorial objects – 'a comparatively new area of discrete mathematics' – see J. Berstel and D. Perrin (2007), 'The Origins of Combinatorics on Words', *European Journal of Combinatorics*, no. 28, pp. 996–1022. What is crucial to note with regard to combinatorics is that it deals only with laws pertaining to transformations upon letters themselves, that is the 'words' it examines are purely planar insofar as they don't involve any function of enunciation at all. The quite astonishing results that such combinatorics generate – such as the relations between 'avoidable' and 'unavoidable', regularities in finite or infinite strings of symbols from finite alphabets, or various theorems in symbolic dynamics – doesn't touch on the uses of *language* as game or name or reference.
44. Kenneth Goldsmith (2011), *Uncreative Writing: Managing Language in the Digital Age*, New York: Columbia University Press.

45. For an archive of Goldsmith's projects, see: http://epc.buffalo.edu/authors/goldsmith/. A savage critique of some of the claims made by the conceptual poets has been levelled by a range of people, including Alec Wilkinson (2015), 'Something Borrowed', *New Yorker*, 5 October, http://www.newyorker.com/magazine/2015/10/05/something-borrowed-wilkinson (accessed 5 January 2016); M. Yankelevich (2012), 'The Gray Area: An Open Letter to Marjorie Perloff', *LARB*, 13 July, https://lareviewofbooks.org/essay/the-gray-area-an-open-letter-to-marjorie-perloff (accessed 23 August 2015); Cathy Park Hong (2015), 'There's a New Movement in American Poetry and It's Not Kenneth Goldsmith', *New Republic*, 2 October, https://newrepublic.com/article/122985/new-movement-american-poetry-not-kenneth-goldsmith (accessed 5 January 2016); Brian Kim Stefans (2015), 'Open Letter to the New Yorker', *New Yorker*, 4 October, http://www.arras.net/fscIII/?p=2467 (accessed 1 February 2016).
46. Christian Bök (2008), *Eunoia*, Edinburgh: Canongate Books, p. 92.
47. See a recent report from Bök himself here: https://vimeo.com/58653647 (accessed 23 August 2015).
48. See their talk for the CalArts Noulipo conference in 2005, available here: http://epc.buffalo.edu/authors/goldsmith/foulipo.html, as well as Goldsmith's response http://epc.buffalo.edu/authors/goldsmith/goldsmith_foulipo.html (accessed 24 May 2016). It is indicative that Goldsmith charges Spahr and Young with 'nostalgia', that is a failure to live up to the terms of the contemporary: in order to maintain the present priority of conceptual poetry against politicised identity critiques, Goldsmith is forced to revivify a centuries-old image of avant-gardism, whose great formula is Rimbaud's 'Il faut être absolument moderne'. Goldsmith's terror of time – let alone of bodies – is legible in this exemplarily symptomatic response.
49. See http://www.anomalouspress.org/14/1.intro.php for a downloadable version of this issue, as well as the interesting commentary by Michael Leong, 'Rats Build Their Labyrinth: Oulipo in the 21st Century' (17 May 2015), at http://ww.hyperallergic.com/206802/rats-build-their-labyrinth-oulipo-in-the-21st-century/ (accessed 23 August 2015).
50. Niall Firth (2016), 'Verse in the Universe: The Scientific Power of Poetry', *New Scientist*, 20 January.
51. See Rae Armantrout (2015), *Itself*, Middletown, CT: Wesleyan University Press; and Joan Retallack (2010), *Procedural Elegies/Western Civ Cont'd*, New York: Roof. See also the essay by A. J. Carruthers (2016), 'Procedural Ecologies: Joan Retallack's "Archimedes' New Light"', *Contemporary Women's Writing*, pp. 1–14. For a cross-over collection edited by none other than Gilbert Adair – the translator of Perec's *La disparition* into English as *A Void* – see https://jacket2.org/feature/metaphor.
52. See https://prezi.com/joh-s2zxir7t/a-turing-test-for-poetry/ for further explanation by Schwartz himself (accessed 17 August 2015).
53. See http://botpoet.com (accessed 17 August 2015).
54. A pdf of Turing's classic paper 'Computing Machines and Intelligence' can be found here: http://orium.pw/paper/turingai.pdf (accessed 17 August 2015).
55. See the excellent review by R. Raley, 'Interferences': http://www.electronicbookreview.com/thread/electropoetics/net.writing (accessed 23 August 2015). Also R. Risam: http://jacket2.org/commentary/poetry-unexecutable-code (accessed 23 August 2015).
56. See 'Rhyme and Reason: Writing Poems in Computer Code', *New Scientist*, 16 December 2014.
57. See http://jacket2.org/commentary/poetry-executable-code (accessed 23 August 2015).

58. Italo Calvino (1986), 'Cybernetics and Ghosts', in Warren Motte (ed.), *Oulipo: A Primer of Potential Literature*, Lincoln: University of Nebraska Press, p. 22.
59. See Brian Rotman (1987), *Signifying Nothing: The Semiotics of Zero*, London: Macmillan.
60. See Marcel Duchamp (1989), *The Writings of Marcel Duchamp*, ed. Michel Sanouillet and Elmer Peterson, New York: Da Capo, p. 31.
61. See Richard Broxton Onians (1988), *The Origins of European Thought: About the Body, the Mind, the Soul, the World, Time, and Fate: New Interpretations of Greek, Roman and Kindred Evidence, Also of Some Basic Jewish and Christian Beliefs*, Cambridge: Cambridge University Press.
62. For the relationships between environmentalism, terrorism and modernism, see Peter Sloterdijk (2009), *Terror from the Air*, trans. Steve Corcoran and A. Patton, Los Angeles: Semiotext(e).

CHAPTER 4

UnSearching for Rue Simon-Crubellier: Perec Out-of-Sync

Darren Tofts

My idea of literature was of something that could and would intervene in reality. Or at least that's the way I thought of it then.

Italo Calvino[1]

When nothing is sure, everything is possible.

Margaret Drabble[2]

All other resemblances to living persons or to people having lived in reality or fiction can only be coincidental.

Georges Perec[3]

Stay, illusion!

Shakespeare[4]

One of the things writing does is wipe things out.

Marguerite Duras[5]

Art consists of limitation.

G. K. Chesterton[6]

I'd rather regret the things I've done than regret the things I haven't done.

Lucille Ball

'A SCHEDULE OF' COMPLICATIONS

While it might seem like a surfeit of epigrams prefacing this tapestry that you are about to Unweave (essay, text, fly specs on a page or screen, the subliminal flicker of codified light), this assemblage of samples already performs what you are about to do in reading this text. It has already said what will have to be, and have been said. All a matter of tense, colliding times, duration and anachrony, it puts the pieces together in the manner of a jigsaw, then takes it apart, out-of-context, out-of-time. Epigrams are at once rhetorical figures of what is to come, other words doing the work for someone else, suggestive, prefatory and oracular. They are a kind of mime or ventriloquism, prolonging entry into another text with the sign-sound proxies of others speaking. Not 'dismantled', 'broken down', 'read' or 'interpreted'. They are gestures out-of-sync.

A label then, on a parcel addressed to *someone*, is another assemblage of Unwords. Its specificity is a contract between signs and atoms, artifice and edifice:

> Monsieur Gaspard Winckler
> 11 rue Simon-Crubellier
> Paris 17 France

In another context its dark borders and curlicue italics would announce a death, notifying a recent absence which can no longer be delivered, made present or signed for. The brittle uncertainty and rigorous ambivalence of the *pharmakon*, the *either/and/or* of writing, becomes the excessive irresolution in print of a street address in a verifiably real city that is nowhere to be found outside page space. Yet, it is *potentially* located somewhere in a city that exists in empirical space if it is sought after with enough suspension of belief as well as its opposite. *Life A User's Manual* is a palimpsest worthy of Lewis Carroll or Jorge Luis Borges in which the map and the territory seamlessly appear to overlap. But there is one minute but not insignificant detail missing in this particular heraldic *mise en abyme*: a glitch marked on a calling card, an address to which we are invited.

Writing, by its own mandate, is an ecology of restrictions, rules, and conventions. While it is 'obliged' (before and after Georges Perec) to perform 'a schedule' of specific and unseen codes and admixtures to ferment its alchemy, it nonetheless complicates everything it touches from reference outside as well as to itself. A previous architect of universes in nutshells, by way of oblique reference to the quantum austerity of another, also wrote from Paris trying to find a path and a destination through its thickets:

> You is feeling like you was lost in the bush, boy? You says: It is a puling sample jungle of woods. You most shouts out: Bethicket me for a stump of a beech if I have the poultriest notions what the farest he all means.[7]

So, while we can find such a reference to Samuel Beckett in *Finnegans Wake*, no matter how hard we harrow the Dantean penance of traversing the seventeenth arrondissement in Paris, our search will never yield a street bearing the name of Simon-Crubellier.

After 'pataphysics and surrealism in that city, before fractal geometry and binary code in others, the Knight's tour of chess served Perec as the architectonic plan for arranging, intertwining and indeed 'intertwingling' detail and more detail.[8] Perec's encyclopaedism reinforces, in the unforgiving facticity of the things it amasses, the unmoving weight of mortar that binds bricks and masonry together in a seven-storey *appartement*:

> The inhabitants of a single building live a few inches from each other, they are separated by a mere partition wall, they share the same spaces repeated along each corridor, they perform the same movements at the same times, turning on a tap, flushing the water closet, switching on a light, laying the table, a few dozen simultaneous existences repeated from storey to storey, from building to building, from street to street. They entrench themselves in their domestic dwelling space – since that is what it is called – and they would prefer nothing to emerge from it; but the little that they do let out – the dog on a lead, the child off to fetch the bread, someone brought back, someone sent away – comes out by way of the landing. For all that passes, passes by the stairs, and all that comes, comes by the stairs: letters, announcements of births, marriages, and deaths, furniture brought in or taken out by removers, the doctor called in an emergency, the traveller returning from a long voyage.[9]

But at the centre of such weight in this closed field of *things* is the aporia of an absent detail beyond the indelible marks of type or the *gramme* of letters.

UNSEARCHING

Artists Norie Neumark and Maria Miranda (collectively known as 'Out-of-Sync') travelled to Paris in 2004 with one determined and interrogative aim in mind: 'Is it possible to bring something that doesn't exist into existence by searching for it?' An inquisitive exercise in the absurd, such rigour tests the credulity of suggestion and suggestibility of a kind that Italo Calvino marvels over at one point in *Cosmicomics*: '"The Dinosaurs are coming back!"'[10] The same artists could have travelled to Dublin in search of number 7 Eccles Street, in a real city described in the voluminous page space of the 'Book of Bloom'. Such fey insistence on the possible would be unnecessary and ridiculed mercilessly by a legion of incisive Joycean wits from Irvine to Zurich. To search for the celebrity streets of Joyce and Perec implies pilgrimages found and lost. But Neumark and Miranda are not interested in bringing Perec's novel to life as street theatre or surrealist dramaturgy. As a video work it is understated in its transparency as a documentary trying to disprove that the street *does not* exist somewhere: Miranda has described the work in this respect as 'ongoing as the search is open-ended and never finished', particularly in a city such as Paris that is indivisibly strange and overwhelmingly familiar.[11] In one moment in the video we see a figurative assemblage being made in an attempt to locate the precise coordinates of Rue Simon-Crubellier on fragments of a street map of the seventeenth arrondissement in Paris. The map is sampled exactly from coordinates detailed in Perec's novel:

> On the sheet there are in fact not one but three sketch-plans: the first, at the top right-hand corner, shows where the building is, roughly half-way along Rue Simon-Crubellier, which cuts at an angle across the quadrilateral formed by Rue Médéric, Rue Jadin, Rue de Chazelles, and Rue Léon Jost, in the Plaine Monceau district of the XVIIth arrondissement of Paris . . .[12]

Despite being armed with such cartographical precision no such address is to be found in the municipality of Paris (not even the seventeenth arrondissement that one literate video interviewee cannily suggests). Other testimony of its possible whereabouts is provided by a toddler who advises the artists to 'go there and go there', then revises the direction 'perhaps there or perhaps there', with decisive and confident hand gestures that are identical in each case. *Searching for Rue Simon-Crubellier* is a gloriously failed quest in which the pursuit of the imaginary and the suggestively elusive is its tentative and fragile goal (an anagram of which, the archaic 'gaol', is a misprision that would have appealed to Perec's lexicographical imagination).

The aesthetic elan of the artists in this work is to shrink the bounds of incredulity and doubt through persistent reinforcement. The medium for this thought experiment is a mediated *dérive* that overlaps page space and urban space. Technologically kitted out with various audio-visual capturing devices, the idea of testimony is visually and assertively reinforced by the assuring rigour of a literary pursuit undertaken simultaneously, consulting the pages of a well thumbed copy of a book they carry around with them: *Life A User's Manual* is talisman, Baedeker and Paris street directory. Along with hunting for snarks in pastoral England, furtively seeking out fairies at the bottom of the garden or the Loch Ness Monster, such forensic vigour may not count for much beyond being a devilish stretch of the truth.[13] But their journey resembles a detective aesthetic that takes them to the reassuringly non-fictive offices of civic officials, map-makers and bureaucrats, the Town Council offices of the seventeenth arrondissement, and even the Office of Town Planning responsible for the naming of streets in Paris. The artists are politely and repeatedly advised that the object of their pursuit is imaginary, to which they counter with the suggestion that it may be the name of an ancient street that has since disappeared and been appropriated by Perec. In testing the bounds of credulity they are persistently met with dogged municipal resistance insisting that it is fictive and not factual. A literate official in the Office for Paris Maps, a former neighbour who knew Perec 'very well as a writer and as a person', decisively underlines the street's fictionality. A walking-talking *Brodie's Notes*, or French version thereof (if such a gauche thing exists), he demystifies any possible truth in the whereabouts of the street by proceeding to describe *Life A User's Manual* as a 'building that is cut down the middle to show everything that happens there'. In itself, this architectonic conceit for a street is a curious metafictional figure for a novel as a building lacking a fourth wall (an image of which features on the cover of most editions of the book in varying forms). While the artists are repeatedly advised that Simon-Crubellier is an imaginary street 'in the framework of a novel', it occupies a lot of civil servant time and effort *searching* for it nonetheless. Throughout *Searching for Rue Simon-Crubellier*, the pursuit of the fabulatory goes viral – a tenuous membrane between making and Unmaking, vanishing, materiality and materialisation.

Avatars of other pursuants of the impossible, Neumark and Miranda nevertheless persist in their quest to find the fictional in the real through the subtle and insidious poetics of suggestion. They do, however, put doubt in many minds, not the least of which is that of the collective viewer of *Searching for Rue Simon-Crubellier*. So, when the imaginary persistently refuses to live up to possibility, there is always Oulipo. The artists finally end up in the book-lined salon of Marcel Bénabou, the Permanent Provisional Secretary of the 'workshop of potential literature'. Having described his enthusiasm for the 'Perec-like' nature of the artists' project, Bénabou flatly declaims that the street does not exist. *Their* work then finishes in an exquisitely reflexive and bookish set piece that features Bénabou's disembodied voice reading from *Life A User's Manual* as his image moves phantom-like through his flat. A heretical Plato in his library, with nothing more to say of 11 Rue Simon-Crubellier, he walks and talks nonetheless.

Such reflexivity of a ludic and mathematical precision is to be expected in relation to any discussion of the fastidiously complex worlds of Georges Perec. While there may indeed be no *outside-text*, in either the most limpid *nouvelle vraisemblable* (*Piers Plowman, Gravity's Rainbow, To the Lighthouse*) or the opacity of well-wrought urns (*Persuasion, The Bostonians, On the Road*), the conundrum of *the who and the what* (after Jacques Derrida) and *what where* (after Samuel Beckett) is nothing so banal as a pursuit or search. Rather, it is a beguiling fuzzy logic, a Gordian knot of UnSearching. But further, not disentangling any more than weaving. The possibility of its impossibility, a momentary half-seeing or half-life is glimpsed fleetingly as if an eye mote courted the imagination or like trying to hold the fragile and fleeting shimmer of a star in focus just long enough to 'see' it, for it *to be* a star.[14] And, this *possibility of impossibility* is the aleatoric *and* highly systematised rule-driven poiesis that motivates the very notion of potential literature as always already to come; it is un-conceived, on the verge of its unlikely possibility. Or not.

UNSIGHTLY/UNSITELY

Searching for Rue Simon-Crubellier is an ideal Sisyphean penance. The artists' knowing pursuit of the non-existent street is a loving labour not of credulity but of fabulation, of testing the bounds of possibility in the minds of the interlocutors they interview in Paris. UnSightly then, in the absence of something seen, UnSitely in an absence un-scène. In her book *Unsitely Aesthetics*, Maria Miranda describes the situation of 'unsitely' as a term that

> pivots on the traditional history of site – from the site/nonsite of Robert Smithson's Spiral Jetty to the decades long history of site-specificity. And is 'un' brought into play to dislodge the fixity of site and to multiply its potential, rather than discard 'site' itself?[15]

When site-specificity is blended with or 'folded into the notion of unsitely'[16] it expands the very question of site, initiating 'new possibilities for artists to work productively at the edges of the art world and its institutions, rather than at its centre'.[17] Accordingly, Out-Of-Sync is a nomadic rather than studio-based collective, working beyond the boundaries of the gallery, mobile and kitted out with myriad audio-visual media, physically embodied in the streets of Paris and simultaneously online elsewhere. Not only Unsitely but unseemly, creating time-based, site-specific and speculative artworks that 'reflect in some ways on the new condition created by the network',[18] as well on the tentative borders of credulity and the possible. No matter how hard the toil, then, the mythical building, unlike Sisyphus' boulder, will fail to appear, and at that moment the journey continues. However, just as Perec's *La Vie mode d'emplois* is fictional, it is just as factual in the crushing weight of detail that amasses a real Paris into words with the precision of an ordnance survey map and a genealogist's patient rigour:

> The exemplary biographies of the five Trévins sisters, unfortunately, do not stand up to close scrutiny, and the reader who smells a rat in these quasi-fabulous exploits will soon have his suspicions confirmed. For Madame Trévins (who, unlike Mademoiselle Crespi, is called Madame despite being a spinster) has no brother, and consequently no nieces bearing her surname; and Célestine Durand-Taillefer cannot live in Rue Hennin in Liège because in Liège there is no Rue Hennin; on the other hand, Madame Trévins did have a sister, Arlette, who was married to a Mr Louis Commine and bore him a daughter, Lucette, who married someone called Robert Hennin, who sells postcards (collector's items only) in Rue de Liège, in Paris (VIIIth *arrondissement*).[19]

Such encyclopaedic detail – *passim* – reassures as well as affirms, as mortar adhering to masonry, a real Paris not only to which it refers, but indexes as well in loving, myopic, and incessantly pedantic detail. Here is the Index entry on 'Paris':

Paris, 18, 19, 33, 34, 40, 48, 50, 83, 97, 108, 112, 113, 117, 128, 134, 145, 161, 170, 186, 187, 193, 198, 199, 203, 204, 208, 214, 229, 231, 237, 245, 246, 249, 252, 258, 261, 269, 270, 273, 274, 280, 290, 303, 312, 321, 328, 356, 358, 401, 403, 404, 406, 419, 421, 438, 441, 445, 449, 452, 479, 480, 482, 483, 499.[20]

That the previously sampled page 450 is not itemised is no facile eye skip, nor is it anything so banal as myopia, especially as, on that page, the speculative and verifiable identity of street names punctuates the paragraph in question – the poetic conceit that underwrites *Searching for Rue Simon-Crubellier* as a holograph as well as the imaginary hologram imposed upon the city of Paris by Neumark and Miranda in *Searching for Rue Simon-Crubellier*. In a novel entirely set in Paris, such bibliographic detail is hardly surprising. What is surprising is that every page is not included in the Index and thereby another heraldic gap is Unwritten into history as fiction (we can be reassured that a 'pataphysical index to the book would surely inventory every single page). The errant page 450 and the street name to which it refers is nonetheless garnered into a sub-category of the boroughs of Paris named in the novel in their own Index entry:

Arrondissements:
Eighth, 450.
Ninth, 237.
Sixteenth, 465.
Seventeenth, 4, 129, 239, 289.
Eighteenth, 456.
Nineteenth, 244.[21]

The Eleventh, suffice to say, is not mentioned.

Inside-text/outside-text. The putatively real and the elusive Unreal. James Joyce's most eloquent and inventive scholiast, Hugh Kenner, similarly inverts the interface between page-space and extra-diegetic space (putatively called 'the real') in one of his many tours through *Ulysses*. In his chapter on Joyce in *The Stoic Comedians*, Kenner underlines the absence of any difference between fact, fiction or the irreal when it comes to the 'thingness' of signification:

> For the reader of *Ulysses* holds a book in his hands. Homer envisaged no such possibility. Consider what it makes feasible. On page 488 we read, 'Potato preservative against plague and pestilence, pray for us.' Now just sixty pages earlier, if we were alert, we may have noted the phrase, 'Poor mamma's panacea', murmured by Bloom as he feels his trouser pocket. And fully 372 pages before that, on the bottom line of page 56, we have Bloom feeling in his hip pocket for the latchkey and reflecting, 'Potato I have'. The serious reader's copy of *Ulysses* acquires cross-references at three points; and Bloom's potato, it is by now commonplace to remark, is but one trivial instance among hundreds of motifs treated very briefly at two or three widely separated points in the book, and not even intelligible until the recurrences have been collated.[22]

It is for such meticulous cross-reference and recapitulation of detail that Kenner distinguishes Joyce from the other stoics that detain his attention (Gustave Flaubert and Samuel Beckett) as the 'comedian of the inventory'.[23] The physical apparatus of the book for Joyce enabled him to materially embody the Thomist principle of *consonantia*, or exact interrelation of parts within the whole, to ensure that any detail would be referred to at least twice. Unlike Perec, Joyce did not append an Index to the text of his metropolis for easy retracing of the poetic repetition and recapitulation of the same detail throughout *Ulysses*' 732 pages.[24] He did, however, build complex series of cross-references and leitmotifs throughout its numbered pages to prompt a dramatic form of reading that *enabled* the assemblage of networks of detail that could be bibliographically remembered through collation, pagination and alphabetisation.

As with Kenner on Joyce, there is here an impeccable enjambment of words and things in Perec. And, with a nod and wink to Michel Foucault and his allegorical pipe, the hierarchical contract of the material and the immaterial that binds them together.[25] In collating such cross-references I had the benefit of being able to consult the Index that appends *Life A User's Manual*. Here the book again blurs fiction and factuality as a form of faction. Indexes imply a code of reference and collation of information that is expected in encyclopaedias or a street directory. In a work of fiction the presence of an index inventories who, what and where is present in the imaginary world of page-space rather than empirical space outside-text. *Ulysses* had no accompanying word reference guide to itself when it was first published and had to wait until 1937 when Miles Hanley did the pitiless work of assembling his *Word Index to Ulysses* – work of a kind that Perec did himself in *Life A User's Manual*. The leitmotif of the jigsaw is a fitting emblem of the novel's totality as *qua world*, this world or a parallel possible world. It is countenanced and measured at the meta-level not beyond the novel (as exegesis, critical commentary, hermeneutical complexity), but in its Index. Hanley's word index is a meta-text belonging to the world of cataloguing and inventory, a word-world outside-text. Perec's, on the contrary, is more like a key or textual legend to identify the miscellaneous pieces in a jigsaw puzzle, whose previous life as seamless traces in an imagistic whole that will have, can and might be put together, fleeting to the eye as an image before being ceremoniously destroyed.

With minutiae such as this it is hardly surprising and somewhat droll to suggest that Miranda and Neumark, like Gaspard Winckler, also had their work cut out for them: the most elusive piece of the dismantled painting-puzzle being the one depicting the whereabouts of number 11 Rue Simon-Crubellier itself (perhaps it was one of Perec's lovingly named 'little chaps').[26] But this is indeed the *work* that is done in *Searching for Rue Simon-Crubellier*, and its complexity is echoed in *Life A User's Manual* in the density of its cross-references within, without and to itself. Lexical collation at such levels of exactitude resembles a form of scholasticism worthy of Flaubert's Bouvard and Pécuchet and their truncated *Dictionnaire des idées recues*. Such rigour transforms both Perec's and Flaubert's works into prodigious compendia that would have met the countenance of Robert Burton. Whether canniness or cruel happenstance, Neumark's and Miranda's lost cause is a *poetic* success. But, it is also a cipher of the novel's most futile Pyrrhic victory, Percival Bartlebooth's lifelong pursuit of extravagant ludic artifice: painting 500 images of harbour scenes throughout the world that are made into jigsaw puzzles by Gaspard Winckler and are eventually destroyed. Tania Ørum has suggested that, in this cork-lined myopia, Bartlebooth is Perec's model of an avant-garde artist of the 1960s, who 'turns his life into a (self-dissolving) art project'.[27] To underline the absurdity of treating life as a gnostic form of art, mortality claims Bartlebooth at the moment of completing his 439th puzzle (499 would have surely been a more exquisitely cruel number, were it not for Perec's considerable forbearance). The contemporary Afterword to this preposterously time-consuming devotion to Unmaking would underwrite the fruitless search of Norie Neumark and Maria Miranda as they travel blindly through the City of Light.

But networks, from ant colonies and flocks of birds to books and databases, are not invulnerable. They are open to attack from viruses, the weather as well as material disintegration. The same is true of oil paintings and crossword puzzles. The life's work of Percival Bartlebooth and Gaspard Winckler is an aesthetic labour of making and Unmaking. The dissembling of Bartlebooth's seaside paintings into jigsaw puzzles to be reassembled and returned to their point of origin and destroyed is an Oulipian conceit in absurdity, an endurance otherwise described by philosophers of the history of ideas as the 'meaning of life', or a Zen-like ludic exercise in what John Cage called 'purposeful purposelessness'.[28] The amassing of detail over the course of two simultaneous lifetimes is verified and denied, made and Unmade:

> Gaspard Winckler had clearly conceived of the manufacture of these five hundred puzzles as a single entity, as a gigantic five-hundred-piece puzzle of which each piece was a puzzle of seven hundred and fifty pieces, and it was evident that the solution of each of these puzzles called for a different approach, a different cast of mind, a different method, and a different system.[29]

And, Bartlebooth's response to the pretzel logic imposed upon him by Winckler is a search for the impossible to give his life meaning. It is also an oblique and anachronistic reference to another pursuit yet to come, a pursuit out-of-sync:

> Bartlebooth found the very essence of his passion in this feeling of being stuck: a kind of torpor, a sort of repetitious boredom, a veiled befuddlement in search of a shapeless something whose outlines he could barely manage to mumble in his mind.[30]

Neumark and Miranda certainly don't mumble in their interviews with the citizens of Paris during their search for Rue Simon-Crubellier. Yet the spectre of that 'shapeless something' is nonetheless always present during these discussions.

Perec tests the burden of incredulity by making it difficult for his reader to *not doubt* that such a street can at least be sought after. It is in the nature of UnSearching that such pursuit is countersigned by a psychological, epistemological and ludic code that searching for the impossible and not finding it is an aesthetic and psychological end in itself. Like an Oulipo experiment in the strict adherence to and rigorous application of rules and constraints, both Perec's novel as well as Miranda's and Neumark's media art work exert pressure on the 'Un': unseeable, unreachable, unsitely, unsightly, yet vigorously pursued nonetheless. So, to further quantify the Un, the search is Unfound and Unfinished.

PRE-UN

Searching for Rue Simon-Crubellier, as with the eponymous street on which it is based, is undoubtedly a brash postmodern work in its playful enjambment of ontology and epistemology, the fictionality of worlds of words and its dogged pursuit of the imaginary in the (putatively) real. Miranda's and Neumark's UnSearching project rests cheek by not so solemn jowl at the posterior end of Perec's formidable pages. Yet there is another, more distant and anterior, work that precedes both of them. In a previous time of reflexive experimentation, British artist Ian Breakwell's *UNWORD* series of live performances (1969–70) engaged with the audio-visual aesthetics and inscrutable semantics of the Un before Perec had even started scribbling *Life A User's Manual*. *UNWORD* has been generically described as a 'film/film document of a series of theatre events'.[31] Art scholar Eve Kalyva is more detailed in her account of the performative and aleatory nature of *UNWORD* as an 'act' that

> takes place in a room filled with paper sheets from ceiling to floor covered with words beginning with the UN-prefix. While projected films and tape recorders play, the artist moves through this 'forest of words' as he called it, biting and shredding them with his teeth . . . Paying attention to the visuality of words, the event acts on both the conceptual dissolution of the words' meaning – now marked, or shall we say 'un-marked' – but also their physical destruction.[32]

The event was filmed by Breakwell's collaborator Mike Leggett, not only as documentation, but also as an incursion into each live event that was visually represented on a suite of still images. Like a palimpsest being written in real-time, *UNWORD* converges the immediacy of anarchic choreography, live performance, and sculptural and painterly elements with images of it being filmed by Leggett.

The Unpredictable element of the work is its 'live' relationship 'within the audience', such that no two performances/screenings are the same. Breakwell evocatively described works such as the UNWORD series as 'process-events or performance events', contrary to 'expanded cinema' as characterised by

Figure 4.2 Mike Leggett filming *UNWORD 4*, Swansea University, Wales, 30 January 1970.

the late filmmaker Steve Dwoskin. Both terms, though, capture the 'constantly shifting' nature of the relationship of the event with its audience.[33] This observation, made originally in 1975, is precursory to both *Life A User's Manual* and *Searching for Rue Simon-Crubellier*, as well as *UnSearching for Rue Simon-Crubellier*.

Searching for Rue Simon-Crubellier is a variation of a hypermediated performance event. It combines the liveness of *vox pop* interviews and the artifice of staged performance (Neumark reading a copy of Perec while sitting on a Métro train, a peripatetic Bénabou in his apartment) with recorded documentary-like sequences (in civic offices, etc.), as well as intra- and extra-textual engagement with the Paris of Perec's pages. Perec's fugitive street as well as the artists' pursuit of it is UnSightly and UnSitely simply because while it is never seen it is always *en scène*, whether in the material pages of a book marked with the vestiges of once wet printer's ink or the virtual *somewhere* within the material division of the French capital defined by another Seine. What is missing in both works is its placement in time (as the object of a search) and space (as a grail that makes its hyperreal incarnation in the seventeenth arrondissement). What Miranda and Neumark are constantly faced with is a famous street's putative and virtual status in lieu of its presence: both are searching for something intransitively. Nothing is found but only sought in a continuous present tense of searching and Unsearching.

Searching for Rue Simon-Crubellier is a talismanic instance of Perec's anticipatory consciousness for media artists in his preoccupation with preposterous complexity, mathematics and the playful permutations of various forms of code. The codework of Australian artist Mez (also known as Mary-Anne Breeze) coincided with the emergence of digital aesthetics in the 1990s. Something of Perec's encyclopaedism and his fastidious obsession with systems and rules is shadowed in works such as *Cut Space* (1995), which parlays the interface between narrative and persistent interruptions that break its flow into sense. Her interest in hypertext as a post-alphabetic form of writing (in works such as *_the data][h!][bleeding t.ex][e][ts* (2001)) is predicated upon the desire to forge a language for an online environment beyond the page, a universe of words not dissimilar to Perec's.[34] Not, though, as a didactic manual of style for making and unmaking media art, or a user's guide to its underlying logics. But, rather, for that very inventory of abstractions to be the subject of art as much as a motivation for its making. Tactical art collective Blast Theory in the UK do just that, exploring 'questions about the meaning of interaction and, especially, its limitations'.[35] Blast Theory have no fixed artistic palette, nor do they work within singular spaces. The province of their largely performative and time-based work is the mixed reality of interconnected media with which we are constantly immersed on a daily basis. Integrating the built and online environment via mobile phone and web-based interfaces, Blast Theory works generate alternative vectors between artists, art, and audiences that are direct expressions of the distributed conditions in which artists now work and most of us live. The complex, nuanced, and integrated networks of connections within Blast Theory's considerable practice over the last twenty years is a hybrid means of bringing together different kinds of space as a manifold event. In this, their poetic and polemical aesthetics are not dissimilar to the method of juggling more *appartements* than you can handle and manage to get away with it: exactly what Perec finesses in *Life A User's Manual*.

As I noted in *Interzone* in 2005, no doubt with Perec's hauntological presence over my shoulder, media art 'didn't simply appear as if from nowhere'.[36] Nor did *Searching for Rue Simon-Crubellier*. It owes as much to the apparatus of the interactive screen, networks and data storage as to the modern novel (Proust, Joyce, Woolf, Faulkner) and the postmodern anti-novel, with its obsessive and compulsive mania for lists and algorithmic rules (Robbe-Grillet, Calvino, Beckett, Duras). It is beyond the modern in its closed and insular world of domestic busy-ness, clutter and overly complex quests. Peripatetic strolls along the boulevards in the manner of Maupassant or Baudelaire, or the *flânerie* of Rimbaud losing himself in the precariousness of the crowd, are a distant memory in Perec's Paris.

So, with Perec and Calvino hovering as a pair of tutelary deities[37] of media and undecidable art in the twenty-first century, 'You are about to begin searching for 11 Rue Simon-Crubellier', etc.

NOTES

1. Italo Calvino and Gregory L. Lucente (1985), 'An Interview with Italo Calvino', trans. Gregory L. Lucente, *Contemporary Literature*, vol. 26, no. 3, p. 248.
2. Margaret Drabble in Carole McKenzie (2013), *Wise Women: Wit and Wisdom from Some of the World's Most Extraordinary Women*, New York: Random House.
3. Georges Perec (1987), *Life A User's Manual*, London: Harvill, p. xi.
4. William Shakespeare (2003), *Hamlet*, New Haven, CT: Yale University Press, act 1, scene 1, line 127.
5. Marguerite Duras (1986), *The Lover*, trans. Barbara Bray, Paris: Editions de Minuit.
6. Gilbert Keith Chesterton in Denis J. Conlin (1989), 'Introduction', *The Collected Works of G. K. Chesterton*, San Francisco: Ignatius Press, p. 24.
7. James Joyce (1975), *Finnegans Wake*, London: Faber & Faber, p. 112.
8. The term 'intertwingled' is one of the many neologisms coined by Ted Nelson to describe the ongoing, web-like interconnectivity of hypertext systems (*Literary Machines*, Sausalito, CA: Mindful Press, 1981, pp. 2/8–2/9).
9. Georges Perec (1988), *Life A User's Manual*, London: Collins Harvill, p. 3.
10. Italo Calvino (1987), *Cosmicomics*, trans. William Weaver, London: Abacus, p. 105.

11. Maria Miranda (2013), *Unsitely Aesthetics: Uncertain Practices in Contemporary Art*, Berlin: Errant Bodies Press, p. 10.
12. Perec, *Life A User's Manual*, p. 4.
13. *Searching for Rue Simon-Crubellier* is a fraught, futile and hysterical pilgrimage cum journey not unlike any number of Monty Python sketches that feature the pursuit of absurd grails and po-faced follies such as 'Tunnelling from Godalming to Java' (1970), 'Cycling Tour of Cornwall' (1972) and 'The Hairdressers Ascent of Mount Everest' (1973). Arguably the most allegorical labour of urban endurance is 'Climbing the North Face of the Uxbridge Road', first televised in 1972.
14. In Arthur Penn's 1976 film *The Missouri Breaks* the eccentric regulator/man hunter Lee Clayton (Marlon Brando), talking in riddles, gives an enigmatic lesson in Unsightliness to the dying cattle rustler Calvin (Harry Dean Stanton): 'You know about this time of year, Indian summer, gettin' there, they say you can see the star of Bethlehem, if you look real good. I've seen it once or twice. But you gotta look away and then gotta look at it see and you gotta just, blink like that, see . . .' Due to the duplicity of ocular parallax the star can never been seen directly, but glimpsed only at the moment of its blurring out of sight. It is sited, temporarily there, but simultaneously not sighted. The last image of Calvin is cruelly unsightly as Clayton throws a metal spike through his right eye.
15. Miranda, *Unsitely Aesthetics*, p. 13.
16. Miranda, *Unsitely Aesthetics*, p. 13.
17. Miranda, *Unsitely Aesthetics*, p. 14.
18. Miranda, *Unsitely Aesthetics*, p. 15.
19. Perec, *Life A User's Manual*, p. 450.
20. Perec, *Life A User's Manual*, p. 545.
21. Perec, *Life A User's Manual*.
22. Hugh Kenner (1974), *The Stoic Comedians: Flaubert, Joyce, and Beckett*, Berkeley: University of California Press, p. 32.
23. Kenner, *The Stoic Comedians*, p. 30.
24. This pagination refers to the first Shakespeare & Company Paris edition of *Ulysses*, published in 1922.
25. Michel Foucault (1983), *This Is Not a Pipe*, Berkeley: University of California Press.
26. Perec, *Life A User's Manual*, p. xvi.
27. Tania Ørum (2006), 'Georges Perec and the Avant-garde in the Visual Arts', *Textual Practice*, vol. 20, no. 2, p. 322.
28. John Cage (1958), *Indeterminacy: New Aspect of Form in Instrumental and Electronic Music*, vinyl record, Folkways: FT 3704.
29. Perec, *Life A User's Manual*, p. 337.
30. Perec, *Life A User's Manual*, p. 337.
31. Entry on Mike Leggett in Rosetta Brooks and John Du Cane (eds) (1972), *A Survey of the Avant-Garde in Britain*, vol. 3, no. 2–15, London: Gallery House Press, p. 32.
32. Eve Kalyva (2009), *Textual Counterparts: A Performative Beyond Visual Attention?* Paper presented at the Association of Art Historians conference, Manchester Metropolitan University, 2–4 April.
33. Steve Dwoskin quoted in Duncan White, 'Expanded Cinema: The Live Record', in A. L. Rees, Duncan White, Steven Ball and David Curtis (eds) (2011), *Expanded Cinema: Art, Performance, Film*, London: Tate, p. 26. I am grateful to Mike Leggett for drawing my attention to the distinction and particularly to Breakwell's understanding of the process and performance elements of the works.

34. See http://www.hotkey.net.au/~netwurker/.
35. See http://www.blasttheory.co.uk/.
36. Darren Tofts (2005), *Interzone: Media Arts in Australia*, Melbourne: Thames & Hudson, p. 10.
37. The phrase is Hugh Kenner's description of the studiously avuncular presence of Jonathan Swift and Laurence Sterne in Joyce's *Finnegans Wake*; see *The Stoic Comedians*, p. 48.

CHAPTER 5

Invoking the Oracle: Perec, Algorithms and Conceptual Writing

Mark Wolff

Recent assessments of contemporary writing have emphasised its relationship to conceptual art and algorithmic processing. According to Craig Dworkin, conceptual art focuses on the initial procedures an artist follows rather than the physical production of art objects.[1] Likewise, conceptual writing '[distances] ideas and affects in favour of assembled objects, rejecting outright the ideologies of disembodied themes and abstracted content'.[2] Scholars such as Marjorie Perloff and Kenneth Goldsmith have used the terms 'unoriginal genius'[3] and 'uncreative writing'[4] to describe a kind of literature that eschews traditional notions of authorship by foregrounding how writing takes place through the appropriation and manipulation of words. Rather than produce new texts that express affect or a sense of self, conceptual writers redeploy existing texts and discern meaning from the massive amounts of information in society. Conceptual writers also use language as data within systems of code, incorporating algorithmic techniques. Referring to Lev Manovich's notion of 'database logic',[5] Dworkin observes that conceptual writing functions as an interface for returning an answer to a particular query or producing a particular output after the application of certain procedures.[6] Algorithmic writing thus designates a kind of conceptual writing that performs computations with pre-existing texts.

The Oulipo is an important precursor to conceptual writing because it devises constraints on writing based on algorithmic processes. Raymond Queneau and François Le Lionnais founded the literary group in 1960 with the publication of the *Cent mille milliards de poèmes*, a collection of ten reconfigurable sonnets by Queneau, and a postface by Le Lionnais that explains the concept behind the immense number of poems made possible by the constraints of the sonnet and a simple algorithm. It is impossible to read 100,000,000,000,000 poems, but the interest in the collection lies in the way Queneau structures the ten initial sonnets to allow an almost unfathomable number of permutations of verses to form potential sonnets. According to Jean-Jacques Thomas, the 'pre-text' of the algorithmic constraint 'becomes the central text to be read [and] relegates the subsequently generated text to a subordinate position'.[7] The Oulipian text is a proof of concept and derives its value not from what it expresses, but from the procedures by which it was generated.

As an Oulipian, Georges Perec took full advantage of the group's experiments developing new structures for writing with rule-based constraints. While he availed himself of all of the Oulipo's procedures, his texts demonstrate more than the potentiality of algorithmic writing. Members of the Oulipo, as well as literary scholars, have emphasised the negotiation between the mechanical constraints of algorithms and the artistic freedom afforded by chance in Perec's writing. The Oulipo often explains the purposeful inclusion of chance in its use of constraints on writing as the effects of the clinamen, a notion developed by the Roman poet and philosopher Lucretius to describe the unpredictable swerving of atoms that allows for creative processes in nature. In an interview in 1981, Perec insists it is important to include anti-constraints within a system of constraints: '[the system] must not be rigid, there must be some play in it, it must, as they say, "creak" a bit; it must not be completely coherent [. . .]'.[8] Paul Braffort, a member of the Oulipo and a computer scientist, attributes a transitional period in the Oulipo's activity (between a first period of experiments with prose and a second period dominated by rigorous mathematical concepts) to Perec's 'exhausting' work, where the role of the clinamen gradually defined itself.[9] Harry Mathews, another member of the Oulipo, offers the following definition:

> For Oulipians, the clinamen is a deviation from the strict consequences of a restriction. It is often justified on aesthetic grounds: resorting to it improves the results. But there is a binding condition for its use: the exceptional freedom afforded by a clinamen can only be taken on the condition that following the initial rule is still possible. In other words, the clinamen can only be used if it isn't needed.[10]

Christelle Reggiani observes that the clinamen serves a dysfunctional role in Perec's texts by preserving the romantic idea of subjective invention, camouflaging the use of constraints and fostering a sense of suspicion in the reader who cannot be sure of what a text by Perec means.[11] For Alison James, 'Perec's texts effectively exploit the possibilities of chance, both tapping into its creative potential and controlling its operation'.[12] Perec combines the use of constraints and clinamens in order to explore how chance affects one's life. Invoking chance within order is not only a technique for writing, but also a philosophical reflection on what it means to live in a world governed in part by the aleatory.[13]

It would seem that the importance of the clinamen for Perec would exclude him from discussions of conceptual writing, where creativity expresses itself through the invention of algorithms for generating texts that cannot be capriciously altered or suspended. It would also seem that Perec showed little interest in harnessing computers as tools for writing. He did not participate directly in any of the Oulipo's experiments with computer-assisted text creation before or immediately after the formation of the ALAMO in 1980.[14] Perec's indifference to computers is somewhat surprising, given that, as Bernard Magné has noted, many of Perec's texts would lend themselves very well to computational media for enacting instances of combinatorial works (such as the 4,096 prose poems for Fabrizio Clerici) and navigating potential hyperlinks within *Life A User's Manual*.[15] Perec had even imagined the possibility of using a computer to write a vast novel based on anthologised selections from famous nineteenth-century authors.[16] Perec did not think technology was sufficiently developed to facilitate the effort, however. Magné suggests that Perec rejected the use of computers because of their potential for excessive power over people's lives and of their lack of power to do anything really creative.[17] Indeed, Perec recognised the computer's ability to perform many operations systematically without error, but he believed that error in a system was required for freedom and creativity, and that programming a computer to err would be very difficult to achieve.[18]

In what follows, I will argue that several of Perec's texts demonstrate an approach to conceptual writing that explores the possibilities of combining rule-based systems with indeterminate exceptions through an approach that aligns with Alan Turing's theory of computation. It should be noted from the outset that I have found no evidence indicating Perec had read anything by or about Turing. Nevertheless, as a member of the Oulipo, Perec did interact regularly with Braffort, and was at least aware of some of the experiments Braffort conducted with computers and writing in the 1970s. More importantly, Perec did not reject computational systems outright and demonstrated openness to their potentiality. His experiments with PALF, his short radio play *The Machine*, the simulated computer output of *The Art and Craft of Approaching Your Head of Department to Submit a Request for a Raise* and his major novel *Life A User's Manual* explore how logic-based constraints, and what we might call oracular interventions, allow the writer to distribute the production of texts among algorithmic and adventitious processes. The constraints he used enabled him to separate mechanical reasoning from indeterminate exceptions in order to define the boundaries of the algorithmic and the incalculable.

Given the interest of Perec and the other members of the Oulipo in the potentiality of algorithms as rule-based procedures for generating texts, the question of the limits of such procedures becomes vital. While it may be possible to devise a procedure to generate a specific output (such as writing a text without the letter 'e'), is it possible to design a procedure that can produce any desired output? Another way of asking this question is what the German mathematician David Hilbert framed as the *Entscheidungsproblem*, or halting problem: given a mathematical proposition, is there a general method for determining if the proposition is provable or not? In 1936, Turing proved that no such method exists, and he did so by showing that such a method would have to be mechanical itself and therefore subject to another halting problem. Turing developed a theoretical construct of what he called an automatic machine (what is now often called a Turing machine) based on simple operations performed sequentially. He did not use an actual machine to demonstrate his proof, in part because the technology at the time could not perform the calculations he envisioned. An automatic machine resembles the functioning of a Teletype through the implementation of a 'head' that moves forward and backward on a linear tape to read, erase and print symbols according to a procedure detailed in an instruction table.[19] Once an automatic machine is initiated, a human operator is not needed to carry out the procedure. An automatic machine is therefore an early definition of a computer program. The equivalent of a computer that can run programs is what Turing called a universal machine, which is composed of a potentially infinite number of automatic machines, each of which is indexed in a master instruction table (much like an operating system today).[20] Turing proved there was no general method to the *Entscheidungsproblem* by constructing a universal machine that used numbers to describe both infinite decimals and instruction tables for calculating infinite decimals. According to Andrew Hodges, Turing exploited a self-referential system: 'The core idea [of Turing's proof] depends on the *self-reference* involved in a machine operating on symbols, which is itself described by symbols and so can operate on its own description.'[21]

Turing investigated the limits of algorithms as techniques for making decisions about propositions, but he also wondered about the relationship between the calculable and the incalculable. After his proof of the undecidability of the *Entscheidungsproblem*, Turing turned his attention to what he called oracle machines, which are theoretical constructs for performing operations that defy computation. Turing himself wrote, 'We shall not go any further into the nature of this oracle apart from saying it cannot be a machine.'[22] Hodges notes that 'the whole point of the oracle-machine is to explore the realm of what cannot be done by purely mechanical processes'.[23] If one begins with an automatic machine and requires an operation that cannot be computed, one can add an oracle to the machine for completing the calculation. The oracle-enhanced machine is still indeterminate (any finite number of oracles added to the machine does not change its indeterminacy), but it is considerably (if not infinitely) more powerful than a purely automatic machine. Hodges explains that Turing developed the idea of the oracle to explain mathematical intuition:

> [For Turing], intuition is in practice present in every part of a mathematician's thought, but when mathematical proof is formalised, intuition has an explicit manifestation in those steps where the mathematician sees the truth of a formally unprovable statement.[24]

The oracle is thus a concept for imagining a more expansive computational process that distinguishes intuition from calculation and allows for a distributed procedure oscillating between insight and method.

The result of such cognitive distribution is the opportunity for humans to explore their intuitions systematically, and to make a more spontaneous and unpredictable use of computation that affirms their freedom. In his outline for the design of a computational machine, Turing anticipated a rewarding experience for those who would eventually program computers:

> Instruction tables will have to be made up by mathematicians with computing experiences and perhaps a certain puzzle-solving ability. [. . .] The process of constructing instruction tables should be very fascinating. There need be no real danger of it ever becoming a drudge, for any processes that are quite mechanical may be turned over to the machine itself.[25]

Rather than draining human work of any interest, programming will allow humans to relegate repetitive and determined procedures to the computer, freeing humans to pursue less predictable outcomes.

Turing's theories of computation can explain the ways in which Perec explores varied uses of automatic and oracular procedures in several of his early works. Before Perec joined the Oulipo in 1967, he and Marcel Bénabou had already begun a long-term project called PALF, or automatic production of French literature. PALF was designed to take any two utterances and transform them, through a reiterative process of mechanical word substitution with a dictionary, into the same utterance.[26] The results of such substitution were always provisional because the results never converged on a single expression. Perec and Bénabou initially explained their unsuccessful experiments as forays into distinct semantic fields (gastronomy, law, religion, military, scatology, finance) dominating discourse.[27] They later understood PALF as evidence that language endlessly conceals its arbitrariness through the instability of the sign: 'If one surrenders indefinitely to this game, one ends up with a never-ending cascade of signifiers [. . .] the number of their arrangements in various definitions is almost infinite.'[28] By replacing words with their definitions from a dictionary, Perec and Bénabou exercised no small degree of discretion in how the text was transformed. In an early outline of their methodology, they insisted on 'perseverance while taking care to demonstrate the greatest rigour and reveal an evident spirit of subversion'.[29] They pursued a structured, but uninhibited, substitution from original word to its definition in a dictionary, with the aim of not only demonstrating the circularity of language but of also challenging established beliefs. This method, according to Bénabou, would be a precursor to the clinamen.[30]

In 1968, Perec collaborated with the Saarländischer Rundfunk and his German translator, Eugen Helmlé, on a radio play entitled *The Machine*. The play simulates a computer reading Goethe's famous poem, 'Wandrers Nachlied II'. The design of Perec's machine strongly resembles the organisation of Turing's universal machine:

> The machine and its system consist of:
> 1. a number of programs that enable it to approach the poem ['Wandrers Nachlied II'] from different directions, to grasp it in all its diverse aspects, and to execute various linguistic operations that present the poem in a new light; and,
> 2. a group of processors that contain:
>   a) the poem,
>   b) a bank of instantaneously retrievable data about the poem's author,
>   c) a comprehensive vocabulary of major world languages,
>   d) several alphabets that are put together according to a phonological key which enables them to form words,
>   e) a syntactical key, i.e., a grammar, and
>   f) a wide selection of poetry from world literature.[31]

> Furthermore, the machine possesses a logic module – the system control. It activates the operations designated by the programs in a certain sequence, and examines their progress. The system control has absolute priority over the processors. It can give them commands such as: stop, wait, forward, backward, return, connect, continue, repeat, etc.
> The programs containing the necessary instructions guaranteeing the correct execution of the various operations are divided into five protocols, which correspond in turn to the five fundamental logical categories that the machine uses in turn in order to analyze the poem.
> Protocol zero (basic knowledge) is essentially statistical in nature: it analyzes and systematizes the linguistic material of the poem in numerical terms.

Protocol one (internal operations) is essentially linguistic in nature: it operates on the lexical material of the poem.
Protocol two (external operations) is essentially semantic in nature: it changes the poem through externally determined restrictions and modifications.
Protocol three is essentially critical in nature: it examines the possible relationships and cross-references between the poem and its author.
Finally, protocol four (explosion of quotations) is essentially poetic in nature: it confronts the poem with the poetry of world literature in order to identify, ultimately, what one might call the essence of poetry.
To the attentive listener it may become clear that this play about language not only describes the functioning of a machine, but also, though in a more concealed and subtle manner, the inner mechanism of poetry.[32]

This lengthy excerpt from the beginning of the play shows how Perec conceived the interaction of the mechanical parts of his reading machine. Moving beyond the tentative experiments of PALF, the machine implements data sources that exceed the information contained within a dictionary and enable it to not only reference multiple languages, but to also form words in those languages with different alphabets. The five protocols correspond to Turing's notion of instruction tables, and the system control functions as a master instruction table governing the interaction of the protocols. The commands of the system control perform the same basic operations of Turing's automatic machine that reads, erases and prints symbols on a tape. Throughout the execution of the system control program with its three processors (each of these components of the machine speaks during the play), specific instructions for computation are preceded by numbers (for example, '211: anagram').[33] These numbers within the system control program are called to invoke other programs as data elements themselves. Such modular structuring of the program resembles the self-reference of Turing's universal machine and demonstrates the use of subroutines, a common practice in software design. Perec clearly understood how computers worked.

What is most striking about the conception of Perec's machine is its almost naive optimism in the power of computation to both analyse Goethe's poem and synthesise it within a canon of world literature. At first, the machine recites the poem and identifies its author.[34] It then performs simple statistical analyses on the typographical contents of the poem (words, punctuation, parts of speech, letters) to break it down into its atomic elements.[35] These straightforward operations through protocol zero lead to a series of deformations of the poem that, while evidently within the realm of the calculable, recast the text in unexpected ways. Recitations of the poem according to different procedures (from left to right in word groups of varying length, from right to left, vertically from top to bottom, horizontally from the last line to the first, and in random word, phonemic and alphabetic order) generate new readings and defamiliarise the text.[36] The machine begins to make references to other authors and texts (the Marquis de Sade, *Waiting for Godot*) while transforming the poem linguistically through word doubling, apocope, redundancy, ellipsis, negation, question and answer, and permutations.[37] The machine continues processing the poem by manipulating phonemes to construct new words and implementing Oulipian constraints, such as isomorphisms and 's plus n' (whereby one replaces every noun with the nth noun that follows it in a given dictionary).[38] Perec even includes PALF as one of the machine's programs.[39] The machine follows instruction tables of ever-increasing linguistic, semantic and literary scope, moving up the scale of its protocols until it begins speaking about other authors and topics related intertextually to the poem.[40] After a dizzying display of encyclopaedic knowledge, the machine ends with various literary references to silence that are punctuated with brief stoppages in its operation. The processing of data by the machine enacts what the poem is about.[41] Perec relates the thrilling experience of reading a poem with a machine that, ostensibly limited to methodical computation, engages with its processors and protocols in ever more complex calculations that humans are unable to follow. The opacity of the machine's inner functioning creates a sense of chance that liberates the human mind to perceive things it might not otherwise notice. For Perec, 'the essence of poetry' can be apprehended through sufficiently elaborate mechanical means. Perec's machine is a black box that enlightens its audience through the felicitous effects of a clinamen emerging through complexity.

Perec pursued another exploration of the potential of computation in 1968, but this time less optimistically. The Humanities Computing Centre of the Centre national de la recherche scientifique (CNRS) commissioned him to write a text that followed all the possible outcomes of a computer program with multiple conditional statements. Raymond Queneau had written a comparable text in 1967 with 'A Story as You Like It' that mimicked a computer by generating a tale as the reader input answers to yes/no questions. Perec was given a complicated flowchart representing what a low-level employee of a large company would need to do in order to ask for a raise. The flowchart's multiple rhombuses and circuitous arrows indicate, as conditional statements, all the permutations of decisions the employee could possibly make. With this prompt, Perec wrote *The Art and Craft of Approaching Your Head of Department to Submit a Request for a Raise*. The title suggests that achieving the desired outcome requires *savoir-faire* instead of *savoir*. This turns out not to be the case: Perec explains that, in one very long sentence written in the second person, the text reproduces the recursion represented by the flowchart:

Instead of telling the story so as to leave the reader free to choose his own route, I have made a LINEAR TRANSLATION of the chart – that is to say, I have followed ONE BY ONE all the steps of the route chosen, going back to the start every time an arrow sent me back there; in other words, I have not allowed myself to utter a proposition before having retraced all those that precede it: the end result is a text of fifty-seven pages built entirely on redundancy.[42]

Queneau's text offers the reader a certain degree of freedom to choose how the story unfolds, but Perec pummels the reader with all possible outcomes. The first lines of the text show the almost stream-of-consciousness quality of following strictly the *if-then* and *go to* statements of the program that would implement the flowchart:

> Having carefully weighed the pros and cons you gird up your loins and make up your mind to go and see your head of department to ask for a raise so you go to see your head of department let us assume to keep things simple – for we must do our best to keep things simple – that his name is mr xavier that's to say mister or rather mr x so you go to see mr x it's one or t'other either mr x is at his desk or mr x is not at his desk if mr x is at his desk it will be quite straightforward but obviously mr x is not at his desk so all you can do is stand in the corridor waiting for him to come back or come in but let us suppose not that he never comes in that case [. . .][43]

The linearity of the text resembles the continuous output of a Teletype, and from this perspective we can compare the implementation of the flowchart to the operation of Turing's automatic machine with its tape moving inexorably forward (with occasional steps backward) toward some eventual outcome. Unlike Perec's machine that can systematically deconstruct and reconstruct a well-known poem for human readers to rediscover and explore, nothing emerges from the repeated actions of the employee following the flowchart's instructions except, as David Bellos observes, the passage of time and the approach of death.[44] Here, computation leads to a dystopian existence. The program simulated in *The Art and Craft of Approaching Your Head of Department to Submit a Request for a Raise* alienates the user and reduces human life to unfulfilling redundancy.

Perec's novel *Life A User's Manual* negotiates between, on the one hand, the optimism of PALF and *The Machine*, and on the other hand the pessimism of *The Art and Craft*. Perec wrote the ninety-nine chapters of the novel using programmatic constraints such as the movement of a knight on a 100-square chessboard, the organisation of 420 elements categorised as forty-two lists of ten items, and the permutations of twenty-one pairs of these lists according to a Greco-Latin bi-square and a pseudo-quenina (an Oulipian procedure invented by Queneau).[45] All of these mechanical constraints determine, to a considerable degree, the content and structure of the novel. Perec used additional constraints of an aleatory nature, such as a reference to something taking place around him as he was writing a particular chapter, and the meta-constraints 'lack' and 'false' which, if invoked (they operated binarily as 'on' or 'off'), either required to him to ignore a programmatic constraint or replace a programmed element with another.[46] The methods by which Perec constructed his novel carry out algorithmic processes that regulate both predictable outcomes that depend on calculations and oracular processes that complicate the calculations. Perec explores the relationship between these two kinds of processes within the novel through the recurring themes of backgammon, puzzle-making and puzzle-solving. The presentation of each of these ludic activities demonstrates the synergy between the computable and uncomputable in creative efforts. As is the case with many Oulipian works, *Life A User's Manual* speaks of the constraints used to generate the text.[47] Perec shows, through the novel, both in the way it was written and in what it is about, how programmatic thinking and computation interact with intuition and insight to lead to discovery.

Backgammon appears twice in the novel. In chapter VIII, the narrator describes the regular matches played by Winckler, who received Bartlebooth's watercolour paintings and made them into puzzles, and Morellet, who took the puzzles Bartlebooth solved and applied a chemical process to restore the paintings to their original state. At this point in their lives, Winckler had finished making Bartlebooth's puzzles and withdrawn from all artistic activity, while Morellet had nothing to do but wait for Bartlebooth to send him solved puzzles. Both men would meet at the same cafe in the evening for a game of backgammon. Unlike the calm reserve he had displayed when he made puzzles for Bartlebooth, Winckler's mood varied wildly during the game:

> Both played heatedly, excitedly, breaking out into exclamations, swearwords, and tempers, which were not surprising in Morellet but seemed quite incomprehensible in Winckler – a man whose calmness verged on apathy, whose patience, sweetness, and resignation were imperturbable, whom no one had ever seen angry; [. . .] such a man, then, was able to seize the board with both hands and send it flying, calling Morellet a cheat and unleashing a quarrel which the café's customers sometimes took ages to sort out.[48]

The narrator does not explain why Winckler fell into these fits of passion. Shortly after his games with Morellet, Winckler seemed to have exhausted his sense of initiative and creativity. In the last year of his life, Winckler stopped going out of his room altogether, and the only activity in which he showed any interest was sorting the hotel labels that Smautf (Bartlebooth's valet) had attached to the mailing containers for the watercolour paintings.[49] After working on this project for a few weeks, he gave up and 'didn't start on anything special again'.[50] Backgammon represents the only occasion where Winckler, the master puzzle-maker, expresses emotion and unpredictability. The reader does not observe him play the game until the final years of his life, however, and he seems to turn reflexively to the methodical thinking he had practised earlier. The deferral (and perhaps repression) of impulsiveness suggests that the years he had spent working for Bartlebooth denied him the opportunity to break free from a constrained life.

Backgammon reappears in chapter XXVII, this time as a futuristic computer game in the lower floor of the duplex apartment belonging to Rémi Rorschach, the television producer. The room is decorated in a modernist, minimalist style with limited furnishings but many strange devices:

> Examples of American gadgetry are strewn about the place, among them an electronic Feedbackgammon, whose players have only to roll their dice and push the numerically corresponding buttons: the counters, circles that light up on the translucent surface, are shifted by microchips built into the board and programmed to follow optimal strategies. (Since each player thus disposes in turn of the best possible offence/defence, the most common outcome of the game is a reciprocal jamming amounting to a draw.)[51]

In this instance of backgammon, the possibility of spirited play is eliminated in favour of pure calculation. The internal circuitry allows players to always make the best possible moves. Chance is thus reduced to the effects of probability: with enough rolls of the dice, the players usually counter each other's moves and neither enjoys a strategic advantage. With the examples of the Winckler-Morellet games and the Feedbackgammon, Perec shows how play without machines can lead to chaos and how play with machines can lead to stasis.

The game of backgammon represents the extremes of creative activity with and without algorithmic constraints. Perec moves beyond this binary opposition to investigate the processes involved in making and solving puzzles. These processes require methodical thinking as well as spontaneous decisions and intuitive guesses. Both Winckler, the puzzle-maker, and Bartlebooth, the puzzle-solver, employ systematic and arbitrary techniques to find solutions to computational problems. Through their creative practices, Perec observes the interaction between the calculable and the incalculable, outlining the limits of each.

Chapter XLIV opens with a description of the art of making puzzles. The narrator begins by explaining that a puzzle is not the sum of its parts, but rather a coherent system that determines its parts according to the uncomputable. A well-made puzzle is composed of pieces that purposely introduce false information to disrupt methodical thinking that would reconstruct the whole.[52] Mechanically produced puzzles present arbitrary levels of challenge, but handcrafted puzzles, like those by Winckler, must subvert any appearance of structure and order. The manner by which he constructs a puzzle cannot follow a method, because to do so would produce regularities that could be apprised and mastered mechanically through reverse engineering (a process often used in software development).

When Winckler receives a painting from Bartlebooth, he initially studies it with no clear idea of how he will make it into a puzzle. He cannot proceed with a fixed pattern, because Bartlebooth would eventually learn the pattern and easily solve the puzzle. Perec distinguishes the almost instinctual processes by which Winckler invents his puzzle from those by which he methodically constructs it. After several days of observation ('like a panther in its cage'), Winckler arrives at a solution, but the narrator does not explain how Winckler does this. Things 'happen very quickly': he places tracing paper on the painting and draws the lines of the cuts for the puzzle pieces rapidly ('in one sweep of the hand'). The rest of the fabrication of the puzzle is technical, 'requiring no further inventiveness'.[53] Winckler must find an answer to the question of how to cut the puzzle through a process that cannot be mechanised. Once the answer is found, the rest follows from mechanisation.

For Bartlebooth, puzzle-solving follows a similar process. When he begins a new puzzle, he is tempted to resort immediately to a logical procedure that resists impulsiveness or subjectivity: 'Each time he vowed to proceed methodically and with discipline [. . .]: this time he was not going to let his passion or his dreams or his impatience get the better of him.'[54] In true Cartesian fashion he seeks to divide the puzzle into smaller problems he can resolve using reason.[55] The problem with such an approach is its predictability: the manner in which Bartlebooth divides problems, if repeated, can lend itself to mechanisation and reduce the puzzle-solver to an automaton. Bartlebooth knows he should 'stay neutral, objective, and above all flexible, that is to say free of preconceptions', but one of these preconceptions is that the puzzle can be solved with a common methodical procedure.[56] 'Bartlebooth [. . .] had to switch his perception, see *otherwise* what [Winckler] had provided to mislead his eyes.'[57] Winckler has the same problem: he must divert his reasoning in making the puzzle to avoid becoming predictable. The method by which Winckler and Bartlebooth find answers to their questions in making and solving puzzles must include an unmechanical component that cannot be systematised. 'The most rigorous methodology, an index of the seven hundred and fifty pieces [of a puzzle], the use of computers or of any other scientific or objective system would not have had much point [. . .].'[58] Each puzzle requires its own oracle machine to be constructed and solved, and there is no way for Winckler or Bartlebooth to abstractly program these oracle machines according to a common set of rules because such a possibility would mean that making and solving puzzles could be mechanised:

> Gaspard Winckler had clearly conceived of the manufacture of these five hundred puzzles as a single entity, as a gigantic five-hundred-piece puzzle of which each piece was a puzzle of seven hundred and fifty pieces, and it was evident that the solution of each of these puzzles called for a different approach, a different cast of mind, a different method, and a different system.[59]

In effect, Winckler and Bartlebooth demonstrate that the *Entscheidungsproblem* holds for puzzles as well as logical systems and machines.

Far from impeding his creativity and reducing him to the slavish application of rules, the use of methodical calculation, along with intuitive guessing, provides Bartlebooth with an exhilarating intellectual experience similar to proving mathematical theorems and inventing computational algorithms. The sense of frustration at not knowing in a definable way the solution to a puzzle is the recognisable start of a computational adventure:

> Bartlebooth found the very essence of his passion in this feeling of being stuck: a kind of torpor, a sort of repetitious boredom, a veiled befuddlement in search of a shapeless something whose outlines he could barely manage to mumble in his mind [. . .][60]

The narrator links these doldrums to the fits of anger displayed by Winckler during his games of backgammon with Morellet.[61] Over an indeterminate amount of time, Bartlebooth attains 'a kind of ecstasy', a peaceful, empty state of mind through intense concentration.[62] In this moment he reaches the awareness of an archer about to shoot an arrow:

> profound oblivion of the body and the target, a mental void, a completely blank, receptive, and flexible mind, an attentiveness that remained total, but which was disengaged from the vicissitudes of being, from the contingent details of the puzzle and its maker's snares.[63]

After hours, days, or weeks of mulling over the puzzle, he is able to solve it in an instant, as if the answer to the question was obvious from the beginning. Bartlebooth succeeds by applying methodical, mechanisable reasoning to insights that come to him unpredictably and spontaneously. Intuition cannot be reduced to a formula, but intuition requires logic to express a unique idea through a well-defined system of parts.

In reflecting on the entirety of his writing, Perec understood his craft in terms similar to the way in which Winckler and Bartlebooth invented and solved puzzles. Perec stated that his first objective was to never write two books that were the same kind: he 'never wanted to reuse a formula, or a system, or an approach already developed in some earlier work'.[64] He recognised that 'this systematic versatility [had earned him] the reputation of being some sort of computer or machine for producing texts'.[65] We can understand the idea of 'systematic versatility' as the clinamen applied to algorithmic writing, where the writer makes use of procedures not to reproduce earlier ways of writing but to veer off in new directions made possible by the results of following procedures. As a consequence of his will to never write twice in the same way, Perec looked forward to '[writing] every kind of thing that it is possible for a man to write nowadays', exploring all genres and engaging as many readerships as possible.[66] He claimed that, apart from these two objectives (never repeat a way of writing and write in every way possible), he did not have master plan as a writer. He did, however, have a reason to write:

> From the books I have written, in the order I have written them, I get the sometimes reassuring and sometimes uneasy feeling [. . .] that they map a path, mark out a space, signpost a fumbling route, describe the specific staging posts of a search which has no *why* but only a *how* [. . .][67]

For Perec, the *why* emerges through a methodical but unpredictable *how* that explores procedures in order to move beyond them and actualise previously unimagined potentiality.

The effects of Perec's writing extend beyond his own *oeuvre*. Jacques Roubaud recognises Perec as the first Oulipian author to completely embrace the use of constraints in all his writing and to identify himself as a writer through the use of constraints.[68] According to Roubaud, the activity of the Oulipo today is largely inspired by Perec's example as a member of the group. When the Oulipo first began, works such as the *Cent mille milliards de poèmes* demonstrated the concept of potentiality but could not move beyond the limits of their constraints: all 100,000,000,000,000 sonnets had already been written potentially and only awaited instantiation. Perec transformed the purpose and consequences of writing under constraint:

> In the after-Perec, it has become automatic, or common practice always to consider both older and newer constraints in light of their potentiality; [. . .] speculating about a constraint's potentiality involves discerning the extent to which it is apt to trigger variations and mutations; the extent to which it

will naturally and productively participate in families of constraints; and, finally, the extent to which it might evolve over the course of time.[69]

The Oulipian writer needs to play with constraints to see where they will lead, and Roubaud identifies this approach to writing as *potentiality in actuality*:

> A displacement in perspective on a constraint, often brought about through its application and the actualization of certain variations, re-inscribes that constraint into a broader family and that re-inscription in turn generates new variations.[70]

Rather than seeking a solution to the *Entscheidungsproblem*, where the outcome would be predetermined by the postulates, the Perecian use of constraints allows for variation and mutation in the procedures for writing as they are implemented. The systematically irregular application of procedures opens the way for creative insight into their potentiality.

Although Perec did not work significantly with computers during his lifetime, his works involving complex systems of constraints entail the same kind of reasoning and inventiveness common to computer programming. Alan Turing demonstrated that no universal machine can calculate all possible instruction tables for automatic machines, and that some automatic machines may not be possible without the intervention of an oracle machine. In other words, computers can be programmed to produce results but human insight must seed the processor with erratic instructions to produce original and meaningful output. Perec's notion of the clinamen in this context refers to the suspension of pure logic and the introduction of irreducible inventiveness that re-engages the machine. Like Turing, Perec thought about logical machines and the way they functioned without much recourse to a computer. He prototyped a conceptual writing programmed with mutable algorithms sparked by imagination.

NOTES

1. Craig Dworkin (2011), 'The Fate of Echo', in Craig Dworkin and Kenneth Goldsmith (eds), *Against Expression: An Anthology of Conceptual Writing*, Chicago: Northwestern University Press, p. xxxiv.
2. Dworkin, 'The Fate of Echo', p. xxxvi.
3. Marjorie Perloff (2010), *Unoriginal Genius: Poetry by Other Means in the New Century*, Chicago: University of Chicago Press, p. 12.
4. Kenneth Goldsmith (2011), *Uncreative Writing: Managing Language in the Digital Age*, New York: Columbia University Press, p. 9.
5. Lev Manovich (2001), *The Language of New Media*, Cambridge, MA: MIT Press, pp. 218–21.

6. Dworkin, 'The Fate of Echo', p. xlii.
7. Jean-Jacques Thomas (1988), 'README.DOC: On Oulipo', trans. Lee Hilliker, *SubStance*, no. 56, p. 28.
8. Georges Perec (1986), 'Clinamen Redux', trans. Warren F. Motte, *Comparative Literature Studies*, vol. 23, no. 4, p. 276.
9. Paul Braffort (1988), 'F.A.S.T.L. Formalismes pour l'analyse et la synthèse de textes littéraires', in Oulipo, *Atlas de littérature potentielle*, Paris: Gallimard, pp. 108–9.
10. Harry Mathews and Alastair Brotchie (eds) [1998] (2005), *Oulipo Compendium*, London: Atlas Press, p. 126.
11. Christelle Reggiani (1999), *Rhétoriques de la contrainte: Georges Perec – l'Oulipo*, Saint-Pierre-du-Mont: Éditions InterUniversitaires, p. 478.
12. Alison James (2009), *Constraining Chance: Georges Perec and the Oulipo*, Evanston: Northwestern University Press, p. 4.
13. James, *Constraining Chance*, p. 225.
14. The ALAMO, or Atelier de Littérature Assistée par la Mathématique et les Ordinateurs (Workshop for Literature Assisted by Mathematics and Computers), was founded by Paul Braffort and Jacques Roubaud, both members of the Oulipo. For an account of early Oulipian experiments with computers, see Mark Wolff (2007), 'Reading Potential: The Oulipo and the Meaning of Algorithms', *DHQ: Digital Humanities Quarterly*, vol. 1, no. 1, available at: http://www.digitalhumanities.org/dhq/vol/001/1/000005/000005.html.
15. Bernard Magné (2007), 'Perec et l'ordinateur', in Henri Béhar et al. (ed.), *Mesures et démesure dans les lettres françaises au XXe siècle*, Paris: Honoré Champion, pp. 410–14.
16. Georges Perec (2003), *Entretiens et conférences*, ed. Dominique Bertelli and Mireille Ribière, vol. 2, Nantes: Joseph K., pp. 133–6.
17. Magné, 'Perec et l'ordinateur', p. 405.
18. Perec, *Entretiens et conférences*, vol. 2, p. 317.
19. Andrew Hodges (2013), 'Alan Turing', in Edward N. Zalta (ed.), *The Stanford Encyclopedia of Philosophy*, available at: plato.stanford.edu/archives/win2013/entries/turing.
20. Hodges, 'Alan Turing'.
21. Hodges, 'Alan Turing' (author's emphasis).
22. Hodges, 'Alan Turing' (cited by Hodges).
23. Hodges, 'Alan Turing'.
24. Hodges, 'Alan Turing'.
25. Alan Turing [1946] (1986), 'Proposal for Development in the Mathematics Division of an Automatic Computing Machine (ACE)', in Brian E. Carpenter and R.W. Doran (eds), *A. M. Turing's ACE Report of 1946 and Other Papers*, Cambridge, MA: MIT Press, p. 44.
26. Georges Perec and Marcel Bénabou (1989), 'Presbytère et prolétaires: Le dossier P.A.L.F.', *Cahiers Georges Perec 3*, p. 17.
27. Perec and Bénabou, 'Presbytère et prolétaires', p. 21.
28. Perec and Bénabou, 'Presbytère et prolétaires', p. 32. My translation.
29. Perec and Bénabou, 'Presbytère et prolétaires', p. 17. My translation.
30. Perec and Bénabou, 'Presbytère et prolétaires', p. 11.
31. Perec, 'The Machine', p. 33.
32. Perec, 'The Machine', pp. 34–5.
33. Perec, 'The Machine', pp. 36–7, 58.
34. Perec, 'The Machine', p. 36.
35. Perec, 'The Machine', pp. 37–8.
36. Perec, 'The Machine', pp. 39–51.

37. Perec, 'The Machine', pp. 52–8.
38. Perec, 'The Machine', pp. 58–69.
39. Perec, 'The Machine', pp. 70–2.
40. Perec, 'The Machine', pp. 72–90.
41. Perec, 'The Machine', pp. 90–3.
42. David Bellos (1993), *Georges Perec: A Life in Words*, Boston: Godine, pp. 409–10.
43. Georges Perec [1968] (2011), *The Art and Craft of Approaching Your Head of Department to Submit a Request for a Raise*, trans. David Bellos, London: Verso, p. 3.
44. David Bellos (2012), 'Georges Perec's Thinking Machines', in Hannah B. Higgins and Douglas Kahn (eds), *Mainframe Experimentalism: Early Computing and the Foundations of the Digital Arts*, Berkeley: University of California Press, p. 46.
45. Hans Hartje, Bernard Magné and Jacques Neefs (1993), 'Une machine à raconter des histoires', in Georges Perec, *Cahier des charges de La Vie mode d'emploi*, Paris: Cadeilhan, pp. 14–25.
46. Hartje, Magné, and Neefs, 'Une machine à raconter des histoires', pp. 19, 26.
47. Oulipo (1988), *Atlas de littérature potentielle*, Paris: Gallimard, p. 90.
48. Georges Perec [1978] (2009), *Life A User's Manual*, trans. David Bellos, Boston: Godine, p. 35.
49. Perec, *Life A User's Manual*, pp. 35–6.
50. Perec, *Life A User's Manual*, p. 36.
51. Perec, *Life A User's Manual*, p. 140.
52. Perec, *Life A User's Manual*, p. 218.
53. Perec, *Life A User's Manual*, p. 221.
54. Perec, *Life A User's Manual*, p. 376.
55. Perec, *Life A User's Manual*.
56. Perec, *Life A User's Manual*, p. 377.
57. Perec, *Life A User's Manual*, p. 378.
58. Perec, *Life A User's Manual*, p. 381.
59. Perec, *Life A User's Manual*.
60. Perec, *Life A User's Manual*.
61. Perec, *Life A User's Manual*, p. 382.
62. Perec, *Life A User's Manual*.
63. Perec, *Life A User's Manual*, pp. 382–3.
64. Georges Perec [2003] (2009), *Thoughts of Sorts*, trans. David Bellos, Boston: Godine, p. 3.
65. Perec, *Thoughts of Sorts*.
66. Perec, *Thoughts of Sorts*, p. 4.
67. Perec, *Thoughts of Sorts*, p. 5.
68. Jacques Roubaud (2004), 'Perecquian OULIPO', trans. Jean-Jacques Poucel, *Yale French Studies*, no. 105, pp. 102–3.
69. Roubaud, 'Perecquian OULIPO', p. 108.
70. Roubaud, 'Perecquian OULIPO', p. 109.

PART II

The Poetics of the Quotidian and Urban Space

CHAPTER 6

Georges Perec and the Significance of the Insignificant

Ben Highmore

Georges Perec died in 1982 at the age of forty-five. What is he for us now, thirty-three years later, in the second decade of the twenty-first century? How do we make him our contemporary? To make Perec's work part of our present-day involves (perhaps counter-intuitively) grasping his project in its historical specificity. It isn't by cherry-picking useable aspects of the work that we will ensure some relevance to its afterlife: rather, it will be by recognising his larger project as a response to a particular historical situation. While Perec's situation in the 1960s and 1970s in France is not ours, it has its hooks in our world. Perec, I think, becomes our contemporary in the act of seeing those hooks, of seeing how a continuity of feeling and mood percolates through historical ruptures, and how changes in mood and feeling activate historical continuities.

There is a simple claim driving this essay, namely that a central aspect of Perec's project was its attempt to register actuality. Which is to say that his project was a form of realism and, like many forms of realism, it was a quest and a question rather than an answer or solution. And, as a question, Perec's realism goes something like this: in a situation where there is no specific artistic style that has a privileged access to reality, where scholarly disciplines are all trying to grasp their slice of reality and claim it as *the* reality, and where the real is saturated by the unreality of the commodity spectacle, how can realism be achieved? Or, slightly differently, and now as a quest rather than a question: if the means of grasping reality (from literature to sociology, from religion to politics) are in doubt, and, if, because of this, there is a suspicion about what in the world should count as significant, then realism might mean revealing the significance of the insignificant.

Perec's work is full of lists of objects and activities, of itemised occurrences and repeated gestures. It is also a constant puzzling and worrying about what to include as part of these itineraries and what to ignore. A crucial worry is that what presents itself as significant (intention or motivation, say, or political and national events) bears the mark of a doxa – an unquestioned assumption of value that reproduces a social order. But Perec's worry doesn't end there, in fact this is its beginning. Suspicion and refusal of the doxa isn't in itself a freedom or a liberation: it offers only an unedited (or uneditable) reality, a melee without shape or end. Without some form of commitment to politics, say, or to the protocols of an analytic approach, what reason could there be for focusing on one thing rather than another, of attending to x while discounting y? Or, more crucially, as his one-time teacher Roland Barthes articulated it, without opting for a position, description is endless, inexhaustible: 'If it were not subject to an aesthetic or rhetorical choice, any "view" would be inexhaustible by discourse: there would always be a corner, a detail, an inflection of space or colour to report.'[1]

Acknowledging the world as inexhaustible is a central aspect of Perec's work in the 1970s, particularly in the project published as *An Attempt at Exhausting a Place in Paris* (first published in French in 1975).[2] But, while this short book might declare its intention to provide an exhaustive description, it actually articulates all the conditions that make such a project impossible. It is in the impossibility of the project and in the waywardness of the descriptions of what is perceived and imagined that Perec offers us a realism engaged not just in describing reality but in describing the activity and limitations of attending to and describing reality. *An Attempt at Exhausting* takes place over three days at various cafes in Place Saint-Sulpice, and starts out by very quickly itemising the buildings, shops, the church, the statue and the fountain in the large square. Instead of concentrating on these elements that could be described as already-marked-as-significant (part of a tourist itinerary, or a list of retail outlets and eateries, and so on), Perec seeks 'to describe the rest instead: that which is generally not taken note of, that which is not noticed, that which has no importance; what happens when nothing happens other than the weather, people, cars, and clouds.'[3] He notes the buses that pass and the different kinds of movement involved in navigating the place: 'waiting, sauntering, dawdling, wandering, going, running toward, rushing (toward a free taxi, for instance), seeking, idling about, hesitating, walking with determination'.[4]

An Attempt at Exhausting a Place in Paris isn't just a valiant effort to attend to the insignificant – it also registers the necessary contingencies involved in this. So, for instance, while watching a bus arrive you miss a car parking: 'Obvious limits to such an undertaking: even when my only goal is just to observe, I don't see what takes place a few meters from me: I don't notice, for example, that cars are parking.'[5] Boredom and the exhaustion of the observer is also another factor that limits any attempt to exhaust the place: 'Buses pass by. I've lost all interest in them.'[6] A problem that accompanies this is repetition: if what you are witnessing is a constant stream of passing passers-by, how often do you register this?

> I again saw buses, taxis, cars, tourist buses, trucks and vans, bikes, mopeds, Vespas, motorcycles, a postal delivery tricycle, a motorcycle-school vehicle, a driving-school car, elegant women, aging beaus, old couples, groups of children, people with bags, satchels, suitcases, dogs, pipes, umbrellas, potbellies, old skins, old schmucks, young schmucks, idlers, deliverymen, scowlers, windbags.[7]

If exhaustion is the aim, would you need to describe each and every vehicle? Or, is it enough to say that there was a fairly constant stream of foot traffic and road traffic? And, how much should description include? As soon as adjectives are introduced, the flat itemising of objects becomes something closer to interpretation: these women are elegant, those people look like windbags. As itemising accumulates, you can hear the echo of frustration, of a creeping misanthropy that emerges out of the Sisyphean task of exhausting description.

Realism, then as now, involves a politics because it stakes a claim on an always contested reality (is reality harmonious or fractious, class-bound or meritocratic, for instance?).[8] But, literature (or art more generally) is not the privileged province of realism. Indeed, it would be hard to think of the varieties of realism within the literature of modernity outside of the realism claims made by sociologists, anthropologists, political economists, psychologists, historians, biologists and so on. Take, for example, Georg Lukács' claims for realism in his book *The Meaning of Contemporary Realism*. Lukács' book promotes a version of critical realism that is set against versions of naturalism (avant-garde and conventional). The key to critical realism, for Lukács, is that the particularity of a character, of a plot, of a situation and of an environment reveals its relationship and position within a larger orchestration of the totality and, in doing so, offers a critical (because it is particular, because it necessarily provides an angle) view of that totality. Realism here requires that the details of the particular are *significant* details for the totality:

> But whether or not the sequence and organization make for an adequate image of objective reality will depend on the writer's attitude towards reality as a whole. For this attitude determines the function which the individual detail is accorded in the context of the whole. If it is handled uncritically, the result may be an arbitrary naturalism, since the writer will not be able to distinguish between significant and irrelevant detail.[9]

The 'arbitrary naturalism' that Lukács points at would include the sort of psychological naturalism (invoking a character's inner voice as a 'stream of consciousness', for instance) of modernist writers such as Virginia Woolf or James Joyce.

What is at stake in disparaging psychological naturalism while promoting a critical realism aimed at unveiling the way that social structures affect and effect lives (a realism based on the way that a singularity of the detail offers access to the generality of the social) is not just a question of style. It is a question of intellectual heritage, socio-political analysis and investigative priorities and propensity. While the 'arbitrary naturalism' of Woolf and Joyce, for instance, might be seen as a reaction against a previous tradition of literature (most obviously, for Woolf, the work of a writer such as Arnold Bennett) it also (and generatively) needs to be seen as aligning itself with an investigative concern found in the work of people such as William James and Bertrand Russell.[10] Similarly, the world of Lukács is unthinkable outside the investigative interests articulated by Marx and Engels, Luxemburg, and Hegel.

In the early 1960s, Perec's position was broadly aligned with Lukács'. Indeed, Perec's important essay, 'For a Realist Literature',[11] pursues a position very close to Lukács' in *The Meaning of Contemporary Realism*. Fundamentally, for Perec, the artwork, by offering an orchestration of the world, provides a coherent depiction:

> What we call an artwork isn't just the rootless creation that the aestheticist work is; on the contrary, it is the most total expression of concrete realities; if literature is a work of art, it is because it organizes and unmasks the world, because it makes the world appear in its coherence beyond its everyday anarchy, while integrating and surpassing the contingencies that render it in the form of the immediate system, with its necessity and its movement.[12]

The methodological basis of this position is a dialectical movement between the general and the particular:

> Because the particular only appears as a function of the general, and because the general can only be grasped as a function of the particular, this self-conscious effort [to write in order to know oneself] that remains a point of departure for all creation (literary or not) can only be a point of departure, and remains useless if it doesn't integrate itself into a larger project involving reality in its entirety.[13]

For Perec, then, realism is the struggle against the formlessness of 'everyday anarchy'. Its role is to find the general in the particular through the seemingly tautological route of recognising that the general can only function in its particularities.

Does this fit with the image we have of Perec? Don't we normally think of Perec as embracing the 'everyday' (and its potential for anarchy) against a (false) coherence offered by conventional narrative forms, or by a political interpretation of society?[14] Doesn't the usual account of Perec suggest that his leftist political leanings became less important in his work, as his work became more ludic in form? Against this, I want to argue that the relationship between the particular and the general, or the detail and the totality, is one that was foundational in his work. But, it was a relationship that was unreconciled and led to an experimental approach to the registering of everyday life.

The question that Perec's work poses is centred on the details of everyday life, and how such details might be meaningful or sensible within a larger social world. What Perec shares with Lukács is a critique of aspects of modernist literature that simply revel in the anarchy of the everyday (in forms of psychological naturalism) and see these as disconnected fragments tied to a monadic understanding of the world. He also seems to recognise in Lukács' writing the importance of realism for attending to moments of dynamic social change. In the late 1950s, Lukács' realism offered a route between the asocial, hyper-modernism of the *Nouveau Roman* (as represented particularly by Alain Robbe-Grillet and Nathalie Sarraute) and the instrumentalism of Jean Paul Sartre's committed literature. But Lukács wasn't the only theoretical voice he was listening to. Indeed, in the way that he navigates across the dilemma of the relationship between the particular and the general his position is perhaps closest to the work of the Marxist philosopher and sociologist Henri Lefebvre.

In 1958, while Perec was undertaking his National Service (as a parachutist), he stayed with Lefebvre at the philosopher's home in Navarrenx.[15] Lefebvre had just published the second edition of his *Critique of Everyday Life*, with the addition of a hundred-page 'Foreword' that clarifies and theoretically develops his understanding of everyday life within capitalist society (which he had first theorised in the 1930s). Indeed, across all the texts that Lefebvre wrote on everyday life it is this 1958 'Foreword' that is the most important in establishing the potential and the problematic of everyday life for critical thinking. In it he offers a definition of everyday life:

> Everyday life, in a sense residual, defined by 'what is left over' after all distinct, superior, specialized, structured activities have been singled out by analysis, must be defined as a totality. Considered in their specialization and their technicality, superior activities leave a 'technical vacuum' between one another which is filled up by everyday life. Everyday life is profoundly related to *all* activities, and encompasses them with all their differences and their conflicts; it is their meeting place, their bond, their common ground.[16]

For Lefebvre, modernity produces the everyday, but not as an integrated realm of the social that is open to reflection, contemplation and public discussion. Instead, it produces it as an unmanaged remainder that provides (potentially at least) a royal road to the totality. This remainder is produced, partly, through an extensive parcelling-out of daily experience into a host of institutions and expertise: to psychology, to sociology, to literature, to health, to professional leisure activities, to social surveys, and so on. The everyday falls between the cracks of such specialisation.

The methodological outcome of Lefebvre's critique is a refashioning of Lukács' rendering of the particular and the general. For Lefebvre, the general is still ultimately important, but the only way to access it is through the social detail – the everyday. In Lukács, the methodological imperative seems to be that the social totality (the general) decrees what would be significant or not. With Lefebvre, the understanding is that everything is significant in as much as it contains (like a fractal) the imprint of the general. He gives the example of a woman buying some sugar to show how a small everyday event connects to history, global trade and memory and that all this is there in the details of everyday life:

> Although what I grasp becomes more and more profound, it is contained from the start in the original little event. So now I see the humble events of everyday life as having two sides: a little, individual, chance event – and at the same time an infinitely complex social event, richer than the many 'essences' it contains within itself.[17]

If everything is touched by the totality because nothing is ultimately autonomous, then what makes Lefebvre opt for one example over another? In theoretical terms, there wouldn't be a privileged realm for moving from the particular to the general, but, in pragmatic terms, there would be very good reasons for not fixing on the sorts of objects and practices that are already seen as significant by those forms of specialisation that remainder the everyday. Indeed, it would be by purposefully seeking out the details of everyday life, details that haven't already been marked as significant, that investigation can, for a while at least, avoid the doxa of established specialism with their already-marked-as-significant objects. In this way, the insignificant provides a trajectory aimed at a totality-yet-to-be-perceived rather than one known in advance. The insignificant (which is always in danger of becoming the new significant) is a heuristic device for exploring emergent generalities and totalities-in-transformation. This is, I want to suggest, what drives Perec's work. I have already briefly looked at the observational work that he conducted in the 1970s but it is perhaps most deliberately explored in his novel from 1965, *Things: A Story of the Sixties*.

FITTED CARPETS AND CHESTERFIELD SETTEES

In Kristin Ross's Lefebvrean cultural history of the decade from the mid-1950s to the mid-1960s ('the years after electricity but before electronics'),[18] Perec's *Things* is called on as an important cultural witness to the changes that France is undergoing. For Ross, French postwar modernisation, particularly evident in the growth of a consumer culture, isn't a slow series of adjustments, it is a pell-mell social reordering and re-orchestrating:

> In the space of just ten years a rural woman might live the acquisition of electricity, running water, a stove, a refrigerator, a washing machine, a sense of interior space as distinct from exterior space, a car, a television, and the various liberations and oppressions associated with each.[19]

In Ross's account, Perec's novel is used to show the way that the child-free heterosexual couple becomes a sign of a new unit of consumption and a new class experience. *Things*, we could say, explores a new territory of consumer culture as it constitutes a crucial aspect of class culture and class experience. This isn't class culture already fashioned in the caldron of industrialisation (a class already known through established forms of significance), it is an emerging class fashioned out of changes in market capitalism, changes in media, changes in the relations of production and consumption, and changes in the nature of work.

Things describes the lives of Jérôme and Sylvie by detailing their material circumstances: their apartment, their work, their furniture and clothes, the food they consume, their groups of friends, their nights out, the films they watch and the magazines they read. Yet, for all that, Jérôme and Sylvie aren't individuated by this extensive itemisation, rather they become generalised in their particularity. They are part of a milieu and are, for us as readers, representatives of this milieu. As the book states:

> They were the 'new generation', young executives who had not yet cut all their teeth, technocrats on the way, but only halfway, to success. Almost all of them came from the lower middle classes, whose values, they felt, were for them no longer adequate. They cast their eyes enviously, desperately, towards the visible comfort, luxury and perfection of the upper middle classes. They had no past, no tradition. There were no inheritances to wait for.[20]

If some expertise was useful for registering this class, it was an expertise that had some agency in fashioning groups as visible entities and as class positions. Exponents of this new knowledge went by the name of *psychosociologues* (psychosociologists), or market researchers in Britain and America. During 1960, Perec worked as a market researcher for the Dutch electronics firm Philips and for the cosmetics company L'Oréal.[21] Market research effected a feedback loop that allowed promoters to shape commodities so as to feed emergent desires and to fashion a subject (a targeted consumer) for these commodities. Market research, then, was a flexible 'social science' with a heightened ability to discover the emergent and produce consumer-class identities based on a liking for such things as high-modernist furniture or Shaker-style kitchen units, or both.

In the novel, Jérôme and Sylvie are both market researchers canvasing opinion about:

> students, fingernails, cough syrup, typewriters, fertilisers, tractors, leisure pursuits, presents, stationery, linen, politics, motorways, alcoholic drinks, mineral water, cheeses, jams, lamps and curtains, insurance and gardening.[22]

In their work, Jérôme and Sylvie feed the world of commodity production in a direct manner, but *Things* is a story that is focused on how a milieu (a milieu that is also Perec's milieu to a certain degree) becomes constituted as consumers. Here the world of commodity promotion is not just tied to the advertising industry but, seen as diffuse, saturating the life-world of a milieu as a vague set of names, moods, feelings and objects. In clothing, it marks a trajectory of class aspiration and class individuation that could mark and make subjects as they pass from adolescence into consumer-adulthood. Initially, Jérôme and Sylvie dress like students, but gradually they attire themselves in textures and textiles that conjure up a rich imaginary of values and sensual arrangements:

> knitwear, silk blouses, shirts by Doucet, cotton voile ties, silk scarves, tweed, lambswool, cashmere, vicuna, leather and jerseywool, flax and, finally, the great staircase of footwear leading from Churches to Westons, from Westons to Buntings and from Buntings to Lobbs.[23]

Needless to say, such a trajectory has no endpoint – there is always a further step on the 'staircase of footwear'.

One of the central arenas for disseminating cultural imaginaries of material culture was the burgeoning magazine industry, particularly magazines such as *L'Express* and *Madame Express*.[24] Perec 'wrote *Things* with a pile of *Madame Express* beside me, and, to wash my mouth out after having read rather too much *Madame Express*, I would read some Barthes'.[25] The new 'lifestyle' magazines offered objects and opinions, holidays and menus:

L'Express held out to them all the signs of comfortable living: thick bathrobes, brilliant unravellings of murky truths, fashionable beaches, exotic cookery, useful tips, intelligent news analysis, the secrets of the gods, places out in the sticks where you could pick up property for almost nothing, the names of the different carillon bells, new ideas, smart outfits, frozen food, elegant accessories, the scandals of polite society, up-to-the-minute advice.[26]

Such magazines, like the world of market research, had a dual role to play, both pandering to the interests of new class identities and concerns, while also bringing that class and its imaginaries into material being. They also emphasised the gap between dream and reality, desire and actuality, through their constant juxtaposition of unspoilt beaches and war reporting, fashion spreads and social exposés. The lifestyle magazine itself was a mobile medium well-fitted to other changes in society. According to Ross:

The growth of the magazine industry after the war bears some relation to the expansion under capitalism of what Lefebvre calls 'constrained time': in this case, the frequent periods of waiting or transition – appointments, commuting – that break up a day and which the portable format, easily digestible prose, and manageable article length of a magazine help fill.[27]

The precarious work of a market researcher (or other service sector workers), with long commutes to different locations, was well-suited to the sort of intermittent and mobile reading experience of magazines.

Things is fashioned out of a couple (Jérôme and Sylvie), a world of work (the casualised employment of market researchers), a medium (lifestyle magazines) and a vast array of material cultural items. It embodies Perec's insistence on describing the world materially rather than imputing an interiority to characters: 'I detest what's called psychology . . . I prefer books in which characters are described by their actions, their gestures, and their surroundings.'[28] But, if we usually think of this interiority as the place for such things as beliefs and values, identifications and desires, Perec seems to suggest that we can find them more materially through attending to the prosaic world of everyday material actuality. In this, his work has the feeling of it being empirical research. In its description of a class – what in France was being called technocrats, or 'hyper-petty-bourgeois'[29] – *Things* describes class not as an identification or a heritage, but as a daily material practice.

In the France of the 1950s and 1960s, the emergence of the 'new middle classes' was a symptom of the staggering changes taking place within homes, within working environments and within global relations (decolonisation and what Lefebvre called neo-colonialism). Writing a few years after *Things*,

Lefebvre sees these changes resulting, not in the eradication of the working-class, but in a new class relation to the totality via consumerism:

> For work and for the worker as subject (individual and collective) the consumer has been substituted who is no longer a subject but a place, that of consumption. Who speaks? The one who teaches consumption, the advertiser, the organizer of the everyday, the one who initiates the coincidence of the image and the situation, between the ideal and the real. To whom does one speak? To the consumer. To his ideal. When one speaks 'to me' it is not to me but to the possible consumer, the ideal.[30]

Consumerism obscures class relations as well as establishing new class identities and moods. And, it is this obscurity that produces a crisis in political identity. In Perec's *Things*, political commitments are worn like clothes, liable to wear and tear and subject to the built-in obsolescence of fashion. Politics has to cope with a new set of allegiances to material life. This is how Perec describes it for the milieu of Jérôme and Sylvie:

> In the past men fought in their millions, and millions still do fight, for their crust of bread. Jérôme and Sylvie did not quite believe you could go into battle for a chesterfield settee. But that was all the same the banner under which they would have enlisted most readily. There was nothing, they thought, that concerned them in party manifestos or in government plans: they would sneer at early retirement pension schemes, increased holiday entitlements, free lunches, the thirty-hour week. They wanted superabundance – Garrard turntables, empty beaches for their eyes only, round-the-world trips, grand hotels.[31]

In concentrating on a material world of what, in the literary and academic world of the 1960s, would have been considered 'insignificant', Perec (and Lefebvre) manage to articulate a general social world that urgently required a new political imaginary. Perec, though, was not the sort of political animal who would work to devise such an imaginary. His work was diagnostic and descriptive. By starting out with insignificant details (fitted carpets, Garrard turntables, chesterfield settees), Perec fashioned a novel of thick description that offered a semiotics of the totality:

> What I wanted [. . .] was for my words to be 'injected' with meaning, loaded with resonance. *Fitted carpet*, for instance: for me, that phrase conveys a whole system of values – specifically, the value-system imposed by advertising. So much so that you could say that, in places, my book *is* a piece of advertising copy; but, obviously, with distance,

and with irony that distance brings. The words I use do not designate objects, or things, but *signs*. They are images. *Things* is a story of poverty inextricably tangled up with the image of wealth.[32]

I think that Perec undervalues the materiality of the things he itemises in his novel. In this he was not alone. This was after all the period when semiology was at its peak. His desire to have phrases like 'fitted carpet' resonate with meaning is precisely the desire to move from the detail to the totality, from the insignificant everyday to the social.

To fashion the general out of the insignificant required that Perec supplement his interest in Lukács' ideas of contemporary realism with ideas percolating through from Roland Barthes and Henri Lefebvre. In recognising the significance of the insignificant in such items as fitted carpets and chesterfield settees, the insignificant is used as a heuristic tool for accessing the social as an emergent form. To see the insignificant as a heuristic methodology Perec had to side with the everyday against an already established understanding of what constituted significance within a known totality. It was by foregrounding the insignificant detail that the social had a chance of becoming visible as an emergent form.

AFTERLIVES

A few years after Perec published *Things*, the anthropologist Paul Rabinow was undertaking his doctoral fieldwork in Morocco. Roughly a decade later, he published a book reflecting on the practices of fieldwork. Trained in the social sciences at the University of Chicago, and well-versed in the structuralist anthropology of Claude Lévi-Strauss, Rabinow went to urban and rural Morocco in search of symbolism and ritualistic activities through which Moroccan culture could be interpreted and understood. But his reflections are aimed instead at the day-to-day activity of interacting with his 'informant' and friend Ali. Rabinow's reflections are about a frustration with the doxa of anthropology (symbolic ritual) and its lack of interest in the much less exotic world of humdrum everyday life. For Rabinow, an argument with Ali reveals just how little he understands of Ali's day-to-day world:

> It is in the less explicitly shaped and less overtly significant areas of day-to-day activity and common-sense reasoning that most cultural differences are embedded. Thematic observation is disturbingly difficult, for these phenomena are everywhere, thereby proving the most opaque to the methodologies we have developed. There are no clear boundaries to conclusively limit and define cultural performance. Ritual certainly

has its complexities, but they are of a different order from those more scattered, fragmentary, and partial orderings which give coherence to social life.[33]

For Rabinow, cultural ritual, the lingua franca of anthropological fieldwork, offered an 'official' interpretation of culture; ritual, in a strong sense, was culture already interpreted, packaged and ripe for consumption. Ritual already knew what was significant and declared it in advance. For an anthropologist, ritual was the doxa of investigation, against which the 'scattered, fragmentary, and partial' orchestrations of the everyday seemed less significant, or even insignificant.

Like Rabinow, Perec (and those with an interest in everyday life) opt to side with the insignificant against that which is already-marked-as-significant. To do so in the name of literature is to plunder the vast terrain of detail that fashions conventional forms of realism without necessarily directing its narrative drive:

> The singularity of description (or of the 'useless detail') in narrative fabric, its isolated situation, designates a question which has the greatest importance for the structural analysis of narrative. This question is the following: Is everything in narrative significant, and if not, if insignificant stretches subsist in the narrative syntagm, what is ultimately, so to speak, the significance of this insignificance?[34]

Perec excavates insignificant stretches of the life-world and makes them his literary terrain. It produced literary forms that reveal the significance of the insignificant. To do this, the foregrounding of the everyday can only be an initial move. Simply to recognise the significance of the insignificant is not enough. The insignificant is inexhaustible and it is formless. The insignificant guards against the doxa of the already-marked-as-significant. But the insignificant is also a lure that invites forms of passive naturalism, or more simply a sort of aimless and endless itemising. What is also needed is a position, a set of limitations, a project.

For Perec, these limitations, and the project that went with them, changed over the years. In an interview from 1981, he connects the mathematical and ludic limitations that Oulipo (the group of experimental writers he belonged to) sought to encourage, not to forms of avant-gardism, but to the much longer history of tradition literature reaching back to forms such as the tanka in Japanese poetry or the alexandrine in European poetry of the baroque and early modern periods. For Perec, the anarchy of modernism broke the formal limitations of literature producing what Lukács saw as arbitrary naturalism. Limitations needed to be imposed so that the everyday didn't result in the refusal of social form: 'Now we are obliged to find new forms, new ways of tracing our way through that thing which is so opaque.'[35] If the insignificant protected writing from the doxa of the disciplines (including literary disciplines), then formal limitations guarded against the endlessness of the everyday detail.

To shift from a sense of knowing what is significant (what should be studied) and to opt instead for a more heuristic foregrounding of the insignificant and everyday is connected to a history that is played out both at the level of ideas (the rise of doubt and suspicion, the belief in knowledge-from-below) and at the level of material actuality (a revolution in communication and technology, an exponentially expanding consumer culture, a superabundance of opportunities for individuating selves, and so on). Perec's historical moment is both ours and not ours. Were we to conduct Perec's experiments now (for instance, *An Attempt at Exhausting . . .*), mobile communication technology would alter both the reality we set out to describe and our attempts at describing it (see Chapter 12, this volume). If the place that Perec describes is a nexus of cars and buses and people who are passing through, such a phenomenological investigation is rendered more complex still when we consider the possible other places that they are also moving through via their wireless communication devices. Similarly, the boredom that befalls the observer in the early 1970s would also have to confront the temptations and habits we have established as electronic twitches around such everyday mobile devices. And what would *Things* look like if it was a story of the 2010s rather than the 1960s? Would it be so thingly? What would be the role of the Internet? How might leisure have changed? And obsessions about bodies and health?

If Perec's time isn't quite ours, it certainly offers a foretaste of our present-day world of endless opportunities to consume (and to consume ideas and opinions as much as shoes and furniture), and where such consumption obscures other possible connections of identity and politics. Perec provides an epistemological invitation that is still key to trying to grasp the details of everyday life as a critical opportunity. It is in his declensions of doubt and belief, of the relationship we have with consumer culture and our desires for a better life, that Perec is still our contemporary.

NOTES

1. Roland Barthes [1968] (1986), 'The Reality Effect', *The Rustle of Language*, trans. Richard Howard, Oxford: Blackwell, p. 145.
2. The book should be seen as part of a much larger project that Perec eventually gave up. Had it been completed, it would have resulted in 288 different texts that would describe (half from memory, half from onsite observation) twelve different places in Paris written

over twelve years (at the rate of two texts per month). See Andrew Leak (2001), 'Paris: Created and Destroyed', *AA Files*, no. 45/46, pp. 25–31, and Georges Perec (2011), 'Lieux: Four Texts by Georges Perec', *AA Files*, no. 45/46, pp. 32–77.
3. Georges Perec [1975] (2010), *An Attempt at Exhausting a Place in Paris*, Cambridge, MA: Wakefield Press, p. 3.
4. Perec, *An Attempt at Exhausting a Place in Paris*, p. 10.
5. Perec, *An Attempt at Exhausting a Place in Paris*, p. 10.
6. Perec, *An Attempt at Exhausting a Place in Paris*, p. 29.
7. Perec, *An Attempt at Exhausting a Place in Paris*, p. 18.
8. The literature on realism is excessive. For a general introduction to realism see Linda Nochlin (1971), *Realism*, London: Penguin, and Peter Brooks (2008), *Realist Vision*, New Haven, CT: Yale University Press. The important debates around realism that took place in the 1920s and 1930s in Germany are well-represented in Theodor Adorno, Walter Benjamin, Ernst Bloch, Bertolt Brecht and Georg Lukács (1980), *Aesthetics and Politics*, London: Verso.
9. Georg Lukács [1957] (1963), *The Meaning of Contemporary Realism*, trans. J. and N. Mander, London: Merlin Press.
10. See Ann Banfield (2000), *The Phantom Table: Woolf, Fry, Russell and the Epistemology of Modernism*, Cambridge: Cambridge University Press; Liesl Olson (2009), *Modernism and the Ordinary*, Oxford: Oxford University Press; and Bryony Randall (2011), *Modernism, Daily Time and Everyday Life*, Cambridge: Cambridge University Press, for useful discussions of the role played by various forms of philosophy and psychology in modernist literature.
11. Georges Perec [1962] (2007), 'For a Realist Literature', *Chicago Review*, trans. Rob Halpern, vol. 54, no. 2–3, pp. 28–39.
12. Perec, 'For a Realist Literature', p. 32.
13. Perec, 'For a Realist Literature', p. 33.
14. Michael Sheringham (2006), *Everyday Life: Theories and Practices from Surrealism to the Present*, Oxford: Oxford University Press, offers the most detailed account of Perec's relationship to 'everyday life' within a French intellectual context.
15. See David Bellos (1999), *Georges Perec: A Life in Words*, London: Harvill Press, p. 192. Lefebvre also introduced Perec to the work of Marcel Mauss and helped Perec get work as a market researcher.
16. Henri Lefebvre (1991), *Critique of Everyday Life: Volume 1*, trans. John Moore, London: Verso, p. 97.
17. Lefebvre, *Critique of Everyday Life*, p. 57.
18. Kristin Ross (1995), *Fast Cars, Clean Bodies: Decolonization and the Reordering of French Culture*, Cambridge, MA: MIT Press, p. 2.
19. Ross, *Fast Cars*, p. 5.
20. Georges Perec [1965] (1990), *Things and A Man Asleep*, trans. Andrew Leak, London: HarperCollins, p. 50
21. Bellos, *Georges Perec*, p. 215. For the importance of market research in Britain see Joe Moran (2008), 'Mass-Observation, Market Research, and the Birth of the Focus Group, 1937–1997', *Journal of British Studies*, vol. 47, no. 4, pp. 827–51, and Colin McDonald and Stephen King (1996), *Sampling the Universe: The Growth, Development and Influence of Market Research in Britain since 1945*, London: NTC Publications.
22. Perec, *Things*, pp. 38–9.
23. Perec, *Things*, p. 39.
24. These are magazines that in the 1960s combined lifestyle advice with social issue articles.

In Britain the equivalent would be a magazine like *Nova* as well as the colour-supplement magazines that started to appear with Sunday papers in the early 1960s.
25. Perec, cited in Andrew Leak (1993), 'Phago-citations: Barthes, Perec, and the Transformations of Literature', *Review of Contemporary Fiction*, vol. 13, no. 1, p. 133. Perec was always asserting the importance of Barthes for his work in the 1960s. If he underplayed the importance of Lefebvre it is probably because it was more diffuse in his work.
26. Perec, *Things*, p. 47.
27. Ross, *Fast Cars*, p. 143.
28. Perec, cited in the introduction to Georges Perec (2009), *Thoughts of Sorts*, trans. D. Bellos, Boston: David R. Godine, p. x.
29. Mark Poster (1975), *Existential Marxism in Postwar France: From Sartre to Althusser*, Princeton: Princeton University Press, p. 217.
30. Henri Lefebvre, writing in 1967 in the book, *Position: contre les technocrates*, cited in Poster, *Existential Marxism in Postwar France*, p. 253.
31. Perec, *Things*, p. 77
32. Marcel Bénabou and Bruno Marcenac [1965] (1993), 'Georges Perec Owns Up: An Interview', *Review of Contemporary Fiction*, vol. 13, no. 1, p. 28. A good deal of what Perec writes about in *Things* is relevant to a more general European context. For the British context of fitted carpets see Judith Attfield (2007), *Bringing Modernity Home: Writings on Popular Design and Material Culture*, Manchester: Manchester University Press, chapters 8 and 11.
33. Paul Rabinow (1977), *Reflections on Fieldwork in Morocco*, Berkeley: University of California Press, p. 58.
34. Roland Barthes [1968] (1986), 'The Reality Effect', *Rustle of Language*, trans. Richard Howard, Oxford: Blackwell, p. 143.
35. Georges Perec and Kaye Mortley (1993), 'The Doing of Fiction', *Review of Contemporary Fiction*, vol. 13, no. 1, p. 96.

CHAPTER 7

What Perec Was Looking For: Notes on Automation, the Everyday and Ethical Writing

Caroline Bassett

I write: I inhabit my sheet of paper, I invest it, I travel across it. I incite blanks, spaces (jumps in meaning: discontinuities, transitions, changes of key).[1]

Perec's writing continually revisits, through its own material operations, specifically through experiments in writing involving a play with constraint, automation and scale, the question of *how* to write. This question may be opened up. At issue is not only how to write, but how to write ethically, and moreover how to write ethically about the everyday. All these questions – and the ways that Perec found to address them – have relevance today.

Perec's work is characterised by an investigation of the very small scale, the insignificant detritus and banal repetitions of a life on the one hand, and a preoccupation with various forms of automation and constraint on the other. The relevant genealogies are well known: Perec's work on the everyday intersects with that of Henri Lefebvre and his associates, who were writing in mid-twentieth-century France. His writing certainly shares with that group a sense of the refractory but elusive qualities of everyday life and a sense of its significance. At the heart of what Lefebvre explored in terms of alienation,[2] and the place we may find ourselves, the everyday, everyday life, is where we are lost and found. Then there is Oulipo, the Workshop for Potential Literature, founded in the early 1960s with members including Italo Calvino and Raymond Queneau. This threw down a 'challenge to chance', experimenting with writing as form and exploiting constraint and its productivity, often through 'mechanical' forms of 'automatism'[3] brought to bear to generate material and operate upon it. This was a writing group to which Perec was most securely attached; membership exceeding life, he remains an Oulipian to this day.

The presence of *both* the small scale *and* the automated – and it is rare that either one is completely absent in his writings – gives Perec's work a particular kind of consistency somewhat at odds with the 'systematic versatility' he cultivated across four 'fields', the sociological everyday, the autobiographical (which deals with his own sad history as an orphaned Jewish child in the Second World War), the ludic, and the fictive;[4] these are Perec's own divisions. This consistency is central to the argument of this chapter, in which I seek to offer a response to the question Perec also asked of himself. This does not concern what he was looking *at* – his work continually excavates, classifies, finds, names and lists this. Rather, the question is what, in his minute investigations of the residue of the everyday – 'the corpses of long since dried up felt-pens, shirts, non-returnable glasses . . . cigar wrappers, tins, erasers, postcards, books, dust and knickknacks . . .' – in his ludic and fictive mode and in his writings on his own life, Perec was looking *for*.[5]

Respecting the division of his work into the given fields of operation would mean asking this question about Perec *either* as the writer of his own life *or* as a sociologist of the everyday, *either* as an exponent of Oulipo ludicity *or* as a writer of fiction. I begin instead by trespassing across these divisions, taking the everyday and the autobiographical to constitute the mutually entangled objects of Perec's attention, and the ludic and the fictive, into which I fold the combinatorial, computational, numerological and narratological modes, to constitute jointly the means and the medium of investigation. Entangling the urban sociology, autobiographical writing, literary works and ludic pieces is not forced here. Michael Sheringham notes that Perec acknowledged a debt to Michel Leiris, who operated between autobiographical and other scales,[6] and the fields of activity Perec set out constitute a highly pervious, if not continuous, terrain. Letting them come closer together is useful, and the various genres constitute a commentary on each other. Perec, it can be said, produced one user manual for 'Life', but many exploring *how* to write about it. My inquiry concerns how this exploration, which is a project of writing, centrally includes the question of how to write the everyday ethically.

This takes us immediately to writing, the medium through which Perec's linguistic *and* his combinatorial/numerological/computational operations and experiments are ultimately articulated. But first it is useful to clarify what it means to talk of 'the computational' in Perec's writing. As David Bellos notes,[7] Perec's actual engagement with computers and computing is very limited – confined to the algorithmically inspired *The Art of Asking Your Boss for a Raise*, and to a radio play and its various broadcast versions. Bellos then argues that, these aside, it is largely as an imaginary that the computational figures in Perec's work. My own sense is that the imaginary matters, but that it is also important to acknowledge the degree to which computational elements, forms and conventions, not fully configured and certainly not amounting to computerised productions, are *operational* (rather than imaginary), even if only operating partially and rarely approaching fully formed algorithmic productions, across much of Perec's work. By operational, I mean to imply that they intervene in what is produced, rather than figuring only as part of what is represented in the writing. Among these operating elements are some returned to later in this chapter – rule-based constraints of many kinds evident in the work and lists, grids and sorts.

Alison James notes that although Oulipo members later produced elaborated works of fiction, the group first set out to fabricate tools 'for use by writers'[8] – and, among them, machine tools of various kinds. Consistent with this general approach, the computational tools Perec uses are rarely imported fully formed but are put together contingently. For Perec, writing in general was never a given, a transparent or a pre-existing tool; rather, it was constantly being tested and remade.

One reason this continuous remaking was necessary was that the everyday, the target of Perec's writing, was itself recalcitrant and fugitive, and finding ways in which it could be sounded out was a struggle. In a discussion of what he termed the infra-ordinary, Perec asks:

> How are we to speak of these 'common things', how to track them down rather, how to flush them out, wrest them from the dross in which they remain mired, how to give them a meaning, a tongue, to let them, finally, speak of what is, of what we are.

Here, then, the question shifts: it becomes, not how to write, but how to write the everyday. It turns out that these are intimately related, since, for Perec, writing a line is also writing a life, a form of inhabitation that may be produced through inscription. As Perec put it, and the link to Michel de Certeau is evident,[9] 'I write. I inhabit my sheet of paper, I invest it, I travel across it . . .'[10] Writing makes bridges to other habitats – '[it] is language that throws a bridge between the world and ourselves . . . expressing the inexpressible . . . and . . . that fundamental relation between the individual and History out of which comes our freedom'.[11] This bridge makes of us historical subjects, free or unfree, justly or unjustly treated, but also joins the personal investigation of the self to the social world. In 'The Work of Memory', for instance, Perec discusses his own life as 'a book, that will belong to others [. . .]', a life story that is 'collective, shareable',[12] and it is what is *common* that he pulls from the 'mire' of the undifferentiated to name, attend to, listen to, let speak, in his writing in *Species of Spaces* (see the indented passage above). Writing is also, and somewhat differently, a way of bridging an impossible gap in Perec's own life. This is the void left by the death of his parents in the Second World War, his father killed, his mother deported to Auschwitz from an internment camp for Jews at Drancy, and lost. Of this, Perec says:

> I write ... because we lived together, because I was one amongst them, a shadow amongst their shadows, a body close to their bodies ... they left in me their indelible mark, whose trace is writing. Their memory is dead in writing ....[13]

The requirement 'to write the everyday' operates as something like an ethical injunction for Perec. And it arises in part because writing responds to a debt – understood in personal terms (the shadow of those others), and as a demand for justice to be done (perhaps by way of a faithful retelling, although faithfulness here is certainly not 'to the tale', as it might be in a narratological ethics, but to the life). The everyday must be written if it is to be found, and it must be found so that it may be written. To begin to untangle and understand this palindromic requirement demands further attention is paid both to the methods of writing Perec develops (the consistency of his writing with its characteristic scales and different forms of tool use) and to his understanding of the everyday.

Undertaking this, I intend to show how ethical writing emerges as, and at the intersection between, various forms of automation and exteriorisation, on the one hand, and the intimate inspection or interior gaze of the infra-ordinary exploration on the other. The micro scale of the infra-ordinary enables oblique perspectives, avoids full-on confrontation, seeks meaning in rubbish, re-composes forms of life from the tiny shreds and fragments left, or from the shape traced around a long missing body. The automated sorts and other loosely computational operations, often structuring the investigations into the infra-ordinary that Perec undertakes, that are also a feature of his writing, meanwhile, operate at a dispassionate or indifferent distance, invoking arbitrary systems and constraints, and they generate a distinctly non-human perspective on the everyday and its materials.

This combination, I will show, is at the heart of a method of investigation and form of writing that is able to grasp the everyday in ways that enable fidelity to its intractable reality to be maintained, and that enable this to be done safely – the latter not only referring to the prosthetic distance that may be provided for the writer, but also in the sense of safe landings, a form of writing staying light in its touch (to adopt Calvino's terms), or 'jumping' away (to use Perec's). This might avoid damage to the writer and avoid doing violence to what is excavated (an experience, a common reality, a brief cohabitation with shadows of the dead, the everyday). Thinking about safety, I am invoking Lilie Chouliaraki's discussion of safety, and relating it also to Roger Silverstone's media ethics of 'proper distance'[14] – both are briefly returned to below.

OUR TIME

Perec's time is not ours, he rarely speaks directly of technology and his engagement with computing was limited, as noted. Nonetheless, Perec's search for a way of writing ethically can speak to ethical issues associated with our digital or post-digital condition, including how we attend to it or name it. Three initial points of connection, each of which are unsettled but remain relevant when they are refracted through the lens I set up in this chapter, are as follows.

First, there is the increased relevance of the micro-scale of Perec's work to everyday life theorists of the media in an era of intimate technologies.[15] Intimate media, redefining bodies, partly through their recomposing them as bodies of data (e.g. as personalised/quantified selves), denaturalise previously 'natural' scales and 'natural' units, and contribute to the redefinition of 'ordinary' space within a 'new spatial economy ... [emerging as] a result of the dynamics between physical and virtual space, between old and new space'.[16] These are issues explored by myself and others.[17] While the focus on the micro-scale might have contributed to Perec's relative eclipse in times focusing on understanding everyday life at individual rather than dividual scales (the world before social media/big data as social data), now it contributes to his rising star.[18]

The second point of connection is the computational itself and the extension of forms of automation to social processes and operations previously thought beyond or below its reach – the friendship algorithms of social media, the rise of game theory, the claimed prioritisation of the game over the narrative, the rise of the list as a cultural form. The essentially imaginary solutions Perec proposed, his play with automated techniques to understand the social world and his interest in exhaustion (capturing 'everything') are now offered in a very different spirit – 'for real' – in the rhetorical claims made for Big Data, with its conspicuously solutionist 'imaginary'.[19]

The third point of connection, pursued most avidly here, relates to Perec's exploration of the 'fragile overlapping'[20] of these two scales and methods, the infra-scale and the computational operation, and their tensioned but productive relationship. Today the dense entanglement of the abstract (big data), and the intimate (the life to which data is increasingly closely coupled), increasingly constitutes the everyday – or threatens to do so – as a closed circuit, an inescapable round. Evidence for unease around this is found in what I call the anti-computational turn, a pervasive anxiety about the form of everyday life in which we now live. In these circumstances, questions that Perec raised around the ethics of writing (how to write the everyday) again become, and in an acute way – as they always were for him too – questions about how to live. The suggestion then, is that Perec's methods constitute an ethical way of 'going about things' that includes machinic and human elements, and that this has significance for thinking about contemporary media ethics in the terrain of the digital/post-digital, particularly as media ethics generalise in conditions of pervasive mediation.

In the second half of this chapter, this basic argument is fleshed out by looking more closely at some of its elements. First, 'Perec's everyday' is explored in relation to associated work and on its own terms across his *oeuvre*. This is undertaken partly as a corrective to widespread assumptions, particularly common in explorations focusing only on the sociological writings, that Perec's work simply celebrates life's small things. Second, I categorise various Perecian writing operations as endotic or exterior. Third, the dynamics this categorisation identifies are remapped onto *W or The Memory of Childhood* and the essay 'Robert Antelme or the Truth of Literature'. Finally, the question of ethical writing and the everyday is directly returned to, with reference to Perec, and to our contemporary situation.

THE EVERYDAY FOR THE EVERYDAY?

Sheringham contrasts the modernist fascination with what Georg Lukács termed the 'miraculous' that may arise *out* of the everyday with the attention paid to the everyday for itself in the work of Lefebvre, de Certeau, Blanchot and Perec.[21] The latter group focused *in* on the flotsam and jetsam (Blanchot's term) of everyday life: on the objects that accumulate, circulate, are forgotten and might be refound;[22] on the nothing that happens, on empty time, that is nonetheless time that passes, and continues to pass, even if it 'lags and falls behind'[23] – which also raises the question of 'for whom' this nothing time is happening.[24] Finding the everyday, obscured or concealed through forms of alienation, forgetfulness, by force of habit, mattered. And, in response, Perec undertakes the various anamnesiac operations characteristic of his work, asking:

> How should we take account of, question, describe what happens every day and recurs everyday: the banal, the quotidian, the obvious, the common, the ordinary, the infra-ordinary, the background noise, the habitual?[25]

THE INADMISSIBLE EVERYDAY

What makes Perec's everyday distinctive? At issue are the stakes in passing from the ordinary to the infra-ordinary ethnography, from the biographical to autobiographical, or from the usual unit – a whole day, a whole practice, a whole body, a whole person, perhaps de Certeau's *Wandersmänner* – to fragments, the fragments that might make up a shape that took up space in the void, or to the list generated of the places that might have been visited. Contra

Adair and others, Perec's infra-ordinary is not isomorphic with the everyday as it is ordinarily given,[26] nor does the mode of scrutiny its excavation demands amount simply to paying close attention. Rather, there are the blanks, the discontinuities and the glitches to take account of.

The writing on everyday life that most closely aligns Perec to the 'Everyday Life' tradition developed in media (and digital media) anthropology, particularly in accounts of media transformation and innovation, deals largely with Perec's adult life, and with spaces and activities of everyday domestic and urban life – notably Paris (*Exhausting a Place*, *Les Choses*) – and with many of the *Species of Spaces and Other Pieces* essays, written in the same vein. This work is often appreciated for what is viewed as a mildly eccentric attention to the microscopic for its own sake, an archaeological dig for small details and a revelation of their value, a rich description made from life's poor things, conspicuous for its conformation to Calvino's virtue of 'lightness'.[27] However, reading Perec's search for 'treasure' as a celebration of the habitual and quotidian, neglects what Perec *also* says – which is that the everyday is, by virtue of its daily inevitability and in its opacity, inadmissible:

> In our haste to measure the historic, significant and revelatory, let's not leave aside the essential: the truly intolerable, the truly inadmissible. What is scandalous isn't the pit explosion, it's working in coalmines. Social problems aren't a matter of concern when there's a strike, they are intolerable twenty-four hours out of twenty-four, three hundred and sixty-five days a year.[28]

This reframes Perec's prioritisation of the everyday, and the infra-ordinary, over its opposite: the event. His approach may enable the ruthlessly leisurely pulling apart of a place in Paris through repetitive micro-description, its exhaustion in the name of cultural geography, or anthropology; but, attention is also paid to this scale because it is at this scale, and at this temporality, that the intolerable occurs, the intolerable that *is* the everyday.

It is useful here to shift from urban sociology to the literary field. First to the 1963 essay in which Perec praises the formal characteristics of Robert Antelme's account of his everyday experiences in a Second World War concentration camp[29] because it exposes the unending everyday in its bare and terrible and incomprehensible bones:

> But we understand nothing. We don't understand the unendingness of hunger. Emptiness, Absence. The body eating itself away. The word 'nothing'. We don't know the camps.[30]

And then, to *W*, an ('anti-')autobiographical account, apparently realist but knowingly undercutting itself, which recounts Perec's early life in occupied

France after the deportation of his mother. There Perec lived in conditions of quasi concealment that operated, in a queasy balance, with the semblance of 'ordinary' life – ordinary in that it contained the banal and the routine, the aunts, the uncles, the games and the plays. In *W*, this 'ordinary' everyday is narrated, but is intercut with sections concerning a fantasy island, a concentration camp[31] where life is organised around sport, and consists of an endless, and endlessly cruel, series of grotesque games. Here failure to enter the lists means starvation, but participating only its delay. The sportsmen have no names, even the race winners inherit parodic identities[32] – the names of their forerunners, and the women run only to organise the order in which they are raped. In this cruel race, where as James aptly puts it, 'chance confirms the law and does not temper it', there is no winning, no escape – and, again, no (chance of) an end. *W*'s narrator tells us that novices from satellite villages, arriving at the camp, find its quotidian reality impossible to grasp:[33]

> Thus ends the novices' first day. The following days will be spent in the same way. [. . .] How can you explain that what he is seeing is not anything horrific, not a nightmare [. . .]? [. . .] this is life, real life, this is what there'll be everyday [. . .]. That's what there is, and that's all.[34]

The competitors, faced with this, maintain hope against all hope 'that there is something else, that the sky can be bluer, the soup better, the Law less harsh'.[35] In *W*, the autobiographically presented elements of Perec's childhood are held at a distance from the fable of the camp, but both are given as memories – and the island story is claimed as a reliable memory of a child's dreamed fantasy, in contrast to what are given as avowedly *unreliable* recollections of 'real' life in occupied France. Both, though, are given to us as unbearable: the early life is forgotten rather than borne, and sportsmen hope against hope that they are in a nightmare that will end.

Across the work, if we listen, we hear again and again that the everyday is, at least in part, inadmissible. But, says Perec – and he says it in the Antelme essay, undertakes it in *W*, and takes it on as the task in his sociological operations – to lay hold on it matters. The everyday has to be, and is, written. This is a matter of justice, and perhaps also of restitution. In the next section I want to explore further some of the tools Perec employs to undertake this writing.

WRITING: A USER'S MANUAL

Perec himself notes that the 'travelling' undertaken in his writing is not smooth. He sought to 'incite' discontinuities and blanks, 'changes of key',[36] glitches: all are aids to the process of tracking, flushing out, wresting from, un-miring and letting speak. These elements, operating to dis-locate, and produce distance, are nonetheless intrinsic to an 'endotic' approach, defined as a form of listening *in* to the self, to be practised on the shards of everyday life that operate below its 'ordinary' surface, that are to be excavated through these processes.

The use of various forms of constraint is central to the production of these discontinuities. Designed to 'refuse chance' in some forms (notably, for instance, the outpourings of 'automatic writing' and, James' point, that Oulipo's stance on chance/anti-chance is conditioned by, and is a response to, surrealism and its focus on the serendipitous outpouring, is apt),[37] constraint nonetheless also embraces the arbitrary. That is, constraint, and particularly the artificial constraint on the writer produced by the invocation of machine rules, may generate new orderings of the material at hand.

These generations are arbitrary rather than serendipitous (they obey orders), but at the same time are dispassionate, may produce something not decided upon in advance and may constitute modes of paying attention not available through human means. These forms of arbitrary intervention include taxonomic operations, the imposition of ludic constraint on writing and the use of the loosely computational techniques already mentioned – lists, grids, algorithms – all of which may dis-assemble the ordinary assemblages of the everyday – its scale, its spatiality and its temporality.

In his useful discussion of endotic anthropology, David Morley, adopting Perec's own terms, sums up the latter's methodology as entailing description, enumeration and inventory.[38] A different way of sorting this is to think about a series of operations along a continuum. This ranges from the interior to, if not the exotic – since Perec used that term to refer anthropology's traditional pursuits in the 'exotic' outside – then the *exterior*.

Perec continually reminds us that what is required is a falling into the self. He says we need 'our own anthropology ... that will speak about us, will look in ourselves ... not the exotic anymore but the endotic'.[39] It is to be remembered that this fall into an interior is always also into common space, that writing takes us into History as well as into the history of the individual, to use Perec's terms.

The self is often approached through objects. As Morley notes, if endotic anthropology turns away from the spectacular[40] it turns *towards* objects, and Perec's writings are often built object by object – bricks, concrete, glass, spoons ... Moreover, non-objects are often objectified as they are brought into his assemblages. They materialise into the shape of that which they refer to and replace – a memory, for instance, covering a void. Objects, indeed, let Perec avoid the void precisely through their quiddity.

Objects can come to speak. Perec wants to *make* them speak, to *force* them to speak – but not firstly *for* themselves. Rather, they are placed in service of the endotic requirement to tune in. Objects thus function chiefly as forms of external memory,[41] working as fragmented repositories that already contain what is 'ours' and may be refound. They may, in this sense, be regarded as an odd form of working memory – they operate to 'make' (human) memory work.

What objects speak of are thus human conditions. Clearly, this is not a study dealing in the radical otherness of objects and we do not wait for their distant hum. And, yet, in gathering objects, organising them, taking notice of them (How many movements? How many spoons?), Perec draws attention to, indeed works with, the ontology of objects, which might be said to present itself in unexpected ways in his work. If objects are to be made to speak of us, they have also to speak of, or to speak as, themselves; there *are* ways in which this is an object-orientated approach perhaps – or, at the least, objects begin already to point to ways in which exterior as well as interior elements are integral to Perec's methodology.

Turning from selves and objects to processes brings me back to computational elements in Perec's writing. First, to the list, one of the basic processes of capture in Perec's work. Bound into the Perecian writing machine, this is an exterior operation that not only complements, but often enables the endotic turn. Perec is a consummate list maker,[42] avowedly influenced by the taxonomical imagination of Borges (and Foucault), and gleefully forces together what were previously incommensurate: scales, objects, events, times, tempos:

> What we need to question is bricks, concrete, glass, our table manners, our utensils, our tools, the way we spend our time, our rhythms.[43]

If the objects collected are often infra-ordinary, being *beneath* general notice, Perec's listing operations sometimes entail a non-commensurate or *over*-determined investment. They are systematically excessive, a bathetics. Consider the attempt to exhaust a place in Paris, or the opening chapter of *Les Choses* with its detailed enumeration of the objects in an over-stuffed room, which constitutes a list in literary form. It is clear that these lists are infra- *and* extra-ordinary, at times hyper-real, generating a parodic ordinary. Ian Bogost, in his recent exploration of the list as the simplest form of ontography, defines it as 'a group of items loosely joined not by logic or power or use' but by 'the gentle knot of the comma'.[44] This formulation gets at how the list, in Perec's hands, can disembed what it collects from its previous contexts and associations, and, in this way, make exterior what was previously contained within the infra-ordinary.

Lists are produced through various operators, algorithms providing principles of selection and inclusion (for example, include if x = Paris, include if x = on my desk, do not include x if x = letter E). What is thus selected into a list or other form of collection may be operated upon further, or re-ordered, each time with the same impartial violence; the result may be *Cent Mille Milliards de poèmes* (Queneau's sonnet) or a four-element recipe in which each element is methodically recombined – the latter constitutes Perec's offering of a bafflingly redundant number of ways to cook a rabbit.[45]

The infra-ordinary is thus found not only through attentive (human) listening in, but through the object and its quiddity, and through the perspectives given by the classificatory process, the algorithm, the sort.

Insisting on the exterior moment as part of the endotic inquiry refocuses questions of attention in Perec's work: the demand is to listen in, but we need to ask what and/or who, or what combinations of natural and unnatural listening are entailed here. Perec's is a computer-assisted, or least a partly automated, listing/listening project. As such it is characterised partly by how it stands off, moves away, as well as how it moves in. It seeks to re-find what was known (and, in this sense, is based on a form of re-familiarisation), but also produces an un-familiar, and if not random or chance-based, then externally programmed or generated, order of things.

THE GRID

This mix of human and non-human attention, which produces a relation neither near nor far, internal nor external, but something defined as an oscillation perhaps, or a series of jumps between interior and exterior elements, is not confined to the sociological writing on the everyday. However, the constraints that structure Perec's more literary works nonetheless take distinctive forms – not least because here the Perecian methodology might be understood as his response to the shortcomings of conventional narrative.

Perec's essay on Robert Antelme, a discussion of the ethics of witnessing and a comment on early Holocaust writing, directly addresses questions of how to write about an unbearable everyday. In it, Perec rejects what he understands to be the false compensations of – perhaps the falsification inherent in – narrative closure and asks how writing seeking to express the inexpressible[46] *should* be undertaken, if not through narrative. He praises Antelme, who, seeking to 'exhaust his particular experience by making it ours', works through the 'imposition of the whole grid of a discovery, of a memory, of a consciousness that goes to the limit'.[47] This grid is interposed between the reader and their pre-configured expectations, and the reality of the camp. It forces the everyday out of the mire, not as a retelling, but *as* the dross and peelings, and endless hunger.

'Robert Antelme or the Truth of Literature' speaks to the more or less autobiographical work, *W*, despite the years that separate them. The constraining grid of writing techniques employed in *W* include the complex connections instantiated between the two main story elements, the play with the narrator's own identity and the distancing entailed in the production of the avowedly fictional camp as the nightmare account of a reality that is not accounted for elsewhere in the text. *W* is in parts ludic in its pleasures – and in its puzzles. The structure of the whole, with its complex quasi-ludic architectural grid, entailing stories within stories and exploiting the nested or dispersed identities of the unreliable narrator with his unreliable memories, disallows forms of identification typically offered in the autobiographical genre.

As David Mitchell points out, *W* is 'ludicrous', grotesquely humorous as well as horrifying.[48] And, as part of that, it is often violent, in terms of its content, and abrupt – in the sense that it is subject to precisely those glitches, disjunctures, jumps that Perc has named as necessary to writing. But the violence here is not that of narrative – there is no foreclosing on the life with the compensations of the tale; no doing violence to the violent experience through its reporting. Rather, this mode of operation involves what, following Claire Boyle, I firstly understand as the active embrace of a certain mode of dispossession, which I take to be a forcing *outside*. Boyle herself goes on to argue that dispossession, certainly central to Perec's experience, constitutes *the* ethical principle informing his autobiographical work.

This chapter has been developing a related but rather different sense of the ethical, one that takes account both of dispossession or exteriorisation and the move inwards. Moreover, this is not an ethics of autobiographical writing only, but extends across the work, as a method of writing the everyday. In conclusion, this is now discussed directly.

ETHICAL WRITING

What has been argued so far is that the ethical dimensions of Perec's writing inhere in the tensioned relationship between rule-based operations – the computational elements of his writing, in which algorithms and rules are used to select and perform operations on groups of 'objects' – and the endotic, a mode of listening in. Both of these enable the infra-ordinary to be explored, and the former assists in the project of the latter. If the infra-ordinary is the only feasible scale at which those 'seeking to lay hold on truth' can operate, then to reach this site thus demands not only introspection but the scales and forms given by remote and automated sensing: a way of touching at a distance or touching down lightly and safely. Where Boyle talks of dispossession, I thus point to the incorporation of the computational process as an actant in a technique of writing that *also* stresses the intimate; it is this combination, the internal and external, put into play, that makes it possible to excavate the everyday without doing unethical violence to its 'truth'.

This ethics also relates to, but differs from, the media ethics of 'proper distance' developed by Silverstone,[49] concerned with viewing and listening, and with responsibility rather than justice (as Daniel Dayan notes)[50] in relation to the global mediapolis, and with the issue of distant suffering as explored by Lilie Chouliaraki.[51] Silverstone's account was focused on questions of narration and representation, of the self to the other, and its responsibilities, drawing on Hannah Arendt. Chouliaraki, engaging with Silverstone, and also with Boltanski's concerns with a politics of 'pity',[52] through a discourse of safety and suffering, does so in relation to 'the news text that reaches our living rooms'.[53] These are thus both accounts of *mediation* and its ethical dilemmas.

Perec is rather differently concerned, as I have shown, with developing a way to *write* the everyday ethically. His *oeuvre* can be viewed as a sustained attempt to develop principles and methods (archaeological, investigative, fictional) that enable him to lay hold of the everyday in writing. This ethics guides collecting, finding, storing, operating – all regarded as parts of writing, forms of an inscription. In this way it might be thought of as a *medium* rather than a media ethics, and is also ontological rather than representational, dealing not with questions of representation but with questions of what are appropriate means of finding, holding and examining the everyday and everyday life – as it is lived and as memory – 'at the point where it actually breaks the surface'.[54]

Perec's deployment of two intertwining and multiple scales, and the distances they produce, which is different from finding an appropriate 'viewing' or even 'receiving' distance (I recognise that this is a selective interpretation of what is a far more nuanced account given in Silverstone's and Chouliaraki's work overall) is thus distinctive. Paul Frosh's critical but appreciative reappraisal of 'proper distance', which rejects the notion of an 'ideal position between mediated closeness and distance'[55] (which Dayan suggests – rightly, I think – would have to be understood as absolute proximity[56]), in favour of asking questions about the proper *across* the range of near and far,[57] is germane here. Specifically, because, by rejecting the search for the ideal 'point' of the proper, Frosh is able 'to theorise the moral possibilities of aspects of mediation that are usually understood as 'impersonal, non-intimate, indifferent', which he argues can be 'morally enabling'.[58]

One reason I find this useful is that it provokes questions about the working of what I would term the 'moral economy of attention' and its possible automation, its complex temporality, its discontinuous or oscillatory characteristics. Moreover, it does this rather than simply naming 'paying attention' as a prerequisite for an ethical engagement between selves and others to be organised. This points back to the paradox at the heart of Perec's own demand that we notice, look, scrutinise, attend, get under the habitual to find the infra-ordinary, while at the same time employing methods that *rely* precisely on *nobody looking*. In the machinic operations integral to Perec's writing, human attentiveness, important elsewhere, is indeed systematically excluded, replaced by the solicitations of machinic indifference – which may attend to the unendurable, capture the inexpressible, bear the intolerable for us, perhaps, and bring the evidence back to the surface, when we may not. In exchange for what may be safely viewed, perhaps, there is what may be bearably approached and touched – and with what tools and by whom or what and for how long, through which grid.

In her discussion of programmed constraint, James says Oulipo offers us a 'paradoxical poetics of necessity grounded in arbitrariness'.[59] I agree that Perec partakes of this poetics, but I would also switch the formulation around to suggest that he also operates a poetics of the arbitrary, grounded in its necessity. Perec *needs* these computational scales in order to operate his endotic inquiries. And they themselves multiply its scales and produce multiple forms of attention so that, while Perec enjoins us to listen in, what is heard in his writing, which listens in partly using prosthetic inhuman means, *may also come from without*. In his excellent account of Perec, Sheringham cites Wittgenstein and Cavell on 'the necessity of the ordinary to explore the ordinary'.[60] But, what Perec shows us perhaps, is that, on the contrary, the ordinary does *not* have this power. Something else, operating beyond and before it, is also required to enable the writing of the everyday.

This may be the case for us, too, in our own times. I began by pointing to three ways in which Perec's work resonated with our own situation: the infra-ordinary engaging with 'dividualisation, the use of automated constraint within increasingly computerised culture and everyday life, and these combinations – the infra-ordinary and the automated – rather neatly mapping on to processes that appear to be accelerating in our everyday world. Perec's development of an ethics of writing, designated as being at once capable of capturing the everyday and of keeping it a safe distance (lightly touched, laid across a grid, approached through objects, operated on through the operation of a law, attended to minutely via the collection of evidential objects), exploits these scales and the different modes of direct or distanced engagement they provide. This is not the place or time to develop these arguments further but, it is interesting at least to point to the contrasts between Perec's conscious play with the possibilities of automation as it intersects with the intimate areas of everyday life and – for instance – the post-digital desire to accept the presence of such technology as a given, but also to put it aside.

NOTES

1. Georges Perec (2008), *Species of Spaces and Other Pieces*, London: Penguin, p. 11.
2. Henri Lefebvre (1991), *The Production of Space*, Oxford: Blackwell.
3. Alison James (2009), *Constraining Chance: Georges Perec and the Oulipo*, Evanston: Northwestern University Press, pp. 109–18.

4. Perec, *Species of Spaces*, p. 141.
5. Perec, *Species of Spaces*, p. 41.
6. Perec, *Species of Spaces*, p. x.
7. David Bellos (2012), 'Thinking Machines', in Hannah Higgins and Douglas Kahn (eds), *Mainframe Experimentalism*, London: University of California Press, p. 38.
8. James, *Constraining Chance*, p. 109.
9. Michel de Certeau (1984), *The Practice of Everyday Life*, Berkeley: California University Press.
10. Perec, *Species of Spaces*, p. 11.
11. Perec, *Species of Spaces*, p. 266.
12. Perec, *Species of Spaces*, p. 133.
13. Georges Perec (2011), *W or The Memory of Childhood*, London: Vintage, pp. 59 and 42; and see Bellos, 'Thinking Machines', p. 62; Marcel Bénabou (2004), 'From Jewishness to the Aesthetics of Lack', in Warren Motte and Jean-Jacques Poucel (eds), *Yale French Studies*, no. 105, p. 27.
14. Roger Silverstone (2006), *The Media and Morality: On the Rise of the Mediapolis*, Cambridge: Polity.
15. See David Morley (2006), *Media, Modernity and Technology: The Geography of the New*, London: Routledge; Caroline Bassett (2012), 'The Real Estate of the Trained-Up Self (Or is This England?)', in Rowan Wilken and Gerard Goggin (eds), *Mobile Technology and Place*, London: Routledge, pp. 104–22; and Ben Highmore, this volume.
16. Bassett, 'The Real Estate'.
17. Iris Tenkink (2006), 'Transformations of Species of Spaces', *Open*, vol. 9, no. 7.
18. Michael Sheringham (2009), *Everyday Life: Theories and Practices from Surrealism to the Present*, Oxford: Oxford University Press.
19. danah boyd and Kate Crawford (2012), 'Critical Questions for Big Data', *Information, Communication and Society*, vol. 15, no. 5, pp. 662–79.
20. Perec, *Species of Spaces*, p. 39.
21. Sheringham, *Everyday Life*.
22. Stephen Clucas (2000), 'Cultural Phenomenology and the Everyday', *Critical Quarterly*, vol. 42, no. 1, pp. 9–10.
23. Clucas, *Cultural Phenomenology and the Everyday*, pp. 9–10.
24. Sheringham, *Everyday Life*, p. 6.
25. Perec, *Species of Spaces*.
26. Kate Morris (2008), 'Perec's Alternative Topography: Figuring Permanence and the Ephemeral in *Lieux*', *Surface*, vol. 4, pp. 31–59.
27. Morley, *Media, Modernity and Technology*, p. 93.
28. Perec, *Species of Spaces*, p. 209.
29. Perec, *Species of Spaces*.
30. Perec, *Species of Spaces*, p. 256.
31. Perec, *W or The Memory of Childhood*.
32. Butler, *Bodies that Matter*.
33. Butler, *Bodies that Matter*.
34. Perec, *W or The Memory of Childhood*, p. 140.
35. Perec, *W or The Memory of Childhood*.
36. Perec, *W or The Memory of Childhood*, p. 11.
37. James, *Constraining Chance*, p. 109.
38. Morley, *Media, Modernity and Technology*.
39. Perec, *Species of Spaces*, p. 210.

40. Morley, *Media, Modernity and Technology*, p. 94.
41. Bassett, 'The Real Estate'.
42. Perec, *Species of Spaces*, p. xx.
43. Perec, *Species of Spaces*, p. 210.
44. Ian Bogost (2012), *Alien Phenomenology, or What It's Like to Be a Thing*, Minneapolis: University of Minnesota Press.
45. Perec, *Thoughts of Sorts*.
46. Perec, *Species of Spaces*, p. 255.
47. Perec, *Species of Spaces*, p. 256.
48. David Mitchell, back cover endorsement for Perec, *W or The Memory of Childhood*.
49. Silverstone, *The Media and Morality*.
50. Daniel Dayan (2007), 'On Morality, Distance and the Other. Roger Silverstone's Media and Morality', *International Journal of Communication*, vol. 1, no. 1, pp. 113–22.
51. Lilie Chouliaraki (2006), *The Spectatorship of Suffering*, London: Sage.
52. Chouliaraki, *The Spectatorship of Suffering*; Paul Frosh (2011), 'Phatic Morality: Television and Proper Distance', *International Journal of Cultural Studies*, vol. 14, no. 4, pp. 383–400.
53. Chouliaraki, *The Spectatorship of Suffering*; Frosh, 'Phatic Morality'.
54. Perec, *Thoughts of Sorts*, p. 16.
55. Lilie Chouliaraki and Shani Orgad (2011), 'Proper Distance: Mediation, Ethics, Otherness', *International Journal of Cultural Studies*, vol. 14, no. 4, pp. 341–5.
56. Roger Silverstone (2004), 'Proper Distance: Towards an Ethics for Cyberspace', in Gunnar Liestøl, Andrew Morrison and Terje Rasmussen (eds), *Digital Media Revisited: Theoretical and Conceptual Innovations in Digital Domains*, Cambridge, MA: MIT Press, pp. 469–89.
57. Frosh, 'Phatic Morality'.
58. Frosh, 'Phatic Morality'.
59. James, *Constraining Chance*, p. 125.
60. Stanley Cavell (1989), 'Declining Decline', *This New Yet Unapproachable America: Lectures after Emerson after Wittgenstein*, Chicago: University of Chicago Press, p. 47.

CHAPTER 8

'Things That Should Be Short': Perec, Sei Shōnagon, Twitter and the Uses of Banality

Anthony McCosker and Rowan Wilken

'The trouble with Twitter: Far from delivering a "wisdom of crowds", social networking sites have created only a deafening banality.' So reads the title to a 2009 article in *The Guardian*.[1] This has become a familiar lament in relation to various forms of social media but is one that is particularly pronounced with respect to Twitter. What seems to be at stake in these critiques is not just that banality proliferates through Twitter, but that this banality is without function or value. As Cornelius Puschman et al. note, due to its focus on 'mundane communication', in its early days Twitter was 'widely lambasted as a cesspool of vanity and triviality by incredulous journalists (including technology journalists)'.[2] Platform developers have since responded: better to hide the banal through algorithms that prefer the intensity of trending topics, and reward certain kinds of expression with visibility.[3] But how can we revalue that element of banality, the intimate access to everyday life-worlds that characterises social media more generally, even if platforms like Twitter have turned toward spectacle, celebrity and breaking news in its place?

This chapter brings together three somewhat disjunctive approaches to banality to rethink the everyday as an object of social research. We consider accounts of Twitter as a 'machinery that produces banality'[4] and the criticisms this attracts, through the lens of Georges Perec and his enduring interest in the musings of the late tenth-century Japanese courtesan Sei Shōnagon and her *The Pillow Book* with its famously intimate observations of her day-to-day life. While Perec never realised his desire to produce a contemporary version of this book,[5] he did identify in Shōnagon's work two specific elements that became crucial in his own writing and his 'new anthropology': (1) an attentiveness to the inner workings of the everyday (the 'infra-ordinary', as he came to call it); and (2) an appreciation of the uses and value of list-making. 'Sei

Shōnagon does not sort; she lists and begins again', he writes, with the list both containing and prising open the ineffable form of everyday intimacy (think shopping or laundry lists, inventories of drink and food consumed and so on).[6]

In this chapter, we aim to present an account of these strands of Perec's work in order to suggest that, through them, we can gain insight into the value of the banalities of the everyday and offer new directions for research via platforms like Twitter. The broader goal here is to consider the ways social science approaches to Twitter (and other social media platforms) continue to grapple with the question of how to study everyday life and the insights it might offer. Perec's work might be as good a guide as any in working through the knotty problem of researching life-worlds in all their banality and as they intersect with social media use. His writing offers a solution to the circular challenge of how to understand the everyday, the ordinary and the banal without either devaluing or hyper-valuing them.

THE 'PROBLEM' OF THE EVERYDAY AND THE BANAL

The everyday has posed a persistent problem for social science that is particularly pronounced in the post-Second World War French tradition reaching back to the late 1950s and 1960s work of Henri Lefebvre in his attempt to rehabilitate 'everyday life as the essential ground of human existence'.[7] As Michael Sheringham points out, this tradition of cultural anthropology came much later to the Anglo sphere where only a minor tradition has questioned what a social science of the banal, the everyday or quotidian would look like when the point is usually to describe complete systems, social structures and large-scale trends. Lefebvre sought to use sociological methods such as the interview to uncover those unknown sectors of social life, where 'detail would be of paramount importance'.[8] Reaching back to the late nineteenth century, Gabrielle Tarde had sought to develop a sociology of the world of detail or the infinitesimal, but it was Émile Durkheim's functional and macro agenda that came to dominate. It wasn't until the growing influence of Lefebvre, the writings of Roland Barthes and the 'reclaiming' of the everyday by cultural anthropologist Michel de Certeau in the early 1970s that the banal and quotidian came to the fore, at least in French social research and scholarship. For Sheringham, however, 'in Georges Perec, the everyday finds its most resourceful explorer and indefatigable champion'.[9]

A feature of the everyday – or, as Highmore puts it, its 'special quality' – is that it is characterised by 'the unnoticed, the inconspicuous, the unobtrusive'.[10] The value of the everyday is precisely its enigmatic and elusive qualities. In Maurice Blanchot's well-known formulation, 'whatever its other aspects, the everyday has this essential trait: it allows no hold. It escapes.'[11] Through its pervasiveness, everyday life tends to be reduced to a platitude, but, as Blanchot adds, 'this banality is also what is most important, if it brings us back to existence in its very spontaneity and as it is lived'.[12] In other words, though it surrounds and consumes us, 'the everyday is extremely difficult to pin down'.[13] This tension poses special challenges for critics of the everyday who must register it as a part of, or inhering in, 'manifold lived experience' without it dissolving into 'statistics, properties, data' when it becomes the object of study.[14] In his work, *Embracing the Ordinary*, Michael Foley, for instance, becomes tangled in this tautology of finding the significance in banality, as a binary switch from the in- to the extra-significant.[15] This predicament becomes all the more difficult to escape in light of the complicated entanglement of the everyday and new modes of public, networked, mobile and social media communication, and this is evident in the early accounts of Twitter and in recent attempts to delineate research methods and a research agenda for Twitter and other social media platforms.

One way out of this bind is to pay attention to Perec's consistent search for a method for writing the everyday that combines sustained observation at local sites with expressive style, form and medium (in working across written genres, radio and cinema):

> What's needed perhaps is finally to found our own anthropology, one that will speak about us, will look in ourselves for what for so long we've been pillaging from others. Not the exotic any more, but the endotic.[16]

Reacting to the media of his day, Perec never stopped advocating the need to reach beyond the 'big event, the untoward, the extra-ordinary'.[17] Beyond this, he asks:

> What's really going on, what we're experiencing, the rest, all the rest, where is it? How should we take account of, question, describe what happens every day and recurs every day: the banal, the quotidian, the obvious, the common, the ordinary, the infra-ordinary, the background noise, the habitual?[18]

In the second decade of the twenty-first century, this resurfaces in the concern for understanding contemporary mobile and social media in their everyday contexts,[19] and in capturing the ordinary intimacies and banalities of life-worlds and media use against the prevailing focus on crisis, protest or viral flow. This move is imperative for navigating our current dilemmas in a world of technological excess and always-on access, of sensors, big data and ubiquitous self-quantification and surveillance, and for helping us to observe contemporary society and to understand the role that services like Twitter play 'within routinized patterns of daily life'.[20]

A SECOND TAKE ON THE BANALITY OF TWITTER

Ideas of Twitter as *breaking* news source and as witness in times of natural disaster or political protest and activism have become common sense. However, tracing the early developments of Twitter, and its transformation as an object of study, Richard Rogers points to the site's deliberate courting of the mundane or the everyday and the intimate:

> Up until November 2009, the question Twitter posed to its users was, 'What are you doing?' In a sense, the question and answers inform the discourse and early study of Twitter as mundane or banal, on the one hand, and highly personal on the other.[21]

The inward, personal orientation of this question lends itself to sharing the banalities of daily life, a practice that subsequently became the subject of scorn, particularly from journalists (how could this be journalism in its indifference and insignificance?). So, at around that time, a widely reported Pear Analytics study[22] categorised around 2,000 tweets to conceive 'tweet types' from the senseless to conversational, self-promotional and so on, claiming forty per cent to be 'Tweets that were "pointless babble", that is, of the "I'm eating a sandwich" type'.[23] This early obsession with the banality of Twitter is now well recorded.[24] It wasn't long after those early reports that the company's development team, and social researchers using the public data Twitter made available, began to preference and promote the platform's role in conveying the urgency of crisis events or political communication. The comment line question shifted its orientation outward to become, 'What's happening?' Nonetheless, the characterisation of Twitter and social media generally as banal persists and runs deep as a criticism of its expressive form and everyday uses.

The scope of these debates hints at the underlying relevance of Twitter's new mode of mediated banality. A year after its launch, technology critic Leisa Reichelt,[25] drawing on earlier ethnographic work on mobile phone use by Daisuke Okabe,[26] used the term 'ambient intimacy' to describe the incidental connection with others' lives afforded by social media platforms and mobile devices. Like many other commentators, Reichelt asked, then, 'Who cares? Who wants this level of detail? Isn't this all just annoying noise?', but she advocated for the 'great value in this ongoing noise'.[27] Access to the details of others' everyday life generates and extends intimacy and this is built around the elegance and immediacy of Twitter's short simple text.[28] Co-founder Jack Dorsey himself intuitively favoured Twitter's role in generating buzz and ambient intimacy, but also equivocated, pointing often to its uses during disasters, events, conferences or political elections, and questioned why he would want to know what his brother is eating.[29] But it wasn't long after the idea of Twitter as ambient intimacy that tech commentators began to lament for its loss, or bemoan Twitter's interference in everyday life and emotional tranquillity. As a typical example of a general disdain for Twitter's public forms of intimacy and banality, in a 2011 blog post, not only does author and UK-based web developer Baldur Bjarnason insist that, 'in short: *Twitter makes us autistic*' through its compromising of the proper capacity to express feeling, but, essentially, 'Twitter is about consumption, the food you eat, the crap you drink, the things you buy, the sites you scan, the books you read, and the TV you watch'.[30] Again, it is upon the question of the access to everyday life, its form and its value, that the critique of Twitter's 'noisy banality' is posed.

The status of social media has generally waxed and waned among cultural and political critics, who waver between its power as an open and distributed site for critical communication, or its numbing generation and circulation of 'cultural effluvia', as Jodi Dean put it,[31] partly at least on the basis of the perceived value of the 'noisy banality' and minutiae of personal experience that it enables. Like many others, Dean emphasises the disconnection between the experience of tweeting and the *experience* that might be tweeted, and laments the co-opting of a community that could have been, and the displacement of action:

> Today people discuss the realities that concern them everywhere and all the time – blogs, Facebook, Twitter, they ooze with the realities of individual concern. Talk. Talk. Talk. Discussion, far from displaced, has itself become a barrier against acts as action is perpetually postponed.[32]

For these reasons, there is defensiveness and cultural anxiety precisely about the value and form of Twitter's banality. Another manifestation of this anxiety is the fear that sacred distinctions between the public and private would start to unravel. Or, from another perspective, we are warned to break out of the hyper-involvement in this technology-induced ambient intimacy, lest we become 'merely' 'a source of fragments to be exploited by others'.[33] In his manifesto-like book, *You Are Not a Gadget*, Jared Lanier offers a list of suggestions for what we can do to not become consumed by those technological developments that have generated an 'open' digital culture:

> If you are twittering, innovate in order to find a way to describe your internal state instead of trivial external events, to avoid the creeping danger of believing that objectively described events define you, as they would define a machine.[34]

Each version of critique of Twitter's and social media's failings takes aim at the significance of its modes of banality. And, in turn, it's not difficult to see how this has come to position Twitter for social researchers along familiar battle lines of quantitative and qualitative methodologies. Twitter offers the promise of big data sets and, yet, its rich seams of information on everyday life are mistrusted or passed over in the rush to find big data gold. Probing the uses of Twitter for social research, Rogers poses the question this way: 'How to consider Twitter as substantive (and thus worthy of serious use and study)? Or does it only offer the banal?'[35] The most common response to this is to refashion Twitter 'as new object of study', in which researchers take up 'the project of de-banalising Twitter by identifying new tweet types, and a new purpose, similar to Dorsey's discussion of where and when Twitter has done well (events, disasters, and elections)'.[36] While this leads to a diverse range of debates about the value and biases of big data drawn from social media use,[37] the search for reliable and reproducible quantitative social media research methods continues as the primary goal for understanding the value of the platform.

So, on the one hand, Twitter is consistently criticised as 'pointless babble', 'useless information' or 'phatic communication'. And these critiques are, of course, too simplistic, as Katrin Weller et al. point out,[38] especially given the anthropological significance that has been given to phatic communication since the 1920s Trobriand Island studies of Bronisław Malinowski.[39] But, on the other hand, both Twitter's developers and scholars working with or on Twitter as a platform defend its role in shaping crisis events and in generating a rich vein of big social data for sophisticated analysis. Both the critique and the counter critique have left a persistent blindness to the everyday in social media research, sustaining a negative valuation of banality that deserves revisiting.

THE FORM OF TWITTER: 'A WORLD OF IMPOSSIBLE DISCOURSES'[40]

To what extent can the banality of Twitter be 'deafening', to paraphrase James Harkin's 2009 claim posed at the beginning of this chapter? This is a question that would have entertained Georges Perec. While, for Harkin, and many others who have echoed him over the years, we have nothing to gain from staring 'at our own narcissistic reflection in a shiny new medium',[41] the question Perec continuously posed was how to make the everyday speak its elusive wisdom. In many ways, Perec's writing within constraints, or, for example, his 'Attempt at an Inventory of the Liquid and Solid Foodstuffs Ingurgitated by Me in the Course of the Year Nineteen Hundred and Seventy-Four',[42] derive their insights from this same methodical organisation and revaluation of the banal details of the everyday. Form of expression is vital to this project.

The networked functionality and publicness of Twitter's short text (and later image-based) observations of daily life drew attention precisely to the role of form in shaping communication. Twitter's unwavering restriction to 140 characters (which, in 2015, was removed for direct messages only) provides a set of productive constraints reminiscent of Perec and the Oulipo. With the introduction of Twitter, after half a decade of the rise of the long-form 'blogsphere', those constraints of message format and character length became associated with immediacy, ephemerality – expressive content that just as quickly comes and goes – and, of course, the virtue of brevity.[43] Described as Twitter's 'underlying sociotechnical grammar', this 140 character restriction has 'opened up a world of impossible discourses', 'discourses that could never have come to pass had the creators of the service not chosen to constrain users' ability to compose messages in this way'.[44] A detailed study of a Twitter dataset from 2008 made strong connections with seventeenth- to nineteenth-century American and European diary writing in terms of topics, particularly in the prevalence of everyday activities, and the use of Twitter within routinised patterns of everyday life.[45] In making these historical connections, Lee Humphreys and her co-authors point to the 'welcomed constraint' that came with small, portable leather-bound journals in the late nineteenth century that limited entries to two or three sentences.[46] Such restrictions later became a large part of the rationale of Oulipo, the deliberate introduction of constraints of form that lead to novelty and invention – introduced, paradoxically, in order to liberate rather than constrain, to foster generative experimentation. Perhaps the most famous of these is Perec's *La Disparition*, rendered masterfully into English by Gilbert Adair as *A Void*.[47]

As artistic or literary expression, such constraints set off pathways of invention and creativity. But, the search for formal method was never just about style for Perec. As with Malinowski's insights into the phatic or connective role of short and seemingly inconsequential exchanges, or Okabe's account of camera phone users' 'traffic in more ambient information' in the exchange of text messages and photos, ethnographers have often recorded their attempts to uncover formal expressive methods for approaching the everyday and banal.

There are other notable accounts of the importance of forms of notation in researching the everyday. In his extended reflection on the function of his own ethnographic fieldwork diaries, and in particular his quick sketches of events, people or things encountered, contemporary anthropologist Michael Taussig scrutinises this vague, ineffable connection between expressive form, everyday life-worlds and lived experience, and anthropological research methods. Of his fieldwork drawings, he says, 'what I have in mind here is a special kind of writing, not poetic or literary – heavens forbid! – but the direct transmission of experience onto the page, usually hurried, abbreviated, and urgent'.[48] The fuzzy edges of experience are never so easily laid down or set in place as writing or text. Like Perec, Taussig's reflections on this question of method seeks to understand the observational encounter and the process of its 'transmission', in precisely those fuzzy attributes of his drawings made in a fleeting moment in time, and in the ethnographer's fieldwork diary more generally. His fieldwork diaries consist of fragments of comments, conversations and observations: 'Events beg for commentary, if not judgment.'[49] These fragments have been celebrated as the prized data an ethnographer brings to the table, but, alongside these written fragments, Taussig also looks to reassess those more underrated forms of expression through his own simple drawings capturing and processing moments, incidents and experiences. Drawing is devalued after childhood, he points out, in a manner that might parallel the way that social scientists devalue the banalities of everyday social media expression, unless it conveys the spectacular or newsworthy event. The anthropologist is telling others' stories and experiences, but filtering them through their own. That is why 'the fieldworker's notebook, with at least one foot in the art of sensuous immediacy, is so valuable as an alternative form of knowledge to what eventually gets into print'.[50]

Perec's inventories and endotic method and style, the anthropologist's fieldwork diaries and Twitter's constrained form each point us toward the world of impossible discourses and their link to the banal and the everyday. It is this everyday, sensuous immediacy that is encapsulated in the ambient intimacy of Twitter's observational, activity-oriented and commentary form, in all its banality. And what Taussig describes of his fieldwork notebooks in capturing experience and context through the sketch as expressive form also resonates with the long history of the personal diary. Perec's interest in the writing style of tenth-century Japanese diarist Sei Shōnagon can also be understood in this sense of providing access to the everyday and the banal through her intriguing formal methods.

THE PILLOW BOOK OF SEI SHŌNAGON: PRECEDENTS OF A FORMAL METHOD

At the end of his short piece on Fashion in 'Twelve Sidelong Glances', Perec introduces a selection from Sei Shōnagon's *The Pillow Book* with a simple 'and so:'.[51] It is an emphatic statement of evidence that would equally suit the use of a meme or illustrative link in an Internet forum or on Twitter. But there is a deeper connection between Perec's reference to *The Pillow Book* and Twitter in his interrogation of fashion in twelve short points. In both her questioning of the routines and trends of tenth-century Japanese court life, and in her formal method of expression, Shōnagon proffers an enduring approach to revaluing banality and repositioning the everyday as a form of popular social analysis. While *The Pillow Book* is understood to belong to the Zuihitsu genre of fragments and personal essays – or 'occasional writings', 'random notes', as Morris describes this genre[52] – following an author's life and surroundings, it can also be placed alongside the tenth- and eleventh-century Nikki Bangaku tradition of literary diary writing. Both traditions were notable for their use of Japanese script rather than Chinese, a shift to the vernacular matching the intimate focus of the prose and the diary form hundreds of years before the emergence of Western diary writing – although, fittingly for Perec's purposes, Zuihitsu writing was said to enjoy much greater variety of form than did writings within the Nikki Bangaku tradition and covered 'everything from reportage and travelogue to poetry, literary criticism, biography, confession, journalism – and so on, almost ad infinitum'.[53] Sei Shōnagon's *The Pillow Book* is thus part of a rich and varied tradition within Japanese culture of writing that seeks to capture the fleeting experiences and ambiences of the everyday.

The Pillow Book, then, stands as exemplary of a mode of attention to things, dispositions and sensations, events and incidents, customs, fashions, processes, times of day or seasons, and so on. These are the often disconnected fragments and experiences of the everyday. The book's notoriety persists more than a thousand years after it was penned because of the light it sheds on the materiality of Japanese life at the level of the infra-ordinary. *The Pillow Book* is well known for its form, its use of lists and enumeration, and the intimate access it affords a millennium later into the everyday life-world of Shōnagon and her court society. And it is remarkable for the way it straddles two very different worlds, the court and life beyond its walls, with clear sensitivities and insightful descriptions of both, conveyed with a lightness of touch and a poetic sensibility, but also at times with irreverence. 'Things That Should Be Short', for instance, sets out a list of thoughts or musings that are elegant in their deliberate constraint but also convey – banally (each less than 140 characters) – observations of the gendered social order within the circles Shōnagon inhabits:

> A piece of thread when one wants to sew something in a hurry.
> A lamp stand.
> The hair of a woman of the lower classes should be neat and short.
> The speech of a young girl.[54]

Thoughts, things and events unfold in simple and elegant form. Coherence of expression doesn't proceed on the basis of narrative, but rather enumeration, initiating or setting off new observations and anecdotes.

There are several aspects of Sei Shōnagon's observations and the textual form of *The Pillow Book* that draw connections centuries later with Georges Perec and with Twitter, but we focus on just two here as a way of illustrating the potential of Perec's method for writing the everyday. The first is the innovative use of lists and listing as the short, sequential, ephemeral and ongoing organisation of elements of the world and everyday experience. The other element concerns both Shōnagon and Perec's manner of accounting for everyday customs through the topic of fashion, to which we will return in the final section. Both of these connections lead toward new methodologies for researching, observing or writing the everyday. They present an anthropology *in situ*, comprised of the fragments of the infra-ordinary.

As Perec points out in 'Thoughts of Sorts / Sorts of Thoughts', 'Sei Shōnagon does not sort; she lists and begins again. One theme sets off one list, of things or of anecdotes. Later, an almost identical theme will produce a different list, and so on.'[55] Groupings of things appear throughout *The Pillow Book*, for instance 'Things Without Merit',[56] 'Outstandingly Splendid Things',[57] 'Things That are Distant Though Near',[58] but also, and even more commonly, Shōnagon lists dispositions or affects, such as, 'Things That Give a Hot Feeling',[59] 'Things That Give a Clean Feeling',[60] 'Things That Give an Unclean Feeling',[61] or 'Things That One Is in a Hurry to See or to Hear'.[62] These groupings form the basis for a particular method of situational and 'ineffable' observation, or a way of seeing and understanding things and states of being. For Perec, too, the joys of enumeration are immeasurable. You can never 'COVER EVERYTHING', and even in trying, something is always 'left out'.[63] Gilbert Adair observes that, clearly for Perec, 'virtually every mode of writing could be regarded as lipogrammatic in its wilful exclusion from the writer's field of vision of so much of the texture of the world'.[64] As part of the world of affect, or the affect of the world, and operating 'prior to any thought of sorting', as Perec puts it, enumeration enacts an intrinsic need to name and collect, 'without which the world ("life") would be unmappable'.[65] In these experiments, there is a tangible link to the questions social researchers seek to ask of Twitter's big data sets: how to map the vastness of social life, events, experiences, while attending to the minutiae of the banalities of everyday social media use. Twitter also presents its units of communication as an infinite list and has its personal curated lists and groupings within hashtag listings, but rarely do we even consider the effect that this formal element has on the platform and its uses.

Perec was drawn to Sei Shōnagon because, like her, he was especially attuned to the effectiveness and significance of lists in revealing what is important in the mundane and quotidian – what he calls the 'infra-ordinary' or 'endotic' (as opposed to the 'extraordinary' and 'exotic'). Following Sei Shōnagon, Perec's creative recuperation of the list form as a textual device and critical tool leads us to a fuller appreciation of how, in Louise Crewe's words, 'the most mundane, ordinary, invisible, and seemingly uninteresting things can be as significant and revealing as the most dramatic'.[66] Across Perec's diverse literary output, lists figure repeatedly in ways that speak directly to their ability to shed light on the inner workings of the everyday – their ability to make the familiar strange[67] – and to reveal the entangled interactions between everyday consumption and personal identity. It is in this second sense that lists operate in his novel *Things: A Story of the Sixties* (*Les Choses*, 1965), a book that the French philosopher Alain Badiou describes as a 'rigorous literary version of the Marxist theme of alienation – especially the prevalence of things over existence'.[68] *Things* tells of the endeavours of Sylvie and Jérôme, a young Parisian couple who, in Bourdieu's terms, attempt to improve their social position in part through the cultural capital they see invested in consumer objects, in the 'things' that they acquire and desire. Perec's telling of this narrative is heavily populated with lists of these semiotically loaded objects of consumer desire, taste and distinction, pointing to the methods of cultural analysis developed around that time by Barthes and Bourdieu.

As market researchers, an attention to fashion drives the protagonists' ecstatic pursuit of the mythologies and signs of cultural objects throughout this 'deeply Barthesian novel', as Barthes' biographer Louis-Jean Calvet puts it.[69] 'They discovered knitwear, silk blouses, shirts by Doucet, cotton voile ties, silk scarves, tweed, lambswool, cashmere, vicuna, leather and jersey wool, flax . . .'[70] However, there is an evident tension between market trends and the lived fashions manifested in the object-worlds of *Things* that flows through to other works, particularly 'Twelve Sidelong Glances'. Such object-lists enable the cataloguing and accumulation of trends, a mapping of consumer life. Through this method, the things themselves and their milieu are brought to the fore.

For Perec, listing thus achieves some of the work of bringing things or events out of context, into new conjunctive relations within categories, but also enforces abrupt disjunctions; and it is here that cultural life-worlds show through. Perec's embrace of lists and listing is a component part in a larger project of his to develop 'an anthropology of everyday life',[71] the loose methodology of which also has much to offer social researchers' attempts to extract everyday experience from new media sites like Twitter.

THE SEARCH FOR A 'NEW ANTHROPOLOGY' OF THE INFRA-ORDINARY

In his study of everyday life, Michael Sheringham refers to the Barthesian methods evident in *Things*:

> Perec's aim is not to create an image but to devise a mode of description that makes a certain level of reality visible, a project that is in some respects phenomenological but whose tactic is rhetorical. There

is an autobiographical dimension [. . .] but it is impersonal rather than individual.[72]

The ambivalence of the uptake of Perec's project in Anglo social sciences hangs on this method of access to the everyday, but also on the implied value of the banal. Howard Becker has offered a challenging, though also somewhat ambivalent, critique of what he calls Perec's 'sociological' method in these and other texts, contrasting Perec's descriptive ethnography with the work that social scientists do. Becker takes aim at the way Perec's detailed listing of objects, people, events and memories eschews narrative and sociological design, referring to Perec's method as 'proto-ethnography' or 'detailed "raw description"'.[73] As Perec asks of the habitual and mundane, 'How are we to speak of [. . .] "common things", how to track them down rather, flush them out, wrest them from the dross in which they remain mired, how to give them a meaning, a tongue [. . .]?'[74]

Yet Becker is also drawn in by the end products of that method: 'As you read Perec's descriptions, you increasingly succumb to the feeling (at least I do, and I think others do as well) that this is important, though you can't say how.'[75] Ultimately, his criticism decries Perec's failure to impose an explicit order on his lists and fragments, perhaps missing the significance of the way they are always bounded and underpinned by a conceptual principle: 'It does not seem to have the kind of cohesion, at least not obviously, that social scientists like to ascribe to a culture, a similarity or interlocking or affinity of the parts to one another.'[76] Interestingly, Becker's lament also echoes those persistent critiques of Twitter's flow of banality. Perec's lists stand as fragments, but fragments that do add up to *something*, as Becker admits: 'The whole is more than the parts.'[77] This ambivalence could just as easily point to the analytical potential Perec found within those fragments, the 'raw description', that can only be understood through the end product. It could be argued that his lists defy the very possibility of presenting the everyday as a cohesive whole and promote instead the everyday in its rich texture, as repetition and disjuncture. This project presents itself as a new anthropology of the everyday, while subverting the functionalist traditions of sociological observation and classification that have dominated since Durkheim.[78]

At the very least, Perec's experiments serve as testimony to his ability to transform the trivial into the poetic – list-making as 'invent-ory'. Importantly, however, Perec makes the shift from the inventory as a pragmatic listing form, 'presenting a simple series of units', 'collected by a conceptual principle',[79] to a more transformative or analytical discursive practice. In all the above cases, Perec deploys listing as method, as an effective lever with which to pry open for inspection the seemingly inscrutable inner workings of everyday spaces, things, memories, in order that they might 'speak of what is [and] of what we are'.[80] Lists play a vital role in actively seeking out and illuminating the banal or quotidian, without overdetermining or fixing its significance once and for all.

Through its enumerated observations on fashion, Perec's 'Twelve Sidelong Glances' offers additional clues as to his methodology of/for the everyday and the banal, and its applicability to Twitter. Again, Perec draws on the thoughts and observations of Sei Shōnagon to provide a subtle critique of the conflation of *trend* and *fashion*, with continued relevance for new media and social science research today. Fashion serves as a source of distinction throughout *The Pillow Book* as it is entwined with the social customs and rituals of tenth-century Japanese life. Shōnagon's observations could even resonate with the kinds of comments a Twitter user might make in shared statements on a daily commute. As a typical example, in 'I Cannot Stand a Woman Who Wears Sleeves of Unequal Width', Sei Shōnagon writes:

> The fashion of unequal sleeves is just as unattractive for men as for women, since it produces the same lop-sided effect. Nowadays everyone seems to have his clothes cut like this, whether he is wearing a fine ceremonial robe or a light summer garment.[81]

Such observations convey custom and social relations, a common manner as well as a sense of the singular and everyday. While Bourdieu was examining the connection between taste and class through the objects and photographs found in suburban homes, Perec was taking Sei Shōnagon as a model for rewriting the ubiquity and, by definition, the dominance of fashion, of manner, of that which needs no justification, as it 'enters into most parts of our everyday lives'.[82] In 'Twelve Sidelong Glances', Perec devotes his attention to understanding these processes in a series of fragments culminating in a reference to Shōnagon's *The Pillow Book*.

> Fashion: the changing and whimsical element in social customs, the element reigning over personal decoration, dress, furnishing, carriages etc. The word properly means *manner*, i.e. the manner which is by definition the right one and which needs no justification.[83]

What starts out for Perec as a list of items *of* fashion becomes the site of a critical exploration of the 'gentle tyranny' of *trends*.[84] In making this important shift, Perec takes inspiration from Shōnagon in seeking to let things themselves speak, to find an alternative to the repetition of trends that could uncover the everyday and the singular as it surrounds objects, spaces, events in their social relations, histories and contexts.

On the surface, fashion and trends speak of 'caprice, spontaneity, fantasy, invention, frivolousness', but for Perec, fashion becomes subsumed within trend, falling 'entirely on the side of violence – the violence of conformism, of obeisance to models, the violence of the social consensus and its veiled scorn for the excluded'.[85] Through Sei Shōnagon's vernacular everyday observations, the sketches of Taussig's fieldwork diaries, and of course Perec's lists, we can draw a methodological line that insists on the revaluation of banality and the everyday. The move in social science research from the banal and mundane qualities of Twitter and other social media to the quantities of big data, aggregates and 'trending topics' highlights what's now at stake. We risk losing site of the manner of the everyday, or the 'changing and whimsical element in social customs'.[86] The problem with trends is that they not only hide but heighten 'the instability of things, the ungraspable, oblivion'.[87] Fashion in this sense 'trivializes lived experience by reducing it to trivial signs, to the trickery of simulated antique gloss or of simulated leather, to the vulgarity of imitations'.[88]

Similarly, trends have come to drive social media flows, while just beneath the surface of those trending flows lies rich life-worlds subjugated by notions of banality. Perec offers a list of alternatives to fashion as trend that could be read as methods for approaching the everyday in social media data: 'variation of periodicity', 'multiplication of fields', 'intensification of incoherence', 'heightened exclusiveness' and the 'function of place'.[89] Ultimately, everyday life is what is left at the edges of trends, in the banal:

> The opposite of fashion is obviously not the unfashionable. It can only be the present – what is there, what is rooted, permanent, resistant, lived-in: an object and the memory of it, a being and its history.[90]

At stake in this search for a new anthropology of the infra-ordinary is a revaluation of banality itself or the mundane life-worlds that might be discarded or derided in the quest for big social data and all its intensities. We lose sight of what Kathleen Stewart calls 'ordinary affects'.[91] This is encapsulated in Perec's interest in, and adaptation of, the observational methods of Sei Shōnagon and in his reference to 'the present', to what's there, permanent and lived in. In Perec and Sei Shōnagon we can see more nuanced kinds of banality and the beginnings of a method for approaching them. What's more, where social science is caught between this need to find significance and understand the intensities of the trends of social media exchange, are we any longer able to leverage such sites' access to the ambient intimacy of daily life, and do we have the methods for bringing it back to life as an appropriate object of social research?

A clue lays in Twitter's expressive form, in the constraints that enable a writing of the everyday as mobile, ephemeral, public media practice. Perec's methods for mapping the infra-ordinary begin with lists and listing. Rather than characters, plot and narrative, Perec begins with objects, spaces, events and moves outward toward a fuller understanding of life-worlds gathered together through them. He takes his cue from Sei Shōnagon, and there are two key elements we can take out of this longer history of diary writing as expressive method and as social observation: the practice of listing and an alternative attention to the *manner* of everyday life (fashion beyond trend). This approach takes Perec toward what he referred to as a 'new anthropology', loosely defined as that was. His writing on fashion and Sei Shōnagon points to its application and brings us back to Twitter as a platform for banality (trends and their Other), and to the need to reconsider the privileging of trends over the everyday. This is the starting point for a different kind of social media research.

NOTES

1. James Harkin (2009), 'The Trouble with Twitter', *The Guardian*, 30 December, available at: http://www.theguardian.com/commentisfree/2009/dec/29/trouble-twitter-social-networking-banality.
2. Cornelius Puschmann, Axel Bruns, Merja Mahrt, Katrin Weller and Jean Burgess (2014), 'Epilogue: Why Study Twitter?', in Katrin Weller, Axel Bruns, Jean Burgess, Merja Mahrt and Cornelius Puschmann (eds), *Twitter and Society*, New York: Peter Lang, p. 425.
3. Taina Bucher (2012), 'A Technicity of Attention: How Software "Makes Sense"', *Culture Machine*, vol. 13, available at: http://www.culturemachine.net/index.php/cm/article/view/470/489.
4. Ilpo Koskinen (2007), *Mobile Multimedia in Action*, New Brunswick, NJ: Transaction Publishers, p. 12.
5. David Bellos (1995), *Georges Perec: A Life in Words*, London: Harvill Press, pp. 582–3, 680.
6. Georges Perec (2009), 'Thoughts of Sorts/Sorts of Thoughts', *Thoughts of Sorts*, trans. David Bellos, Boston: Verba Mundi, p. 130.
7. Michael Sheringham (2006), *Everyday Life: Theories and Practices from Surrealism to the Present*, Oxford: Oxford University Press, p. 134.
8. Sheringham, *Everyday Life*, p. 136.
9. Sheringham, *Everyday Life*, p. 248.
10. Ben Highmore (2002), *Everyday Life and Cultural Theory: An Introduction*, London: Routledge, p. 1.
11. Maurice Blanchot (1987), 'Everyday Speech', trans. Susan Hanson, *Yale French Studies*, 73, p. 14.
12. Blanchot, 'Everyday Speech', p. 13.
13. Fran Martin (2003), 'Introduction', in Fran Martin (ed.), *Interpreting Everyday Culture*, London: Hodder Arnold, p. 2.
14. Sheringham, *Everyday Life*, p. 360.
15. Michael Foley (2012), *Embracing the Ordinary: Lessons from the Champions of Everyday Life*, London: Simon & Schuster.

16. Georges Perec (1999), 'Approaches to What?', in *Species of Spaces and Other Pieces*, ed. and trans. John Sturrock, Harmondsworth: Penguin, p. 210.
17. Perec, 'Approaches to What?', p. 209.
18. Perec, 'Approaches to What?', pp. 209–10.
19. Caroline Bassett (2003), 'How Many Movements?', in Michael Bull and Les Black (eds), *The Auditory Culture Reader*, Oxford: Berg, pp. 343–54.
20. Lee Humphreys, Phillipa Gill, Balachander Krishnamurthy and Elizabeth Newbury (2013), 'Historicizing New Media: A Content Analysis of Twitter', *Journal of Communication*, vol. 63, no. 3, p. 427.
21. Richard Rogers (2014), 'Foreword: Debanalising Twitter: The Transformation of an Object of Study', in Katrin Weller, Axel Bruns, Jean Burgess, Merja Mahrt and Cornelius Puschmann (eds), *Twitter and Society*, New York: Peter Lang, p. xii.
22. Pear Analytics (2009), *Twitter Study – August 2009*, San Antonio, CA: Pear Analytics, available at: http://pearanalytics.com/wp-content/uploads/2012/12/Twitter-Study-August-2009.pdf.
23. Rogers, 'Foreword', p. xii.
24. Noah Arceneaux and Amy Schmitz Weiss (2010), 'Seems Stupid Until You Try It: Press Coverage of Twitter, 2006–9', *New Media and Society*, vol. 12, no. 8, pp. 1262–79; Pear Analytics, 'Twitter Study – August 2009'.
25. Leisa Reichelt (2007), 'Ambient Intimacy', *disambiguity.com*, 1 March, available at: http://www.disambiguity.com/ambient-intimacy/.
26. Daisuke Okabe (2004), *Emergent Social Practices, Situations and Relations Through Everyday Camera Phone Use*, paper presented at Mobile Communication and Social Change, the 2004 International Conference on Mobile Communication in Seoul, South Korea, 18–19 October, available at: http://www.itofisher.com/mito/archives/okabe_seoul.pdf.
27. Reichelt, 'Ambient Intimacy'.
28. As Michele Zappavigna writes, 'personal expression of routine experiences has never been subject to real-time mass dissemination in the way that we are currently witnessing' as a result of microblogging. Michele Zappavigna (2012), *Discourse of Twitter and Social Media: How We Use Language to Create Affiliation on the Web*, London: Bloomsbury, p. 37.
29. Quoted in Rogers, 'Foreword', p. xiii.
30. Baldur Bjarnason (2011), 'The Loss of Ambient Intimacy', *baldurbjarnason.com*, 15 September, available at: http://www.baldurbjarnason.com/notes/the-loss-of-ambient-intimacy/.
31. Jodi Dean (2005), 'Communicative Capitalism: Circulation and the Foreclosure of Politics', *Cultural Politics*, vol. 1, no. 1, p. 52.
32. Jodi Dean (2010), 'Affective Networks', *Media Tropes*, vol. 2, no. 2, p. 34, available at: http://www.mediatropes.com/index.php/Mediatropes/article/view/11932/8818.
33. Jared Lanier (2010), *You Are Not a Gadget*, New York: Alfred A. Knopf, p. 17.
34. Lanier, *You Are Not a Gadget*, p. 17.
35. Rogers, 'Foreword', p. xiii.
36. Rogers, 'Foreword', p. xviii.
37. danah boyd and Kate Crawford (2012), 'Critical Questions for Big Data: Provocations for a Cultural, Technological, and Scholarly Phenomenon', *Information, Communication and Society*, vol. 15, no. 5, pp. 662–79.
38. Katrin Weller, Axel Bruns, Jean Burgess, Merja Mahrt and Cornelius Puschmann (2014), 'Twitter and Society: An Introduction', in Katrin Weller, Axel Bruns, Jean Burgess,

Merja Mahrt and Cornelius Puschmann (eds), *Twitter and Society*, New York: Peter Lang, pp. xxix–xxxviii.
39. Bronisław Malinowski [1922] (2014), *Argonauts of the Western Pacific*, London: Routledge.
40. Puschmann, Bruns, Mahrt, Weller and Burgess, 'Epilogue', p. 428.
41. Harkin, 'The Trouble with Twitter'.
42. Georges Perec (1999), 'Attempt at an Inventory of the Liquid and Solid Foodstuffs Ingurgitated by Me in the Course of the Year Nineteen Hundred and Seventy-Four', in *Species of Spaces and Other Pieces*, ed. and trans. John Sturrock, Harmondsworth: Penguin, pp. 244–9.
43. Arceneaux and Schmitz Weiss, 'Seems Stupid Until You Try It'.
44. Puschmann, Bruns, Mahrt, Weller and Burgess, 'Epilogue', p. 428.
45. Humphreys, Gill, Krishnamurthy and Elizabeth Newbury, 'Historicizing New Media'.
46. Humphreys, Gill, Krishnamurthy and Elizabeth Newbury, 'Historicizing New Media', p. 416.
47. Georges Perec (1995), *A Void*, trans. Gilbert Adair, London: Harvill Press.
48. Michael Taussig (2011), *I Swear I Saw This: Drawings in Fieldwork Notes, Namely My Own*, Chicago: University of Chicago Press, p. 19.
49. Taussig, *I Swear I Saw This*, p. 51.
50. Taussig, *I Swear I Saw This*, p. 49.
51. Georges Perec (2009), 'Twelve Sidelong Glances', *Thoughts of Sorts*, trans. David Bellos, Boston: Verba Mundi, p. 40.
52. Ivan Morris (1991), 'Introduction', in Sei Shōnagon, *The Pillow Book of Sei Shōnagon*, ed. and trans. Ivan Morris, New York: Columbia University Press, p. 11.
53. Steven D. Carter (2014), 'Introduction', in Steven D. Carter (ed. and trans.), *The Columbia Anthology of Japanese Essays: Zuihitsu from the Tenth to the Twenty-first Century*, New York: Columbia University Press, p. 2.
54. Sei Shōnagon (1991), *The Pillow Book of Sei Shōnagon*, ed. and trans. Ivan Morris, New York: Columbia University Press, p. 201.
55. Perec, 'Thoughts of Sorts/Sorts of Thoughts', p. 130.
56. Shōnagon, *The Pillow Book*, p. 159.
57. Shōnagon, *The Pillow Book*, pp. 159–62.
58. Shōnagon, *The Pillow Book*, p. 181.
59. Shōnagon, *The Pillow Book*, p. 143.
60. Shōnagon, *The Pillow Book*, p. 168.
61. Shōnagon, *The Pillow Book*, p. 168.
62. Shōnagon, *The Pillow Book*, p. 173.
63. Perec, 'Thoughts of Sorts/Sorts of Thoughts', p. 131.
64. Gilbert Adair (2009), 'The Eleventh Day: Perec and the Infra-ordinary', *Review of Contemporary Fiction*, vol. XXIX, no. 1, Spring, p. 188.
65. Perec, 'Thoughts of Sorts/Sorts of Thoughts', p. 131.
66. Louise Crewe (2011), 'Life Itemised: Lists, Loss, Unexpected Significance, and the Enduring Geographies of Discard', *Environment and Planning D: Society and Space*, vol. 29, p. 44.
67. Highmore, *Everyday Life and Cultural Theory*, p. 12.
68. Alain Badiou (2012), *The Rebirth of History: Times of Riots and Uprisings*, trans. Gregory Elliott, London: Verso, p. 20, note 1.
69. Jean-Louis Calvet (1994), *Roland Barthes: A Biography*, trans. Sarah Wykes, Bloomington, IN: Indiana University Press, p. 141.

70. Georges Perec (1991), *Things: A Story of the Sixties* with *A Man Asleep*, London: Harvill Press, p. 39.
71. Editorial note added to Georges Perec (1999), 'Notes on What I'm Looking For', in *Species of Spaces and Other Pieces*, ed. and trans. John Sturrock, Harmondsworth: Penguin, p. 142, note §.
72. Sheringham, *Everyday Life*, p. 253.
73. Howard Becker (2001), 'Experiments in Social Description', *Ethnography*, vol. 2, no. 1, p. 73.
74. Perec, 'Approaches to What?', p. 210.
75. Becker, 'Experiments in Social Description', p. 71.
76. Becker, 'Experiments in Social Description', p. 74.
77. Becker, 'Experiments in Social Description', p. 69.
78. Roy Boyne (2006), 'Classification', *Theory, Culture and Society*, vol. 23, no. 2–3, pp. 21–30.
79. Robert E. Belknap (2004), *The List: The Uses and Pleasures of Cataloguing*, New Haven, CT: Yale University Press, pp. 2, 3.
80. Perec, 'Approaches to What?', p. 210.
81. Shōnagon, *The Pillow Book*, p. 252.
82. Perec, 'Twelve Sidelong Glances', p. 37.
83. Perec, 'Twelve Sidelong Glances', p. 34.
84. Perec, 'Twelve Sidelong Glances', p. 33.
85. Perec, 'Twelve Sidelong Glances', pp. 36–7.
86. Perec, 'Twelve Sidelong Glances', p. 34.
87. Perec, 'Twelve Sidelong Glances', p. 39.
88. Perec, 'Twelve Sidelong Glances', p. 39.
89. Perec, 'Twelve Sidelong Glances', pp. 38–9.
90. Perec, 'Twelve Sidelong Glances', p. 40.
91. Kathleen Stewart (2007), *Ordinary Affects*, Durham, NC: Duke University Press.

PART III

Ludic Intensities and Creative Constraints

CHAPTER 9

Perec and the Politics of Constraint

Alison James

Georges Perec's literary legacy perhaps resonates most strongly for the current members of the Oulipo, or Workshop for Potential Literature (*Ouvroir de littérature potentielle*). Perec joined the group in 1967, seven years after its founding by Raymond Queneau and François Le Lionnais, during a moment of generational transition that had begun with the 'co-opting' of the poet Jacques Roubaud in 1966. Subsequently, Perec's legendary formal virtuosity and (in his own words) 'systematic versatility'[1] have become at once an inspiration and an obstacle for members of the 'third generation' of Oulipians – those writers who joined the group after Perec's demise in 1982. In the collective Oulipo volume *Moments oulipiens*, both Jacques Jouet and Anne Garréta wryly cite the catchphrase 'Georges thought of that already' (*Georges y avait pensé*), a refrain that inevitably greets the writing proposals of the group's eager new recruits.[2] This version of what Harold Bloom called the 'anxiety of influence' reflects Perec's pivotal role in the Oulipo's history. That is, his exhaustive approach to the possibilities of literary constraints risked exhausting the group's experimental project while ultimately pushing its writers in new directions.

If the group has since moved out from under the shadow of mourning, Perec nevertheless continues to haunt Oulipian production. Death, we should recall, does not exclude Oulipo members from the group, but merely excuses them from attending the regular meetings. Perec's impact is visible not only, or perhaps not even primarily, on the level of constraints (the lipogram of *A Void* and its monovocalic counterpart *The Exeter Text* being the most spectacular examples in his body of work). It is also manifest in Perec's production of what Marcel Bénabou has called 'epidemic' creations, a set of endlessly generative works that continue to inspire imitations and rewritings.[3] Thus

Perec's *Je me souviens* (itself inspired by Joe Brainard's *I Remember*) is the model, or countermodel, for Jacques Jouet's *Exercices de la mémoire* (*Memory Exercises*), Jacques Bens's *J'ai oublié* (*I Forgot*), and Garréta and Valérie Beaudouin's *Tu te souviens...?* (*You Remember...?*).[4] His short story *The Winter Journey*, written in 1979, gave rise to a series of sequels that are now gathered in the collective volume *Winter Journeys*, a volume which, even as it problematises the idea of literary origins, inscribes a text by Perec as the source of an Oulipian mythology.[5] These examples might lead us to modify Roubaud's suggestion that the Oulipians are characters in 'an unwritten novel by Queneau';[6] perhaps, rather, the members of the group are now characters in an open-ended, infinitely extensible Perec novel.

PIVOTAL PEREC

For Perec, joining the Oulipo meant choosing a path and an identity as a writer at a pivotal moment in his career. Indeed, he once described himself as 'a product of the Oulipo', 'ninety-seven percent' dependent on the group for his existence as a writer.[7] Conversely, his participation also determined the Oulipo's direction and identity at a crucial moment in the group's history. The Oulipo poet Roubaud divides the history of the group into the 'pre-Perecian', 'Perecian' and 'post-Perecian' periods, with the second of these stretching from 1969, the year of the publication of Perec's *A Void*, to the culminating moment of his *Life A User's Manual* in 1978.[8] Perec, according to Roubaud, revealed the full potential of the group by inventing the figure of the Oulipian author; the latter is someone 'who casts constraint in the service of all his activities as a writer', and 'responds as [an Oulipian author] to the social endeavour, regardless of whether his service is private or public'.[9] As the first truly Oulipian author, Roubaud argues, Perec transformed the Oulipo itself into a 'collective work', while he also created (with *Life A User's Manual*) an unsurpassed Oulipian masterwork.[10] Perec appears in this account as both exception and exemplar, at once apparently inimitable, since no Oulipian has yet equalled him (though Roubaud does admit a possible exception for Jacques Jouet), and a model for the aspiring Oulipian.

Perec's work also marks a turning point in the group's reception, helping to determine its emergence into full public visibility in the 1970s (with the 1973 anthology *La Littérature potentielle*), as well as its more recent respectability as a topic for academic research in France and beyond.[11] If Perec revealed to the Oulipo the full literary possibilities of constraints, he also came to represent for many general readers the accessible and acceptable face of the Oulipo. The beginning of the twenty-first century has seen the solidification of this positive general consensus around Perec's works in France and beyond, even among some of the group's harshest critics. Thus, in an otherwise scathing attack on Oulipian poetics, the poet Henri Meschonnic deems Perec a 'strong exception' to the mediocrity of the group's conception of literature.[12] In their 2012 essay-pamphlet, *The End of Oulipo?*, Scott Esposito and Lauren Elkin treat Perec as one of the 'strong Oulipians', and his work as a benchmark against which other members of the group are measured (and judged to be lacking his 'seriousness of purpose'[13]).

Beyond his prodigious skill as a manipulator of forms, Perec's status as the Oulipian author par excellence can be attributed to a number of additional factors. One of these is the way in which his work motivates formal constraint as a traumatic symptom, a mark that bears witness to the experience of loss and absence. The paradigmatic example here is the absent 'e' of *A Void* which stands for the absent *eux*, 'them', the parents who were killed during the Second World War. Numerous other instances of formal-semantic patterning can be linked to Perec's autobiographical utterances. The critic Bernard Magné calls these textual markers *autobiographemes*; they include motifs of rupture and absence, bilateral symmetries, bilingualism and numbers such as 11 and 43 (which are linked to the date of Perec's mother's deportation).[14] Never merely formal in nature, such half-hidden, half-revealed marks are the symbolic and expressive traces of loss and lack, while they also transform the pressures of historical necessity into creative freedom. This powerful transmutation attests to Perec's problematic relation to history, and to his paradoxical position as a witness deprived of memory; he can account for the past only indirectly.[15] Perec's work thus imbues literary play with a deep seriousness and gives it both personal and political weight.

Another factor that determines the politics of constraint is Perec's ambiguous strategy of at once hiding and revealing constraints, the psychological basis of which may lie, as he suggests in *W or The Memory of Childhood*, in the child's simultaneous desire and fear at once to be found and to stay hidden in the game of hide-and-seek.[16] In this respect, Perec's work gestures toward two opposite extremes of Oulipian reception: one oriented toward the generative concept, the other toward the text as final product. For instance, Perec's *A Void* is often cited for its famous lipogrammatic constraint but is less often read as a novel. Governed by a constraint that is at once easily described and difficult to execute, *A Void* might be considered the quintessential Oulipian work, more notorious now than the inaugural Oulipian text that once held this status, Queneau's *A Hundred Thousand Billion Poems*.[17] Perec's *Life A User's Manual* is the other obvious candidate for the title of Oulipian masterpiece, but for different reasons: unlike *A Void*, it is often read as a 'straight' novel, and even as a realist work, without any knowledge of the combinatorial system that underlies the text. These two cases place Perec in a variable position between what Roubaud calls the 'Queneau pole', on the one hand, which favours the text built on invisible constraints (the 'scaffolding' that is then removed), and the 'Le Lionnais pole', on the other, which emphasises the discovery and disclosure of constraints and structures for their own sake.[18] In fact – and this echoes Roubaud's point about the Oulipian author – the conceptual dimension of Perec's work is always oriented toward the goal of literary creation. Perec is a writer of actualised Oulipian literature rather than an inventor of structures for potential literature. Nonetheless, the constraint is never a mere means to an end but determines both the shape of the work and the latter's relation to the reader.

TOWARDS A UNIVERSAL DICTIONARY OF LETTERS

Perec's success can thus be attributed less to his skill at deploying spectacular forms than to his occupying an aesthetic 'middle position', situated both between the extremes of Oulipian practice and, more broadly, between 'mainstream' narrative fiction and the experimental margins. This negotiation at once renders him accessible to many readers and makes him a target of criticism for some – whether he is rejected as a frivolous formalist or, at the other end of the spectrum, berated for being too 'conservative' and traditional in his approach to literary experiment.

In this respect, Perec's work exemplifies some of the ambiguities of Oulipian practice more generally. The group's international reception brings some of these questions to the surface, while also producing misunderstandings: experimental writers criticise its attachment to narrative convention whereas lyric poets align it with conceptual mind games and the refusal of affect.[19] In the proceedings of the CalArts '*noulipo*' conference held in October 2005, several North American experimental writers, and even admirers of the group, find Perec and the Oulipo to be insufficiently 'avant-garde' or 'radical'. Christian Bök, whose monovocalic poems in *Eunoia* are directly inspired by Georges Perec's *A Void*, criticises the Oulipo on both political and aesthetic grounds: first, the group does not make explicit its political stance;[20] second, its interest in 'obsolete, literary genres' and its 'grammatical, referential bias' make its work insufficiently radical.[21] This second objection is also voiced by the conceptual writer Kenneth Goldsmith, whose work deliberately pursues 'uncreativity' – whether by recording all his own words for a week (*Soliloquy*),[22] noting down all his movements and gestures for a day (*Fidget*),[23] transcribing weather and traffic reports (*The Weather*; *Traffic*)[24] or retyping a copy of *The New York Times* (*Day*).[25] Goldsmith concedes that the Oulipo's conceptual aspect is promising, but asserts that in implementing constraints Oulipians embraced a 'blandly conservative narrative fiction'.[26] In *The End of Oulipo?*, Elkin and Esposito criticise the Oulipo's alleged failure to resist mainstream consensus but praise Perec's 'disruptive use of language and a more conscious approach to the everyday world'.[27] Perec thus represents for some readers the 'original, revolutionary roots'[28] of the Oulipo, while for others his attachment to the form of the novel indicates literary 'conservatism' or a failure of conceptual nerve.

Such responses often conflate issues of political and aesthetic radicalism in ways that have to do in part with the contours of the North American literary landscape but are not limited to this context. Indeed, the claim that poetic revolution and political revolution are inseparable is rooted in the history of the avant-garde. Nevertheless, as Daniel Levin Becker notes in his lively account of the group, *Many Subtle Channels*, 'these were never the terms the Oulipo set for itself'.[29] Rather, the Oulipo deliberately detaches itself from the history of the French avant-garde, particularly surrealism (in which Queneau and others had participated): 'The alternative to Breton's mandatory commingling of literature and class struggle [. . .] is the voluntary withdrawal that makes the Oulipo, by design, collectively disengaged.'[30] If the group's rules mean that no one can be excluded for political reasons, it is also possible that this apparently apolitical stance might dissuade potential members from joining in the first place.[31]

The Oulipo refuses either to amalgamate aesthetics and politics or to adhere to an agonistic conception of literature. 'Perhaps we aren't so very "anti"' is Queneau's response, in the course of one of the early Oulipo meetings, to Claude Berge's characterisation of Oulipian practice as 'anti-chance'.[32] If Queneau thus resists casting the Oulipo's relationship to surrealism (and, in particular, to the surrealists' fascination with chance) in wholly oppositional terms, it is in order to position the group's project not against, but outside the conflictual history of the literary avant-garde in favour of a transhistorical – but not ahistorical – understanding of the 'potentiality' of forms. This utopian ambition explains both the wide international resonance of the group's work and an ambivalent reception in which significant divergences hinge on the Oulipo's relationship with history, politics and the avant-garde.

Aesthetically, the Oulipo has a strong sense of literary tradition without being 'classicist' or 'anti-modern'.[33] As Queneau states, it is not so very 'anti' at all. Politically, the group resists straightforward identifications between literary history and national history. This search for a 'third way' of sorts can be found in Roubaud's *Poetry, Etcetera: Cleaning House*, where Roubaud explores the political implications of literary forms and distances himself from Louis Aragon's idea of 'national poetry'. Aragon, in turning away from his earlier surrealist free verse, had linked the traditional forms of the alexandrine and the sonnet to French history, and contrasted the forms of literary tradition with the 'formal individualism' of much modern poetry.[34] Roubaud formulates an alternative to this modernism-traditionalism binary by connecting form to language, and specifically to the memory of a language, rather than to the history of a nation.[35] However, faced with the globalisation of the literary market and the dominance of the English language, poetry written in the dominated languages is under threat. In response, Roubaud suggests a defence of the multiplicity of languages but also, as a semi-joke, offers a 'sonnet' written in binary code that 'can easily cross all borders'.[36] Read as an ironic gesture, this poem demonstrates the inseparability of poetry and language, and the impossibility of becoming a universal poet. On the other hand, it recalls Roubaud's own 'theory of abstract rhythm' formulated with Pierre Lusson.[37] To an extent, the Oulipian project involves precisely this kind of generalising move: Oulipian potentiality entails abstracting the particulars of literary form from both nationhood and history, and, to a lesser extent, from language.

Perec's *History of the Lipogram* offers another exemplary case of the Oulipo's simultaneous historicising and dehistoricising of formal constraint. In this essay, Perec situates his novel *A Void* (*La Disparition*)[38] in a long line of 'formal mannerisms' that have traversed Western literature 'since time immemorial' but are dismissed by traditional literary history.[39] Adopting a mock-academic style that does not preclude seriousness of purpose, he cites examples ranging from ancient authors (Lasus of Hermione and Nestor of Laranda) to twentieth-century writers (Ernest Vincent Wright), observing in passing that 'The list that the Oulipo intends to elaborate of its "plagiarists by anticipation" might very well constitute in the end a new Universal Dictionary of Letters'.[40] National history does make a discreet appearance in Perec's essay, for instance when Perec cites the case of Salomon Certon, an author of lipogrammatic sonnets who narrowly escaped the Saint Bartholomew's Day Massacre.[41] Nevertheless, the essay as a whole offers a disparate and dispersed account of Western history, tracing a story that has a utopian dimension. Against the central tenets of institutionalised literary scholarship, Perec traces a transversal line that intersects with different languages and traditions and is very far from any kind of linguistic or formal purism. The imagined Oulipian Universal Dictionary of Letters projects an alternative literary history and a transhistorical community of writers.

Of course, as in Roubaud's poetics, such universalism has its limits. The potentiality and the difficulty of any given constraint are variable across languages, as Perec observes with respect to the lipogram (omitting the letter 'e' does not have the same consequences in French, Spanish and English). Nevertheless, recent years have seen the international success, especially in the English-speaking world, of Oulipian forms that are translinguistic, or at least widely translatable: the lipogram, monovocalic poetry, S+7, etc.[42] The risk is here that the stakes of Oulipian decontextualisation itself become decontextualised – such that the result is not a Universal Dictionary of Letters but, rather, the appropriation of the constraint as an 'avant-garde' break with tradition or as 'conceptualist' anti-aesthetics.

CONSTRAINT AND COMMUNITY

What Levin Becker calls the 'voluntary withdrawal' or 'collective disengagement' of the Oulipo is not only an anti-dogmatic stance, but also, paradoxically, a form of universalism that has as its horizon the idea of a literary community. Jacques Rancière's work on the politics of aesthetics may serve to shed light on this complex position. Rancière rethinks the modernist autonomy of the work of art by situating politics precisely at the nexus of autonomy and community, defining aesthetics as 'a thinking of the sensory configuration able to establish a community'.[43] Yet, the poet's isolation, as Rancière argues of Mallarmé, means that the reunion of poet and audience can only take place in an imagined future. Vincent Kaufmann, in a fascinating book on the poetics of the avant-garde, situates the Oulipo firmly within this Mallarméan lineage, as 'the last in a line of groups who wish to bring into being a total book whose existence would coincide with that of an ideal community'.[44] For the Oulipo, as for the historical avant-garde, this ideal community is prefigured by the actual community of the group and the modes of coexistence that it produces. Nowhere is this clearer than in the Oulipo's insistence on the harmony of a collective identity that continues to accommodate individual difference.

In the light of this utopianism, it is tempting to separate the Oulipo's mobile, relatively transnational forms and procedures from the Oulipo as a specific entity, that is to distinguish the group in its collective mode of being from its poetic 'products'. Yet the Oulipo's achievement lies precisely in the collective creation of shared constraints, not simply in the sum of the work of its individual members. As Christophe Reig notes, the dynamics of the group's activity is grounded in a tension between the closure of the limited community and the 'exoteric' movement that places poetic language back into the public sphere.[45] The Oulipo functions as a private society that (increasingly since the 1970s) makes its procedures and proceedings visible, through publications, readings and other forms of public intervention. As 'potential literature', the Oulipian constraint becomes public property, prior to its reprivatisation by an author as 'scaffolding' for an actual work.

The group functions according to a model of community that is not directly political but is nevertheless grounded in a shared ethos that cannot be entirely divorced from politics. This ethos is in part determined by a shared history: Peter Consenstein mentions a moment in 1997 when the Oulipo, citing the suffering of several of its members under Nazism, took a public stand against the far-right *Front national* party (which was holding a rally in Strasbourg on the same day that the group was scheduled to give a reading).[46] The Oulipo member Garréta notes that the Oulipo, whatever the political engagement of its individual members, is concerned with literature and not with collective protest. Yet she goes on to suggest that the ethos of the group reveals a concern with political form, such that the group both is and is not politics/political: 'est et n'est pas (de la) politique'.[47] While this claim remains somewhat enigmatic, the hesitation between the adjectival and substantival meanings of the French *politique* points in two directions: to the political potential of constraint, and to the group's mode of existence as a (potentially) political entity.

The Oulipo exists both as an embodied community and as a textual community actualised by a collective signature, 'Oulipo' as author.[48] In an article on Oulipian politics, Reig focuses on the group as a community that produces mobile texts and increasingly operates in the public sphere; its public readings and writing workshops stake a claim for a place for the writer in the *polis*.[49] It is also possible to locate the political – or, at least, a potential politics – in the constraint itself. Some semantic constraints have in-built political implications; a case in point is Garréta's *Sphinx*, in which the constraint consists in the absence of gender markers that would allow us to identify the two main characters in a love story.[50] At another level, Christelle Reggiani has argued that Oulipian formalism, exemplified by the work of Perec, espouses a poetics of the enigma that belongs to a particular national and political history: in the context of postwar and postcolonial France, a nation deprived of its former relation to history, we see a privatisation of the author's discourse, a withdrawal into a secretive rhetoric addressed to a limited community of readers who have a special affinity for the work.[51] Perec's 'autobiographemes' perfectly illustrate this restricted rhetorical mode: as the encryption of an extratextual reality at the level of formal structures, these autobiographical markers are legible only to a certain kind of reader – one who already knows they are there and has been initiated into the world of Perec's work.

This kind of semi-private rhetoric, particularly as it occurs in *Life A User's Manual*, produces varying critical responses. It has led some critics to complain of the 'elitism' inherent in this use of constraint, which does not allow all readers to participate in the game on equal terms.[52] However, whatever its relevance for the Oulipo as a whole (and it is difficult to generalise about this eclectic and idiosyncratic company of writers), such an insistence on the enigmatic and secretive nature of constraint surely overemphasises the hermetic nature of Perec's writing and fails to account for the accessibility and impact of his work. It is undeniably the case that Perec adopts strategies of semi-invisibility in order to avoid the pitfalls of a hypervisibility of form.[53] However, this approach also allows his works to operate at multiple levels in order to engage different communities of readers, ranging from aficionados of formal games to devotees of popular novels. Perec's novel thus exemplifies a poetics of compromise that is also a poetics of proximity, of friendly collusion with the reader. Perec's use of constraints is in this sense profoundly democratic; it is an invitation to participate in the game.[54]

Perec's politics, of course, is not only to be located in the rhetoric of constraint. Political concerns are present in his writing from his contributions to the Marxist *Ligne générale* (*General Line*) project in the early 1960s to his participation in the leftist sociological journal *Cause commune* (*Common Cause*) in the 1970s.[55] In his multi-dimensional body of work, Perec unmasks the fetishised objects of consumer culture (*Things*), engages with the traumas of European history (*W or The Memory of Childhood*), attempts to grasp the unnoticed world of the 'infra-ordinary' (*An Attempt at Exhausting a Place in Paris*), and questions our modes of inhabiting space (*Species of Spaces*). Distinguishing in 'Statement of Intent' between the sociological, autobiographical, ludic and novelistic aspects of his work, Perec describes himself as a farmer cultivating 'four different fields, four different modes of questioning, which, in the last analysis, perhaps address the same problem, but approach it from different perspectives'.[56] What the general 'problem' is ultimately remains unspecified, except that it aims toward a certain image of literature that can never be grasped entirely.[57] Perec echoes Mallarmé's fantasy of the total book, which can be linked, as we have seen, to the notion of an ideal community. Yet Perec combines this utopian projection with a tentative exploration of literature's available space in the present. His modest cultivation of his 'fields' entails a commitment to common causes and things (*causes/choses communes*), and a belief in the shared world of reader and writer.

POTENTIALITIES

Both real and imagined communities of writers and readers are the protagonists of the Oulipo's collective hyper-novel, *Winter Journeys* (*Le Voyage d'hiver & ses suites*), inspired by Perec's 1979 short story. Perec's initial novella, *The Winter Journey*, is a tale of monomania that would not have been out of place in *Life A User's Manual*. The literature professor Vincent Degraël (a name that aptly evokes, like that of Percival Bartlebooth in *Life A User's Manual*, the fabled quest for the Holy Grail) accidentally discovers a book titled *The Winter Journey*. Published in 1864 by an unknown author, Hugo Vernier, this text reveals itself to be the source of the work of numerous great French poets of the end of the nineteenth century who shamelessly plagiarised it. After this copy of Vernier's text disappears during the Second World War, Degraël devotes the rest of his life to searching, in vain, for traces of the elusive poet. He dies in a psychiatric hospital.

Perec's story of copying, obsession and lost origins can be read as a parable of the Oulipian notion of 'anticipatory plagiarism'[58] and also as an exemplary 'fictional speculation on literary history' which raises questions about authorship, originality, interpretation and the temporality of literature.[59] In this respect, it is reminiscent of Jorge Luis Borges' essay 'Kafka and His

Precursors', in which the narrator recognises Kafka's idiosyncratic voice in works written before Kafka's, or, in a fictional mode, of the same author's 'Pierre Menard, Author of the Quixote', in which the eponymous writer attempts to recreate Cervantes' text line for line (incidentally, we should note that Borges' work is one of the sources of pre-programmed quotations in Perec's *Life A User's Manual*).[60] As for Perec and his successors, the meaning of *The Winter Journey* is transformed by its Oulipian sequels, which begin in 1992 with Roubaud's *Le Voyage d'hier* (*Yesterday's Journey*) and follow at a varying pace until Levin Becker's *Le Voyage obscur* (*The Obscure Journey*) of 2013 which closes the published collection. The series continues beyond the volume – the twenty-second episode in the saga, Michèle Audin's *La Vérité sur 'Le Voyage d'hiver'* (*The Truth about* The Winter Journey) appeared in 2014. Following a typically Oulipian logic of semi-privacy, the sequels first appear in the limited-edition series *La Bibliothèque oulipienne*, before being assembled in more widely available volumes. Attributed, significantly, to 'Georges Perec/Oulipo', a first limited-edition paperback titled *Winter Journeys* was published in English by Atlas Press in 2001. An expanded version followed in 2013, the same year that a French version was also published by the Éditions du Seuil.

Although the Oulipian sequels take Perec's original narrative in multiple thematic directions and adopt varying genres and tones, considered as a whole they transform the original tale of individual obsession into the saga of a collective conspiracy. In this context, although not required of all members, writing a 'winter journey' becomes an Oulipian rite of passage that confirms the individual's entry into a semi-secret society. This association of literary community with communal conspiracy might call to mind earlier group formations such as Georges Bataille's secret society *Acéphale*, whose 1936 inaugural essay was titled precisely *The Sacred Conspiracy*.[61] It also has echoes of Borges' story 'Tlön, Uqbar, Orbis Tertius', in which an alternative cosmos, complete with its own laws, is created by 'a secret society of astronomers, biologists, engineers, metaphysicians, poets, chemists, algebraists, moralists, painters, geometers [. . .] guided and directed by some shadowy man of genius'.[62] Yet, the Oulipo develops this idea of the restricted community, not as a form of cultural resistance or metaphysical speculation, but according to its own particular spirit of playful emulation. Blurring the boundary between fact and fiction, the group draws writers beyond the group, including Cortázar, into the plot.[63] To an extent, the volume appeals to a privileged audience of Oulipo members and initiated readers via various private jokes, such as the use of pseudonyms (Reine Augure, Mikhaïl Gorliouk and Hugo Vernier himself). However, the ordinary reader's struggle to distinguish Oulipian history from Oulipian fiction surely contributes to the fascination exercised by this work. In constructing a partly fictional identity, a collective mythology (and mystification), the Oulipo invites the complicity of the reader, while also inscribing itself within a larger history of modern literature. The sequels elaborate on Perec's tale by uncovering alleged new instances of literary and artistic borrowing, developing fictions on the basis of playful variations on the original title: *Le Voyage d'Hitler, Le Voyage d'Hoover, Le Voyage du ver, Un Voyage divergent . . . (Hitler's Journey, Hoover's Journey, The Worm's Journey, A Divergent Journey)*.

In elaborating the multi-faceted fiction of Hugo Vernier's symbolist *Urtext*, the Oulipian community works through its relationship to its own lost genius, Perec – the illustrious precursor who is both model and obstacle, and who is even cast, in Levin Becker's contribution, as a mastermind operating behind the scenes:

> Perec thought of everything, as usual: what seems to be the chaos of our chasing and misdirecting and leapfrogging over one another is in fact the patient unfolding of a meticulously plotted novel [. . .][64]

It is certainly the case that the multiple stories, in dialogue with each other, unfold narrative possibilities present in Perec's original text. However, *Winter Journeys* is an open-ended, mobile novel. It is less a constrained work, in strictly formal terms, than an illustration of literary potentiality as such. It is in this respect that we might align Perec with his creation, the mysterious Hugo Vernier – if we see Vernier not as the hapless victim of plagiarism or the overwhelming predecessor who has already thought of everything, but rather as the writer who has something to offer to everyone. Perec, via Vernier, becomes the patron saint of potentiality.

NOTES

1. Georges Perec (2009), 'Statement of Intent', in *Thoughts of Sorts*, trans. David Bellos, Boston: David R. Godine, p. 3
2. Oulipo (2004), *Moments oulipiens*. Bordeaux: Le Castor Astral, pp. 84, 143. On Perec's legacy among contemporary Oulipians, see in particular Camille Bloomfield (2011), 'L'héritage perecquien chez les jeunes oulipiens: Anne F. Garréta, Ian Monk, Hervé Le Tellier et Jacques Jouet', in Maryline Heck (ed.), *Filiations perecquiennes, Cahiers Georges Perec*, no. 11, Bordeaux: Le Castor Astral, pp. 19–32.
3. Marcel Bénabou (2011), 'Petit complément à l'adresse présidentielle', in Carole Bisenius-Penin and André Petitjean (eds), *50 ans d'Oulipo: de la contrainte à l'œuvre*, *La Licorne*, no. 100, Rennes: Presses Universitaires de Rennes, p. 26.
4. Georges Perec (1978), *Je me souviens*, Paris: Hachette; Jacques Jouet (1996), *Exercices de la mémoire*, no. 82, Paris: La Bibliothèque oulipienne; Jacques Bens (1997), *J'ai oublié*, no. 88, Paris: La Bibliothèque oulipienne; Anne F. Garréta and Valérie Beaudouin (2007), *Tu te souviens . . .?*, no. 160, Paris: La Bibliothèque oulipienne.
5. Georges Perec and the Oulipo (2013), *Winter Journeys*, London: Atlas Press; Georges Perec and the Oulipo (2013), *Le Voyage d'hiver & ses suites*, Paris: Seuil.

6. Jacques Roubaud (1991), 'L'Auteur oulipien', in Michel Contat (ed.), *L'Auteur et le manuscrit*, Paris, Presses Universitaires de France, p. 83.
7. Georges Perec (2003), 'Queneau et après', round table discussion at Rouen, 29 November 1980, in *Entretiens et Conférences*, ed. Dominique Bertelli and Mireille Ribière, vol. 2, Nantes: Joseph K., pp. 148–9.
8. Jacques Roubaud (2004), 'Perecquian OULIPO', *Yale French Studies*, trans. Jean-Jacques Poucel, New Haven, CT: Yale University Press, p. 99.
9. Roubaud, 'Perecquian OULIPO', pp. 102–3.
10. Roubaud, 'Perecquian OULIPO', p. 103.
11. For instance, the French National Research Agency funded the collective 'DifDePo' project that focuses on Oulipian history, poetics and aesthetics; the Bibliothèque nationale de France held an important exhibition on Oulipo from November 2014 to February 2015.
12. Henri Meschonnic (2001), *Célébration de la poésie*, Lagrasse: Verdier, p. 121.
13. Lauren Elkin and Scott Esposito (2013), *The End of Oulipo? An Attempt to Exhaust a Movement*, Winchester: Zero Books, p. 9.
14. Bernard Magné (1997), 'L'autobiotexte perecquien', in *Cahiers Georges Perec*, no. 5, Bordeaux: Le Castor Astral, pp. 5–42.
15. 'I have no childhood memories' is the famous opening of the autobiographical section of Georges Perec (1987), *W or The Memory of Childhood*, trans. David Bellos, Boston: Godine, p. 6. The fictional section of the book represents an attempt to imagine the concentration camp where Perec's mother was murdered, but which the young Perec did not himself experience.
16. Perec, *W*, p. 7.
17. Raymond Queneau (1960), *Cent mille milliards de poèmes*, Paris: Gallimard.
18. Roubaud, 'L'Auteur oulipien', p. 81.
19. To cite just one recent example, the poet Calvin Bedient condemns Oulipian 'conceptualism' for its supposed rejection of affect and imagination, which he links to 'political compliance or social under-concern'. Calvin Bedient (2013), 'Against Conceptualism: Defending the Poetry of Affect', *Boston Review*, 24 July, available at: http://www.bostonreview.net/poetry/against-conceptualism.
20. Christian Bök (2007), 'Oulipo and Its Unacknowledged Legislation', in Christine Wertheim and Matias Viegener (eds), *The Noulipian Analects*, Los Angeles: Les Figues Press, p. 157.
21. Christian Bök (2007), 'UbuWeb and Intentional Freedom', in Christine Wertheim and Matias Viegener (eds), *The Noulipian Analects*, Los Angeles: Les Figues Press, p. 222.
22. Kenneth Goldsmith (2001), *Soliloquy*, New York: Granary Books.
23. Kenneth Goldsmith (2000), *Fidget*, Toronto: Coach House.
24. Kenneth Goldsmith (2005), *The Weather*, Los Angeles: Make Now Press; Kenneth Goldsmith (2007), *Traffic*, Los Angeles: Make Now Press.
25. Kenneth Goldsmith (2003), *Day*, Great Barrington: The Figures.
26. Kenneth Goldsmith (2001), 'Interview with Erik Belgum', *Read Me*, no. 4, available at: http://wings.buffalo.edu/epc/authors/goldsmith/readme.html.
27. Elkin and Esposito, *The End of Oulipo?*, p. 75.
28. Elkin and Esposito, *The End of Oulipo?*, p. 61.
29. Daniel Levin Becker (2012), *Many Subtle Channels: In Praise of Potential Literature*, Cambridge, MA: Harvard University Press, p. 286.
30. Levin Becker, *Many Subtle Channels*, p. 28.
31. According to Paul Fournel, Julio Cortázar declined an invitation to join the group: 'We were not sufficiently Guevarist for his liking'. David Caviglioli (2014), 'Oulipo: le cercle

des poètes farfelus', *Le Temps*, 19 November. For more speculation on the possible reasons for Cortázar's refusal, see also Levin Becker, *Many Subtle Channels*, p. 198.
32. Quoted in Jacques Bens (1980), *OuLiPo 1960–63*, Paris: Christian Bourgois, p. 136.
33. For the claim that Oulipian practice is a form of 'neo-classicism', see Marc Lapprand (1998), *Poétique de l'Oulipo*, Amsterdam: Rodopi, pp. 150–8. On modernism and the anti-modern, see Antoine Compagnon (2005), *Les antimodernes: de Joseph de Maistre à Roland Barthes*, Paris: Gallimard.
34. Louis Aragon (1954), *Journal d'une poésie nationale*, Lyon: Les Écrivains Réunis, p. 111.
35. Jacques Roubaud (2006), *Poetry, Etcetera: Cleaning House*, trans. Guy Bennett, Los Angeles: Green Integer, p. 21.
36. Roubaud, *Poetry, Etcetera*, pp. 29–30.
37. Jacques Roubaud (1991), 'T.R.A.(M,m) (question d'une poétique formelle, I)', *Mezura*, no. 24, Paris: Publications Langues O.
38. Georges Perec [1969] (1994), *A Void (La Disparition)*, trans. Gilbert Adair, London: Harvill.
39. Georges Perec (1986), 'History of the Lipogram', in *Oulipo: A Primer of Potential Literature*, ed. and trans. Warren F. Motte, Lincoln: University of Nebraska Press, p. 99.
40. Perec, 'History of the Lipogram'.
41. Perec, 'History of the Lipogram', p. 102.
42. For examples, see Christine Wertheim and Matias Viegener (eds) (2007), *The Noulipian Analects*, Los Angeles: Les Figues Press; as well as Jean-Jacques Poucel (n. d.), 'Feature: Oulipo', *The Drunken Boat*, available at: http://www.drunkenboat.com/db8/oulipo/feature-oulipo.
43. Jacques Rancière (1996), *Mallarmé: la politique de la sirène*, Paris: Hachette, p. 27.
44. Vincent Kaufmann (1997), *Poétique des groupes littéraires (Avant-gardes 1920–1970)*, Paris: Presses Universitaires de France, p. 12.
45. Christophe Reig (2011), 'Oulipo-litiques', in *Poésie et politique au XXe siècle*, Paris: Hermann, p. 79.
46. Peter Consenstein (2002), *Literary Memory, Consciousness, and the Group Oulipo*, Amsterdam: Rodopi, pp. 227–8.
47. Oulipo, *Moments oulipiens*, p. 149.
48. On the collective signature see Reig, 'Oulipo-litiques', p. 76, and Camille Bloomfield (2011), 'L'Oulipo dans l'histoire des groupes et mouvements littéraires: une mise en perspective', in Carole Bisenius-Penin and André Petitjean (eds), *50 ans d'Oulipo: de la contrainte à l'œuvre*, *La Licorne*, no. 100, Rennes: Presses Universitaires de Rennes, p. 38.
49. Reig, 'Oulipo-litiques', p. 76.
50. Anne F. Garréta (1986), *Sphinx*, trans. Emma Ramadan, Dallas, TX: Deep Vellum.
51. Christelle Reggiani (2008), *Éloquence du roman: rhétorique, littérature et politique aux XIXe et XXe siècles*, Geneva: Droz, pp. 170–1.
52. Benoît Peeters (1985), 'Échafaudages', *Cahiers Georges Perec*, no. 1, pp. 178–91. See also Bernard Magné's analysis of the 'paradoxical clue' in Bernard Magné (1993), 'Les Cahiers des charges de Georges Perec', *Le Magazine littéraire*, no. 316, p. 72.
53. 'The trouble is that when you see the constraint, you no longer see anything but the constraint' *('L'ennui, quand on voit la contrainte, c'est qu'on ne voit plus que la contrainte')*. Georges Perec in Claudette Oriol-Boyer (1981), 'Ce qui stimule ma racontouze ...' in Perec, *Entretiens et conférences*, vol. 2, p. 171 (author's translation).
54. On this 'democratic' aspect of Perec's works, see Claude Burgelin (1989), 'Le phénomène Perec', *Esprit*, no. 151, pp. 65–75.
55. Georges Perec (1992), *L.G. Une aventure des années soixante*, Paris: Seuil; Paul Virilio,

Georges Perec, Jean-Michel Palmier and Jean Duvignaud (1972–3), *Cause commune*, no. 1–7.
56. Perec, 'Statement of Intent', p. 3.
57. Perec, 'Statement of Intent', p. 5.
58. François Le Lionnais introduces this notion in his Second Manifesto: 'Occasionally, we discover that a structure we believed to be entirely new had in fact already been discovered or invented in the past, sometimes even in a distant past. We make it a point of honour to recognise such a state of things in qualifying the text in question as "plagiarism by anticipation".' François Le Lionnais 'Second Manifesto', in Warren F. Motte (ed. and trans.) (1986), *Oulipo: A Primer of Potential Literature*, Lincoln: University of Nebraska Press, p. 31.
59. Jean-Louis Jeannelle (2009), 'Perec et le divers de l'histoire littéraire: sur *Le Voyage d'hiver*', dans 'Fictions d'histoire littéraire', *La Licorne*, no. 86, Rennes: Presses Universitaires de Rennes, p. 173.
60. Jorge Luis Borges (2000), 'Kafka and his Precursors', in *Selected Non-Fictions*, ed. Eliot Weinberger, trans. Esther Allen and Suzanne Jill Levine, New York: Penguin, pp. 363–5; Jorge Luis Borges (1999), 'Pierre Menard, Author of the Quixote', in *Collected Fictions*, trans. Andrew Hurley, New York: Penguin Books, pp. 88–95; Georges Perec (1993), *Cahier des charges de* La Vie mode d'emploi, ed. Hans Hartje, Bernard Magné and Jacques Neefs, Paris: CNRS Éditions/Zulma, p. 16.
61. Georges Bataille (1985), 'The Sacred Conspiracy', *Visions of Excess: Selected Writings 1927–1939*, ed. and trans. Allan Stoekl, Minneapolis: University of Minnesota Press, pp. 178–81.
62. Jorge Luis Borges (1999), 'Tlön, Uqbar, Orbis Tertius', in *Collected Fictions*, trans. Andrew Hurley, New York: Penguin Books, p. 72.
63. Mikhaïl Gorliouk (2013), 'If on a Night a Winter's Traveller', in Georges Perec and the Oulipo, *Winter Journeys*, London: Atlas Press, p. 176; Frédéric Forte (2013), 'The Journey of Dreams', in Georges Perec and the Oulipo, *Winter Journeys*, London: Atlas Press, pp. 190–5.
64. Daniel Levin Becker (2013), 'The Obscure Journey', in Georges Perec and the Oulipo, in *Winter Journeys*, London: Atlas Press, p. 343.

CHAPTER 10

The Architecture of Constraint and Forgetting

Sandra Kaji-O'Grady

ARCHITECTURE AND ITS INFATUATIONS WITH PHILOSOPHERS AND WRITERS

Each of the major thinkers of the late twentieth century engages architecture in some way, be that as subject, metaphor, evidence or ground. Fredric Jameson discerns in the Bonaventure Hotel the evidence of epistemic change, as does Peter Sloterdijk with the Crystal Palace.[1] Roland Barthes finds the Eiffel Tower an exemplary artefact for understanding mythology, and Jacques Derrida elaborates deconstruction through Bernard Tschumi's Parc de la Villette and Daniel Libeskind's Jewish Museum. In turn, contemporary architects have demonstrated a voracious appetite for ideas from philosophers and writers, employing these as inspiration for design as much as for their explicatory potential on metaphysical, epistemological or aesthetic questions. Indeed, the past fifty years are coloured by architecture's successive engagements with continental and critical thought. Derrida's influence upon mainstream architecture begins with his 1982 collaboration with Peter Eisenman for the Parc de la Villette competition, reaches its zenith in the Deconstructivist Architecture exhibition at MOMA in 1988, and, in 2012, he is the subject of a conference that 'hopes to re-establish the connections' with his work.[2] Bernard Cache's *Earth Moves*[3] saw the first applied investigation of Gilles Deleuze's concept of the 'fold' in architecture, yet, by the 2004 special issue of *Architecture Design* on 'Folding in Architecture',[4] such Deleuzian concepts as the 'fold', 'smooth space' and 'faciality' had been reduced to 'a prescriptive repertoire of formal manoeuvres'.[5]

These transactions have some enduring legacy after architects have exhausted the formal tropes generated by their readings of each thinker or writer. There is a healthy industry in explaining (or advocating) specific thinkers to subsequent generations, exemplified in Routledge's 'Thinkers for Architects' series. Launched in 2007 with *Deleuze and Guattari for Architects* by Andrew Ballantyne, it includes titles on Henri Lefebvre, Charles Goodman, Michel Foucault, Hans-Georg Gadamer, Jacques Derrida, Walter Benjamin, Pierre Bourdieu, Homi K. Bhabha, Luce Irigaray, Gilles Deleuze and Félix Guattari, and Martin Heidegger. A volume on Paul Virilio is forthcoming. In a similar vein, albeit slimmer, Leopold Lambert's 2013 'Funambulist Pamphlets', published by Punctum Books, include volumes on Michel Foucault, Baruch Spinoza and Gilles Deleuze. Those whose architectural shadows are longest have attracted multiple retrospective texts. Deleuze, for example, is the subject of *Deleuze and Space*, *Architecture for a Free Subjectivity: Deleuze and Guattari at the Horizon of the Real*, *Deleuze and Architecture*, *Deleuze and Guattari on Architecture*[6] and innumerable essays and conferences.

Georges Perec is the worthy subject of the present book, which assesses his impact across several cultural domains, yet at this point it is inconceivable that he would be graced with a title in the 'Thinkers for Architects' series. Is it that his writings on space and the city are too literary or oblique? Is it that they have yet to be introduced to an architectural audience? Did his early death mean that there is insufficient material to warrant a retrospective? None of the above is a plausible reason for his relative scarcity in architectural discourse. Architects have never been put off by the literary or poetic. James Joyce, Franz Kafka, Jorge Luis Borges and Italo Calvino, among others, have each been enjoyed for their experimentation, their references to architecture, and their views on the city. Kafka's *The Castle* is the undisguised model for architect Ricardo Bofill's housing project, El Castell. Kafka has been a popular reference point, too, in architectural education, 'because the narrative space in Kafka's texts has ambiguous, incomplete, non-functional, non-geometric and unusual peculiarities that allow students to explore and experience space in new ways'.[7] Calvino has also been heavily mined by architects, notably Rem Koolhaas and Bernard Tschumi, and his ongoing appeal is borne out by 'the presence on architecture and urbanology syllabuses, for instance, of his seminal *Invisible Cities*'.[8] The counter-utopias imagined by the Italian radical architects and the French megastructuralists of the 1960s are reflected in Calvino's imagined cities, especially those that levitate. In turn, Calvino's fictional 'cities' have spawned architectural fantasies.

Calvino was a friend of architectural historian Joseph Rykwert and urban planner Gianni Celati, and also Perec.[9] Calvino regarded Perec's 1978 *Life A User's Manual* to be 'the last real "event" in the history of the novel so far'.[10] In his discussion of *Life*, Calvino stressed the fact that 'for Perec, the construction of a novel according to fixed rules, to constraints, by no means limited his freedom as a storyteller, but stimulated it'.[11] Like Perec, Calvino substitutes a conventional narrative or plot in his novels with a rigorous structure that he likens to its architecture, so much so that he admits that in *The Castle of Crossed Destinies*, 'the architecture is the book itself'.[12] Unlike Calvino, Perec has inspired choreography and art, but not – as far as I know – works of architecture.[13] This relative disinterest is anomalous given the architectonic structure of his writings, the detailed attention given to buildings and cities, his Parisian pedigree, his friendships with influential thinkers in architecture and urbanism such as Virilio, Lefebvre and Calvino, and, of course, the appetite the architectural discipline has for writing that offers fresh perspectives on questions of space and inhabitation. It is even more curious given that his posthumous introduction to an English-speaking architectural audience was so extraordinarily auspicious.

PEREC'S POSTHUMOUS GRAND DEBUT IN ARCHITECTURE

In 2002, issues 45 and 46 of *AA Files* – the journal of the Architecture Association, one of the most significant venues of architectural discourse since its launch in 1981 – were dedicated to the author. It was titled 'P is for Perec and Paris'. It was in the *AA Files* that Derrida's critique of Tschumi's competition-winning project for La Villette, 'Point de Folie – Maintenant l'Architecture', brought the philosopher a new audience in 1986. The journal was also the venue for Paul Hirst's attempt, in 1993, to remedy the neglect of Foucault 'in obvious contrast to [. . .] his contemporary Jacques Derrida' in 'Foucault and Architecture'.[14] These essays fuelled the development of a sustained architectural discourse around each philosopher.[15] Despite the unprecedented dedication of a whole issue – indeed, a double issue – it failed to generate further interest in Perec among architects. His 'failure to launch' in the discipline can be ascribed partly to bad timing and partly to the way in which Perec's work was presented. It is worth revisiting this double issue to locate those moments where Perec's *oeuvre* may yet find fertile ground in architecture.

Perec's appearance in *AA Files* appears to be prompted by the publication in English of *Life A User's Manual* in 1996 and *Species of Spaces* in 1997. These had generated interest among a small circle of architects who contributed to the double issue. William Firebrace, an architect, academic and graduate of the AA had earlier in 2002 e-published his first book, *Specious Spacious*, based on Perec's prose. Enrique Walker was a doctoral student at the AA, undertaking a thesis on Perec's *Lieux* project that he completed in 2012.[16] It likely helped also that the French Ministry for Foreign Affairs financially supported the publication and that its editor at the time, Mark Rappolt, now co-editor of *Art Review*, had trained as an art historian not as an architect.[17]

The two volumes centre on four pieces from the abandoned work, *Lieux* (*Places*), begun in 1969 and translated and published here for the first time: 'Scene in Italie', 'Glances at Gaîté', 'Comings and Goings in rue de l'Assomption' and 'Stances on Mabillon'. These are interspersed with texts and photographs by others that veer from hagiography to homage. Harry Mathews, Jacques Roubaud, Jacques Jouet, Hugo Brandt Corstius, Marcel Bénabou and Ian Monk – most of whom were fellow members of the Oulipo – contribute original prose. Terry Smith (who confesses that he had never heard of Perec before the commission) writes a travel diary ostensibly in the style of *Lieux*. There are interviews with Paul Virilio and Pierre Getzler. Urbanist and philosopher, Virilio, met Perec in 1971 when on the editorial board of the new journal *Cause Commune*. Virilio went on to commission *Species of Spaces* for his book series *L'Espace critique*. Virilio reports that conversations had with his friend always took place while walking so that they 'never condensed into anything face-to-face. But continued side by side.'[18] Getzler participated with Perec in a small group of intellectuals called *La Ligne générale* and took photographs of and for Perec. He admits that Perec 'didn't really know what he wanted' from the photographs he instructed Getzler to take of Mabillon.[19] If Perec's ambition was 'flat writing', this is not what is returned to him in the *AA Files*, for it is coloured by personal recollections.

The *Lieux* project centred on twelve Parisian locations. Each was to be described in situ in one month and once again from memory, according to an algorithmic constraint, so that no place was described twice in the same month. Each of these writings was to be sealed in a dated and labelled envelope. The intention was to open the archived writings twelve years later (when each place had been written about once in each month), but Perec abandoned the incomplete project in 1975. *Lieux* was meant to register three kinds of ageing, 'The aeging of places, the aeging of my writing, and the ageing of my memories.'[20] The pieces published in the *AA Files* reveal only part of this ambition. The city – its fabric, people, goods and comings and goings – are recounted alongside his own movements and memories. Buildings are frequently described in terms of changes that have taken place or appear to be underway. Take the following, for example, 'No. 7: A small private house. It is difficult to tell whether it is being done up or demolished.'[21]

Perec seemed to want to reveal ordinary facts without embellishment. Moving systematically along each street, he avoided undue attention on one site over another, or any obvious act of authorial selection or exclusion. Naming each address in turn ensures the reader understands this self-imposed method. We also are left in no doubt as to its burden on the author. At one point, as he attempts to record each of the posters and flyers on the hoarding of a building site, Perec resorts to 'etc.', confessing 'I'm sick of noting them all down'. The reader is also likely to falter in the face of the sheer proliferation of facts. As Gilbert Adair wonders, 'why does Perec bother recording any of these minutiae; or rather, from the reader's own point of view, why am I bothering to read such a book?'[22] The point of the meticulous descriptions is that while they imply the possibility of an exhaustive inventory, at the same it is made clear that this ambition is unfulfillable. There is no encompassing truth by which to capture the heterogeneity of the city. Perec's city is without 'scents, no urine, no sounds, no shouts [. . .] he's in a silent film, and it's in black and white'.[23] Getzler suspects that, for Perec, the objects he observes are merely 'pegs, where you can hang quotations, memories'.[24] This may be so, but the personal memories are described in the same indifferent tone as inert objects, for example, 'the flat where Martine Carol used to live', or 'no. 18 is where my aunt and uncle used to live'.[25]

MISREADINGS AND REREADINGS

Perec's sociological concerns are less evident in *Lieux* than in other writings, although the project does exhibit an underlying anxiety around the destruction of the city. As Kate Morris observes, one of the limitations of literary scholarship on Perec is that it 'has tended to focus on memory and writing rather than his sociological concerns about space and the peculiar way they are written'.[26] Morris finds it 'striking [. . .] the extent to which space and urban geography are taken as givens in literary studies of Perec's work'.[27] Morris laments that Perec's desire to preserve the past and bear witness is too quickly tied to the author's personal experience of the Holocaust, thus defusing its wider challenge. It is easy to see why this occurs. Perec himself described writing as a battle against forgetting:

> To write: to try meticulously to retain something, to cause something to survive: to wrest a few precise scraps from the void as it grows, to leave somewhere a furrow, a trace, a mark or a few signs.[28]

Alternatively, the *Lieux* are dismissed as 'wearisome and futile reproductions of urban space that do not speak to larger literary or cultural issues'.[29]

For Morris, a more apt reading is that Perec's writings 'emphasize the perpetual un-becoming of those spaces themselves in contrast to an equally prevalent discourse of urban development that is also found in the texts'.[30] The texts reveal an essential truth about cities rather than a personal pathology. His recording of the advertisements, posters and public texts embedded in the city expose conflicting discourses of ownership and inhabitation. They show the myriad objects and texts competing for our attention and unsettling our sense of a coherent place. Perec makes salient that 'the dialectical obverse of "making new" is the process of disintegration and un-becoming that makes development projects necessary and which also inevitably follows them'.[31] He reminds us that destruction and decay are the necessary pre-conditions for what architectural theorist and historian Francesca Hughes satirically calls 'the anti-entropic duties of the architect'.[32]

Yet, these lessons for architects are not brought out in the special issue. In the preface, Andrew Leak asks, 'What can these texts mean to us today?' But his attempt at an answer does not refer to what they might mean outside of literature. Perec is presented here as if he is essentially interested in writing, and only one aspect of his writing is made apparent. Perec outlined four modes in which he wrote: sociological, autobiographical, ludic and fictive. The fragment of his writing in the special issue, however, does not reveal this range of interests to the novice reader. His *oeuvre*, narrowed to the *Lieux* fragments, is reduced to a lesson in the acute and systematic observation of the city, its buildings and material ephemera. For architects, reading literature, or 'reading' the quotidian world, is invariably premised as a precursor for action in it. It is difficult to see how a projective trajectory could be derived from these texts, even if readers discern that their overriding message is the inevitability of the cycle of destruction and development.[33] Faced with texts that Perec himself had abandoned, and with no discussion as to how they might be of use in making the city, it is unlikely that many were tempted to delve further into his *oeuvre*.

It is extremely unlikely, too, that architectural audiences encountered alternative views on the potential significance of Perec in the field. Morris's essay, 'Perec's Alternative Topography',[34] was published in a short-lived journal for the visual arts by postgraduate students at the University of California, Irvine. She was an English literature graduate working as an editor in Canada. Peta Mitchell's 'Constructing the Architext: Georges Perec's *Life A User's Manual*' was published in the Canadian literary journal *Mosaic* and, at the time of publication, Mitchell was a lecturer in English at the University of Queensland. Both authors and their essays were far from the geographical and disciplinary centres of architectural discourse.

Mitchell notes that, from the mid-1970s, in both architecture and literature, the concept of a unified work was replaced with that of 'textuality' – 'parody and citationality became key concepts, and, moreover, both came to be informed by a kind of Lyotardian game theory'.[35] She argues that Perec's novel, *Life A User's Manual*, departs from the French tradition of drawing upon architecture for its verisimilitude so as to provide a kind of grounding. The novel is not a search for the real but, rather ironically, 'denies the very possibility of originality'.[36] It is, for Mitchell, the quintessential 'architext', a book in which structure and theme, book and building, are one. She describes how the constraints Perec uses to structure the novel – the ten-by-ten chessboard-like grid of the apartment building, the knight's tour through the apartment and the hundred-year time frame for the novel – have their parallel in the totalising plans of architects and urbanists, such as Georges-Eugène Haussman, within whose grid the Parisian apartment building is set. The difference is that, whereas totalising architecture is doomed to failure, Perec's system of constraints fails by design. Its failure is an opening for the reader and for order and chaos, and the ideal and the quotidian, to rub productively against each other.

Hughes, revisiting *Life A User's Manual* in 2014, follows David Bellos, the book's translator, in considering the novel a kind of 'machine' that writes the book. She compares Perec's literary machine with the debates that have taken place in biology over the relationship between DNA as information and RNA as material. The 'looped architecture' of instruction and perambulation in Perec's lesser-known *The Art and Craft of Approaching Your Head of Department to Submit a Request for a Raise* – in which Perec appropriates a computing flowchart – Hughes finds to be comparable with current understandings of biological coding. It does away with the distinction between process and product. Hughes writes:

> The revival of observation [. . .] not only drew the newly observing molecular biologist away from the hegemony of genetic determinism but brought back the spectacle of the phenomena and, with it, the value of the particular [. . .][37]

Hughes' book is a rather wild detour itself between the general and the particular, in which Perec serves an argument against precision in architecture that is already made and won well before Perec makes an appearance in the text.

ARCHITECTURAL DESIGN AND COMPOSITIONAL CONSTRAINTS

Perec's engagement with compositional constraints has obvious synergies and attractions for architecture that have been taken up by just one architect at the heart of the discipline – Walker, formerly the doctoral student at the AA who had interviewed Virilio for the double issue. Now (at the time of writing) at the Graduate School of Architecture, Planning, and Preservation at Columbia University, Walker tests the Oulipian method in his design teaching. In a studio series entitled 'Under Constraint' (2003–6), students examine the use of self-imposed constraints. In the subsequent studio series, 'The Dictionary of Received Ideas' (ongoing since 2006), students 'examine received ideas – in other words, ideas which have been depleted of their original intensity due to recurrent use'.[38] Through the deliberate use (or misuse) of familiar design operations and conceptual strategies, the goal is to open up otherwise precluded possibilities for architectural design and architectural theory. It is played as a game in rounds of three in which the building blocks are three, seemingly incompatible, received ideas from which the students develop a hybrid and unexpected outcome. The results can be seen in Figures 10.1, 10.2 and 10.3.

In 'Under Constraint' (2010), Walker lists the numerous writers and filmmakers who have worked productively with predetermined constraints, including Perec, before proposing:

> Subjected by definition to a regime of external forces, architecture has dismissed self-imposed constraints as a productive device. While it has overly submitted to a practice of problem-solving, it has demonized any constraint as a limitation to architectural imagination. Architecture tolerates voluntary constraints only when these forces appear as feeble, yet, used to a regime of dependency, still masking them ultimately under a narrative of necessity, and in so doing hindering their potential. The practice of self-imposed (and therefore arbitrary) constraints entails deliberately formulating the problem; an uncompromising decision which, if properly calibrated, may release otherwise unexpected paths of production.[39]

Further:

> Self-imposed – and therefore arbitrary – constraints can potentially mobilize the forces of architectural imagination. Not only do they grant great freedom; if properly calibrated, they can also release otherwise unenvisaged paths of production.[40]

Walker's belief that architects have dismissed the introduction of compositional constraints is not entirely true and his case would be much stronger if he used the work of his predecessors as evidence. While there is no equivalent in architecture of music's Total Serialism or literature's Oulipo, and although Perec may not be the direct source, he has had his fellow travellers in the design discipline. These span from Walter Netsch and John Hejduk in the 1960s to Eisenman and Tschumi in the 1970s and 1980s, to the parametric architecture of the 1990s. I will describe each briefly.

Netsch is an architect both misunderstood and largely forgotten. Netsch joined SOM – a large American commercial practice not given over to the fanciful – in 1947. He was a maverick there and soon had his own autonomous studio away from SOM headquarters.[41] His first significant project at SOM was the United Air Force Academy in Colorado Springs. To this, Netsch

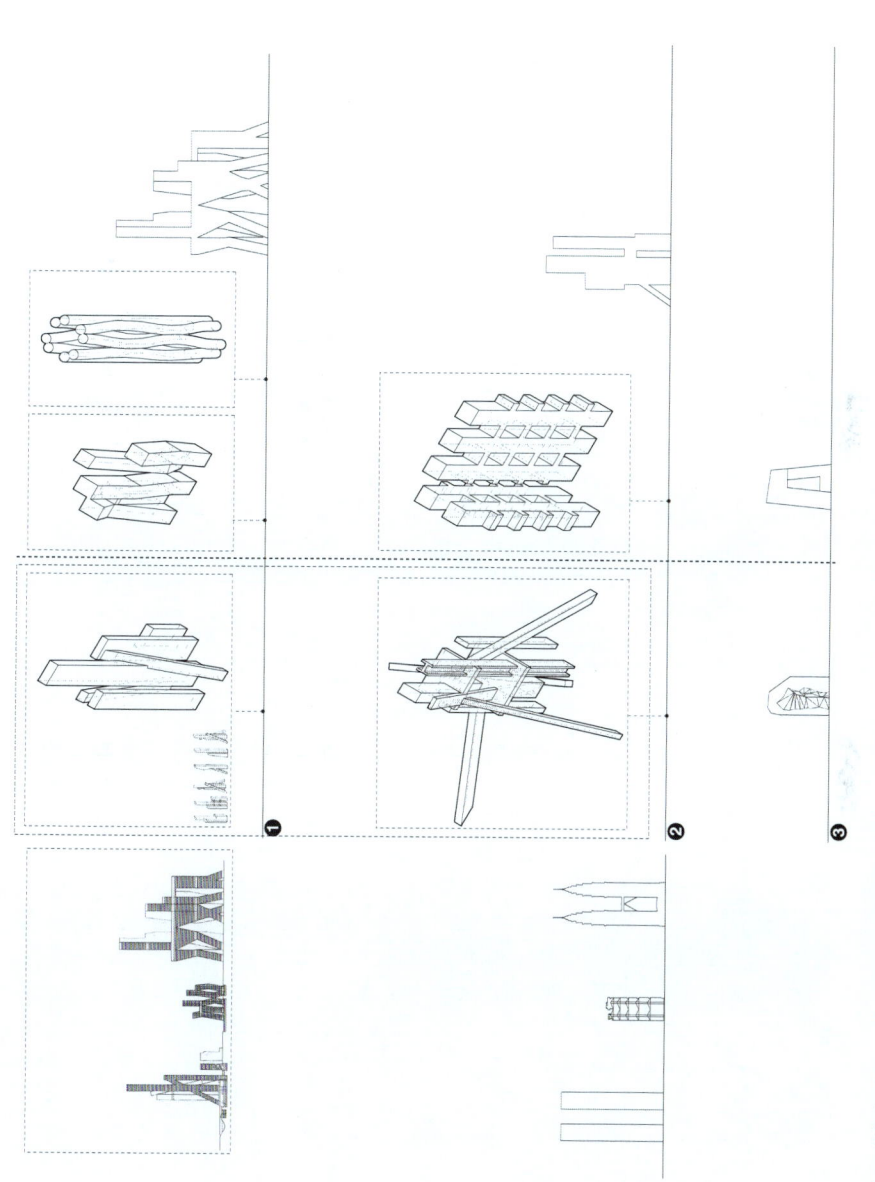

Figure 10.1 Student Lluis Alexandre Casanovas Blanco's work from Enrique Walker's Spring 2012 Advanced Architecture Studio IV The Dictionary of Received Ideas, at the GSAPP.

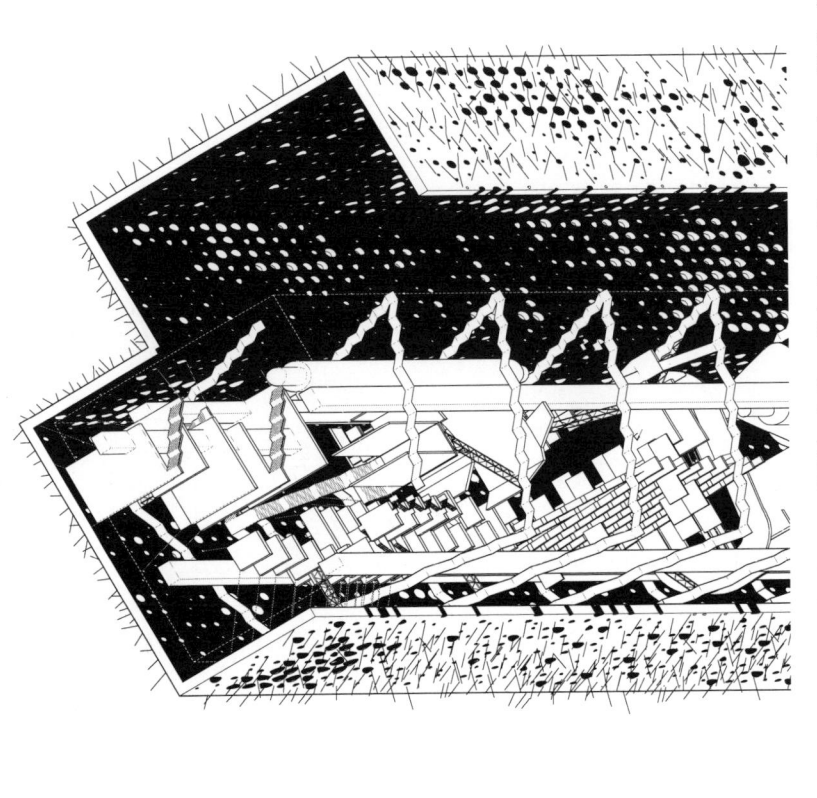

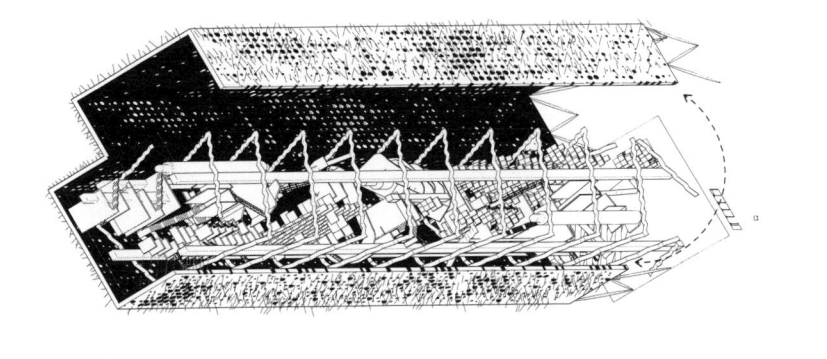

Figure 10.2 Students Emanuel Admassu, Lluis Alexandre Casanovas Blanco, Idan Naor and Eduardo Rega Calvo's work from Enrique Walker's Spring 2012 Advanced Architecture Studio IV The Dictionary of Received Ideas, at the GSAPP.

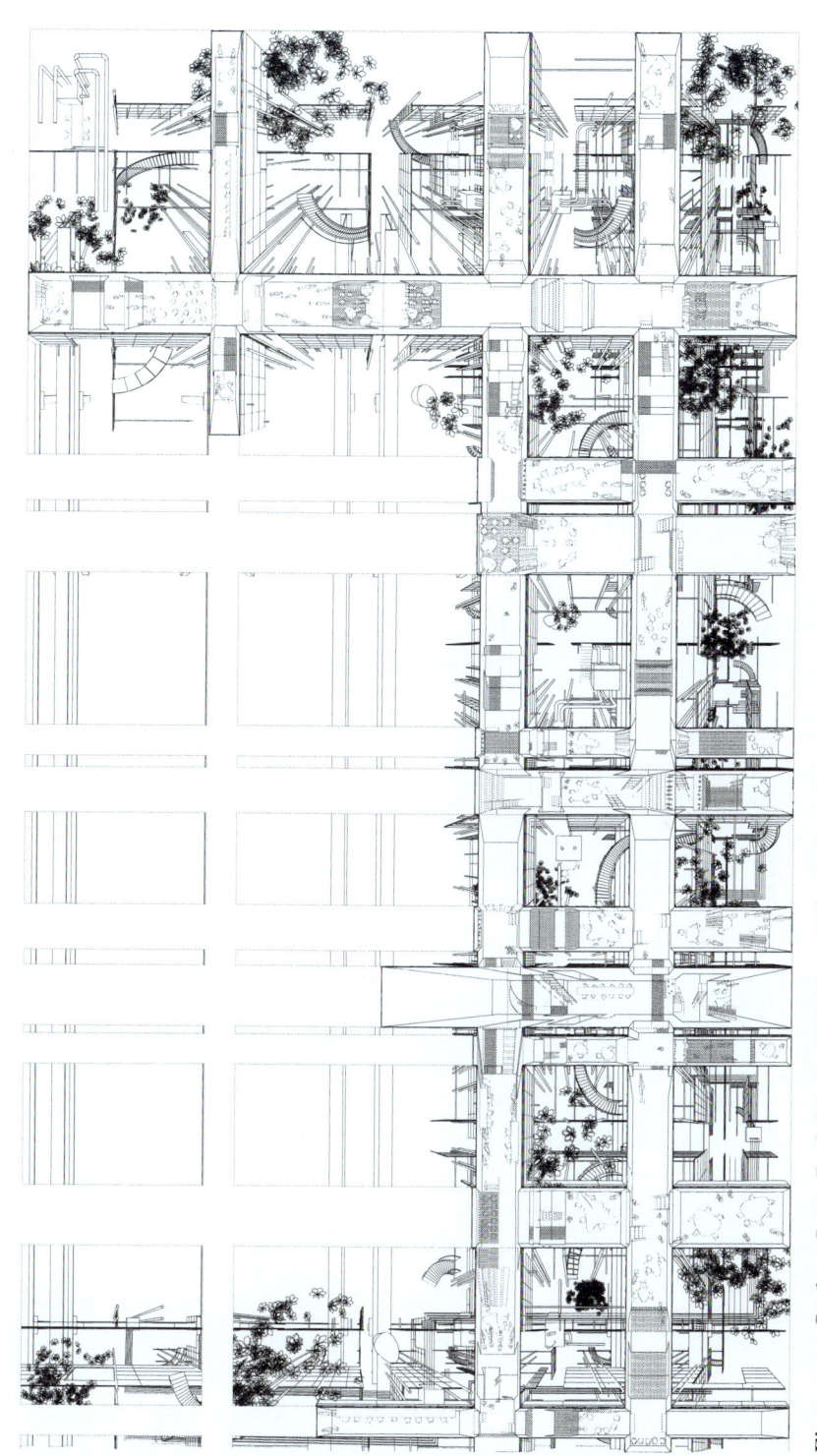

Figure 10.3 Students Laura Buck, Myung Shin Kim, Alejandro Stein and Rui Wang's work from Enrique Walker's Spring 2014 Advanced Architecture Studio IV The Dictionary of Received Ideas, at the GSAPP.

applied a proportioning system based on a seven-foot module, which he subsequently developed into something he called field theory. Field theory was a departure from the Miesian aesthetic of SOM, but shared with it the assumption, even insistence, that any project site be empty before design work begins. As Netsch explains, 'Field theory can't or won't deal with existing context, it needs to makes [sic] its own fresh start. The operative ground condition for field theory is tabula rasa.'[42] More specifically, field theory was a solipsistic method for ordering space and architectural elements according to a consistent repetition or modularity. It entailed the establishment of predetermined parameters and their internal relationships. Netsch insisted that, 'Correctly developed, the diminution of choice ceases to be limiting in character, but rather becomes the refined crystallization of the creative art.'[43] Field theory became associated with Netsch's favourite formal device – the rotated square, repeated and overlapped at multiple scales.

The consequences of maintaining an overarching 'continuous proportional system' sometimes impacted on functionality.[44] Librarian William Jones describes Netsch's Behavioural Sciences building at the University of Illinois as aesthetically unified but possessing a 'bewildering layout' and as 'a maze of confusing interior corridors and awkwardly shaped offices'.[45] Jones believes that the subordination of function to Netsch's rigid geometry was averted at the Northwestern's Science-Engineering Library because of the planning committee's insistence on functional space. He advocates that other librarians keep a tight reign on their architects.[46] Possibly even those buildings untouched by forceful client committees were something of a compromise for Netsch, and he sought a purer realisation for field theory. This came in the invention of a 'design game' for which he was granted a patent in March 1987 – *US 4651993 Design game and modules for use therein*. The game uses a plurality of series of flat pieces of the same shape – equilateral polygons – progressive in size and of a predetermined number. The size progression is precisely determined. The game is essentially an educational puzzle intended to allow children to produce an unlimited number of abstract or quasi-representational designs of 'pleasing aesthetic effect'.[47] Netsch's approach is something like the structure of *Life*, minus the life. The abundant contents of each apartment – the life that threatens to spill over its constraining order at any time – delighted Perec but repulsed Netsch.

In the mid-1950s, while teaching at the University of Texas in Austin, architect John Hejduk developed a design puzzle for his students of working within the self-imposed cage of a nine-square grid. Hejduk's 9SG exercise quickly became *de rigueur* for students in the early years of architectural education where the elimination of programme, materiality and site made the problem tightly focused and, like Netsch's game, highly abstract and aesthetically pleasing. Hedjuk described the 9SG as 'one of the classic, open-ended problems', reductive and constraining, but also capable of generating infinite scenarios.[48] In his own work, Hejduk explored the potential of designing through the reductive context of an abstract plan diagram and a limited kit of parts in the Texas Series of houses (1954–63) and the Diamond Series (1962–7). Hejduk was influenced, through his colleagues Colin Rowe and Robert Slutzky, by Rudolf Wittkower's 1949 argument that Palladio's eighteenth-century villas were based on a similar consistent organisational schema – suggesting that self-imposed formal constraints have a long history in architecture.[49]

Subsequent experiments by Eisenman in his House projects (1967–75) draw heavily on Hejduk, and are equally informed by a group of artists who in 1967 and 1968 were experimenting with serial methods, Sol LeWitt in particular but also Donald Judd and Mel Bochner. Eisenman's parallel experiments in architecture get caught up in a lively discourse around architectural representation, meaning and authorship. In *The Architectural Uncanny* (1992), Anthony Vidler suggests two different ways of understanding Eisenman's houses. One is to the see the series of projects as 'an exercise in the rational exploration of certain pre-established formal constructs: a self-conscious logical sequence with a beginning and an end'.[50] Alternatively, Vidler proposes that it is plausible to see them as 'posed self-consciously against anthropomorphic analogies, closed formal systems and functionalist derivations', in such a way that these designs 'overturn the classical system of representation'.[51] Others were affronted. Critics deride his serial houses as mere sculpture because they do not derive their purpose from the function or meaning of inhabitation and the logical processes of building. Michael Sorkin finds House El Even Odd to be far 'from any reasonable standard of legibility as habitable architecture' and dismisses them as socially irresponsible, culturally irrelevant and arbitrary.[52]

Undeterred, in his design for the Memorial to the Murdered Jews of Europe, Eisenman more directly evokes both LeWitt and Perec and links the predetermined constraint with the banal and inherent chaos. He writes:

> The context of the Memorial to the Murdered Jews of Europe is the enormity of the banal. The project manifests the instability inherent in what seems to be a system, here a rational grid, and its potential for dissolution in time. It suggests that when a supposedly rational and ordered system grows too large and out of proportion to its intended purpose, it in fact loses touch with human reason. It then begins to reveal the innate disturbances and potential for chaos in all systems of seeming order, the idea that all closed systems of a closed order are bound to fail.[53]

The grid is a consistent formal trope in Perec's, Hejduk's and Eisenman's compositions. It is an initial means of production that guides the viewer through the work but, at the same time, is under constant deformation. As much as the grid holds or structures it produces movement across itself. The grid is also found in Tschumi's 1986 design for the Parc de la Villette with its superimposition of three principles of organisation: a grid of points that locate the follies, the axial lines of circulation and the expansive neutral surfaces of the park. Tschumi proposes that the transformational sequence entailed by the design process is based on a 'precise, rational set of transformational rules and discrete architectural elements'.[54] He likens this process of recombining fragments through a 'series of permutations' to the writings of Queneau and Perec.[55] Claiming to avoid 'pure formalism', Tschumi subjects space, movement, form and programme to a set of mechanical operations in which each parameter is independent, proposing 'as sequences of events do not depend on spatial sequences (and vice versa), both can form independent systems, with their own implicit schemes or parts'.[56] The dissociations and complexities of layering three disparate systems animate and disrupt the grid. It is a brilliant exercise with the theoretical richness of *Life A User's Manual* – yet, perhaps, like some of the Oulipian texts, the idea is less rewarding than the outcome. The scale of the park and the distance between the follies produces an experience less compelling than the limited edition folio of drawings. After Parc de la Villette, Tschumi abandoned these methods.

In the new millennium, Serial Art has attracted considerable historical revision, for example Anne Rorimer's chapter, 'Systems, Seriality, Sequence', in her *New Art in the 60s and 70s: Redefining Reality* (2001). In architecture, the experiments of a previous generation in predetermined rule-bound techniques are largely overlooked. Architects using rule-based procedures coupled with software for 'parametric' design have suggested their work extends from the serial music of Schoenberg and Boulez rather than architectural antecedents. Sanford Kwinter, for example, describes Eisenman's design process as 'Boulez-like total serialism' in its 'rigid positions or relations' and positions his own work as more responsive.[57]

Kwinter's assessment of Eisenman's formalism comes just three years after the publication of the *AA Files* issue on Perec. Perec, of course, never held rigidly to the compositional relations and rules he set up – there are just ninety-nine apartments described in *Life* when there should have been 100. He sought the anomalous in the methodical, what Deleuze describes as the *clinamen* – the Lucretian notion of the unpredictable swerve that atoms take in space. This indeterminacy, according to Lucretius, provides the 'free will which living things throughout the world have'.[58] For the Oulipo, the clinamen could only be employed if it was not required, that is if the constraints could actually be fulfilled.[59] I would argue that Eisenman and Tschumi were equally invested in the interruption, the error and the impossibility of perfect systematisation. Indeed, they had little choice if they were to persist in architectural practice and not, like Netsch, resort to designing games.

Yet, while Eisenman's and Tschumi's experiments with predetermined rules were fruitful, during the period that followed Perec's introduction to a new audience, architects were increasingly moving away from any position that asserted the autonomy of the discipline. Autonomy, as Alejandro Zaera-Polo notes, enables the development of disciplinary codes in the absence of external attachments but 'limits the transformative potential of the discipline'.[60] It is this transformative potential that architects have sought in the past two decades. An initial period of formalist parametric experimentation in the digital has given way to the adoption of parameters directed at material and environmental performance. The formalist conviction that messing with the conventions of representation of language and text, image or object is in itself disruptive of the political status quo holds little sway. Walker's plea for the potentialities of Perec's method will not find adopters until it is recombined – as it was for Perec – with social critique and new technologies.

CONCLUSION

I would like to conclude with a lesson from the visual arts. The descriptive mode of recording the city that Perec purported to carry out anticipates the impassive but systematic eye of Google Street View: the car-mounted camera recording nine images every ten metres. Street View offers an archive of frozen images of ordinary streets and the life that takes place in them for artists such as Doug Rickard. Rickard's *New American Picture* (2012) crosses Oulipian methodology with photographic social documentary.[61] Rickard's initial search criteria was 'Martin Luther King', yielding all those streets, boulevards and parks named after the black activist, almost all of which were in poor black neighbourhoods. From Google Street View, Rickard extracted around 10,000 images. Selected images were rephotographed, cropped and Google's proprietary markers removed in Photoshop. Of these images, seventy-nine were chosen for an Aperture monograph, and twenty archival pigment prints were exhibited at the Yosse Milo Gallery, New York City.

The aspect of change that preoccupied Perec in the *Lieux* project is here embedded in the ways in which even the photographs in this project are now outdated by Google Street View's upgraded camera technology. Furthermore, Rickard's works have unwieldy titles that register the geographical coordinates, the date of the Google photograph and the date of his reproduction of it, for example *#32.700542, Dallas, TX. 2009* (2010). Rickard's project seems to me to update Perec's *Lieux* in a way that is immediately accessible and resonant with a new generation of architects and artists. To see the two side by side is to comprehend how the imposition of parameters and rules might be combined with extraordinary reservoirs of available data about the city and its flows of people, goods and money. More than ever, Perec's combination of the algebraic with the phenomenal and the geometric with the social offers rich ways for the re-presenting and re-making of the built world.

NOTES

1. Peter Sloterdijk (1997), 'The Crystal Palace', *Public 37*, York Digital Journals, pp. 11–16; Frederic Jameson (1991), *Postmodernism, or, The Cultural Logic of Late Capitalism*, Durham, NC: Duke University Press, pp. 38–45.
2. *Architecture of Deconstruction: The Specter of Jacques Derrida* (2012), Faculty of Architecture at the University of Belgrade on 25–27 October, available at: http://labont.it/aod-architectur-of-deconstruction-the-specter-of-jacques-derrida.
3. Bernard Cache (1995), *Earth Moves: The Furnishing of Territories*, Cambridge, MA: MIT Press.
4. Greg Lynn (ed.) (1993), 'Folding in Architecture', *Architectural Design*, vol. 63, no. 3/4.
5. Douglas Spencer (2011), 'Architectural Deleuzism', *Radical Philosophy*, vol. 168, July/August, available at: http://www.radicalphilosophy.com/article/architectural-deleuzism.
6. Ian Buchanan and Gregg Lambert (eds) (2005), *Deleuze and Space*, Toronto: University of Toronto Press; Simone Brott (2011), *Architecture for a Free Subjectivity: Deleuze and Guattari at the Horizon of the Real*, Farnham: Ashgate; Helene Frichot and Stephen Loo (2013), *Deleuze and Architecture*, Edinburgh: Edinburgh University Press; Graham Livesey (2015), *Deleuze and Guattari on Architecture*, New York: Routledge.
7. Beyhan Bolak Hisarligil (2012), 'Franz Kafka in the Design Studio: A Hermeneutic Phenomenological Approach to Architectural Design Education', *International Journal of Art and Education*, vol. 31, no. 3, p. 257.
8. Dani Cavallaro (2010), *The Mind of Italo Calvino: A Critical Exploration of His Thought and Writings*, Jefferson, NC: McFarland, p. 4.
9. Letizia Modena (2011), *Italo Calvino's Architecture of Lightness: The Utopian Imagination in an Age of Urban Crisis*, New York: Routledge, pp. 80–1.
10. Italo Calvino (1988), *Six Memos for the Next Millenium*, Cambridge, MA: Harvard University Press, p. 121.
11. Calvino, *Six Memos for the Next Millenium*, p. 123.
12. William Weaver, Damien Pettigrew and Italo Calvino (1992), 'Interview: The Art of Fiction No. 130', *Paris Review*, no. 124, Fall, available at: http://www.theparisreview.org/interviews/2027/the-art-of-fiction-no-130-italo-calvino.
13. Creative works in homage to Perec were a feature of the conference *Species of Spaces: Transdisciplinary Approaches to the Work of Georges Perec*, Teesside University, 28 March 2014, available at: http://www.tees.ac.uk/sections/news/pressreleases_story.cfm?story_id=4450&this_issue_title=September%202013&this_issue=244.
14. Paul Hirst (1993), 'Foucault and Architecture', *AA Files*, vol. 26, p. 52.
15. Jacques Derrida (1986), 'Point de Folie – Maintenant l'architecture', *AA Files*, vol. 12, pp. 66–75.
16. Enrique Walker (2012), 'The Scaffolding (Georges Perec's Lieux)', PhD thesis, Open University.
17. Mark Rappolt was the *AA Files* second editor. Its first, Mary Wall, edited issues 1–40. Rappolt edited issues 41–9 and was succeeded by David Terrien, now his co-editor at *Art Review*. Rappolt studied eighteenth-century public sculpture in France, which led him to

an interest in town planning and from there to the Architectural Association. He is now focused on art. 'In Conversation with Mark Rappolt' (2013), *Debut Magazine*, 5 June, available at: http://www.debutcontemporary.com/in-conversation-with-mark-rappolt/.
18. Paul Virilio (2002), 'A Walking Man', trans. Clare Barrett, *AA Files*, no. 45/46, p. 136.
19. Jean-Charles Depaule and Pierre Getzler (2002), 'A City in Words and Numbers', trans. Clare Barret, *AA Files*, no. 45/46, pp. 117, 124.
20. Georges Perec and Kate Mortley (1993), 'The Doing of Fiction', *Review of Contemporary Fiction*, vol. 13, no. 1, p. 27.
21. Georges Perec (2002), 'Comings and Goings in rue de l'Assomption', trans. Andrew Leak, *AA Files*, no. 45/46, p. 59.
22. Gilbert Adair (1993), 'The Eleventh Day: Perec and the Infra-ordinary', *Review of Contemporary* Fiction, vol. 13, no.1, p. 105.
23. Depaule and Getzler, 'A City in Words and Numbers', p. 127.
24. Depaule and Getzler, 'A City in Words and Numbers', pp. 117, 124.
25. Perec, 'Comings and Goings in rue de l'Assomption', p. 58, p. 59.
26. Kate Morris (2008), 'Perec's Alternative Topography: Figuring Permanence and the Ephemeral in Lieux', *Octopus*, vol. 4, p. 34.
27. Morris, 'Perec's Alternative Topography', p. 33.
28. Georges Perec (1997), 'Species of Spaces (1974)', in *Georges Perec, Species of Spaces and Other Pieces*, ed. and trans. John Sturrock, Harmondsworth: Penguin, p. 91.
29. Perec, 'Species of Spaces', p. 45.
30. Perec, 'Species of Spaces', p. 48.
31. Perec, 'Species of Spaces', p. 56.
32. Francesca Hughes (2014), *The Architecture of Error: Matter, Measure, and the Misadventures of Precision*, Cambridge, MA: MIT Press, p. 163.
33. Anthony Vidler (2007), 'Reading the City: The Urban Book from Mercier to Mitterand', *PMLA*, vol. 22, no. 1, Special Topic: Cities, p. 235.
34. Kate Morris (2008), 'Perec's Alternative Topography: Figuring Permanence and the Ephemeral in Lieux', *Octopus*, vol. 4.
35. Peta Mitchell (2004), 'Constructing the Architext: Georges Perec's Life a User's Manual', *Mosaic*, vol. 37, no. 1, p. 2.
36. Mitchell, 'Constructing the Architext', p. 3.
37. Hughes, *The Architecture of Error*, p. 209.
38. Enrique Walker (2014), 'Dictionary of Received Ideas', *Columbia Abstract*, Columbia University, available at: http://abstract20122013.gsapp.org/dictionary-of-received-ideas/.
39. Enrique Walker (2010), 'Constraints', in *Architecture as a Craft: Architecture, Drawing, Model and Position*, M. Riedijk (ed.), Amsterdam: SUN Architecture Publishers, pp. 25–34.
40. Enrique Walker (2005), 'Decisions', *Volume*, no. 1/1, p. 68.
41. David Goodman (2005), 'Systematic Genius: Walter Netsch and the Architecture of Bureaucracy', in Charles Waldheim, and Katrina Rüedi Ray (eds), *Chicago Architecture: Histories, Revisions, Alternatives*, Chicago: University of Chicago Press, pp. 261–84.
42. Martin Felsen and Sarah Dunn (2005), 'Walter Netsch: Field Theory', in Charles Waldheim and Katrina Rüedi Ray (eds), *Chicago Architecture: Histories, Revisions, Alternatives*, Chicago: University of Chicago Press, p. 254.
43. Walter A. Netsch (1958), 'Objectives in Design Problems', *Journal of Architectural Education*, vol. 13, no. 2, p. 46.
44. Walter A. Netsch (1980), 'A New Museum by Walter Netsch of SOM Given Order by His Field Theory', *Architectural Record*, no. 167, p. 118.

45. William G. Jones (1990), 'Academic Library Planning: Rationality, Imagination, and Field Theory in the Work of Walter Netsch – A Case Study', *Academic Library Planning: College and Research Libraries*, May, p. 217.
46. Jones, 'Academic Library Planning', p. 219.
47. Walter A. Netsch (1987), *Patent US 4651993 A, Design Game and Modules for Use Therein*, 24 March.
48. John Hejduk (1985), 'Frame 7', *Mask of Medusa*, New York: Rizzoli, p. 129.
49. Rudolf Wittkower (1962), *Architectural Principles in the Age of Humanism*, New York: W. W. Norton.
50. Anthony Vidler (1992), *The Architectural Uncanny: Essays in the Modern Unhomely*, Cambridge, MA: MIT Press, p. 118.
51. Vidler, *The Architectural Uncanny*, p. 118.
52. Michael Sorkin (1991), *Exquisite Corpse: Writings on Buildings*, London: Verso, p. 38.
53. Peter Eisenman (2005), 'The Silence of Excess', *Holocaust Memorial Berlin: Eisenman Architects*, Baden: Lars Müller, p. 4.
54. Bernard Tschumi (1983), 'Sequences', *Princeton Journal*, no. 1, p. 20.
55. Bernard Tschumi (1984), 'Madness and the Combative', *Precis*, no. 5, p. 153.
56. Tschumi, 'Madness and the Combative', 153.
57. Sanford Kwinter (1996), 'Can One Go Beyond Piranesi?', in Cynthia Davidson (ed.), *Eleven Authors in Search of a Building: The Aronoff Center for Design and Art at the University of Cincinnati*, New York: Monacelli Press, p. 158.
58. Lucretius, ii, 251 (1994), trans. Brad Inwood and L. P. Gerson, *The Epicurus Reader*, Indianapolis: Hackett, p. 66.
59. Harry Mathews (1998), 'Clinamen', in Harry Mathews and Alastair Brotchie (eds), *Oulipo Compendium*, London: Atlas Press, p. 126.
60. Alejandro Zaera-Polo (2008), 'The Politics of the Envelope: A Political Critique of Materialism', *Volume*, no. 17, p. 79.
61. Doug Rickard, *Artist Website: Doug Rickard*, available at: http://www.dougrickard.com/.

CHAPTER 11

Georges Perec: A Player's Manual

Thomas Apperley

This chapter explores the well-established attribute of playfulness in Perec's work, a quality exemplified in his 1978 novel, *Life A User's Manual*.[1] In Perec's *oeuvre*, *Life A User's Manual* is the culmination of experimentation with writing through play, games, rules, constraints and contingency. In addition to the many commentators that have noted his interest in play, Perec himself acknowledged that the ludic was one of the techniques of inquiry he used in his writing.[2] The themes and structure of the novel resonate with contemporary discussions of player agency, through the creative use of contingency and constraint in relation to an algorithmic structure, and this attribute of playfulness and experimentation in his work suggests an unintended and enduring afterlife for Perec's work in Game Studies and critical literature on digital games. Perec's work also flags an important and enduring issue for Game Studies: the contentious role that the digitally coded algorithm has in shaping player agency.

No research on Perec can proceed without covering ground opened for exploration by David Bellos's excellent biography, *George Perec: A Life in Words*. By looking across Perec's *oeuvre*, Bellos establishes that play and games have an important place in his life and works.[3] By tracing the ground laid by Bellos, this chapter moves in new directions to explore the unusual parallels between Perec's work and the concerns of Game Studies. As Marcel Bénabou notes, it is extremely difficult to make an overarching claim about Perec's *oeuvre* with any interpretation of his work being 'only one of the possible "Perecquian Paths"' that may be taken.[4] To use the metaphor of the humble filing card database of which Perec was a master: by pushing a pin through our stack of cards, we can expose new relations from existing data.

This examination begins by fleshing out the contexts from which Perec's attentiveness to the ludic arose: his childhood and early experiences; his day job as an archivist and database designer; and his experimentation with constrained writing through his association with Oulipo. The chapter then proceeds to examine the writing process he used in *Life A User's Manual*, and how these processes are emphasised through the themes of the novel, particularly the failed attempts by the novel's protagonist to create an overarching, programmatic vision of life.

PEREC AND GAME STUDIES

McKenzie Wark was the first to note the peculiar relevance of Perec to the emerging discipline of Game Studies.[5] In particular, he has suggested that the portrayal of a 'perverse "ludic" universe' in *W or The Memory of Childhood*,[6] is of particular significance for scholars of digital games. The novel, through its elaborate descriptions of a sporting community, gradually exposes the connection between play, competition, sadism, control and fascism.[7] This point resonates strongly with contemporary scholarship of digital games that considers their connection with control.[8] The novel also has an element of structural play as it requires the reader to reassemble the multiple parallel narratives.[9] Briefly, one of the interwoven storylines of *W or The Memory of Childhood* explores the 'horrifying absurdities of sport',[10] through a 'parody of a "ludic" society'.[11] This playful element, in concord with other parallel storylines, is used to explore some aspects of the experience and concept of 'lack'[12] and serves as a monument or site of mourning to Perec's parents. Both his parents died during the Second World War, his father during the invasion of France by the Germans and his mother after being deported to Auschwitz.[13] *Life A User's Manual*, in which play is a central theme, examines further aspects of the ludic. While *W or The Memory of Childhood* could be considered a 'parable of corrupted play',[14] an illustration of the creative element of play destroyed by absolute adherence to the rules, in *Life A User's Manual* play and chance become techniques for operating creatively within rule-based systems.

In part, the relevance of Perec for Game Studies is derived from the context in which he writes. This is prior to widespread domestic ownership of computers and video game consoles, yet also when there was burgeoning interest among intellectuals regarding the social impact of these technologies.[15] Perec is linked to a number of his scholarly contemporaries through a common concern with the rapidly changing French lifestyle in the post-Second World War period such as: the reorganisation of rural workforces into 'new towns',[16] the growth of 'post-industrial' forms of labour,[17] and the increasing prevalence of advertising in public and private spaces.[18] Information technologies were just in the process of being introduced to many industries and government administration systems. They were in the early stages of being adopted as forms of entertainment, through videogame arcades open to the public and domestic use of videogame consoles and early home computers. In the mid-1970s they were still far from becoming genuinely pervasive and ubiquitous. Yet, terms like Lefebvre's 'Bureaucratic Society of Controlled Consumption'[19] and Touraine's 'Post-Industrial Society'[20] gestured, alongside Perec's work, towards a new understanding of the centrality of information technology in everyday life.

As contemporary culture moved towards a logic that is variously described as 'algorithmic',[21] 'computational'[22] or of 'control',[23] the core concern with the centrality of information technologies remained, but intensified in response to their increasing ubiquity and pervasiveness. As bodies, space and time became increasingly coordinated by information technologies, the social practices of play – particularly digital play – came to be experienced and understood less and less as something that stood apart from other spheres of life. While 'play' had often been considered a critical and disruptive force in twentieth-century studies,[24] information technology effectively recuperated play into the logic of domination.[25] Alexander Galloway provides a persuasive account of this issue in *Gaming: Essays on Algorithmic Culture*, where, through a discussion of *Sid Meier's Civilization III*, he argues that digital games illustrate the disjuncture between textual or ideological analysis and a critique of the algorithmic processes of the software. While the game can be 'read' by the player, each action taken or choice that they make is signalled to the computer as a new piece of data to include in its algorithm. The action might mean something significant to the player, but in the game software it is only recognised mathematically. The bottom line is that all potential meanings and actions are constrained and contained within the algorithm, play is no longer 'outside' and it has lost its potential for critique.

This stance is not adopted by all game scholars. Digital anthropologist Thomas Malaby emphasises that play is characterised by the generation of 'new practices or new meanings, which may in turn transform the way the game is played'.[26] This chapter argues that, in *Life A User's Manual*, Perec implicitly adopts a similar position and even offers scope for questioning the dominant computational logic of our era, even if it is a muffled echo emanating from a past less inundated by information technologies. Thus, Perec's novel speaks to what has become an ongoing issue for Game Studies: to what extent can the acts of the player be considered creative if they are within the parameters of a digitally coded algorithm?

FROM PLAY TO WORK: PEREC, OULIPO AND THE DATABASE

Play had an important role in Perec's family life. While he lost his parents at an early age, he knew of his father's love of cards and gambling from his paternal aunt and adoptive mother, Esther Bienenfeld.[27] Card games were an important part of family gatherings,[28] and also served a significant function in the pearl trading business of his uncle, David Bienenfeld.[29] As an adult, Perec often made mention of his passion for cards, jigsaw puzzles and board games like *Monopoly* and *Scrabble* in his unpublished writings and notes.[30] In his early days as a student of History at the Sorbonne (1955–6) he developed an 'obsession' with pinball – which was known colloquially as *flippers* or *tilts* – that came to border on 'addiction'.[31] It was during this period of fascination with *tilts* that he began to use a ludic metaphor to describe his life:

> Georges would often hold forth mock-philosophically that his life could be compared to the brief and violent path of a ball in a tilt, rejected unpredictably by one blinking spring-loaded pin after another before plunging – too soon! – into the black hole where all balls must eventually come to rest.[32]

The material traces left on his body during these binges with pinball – 'blisters on his button fingers and sores on his thumbs' as well as 'headaches' – helped him to ignore the other forms of pain in his life.[33] His metaphor for life through *tilts* emphasises the senseless, even brutal, elements of play that were later explored in *W or The Memory of Childhood*.

As he drifted away from study into a more bohemian, intellectual lifestyle, Perec cultivated a group of friends, dubbed the 'magnetic bunch', who shared his passion for games and jigsaw puzzles.[34] But, despite his clear enjoyment of their shared pastimes, Perec was not usually the outstanding champion:

> Perec was a player from the start, and could lose himself totally in a game of poker, belote, *le barbu*, bridge, Scrabble, Monopoly, or patience. Oddly enough, he was never more than a mediocre player of any of these games, and often lost to friends with more guile, or more skill, or perhaps just more brains. He was never much of a cheater, except when playing against himself.[35]

His obsession with playing games sometimes led to friction among the group.[36] But it was his preoccupation with the Japanese board game *Go* that eventually raised the concern of his closest confidants.[37] *Go* was far more than just a distraction for Perec. In Chapter 94 of *Life A User's Manual*, 'On the Stairs, 12', the *Go* position 'Ko' is listed as one of the items found on the staircase in the form of 'seven marble lozenges, four black and three white'.[38] The rule of Ko is significant as it overrides the typical rules for the placement of *Go* pieces by preventing a stalemate where the exchange of pieces can continue indefinitely. As an intervention designed to break a deadlock, Ko is particularly evocative considering that Perec argued that playing *Go* can be compared to writing.[39] If *Go* can be compared to writing, then a variation in the rules like Ko suggests that it is appropriate to 'break' or change the rules in order to proceed. Employing rules to constrain writing was not simply about following rules and discovering where that would take him, it was also about *developing new rules that refined the process* and moved him onto new challenges, rather than rehearsing and repeating the same old moves. Making meta-rules for how to write became almost important as writing itself, and became an increasingly important part of his exploration of contingency in his writing.[40]

From 1961 to 1978, Perec worked for a large neurophysiology research laboratory in Paris as a *documentaliste* (archivist). His first role was to design an indexing system for the specialised scientific journals to which the laboratory subscribed. He quickly developed a fascination for indexing systems and the system of indexing he eventually implemented, 'Flambo', was greatly admired by his scientific colleagues.[41] In 1965, his laboratory moved to larger premises and Perec was tasked with developing a larger, more elaborate database, which he called 'Peekaboo'. The new database included a few ludic touches: one index card described his novel *Things: A Story of the Sixties*, and he often introduced humorous errors into bibliographies and texts he was working on for his scientific colleagues.[42] Such high jinks suggest Perec was already thinking about how to apply knowledge and skill he had for database design to create game-like structures which would allow him to explore fiction in a procedural, generative and ultimately playful manner. It appears he was reasonably invested in experimenting with this disruptive playfulness, because, while his colleagues took his antics with good humour, Perec wasted precious writing time removing these glitches he had deliberately introduced.[43] Through playing around with databases and simple algorithms, Perec discovered new ways to engineer contingency in order to uncover chance connections, relations and patterns between various ideas, people, objects and events.

In late 1968, Perec was commissioned by the Computing Service of the Humanities Research Centre in Paris to 'explore the literary potential of the algorithm'.[44] Perec's task was to turn an algorithm, in the form of a flow chart that represented the steps to be taken in order to obtain a pay raise by a lowly member of a large bureaucracy, into a literary work. This was eventually published in 1968 as *The Art and Craft of Approaching Your Head of Department to Submit a Request for a Raise*; a revised version of the literary algorithm found its way into *Life A User's Manual*. Chapter 98, 'Réol, 2', describes the tragic-comic tale of Maurice and Louise Réol, and Maurice's year-long efforts to secure a raise in the face of crippling household debts.[45] This successful experiment in literary computing ironically presages the outmoding of Perec's archival skills. By 1975, Perec's role as a virtuoso index card database designer and manager had become rather precarious.[46] By this time, newer databases were managed using computers and his once lauded Peekaboo system became old-fashioned. Perec refused to undergo retraining as a computer database operator and, as he had tenure at the laboratory as an archivist, was able to ignore the pressure from his colleagues to resign, which created 'an awkward, irksome stalemate'.[47] Indeed, this stalemate shaped Perec's everyday experience while he was writing the manuscript for *Life A User's Manual* and continued until he was able to retire and write full-time in 1978, following the success of the novel.

Perec joined Oulipo or *Ouvroir de Littérature Potentielle* (Workshop for Potential Literature) in 1967.[48] The Oulipo met regularly in Paris from 1960, headed by Raymond Queneau, and together the group members conducted an exhaustive investigation of existing formal languages – mathematics, logic, computer science and chess – and how they might be used in poetry, and developed and explored various techniques of constrained writing. Constrained writing involved writing according to particular set rules, which, while limiting, also stimulated novel approaches and ideas through happenstance. While his interest in play and experimental writing predated his involvement with Oulipo,[49] Perec's involvement in the group helped him to cement his interest in rules for writing and provided him with a strong and supportive intellectual context to explore his interest in using games and play to create situations of contingency and unpredictability that would inspire his writing. Play became increasingly central to Perec's work after the publication of *Things: A Story of the Sixties* in 1965, although he had made reference to writing as a kind of game as far back as the 1950s. By 1967, when Perec was working on *A Void*, he was already insisting on a ludic approach to writing.[50] This novel was famously written without once using the letter 'e', a writing constraint that had begun as a word game that he played with his friends from 1967 onwards, which he also hoped would help him to overcome writer's block.[51] Perec's commitment to using constraints was peculiar; he was also fascinated by the notion that these constraints could be selectively ignored, that he could judiciously cheat against his own self-imposed rules.[52]

In other words, play had a crucial role in Perec's life – and not just as a memory from childhood. Beginning as a method of escapism or avoidance, play soon became something more significant: through the influence of Oulipo, he also began to experiment with playful forms of writing through the use of constraints or rules that shaped how or what he could write. During the course of his day job, Perec played with the organisation of databases until computers replaced the index card systems that he had helped design. These experiences demonstrate that *Life A User's Manual* was the culmination of many experiments he had undertaken with the use of technologically generated constraints to bring novel and inspiring contingencies to his writing process.

PLAYING *LIFE A USER'S MANUAL*

The book is structured through multiple constraining grids.[53] These are variously described as 'rigorous formal structures'[54] or 'pre-textual machinery',[55] or as a 'structure-machine'[56] or 'combinatory algorithm'.[57] These grids directed the novel's creation through the 'interplay of algorithm and literature'.[58] Constraint guided the 'creative effort'.[59] However, Perec's rules and systems did not rigidly dictate the content of the novel.[60] He also allowed himself considerable flexibility to subvert the rules of the system when he needed too. This was done by deliberately introducing 'mistakes' by breaking the rules he set for himself,[61] which established a considerable scope for creative freedom, 'in spite of the apparent rigidity of his lists'.[62] In *Life A User's Manual*, Perec both works within and plays with constraints. This can be found both in the structures and processes of his writing and in the literary themes of the novel.[63]

The structure of the novel's ninety-nine chapters is elaborated through a game-like procedure that mimics a chess puzzle. Each chapter focuses on describing one room and its contents and inhabitants, both past and present. The apartment building described in the novel – 11 Rue Simon-Crubellier – has ten levels (including a basement and two attic levels under the eaves of the roof) and Perec sets out to describe ten rooms from each of the ten levels which he maps out as a ten-by-ten grid.[64] He then proceeds to move around the grid of rooms, like a knight on a (extra-large) chessboard. By visiting each room – bar one – once, Perec replicates a classic chess puzzle, 'the Knight's Tour', using the puzzle to structure his novel. He also used a mathematical procedure, the 'bi-square', to set parameters over what would be included in each of the individual chapters (and rooms). This 'elaborate machinery' was used to dictate which items from forty-two lists were to be included in each chapter.[65] Perec had previously experimented with algorithms during his work on the short film *Les Lieux d'une fugue* (1975),[66] but for *Life A User's Manual* he employed a mathematician to develop a suitable algorithm for him to use to distribute the contents of the chapters.[67]

The central motif of the novel is the jigsaw puzzle.[68] The novel is carefully structured around this motif, leading it to be described as a 'novel-puzzle',[69] or 'static jigsaw puzzle', with each chapter constituting a piece.[70] Perec introduces this motif in the preamble to the novel which examines the art of jigsaw puzzles: 'Despite appearances, puzzling is not a solitary game, every move the puzzler makes, the puzzle-maker has made before.' The significance of jigsaws is highlighted later in the novel when the passage from the preamble is repeated in Chapter 44, 'Winckler, 2'.[71] This repetition emphasises the importance of the jigsaw puzzle as a framing device for the novel, while also highlighting the conflict between puzzle-maker and puzzler, which also symbolises the relationship between Perec and the reader of the book.[72]

A key character of the book, the eccentric British millionaire Percival Bartlebooth, has devised a programmatic schedule for his life.[73] This schedule is designed around the regular completion of jigsaw puzzles. Bartlebooth's attempt to execute absolute control over his life has also structured the lives of various inhabitants of the building: his assistant Smauft, who accompanied him on his travels around the globe to paint the watercolours which are made into jigsaw puzzles; Morellet, the chemist that restored the completed puzzles to a single canvas; Madame Hourcade, who made the puzzle boxes; and Valène, the artist that taught Bartlebooth how to paint. The most important employee is Gaspard Winckler, an artisan who creates a series of five hundred 750-piece jigsaw puzzles for Bartlebooth and, as the novel unfolds, is revealed to be his employer's nemesis.

Gaspard Winckler, the puzzle-maker, is a crucial figure in *Life A User's Manual*. He is an extremely skilled craftsman who works traps and perceptual illusions into the jigsaw puzzles he designs. Through his crafts, he establishes a dialogue with Bartlebooth, playing upon the expectations that Bartlebooth had developed over the previous puzzles he had completed. Despite working on the puzzle 'methodically', with the 'Cartesian rigour' of a 'chess player', 'each of Winckler's puzzles was a new, unique, and irreplaceable adventure for Bartlebooth'.[74] The character of Winckler (in name at least) also appears as Perec's slightly fictionalised alter-ego in the semi-autobiographical *W or The Memory of Childhood*. The presence of this character in both novels, *Life* and *W*, suggests that the connection between the two novels is not simply around the theme of play,[75] but also of creativity, as the creative processes of Winckler the puzzle-maker have much in common with those of Perec while he wrote *Life A User's Manual*.

In *Life A User's Manual*, Perec emphasises Winckler's skill and artistry, devoting several detailed passages to the technical processes of devising Bartlebooth's puzzles, itemising the inventory of Winckler's workshop and describing some of his other craft projects. He homes in on the specificity of the various jigsaw puzzle pieces, intimately describing various standard shapes and noting how Winckler preferred also to include unique shapes: 'a python, a mountain cat, and two fully formed elephants, one of the African (long-eared) variety, the other Indian, or a Charlie Chaplin'.[76] Through his skill in puzzle-making, Winckler has escaped the boredom of this apparently repetitive task[77] and usurped the 'authorship' of Bartlebooth's project.[78] For Game Studies,

Perec's interest in the artistry of the jigsaw puzzle has parallel's with the struggle to conceptualise digital games. The experience of playing digital games involves the integration of technical forms of information with audio, narrative and visual information; similarly, completing a jigsaw puzzle requires the integration of information from multiple sources. However, Perec suggests the experience of doing the jigsaw is just as much about understanding the forms of the individual pieces as it is about the fragment of the picture contained on each piece or, indeed, the picture as a whole. Here Perec's point resonates with Galloway's: the structural element of the jigsaw – the puzzle piece – is the key determining factor in the experience of doing a jigsaw. For digital games, this has strong resonance with the notion that their visual and narrative elements might also be more effectively understood in relation to the structures of software. The genius of *Life A User's Manual* is in how Perec is able to expose the inner mechanisms that he has used to create the novel, whereas digital games – and most other everyday software – still mostly conceal their inner workings. Perec's novel is a useful reminder that *process and product are not necessarily tidily discreet*, a point which is just as salient for scholars of digital games.

In a 1978 interview published in *Le Monde*, Perec states: 'Writing a novel is not like narrating something related directly to the real world. It's a matter of establishing a game between reader and writer'.[79] The 'game' that is established in *Life A User's Manual* is described by David Bellos as taking place between Bartlebooth, Valème and Winckler.[80] Space precludes discussion of Valème but, particularly for the theme of authorship, the relationship between Winckler, the puzzle master (Perec) and Bartlebooth (the reader) is crucial, as it sets up a game between Perec and the reader.[81] In the competition between Winckler and Bartlebooth (but not necessarily between Perec and the reader), the puzzle-maker bests his employer. This is because Winckler's puzzles are unexpectedly difficult, forcing Bartlebooth to proceed more slowly than his schedule had anticipated, and also due to unforeseen circumstances and human fragility as he gradually lost his sight, making it even more difficult to complete the puzzles to schedule. Ultimately, Bartlebooth dies without completing his goal. In the execution of the process of completing his task, it is apparent that he was immersed in a programmatic logic which could not account for human frailty, error or 'inevitably changing circumstances'.[82] Ultimately, Bartlebooth fails at this game because he cannot reincorporate the fragments *according to his programme*. Perec, however, builds errors into his novel, celebrating failure by recognising how it can be used creatively to take a project beyond the limits imposed by systemic logic. Accordingly, for Game Studies, this relationship suggests, along the lines of Malaby, that contingency is a reservoir of creativity for game players. Indeed, any scholarly exploration of game cultures will attest to myriad and elaborate practices which are developed by players rather than designed.[83]

W or The Memory of Childhood adhered strongly to the internal logics of the constraints he imposed on his writing. However, in *Life A User's Manual*, by embracing the mistake, Perec demonstrates a different approach to the technique. He was fascinated by 'writing with rules and with the exhaustive completion of self-devised schemes and grids', but always sought to 'communicate a human experience of the world' through this process.[84] The playful structures of the novel did not dictate, they were to provoke the aleatory.[85] By playing with the rules he imposed, Perec explored the possibilities of contingency and constraint within the dominant logic of the 'bureaucratic society of controlled consumption'. He demonstrated how space for life and lived experience was carved out from within the machine-like structures of directives and procedures.

CONCLUSION

Several elements of Perec's life suggest a special place for play in his work. His own well-documented interest in games and puzzles was later shaped and turned towards literature and work through his involvement with Oulipo and his employment as a database designer and archivist. This provides a biographical backdrop for understanding the centrality of play in *Life A User's Manual* which deploys play as a key metaphor that frames and organises both the process through which the novel was written and its finished form. Written at a tipping point between the computer being largely confined to government and a few industries and becoming an everyday workplace and domestic appliance, the novel demonstrates how contingency within a system can provide space for creative acts. This issue endures in Game Studies. While the digital networks of gaming online worlds are shaped by algorithms, *Life A User's Manual* would insist that players can do something more than just enact a pre-existing potential, they may also develop new practices which are formed through contingency and discovery.

ACKNOWLEDGEMENTS

Thanks to Rafael Bienia, Hugh Davies, Robbie Fordyce, Christian Gelder, Laurie Johnson, Veli-Matti Karhulahti, Thomas Malaby, Laetitia Nanquette and Samuel Tobin for their comments on an earlier version of this chapter.

NOTES

1. Kimberly Bohman-Kalaja (2007), *Reading Games: An Aesthetics of Play in Flann O'Brien, Samuel Beckett and Georges Perec*, Victoria, TX: Dalkey Archive Press; David Gascoigne (2009), *The Games of Fiction: Georges Perec and Modern French Ludic Narrative*, Oxford: Peter Lang; Alison James (2009), *Constraining Chance: Georges Perec and the Oulipo*, Evanstown: Northwestern University Press.
2. Michael Sheringham (2006), *Everyday Life: Theories and Practices from Surrealism to the Present*, Oxford: Oxford University Press, p. 248.
3. Bellos's observation is supported by several recent book-length projects that mark the connection between Perec, play and chance: Bohman-Kalaja, *Reading Games*; Gascoigne, *The Games of Fiction*; James, *Constraining Chance*.
4. Marcel Bénabou (2004), 'From Jewishness to the Aesthetics of Lack', trans. Brian J. Reilly, *Yale French Studies*, no. 105, p. 22.
5. McKenzie Wark (2006), *Gamer Theory*, Cambridge, MA: Harvard University Press, p. 116; McKenzie Wark (2012), *Telethesia: Communication, Culture and Class*, Malden, MA: Polity, p. 91.
6. Gascoigne, *The Games of Fiction*, p. 182.
7. Philippe Lejeune (2009), '*W or The Memory of Childhood*', trans. David Bellos, *Review of Contemporary Fiction*, vol. 29, no. 1, p. 164.
8. See: Thomas Apperley (2010), *Gaming Rhythms: Play and Counterplay from the Situated to the Global*, Amsterdam: Institute of Network Cultures, p. 37; Alexander Galloway (2007), 'StarCraft, or Balance', *Grey Room*, vol. 28, p. 87.
9. Gascoigne, *The Games of Fiction*, p. 173.
10. Warren Motte (1984), *The Poetics of Experiment: A Study of the Work of Georges Perec*, Lexington, KY: French Forum, p. 56.
11. Gascoigne, *The Games of Fiction*, p. 309.
12. Bénabou, 'From Jewishness to the Aesthetics of Lack', pp. 20–35; Marcel Bénabou (2009), 'Perec's Jewishness', trans. David Bellos, *Review of Contemporary Fiction*, vol. 9, no. 1, pp. 148–62.
13. Warren Motte (2004), 'The Work of Mourning', *Yale French Studies*, no. 105, pp. 56–71.
14. Bohman-Kalaja, *Reading Games*, p. 202.
15. Michael Sheringham (2000), 'Attending to the Everyday: Blanchot, Lefebvre, Certeau, Perec', *French Studies*, vol. 54, no. 2, p. 187–99. See also: David Bellos (1993), *Georges Perec: A Life in Words*, Boston: David R. Godine, p. 292; Michael Sheringham (2005), 'The Project and the Everyday: François Bon's Experiments with Attention', in Johnnie Gratton and Michael Sheringham (eds), *The Art of the Project: Projects and Experiments in Modern French Culture*, New York: Berghahn, pp. 188–203; Sheringham, *Everyday Life*, p. 248.
16. Henri Lefebvre (1995), *Introduction to Modernity: Twelve Preludes, September 1959–May 1961*, trans. John Moore, London: Verso.
17. Alain Touraine (1971), *The Post-Industrial Society*, New York: Random House.
18. Guy Debord (2000), *Society of the Spectacle*, Kalamazoo: Black & Red.
19. Henri Lefebvre (1971), *Everyday Life in the Modern World*, trans. Sacha Rabinovitch, New York: Harper.
20. Touraine, *The Post-Industrial Society*.
21. A. Aneesh (2006), *Virtual Migration: The Programming of Globalization*, Durham, NC: Duke University Press; Alexander Galloway (2006), *Gaming: Essays on Algorithmic Culture*, Minneapolis: University of Minnesota Press.

22. David Golumbia (2009), *The Cultural Logic of Computation*, Cambridge, MA: Harvard University Press.
23. James R. Beniger (1986), *The Control Revolution: Technological and Economic Origins of the Information Society*, Cambridge, MA: Harvard University Press; Giles Deleuze (1995), *Negotiations*, New York: Columbia University Press.
24. For example: Graeme Kirkpatrick (2013), *Computer Games and the Social Imaginary*, Cambridge: Polity Press; Sven Lütticken (2010), 'Playtimes', *New Left Review*, no. 66.
25. Apperley, *Gaming Rhythms*; Kirkpatrick, *Computer Games and the Social Imaginary*; Lev Manovich (2008), 'The Practice of Everyday (Media) Life', in Geert Lovink and Sabine Niederer (eds), *Video Vortex Reader: Responses to YouTube*, Amsterdam: Institute of Network Cultures, pp. 33–42.
26. Thomas Malaby (2007), 'Beyond Play: A New Approach to Games', *Games and Culture*, vol. 2, no. 2, p. 103.
27. Bellos, *Georges Perec*, p. 29.
28. Bellos, *Georges Perec*, p. 34.
29. Bellos, *Georges Perec*, p. 113.
30. Bellos, *Georges Perec*, cards (pp. 113, 137, 239, 282, 300, 302, 344, 395, 405), jigsaw puzzles (p. 302), *Monopoly* (pp. 91, 239, 344), *Scrabble* (pp. 239, 273, 282, 290, 344, 533).
31. Bellos, *Georges Perec*, p. 138.
32. Bellos, *Georges Perec*, pp. 137–8.
33. Bellos, *Georges Perec*, p. 138.
34. Bellos, *Georges Perec*, p. 282.
35. Bellos, *Georges Perec*, p. 344.
36. Bellos, *Georges Perec*, p. 248.
37. Bellos, *Georges Perec*, p. 335, p. 408.
38. Georges Perec (2008), *Life A User's Manual*, trans. David Bellos, London: Vintage, p. 467.
39. Pierre Lusson, Georges Perec and Jacques Roubaud (1969), *Traité invitant à la découverte de l'art subtil du go*, Paris: Christian Bougois. See also Motte, 'Georges Perec on the Grid', pp. 823–4.
40. For discussion of meta-rules in digital games see: Marcus Carter, Martin Gibbs and Mitchell Harrop (2012), 'Metagames, Paragames and Orthogames: A New Vocabulary', in the *Collected Papers of Foundations of Digital Games*, Raleigh, North Carolina, May 29–June 1.
41. Bellos, *Georges Perec*, p. 255.
42. Bellos, *Georges Perec*, p. 259.
43. Bellos, *Georges Perec*, p. 262.
44. Bellos, *Georges Perec*, p. 409.
45. Perec, *Life A User's Manual*, pp. 484–93.
46. Bellos, *Georges Perec*, p. 290.
47. Bellos, *Georges Perec*, p. 266.
48. Motte, 'Georges Perec on the Grid', p. 821.
49. Bellos, *Georges Perec*, p. 344.
50. Sheringham, *Everyday Life*, p. 252.
51. Bellos, *Georges Perec*, p. 395.
52. Bellos, *Georges Perec*, p. 596.
53. Motte, 'Georges Perec on the Grid', p. 822.
54. Bohman-Kalaja, *Reading Games*, p. 161.
55. Gascoigne, *The Games of Fiction*, p. 200.
56. Bohman-Kalaja, *Reading Games*, p. 163.

57. James, *Constraining Chance*, p. 142.
58. Motte, 'Georges Perec on the Grid', p. 832; see also Gascoigne, *The Games of Fiction*, p. 215.
59. Motte, 'Georges Perec on the Grid', p. 832.
60. Gascoigne, *The Games of Fiction*, p. 203; Motte, 'Georges Perec on the Grid', p. 822.
61. Bohman-Kalaja, *Reading Games*, p. 171; James, *Constraining Chance*, p. 142.
62. Bohman-Kalaja, *Reading Games*, p. 171.
63. James, *Constraining Chance*, p. 156.
64. Perec, *Life A User's Manual*, p. 501. See also Bohman-Kalaja, *Reading Games*, pp. 162–3.
65. Bellos, *Georges Perec*, p. 603.
66. Motte, 'Georges Perec on the Grid', p. 830.
67. Sheringham, *Everyday Life*, p. 258.
68. Bohman-Kalaja, *Reading Games*, p. 201; Motte, 'Georges Perec on the Grid', p. 829.
69. Bohman-Kalaja, *Reading Games*, p. 165.
70. Gascoigne, *The Games of Fiction*, p. 219.
71. Gascoigne, *The Games of Fiction*, p. 243; James, *Constraining Chance*, p. 180.
72. Bohman-Kalaja, *Reading Games*, p. 216; Gascoigne, *The Games of Fiction*, p. 235.
73. Gascoigne, *The Games of Fiction*, p. 240.
74. Perec, *Life A User's Manual*, pp. 332–3.
75. Bohman-Kalaja, *Reading Games*, p. 215.
76. Perec, *Life A User's Manual*, pp. 334.
77. Bohman-Kalaja, *Reading Games*, p. 227.
78. Gascoigne, *The Games of Fiction*, p. 242.
79. Georges Perec (1978), 'Interview with Jacqueline Piatier', *Le monde*, 29 September.
80. Bellos, *Georges Perec*, p. 632.
81. Bohman-Kalaja, *Reading Games*, p. 199; Gascoigne, *The Games of Fiction*, p. 271; Motte, 'Georges Perec on the Grid', p. 823.
82. Bohman-Kalaja, *Reading Games*, p. 219.
83. Apperley, *Gaming Rhythms*; Mia Consalvo (2007), *Cheating: Gaining Advantage in Videogames*, Cambridge, MA: MIT Press; Alan Meades (2015), *Understanding Counterplay in Video Games*, New York: Routledge.
84. David Bellos (2011), 'Introduction', in Georges Perec, *The Art and Craft of Approaching Your Head of Department to Submit a Request for a Raise*, trans. David Bellos, London: Vintage, p. xix.
85. Bohman-Kalaja, *Reading Games*, p. 208.

PART IV

Productive Problems of Description and Transcription

CHAPTER 12

'An Attempt at Exhausting an Augmented Place in Paris': Georges Perec, Observer-Writer of Urban Life, as a Mobile Locative Media User

Christian Licoppe

> So now, at a time when others are asleep, Mr G. is bending over a table, darting on to a sheet the same glance that a moment ago he was directing towards external things ... And the external world is reborn upon his paper.[1]

INTRODUCTION

The modern metropolis has been aptly described as a place of, and a place for, strangers,[2] where strangers are expected to be 'thrown together'.[3] Charles Baudelaire's *flâneur* heralded the rise to dominance of the modern metropolis in the Western world. The way he used his leisurely gait functioned as a political sign of resistance against capitalistic and consumer concerns in the metropolis. On an experiential plane, the *flâneur* could immerse himself in the joys of being thrown together with anonymous strangers, of being an anonymous body lost in the crowd – that is, in the random flow of a multitude of other strangers:

> The crowd is his element, as the air is that of birds and water of fishes. His passion and his profession are to become one flesh with the crowd. For the perfect *flâneur*, for the passionate spectator, it is an immense joy to set up house in the heart of the multitude, amid the ebb and flow of movement, in the midst of the fugitive and the infinite. To be away from home and yet to feel oneself everywhere at home; to see the world, to be at the center of the world, and yet to remain hidden from the world – impartial natures which the tongue can but clumsily

define. The spectator is a prince who everywhere rejoices in his incognito.[4]

His delight was primarily visual, and his experience framed as an unpredictable succession of sights, which could be presented as lists of events intelligible to all, that is to any other stranger in the crowd. The *flâneur*'s conduct and the way it could be described systematically conjured up 'the "seen" and "witnessed" character of space and particularly urban space':[5]

> He delights in fine carriage and proud horses, the dazzling smartness of the grooms, the expertness of the footmen, the sinuous gait of the women, the beauty of the children, happy to be alive and nicely dressed – in a word, he delights in universal life.[6]

One century later, such an experience had become banal, no longer the stuff of a deeply aesthetic enjoyment. Understanding the behaviour of strangers in crowds had become a topic for interactionist sociology and the nascent Urban Studies. William H. Whyte thus tried to document visually the embodied arrangements of passing strangers on busy urban plazas in large American cities in an interesting early use of 'video-as-data'.[7] At around the same time, Erving Goffman was trying to bring to light the 'interaction order' which characterises 'interactions in public', and which, for instance, gives rise to expected displays of 'civil inattention' in the mingling of mobile strangers on the street.[8] Goffman's attention to the visual surface organisation of interactions in public also testified in its way to the centrality of 'the "seen" and "witnessed" character' of urban public places and the life forms they support. However, visuality and gaze are social constructions. Goffman showed how the fact that any event which occurs in the open could be treated as a spectacle for disengaged onlookers is a, if not the, constitutive feature of urban spaces and interactions in public as such:

> When individuals are engaged in playing a sport or a board game, repairing a car, or constructing a building, bystanders will often blatantly watch the proceedings and be suffered in this status of onlookers by those upon whom they are looking. It is this onlooker status that becomes available whenever one has an accident or creates a scene; indeed the creation of these rights of open looking constitutes one of the chief costs of getting into trouble in public.[9]

At about the same time, in Paris, Georges Perec was engaged in a literary project which seemed to resonate deeply with the urban sociology of the time. He decided to sit at the terrace of a Parisian cafe three days in a row in 'an attempt at exhausting a place in Paris'. His aim was to try to describe everything that would pass or happen in front of his eyes in Place Saint-Sulpice, 'everything' being here taken as a string of ordinary and visual happenings:

> My intention in the pages that follow was to describe the rest instead: that which is generally not taken note of, that which is not noticed, that which has no importance: what happens when nothing happens other than the weather, people, cars and clouds.[10]

Though it retains a link with Baudelaire's writer-*flâneur*, the experience of which also involved an enumeration of encounters from a disengaged perspective, Perec's endeavour nevertheless differs in two important respects. First, it is framed as an attempt at exhaustiveness, that is as a consciously self-defeating effort to encompass the whole of the fleeting urban experience and to account for it in writing. Second, Perec as a writing observer does not delight in the spectacle he recounts, nor does he glamorise his experience. Perec's inventories are written in a monotonous tone, mostly devoid of emotion. As I will discuss below, the force of his attempt is founded on the coherence of his stance as a neutral onlooker, both when gazing at Saint-Sulpice square and when writing, and the framing of the reader as a similar onlooker, precisely achieved through the 'neutral' and impersonal commonsensicality of his descriptions. In that sense, Perec's literary project parallels Goffman's urban sociology in extolling the city as a place for anonymous crowds, the conduct of which is designed to be open and meaningful to the neutral and disengaged onlooker. Both authors insist on urban locales as lived public places, and highlight the onlooker's stance as constitutive of their 'public' character.

In this chapter, I will use Perec's work as a starting point for a thought experiment. I will try to imagine a high-tech reincarnation of Perec equipped with a smartphone and himself an active user of mobile locative media, who would attempt today to emulate his earlier, unconnected counterpart's project in Place Saint-Sulpice. The point of such a thought experiment is to make perceptible some of the shifts which the possible – and probable – development of mobile locative media might bring to the framing of the city as an assemblage of public places criss-crossed by large fluxes of anonymous bodies and vehicular units, always open to the impersonal and commonsensical gaze of the onlooker. Unlike the contemporary metropolis, the future augmented city will instead appear as a set of hybrid ecologies, simultaneously public and 'parochial'[11] and populated by 'pseudonymous strangers', that is hybrid entities who have the visual appearance of embodied anonymous strangers but who are also simultaneously available on screen as individualised digital personae. An attempt by a connected Perec to exhaust an augmented public place would thus constitute a very different kind of project involving descriptions of augmented urban places yet to be designed, and whose literary coherence would be of a different order.

To give a concrete character to such a thought experiment, I have imagined that our connected Perec is also an active user of Foursquare. Although the mobile application evolved into a spatial search and recommendation application in 2014,[12] Foursquare was initially a location-aware mobile social networking application in which people could formulate places in generic or personalised terms,[13] localised within the application, and into which they could check when nearby. The social meaning of such an action has been the object of extensive research.[14] Moreover, the application involved some gamification of mobile social networking, as it allowed competition between users who could become virtual 'mayors' of such virtual places if they were the ones to check into them the most.[15] Beyond the particulars of its design, Foursquare will be taken here as a typical exemplar of location aware mobile social networking media, prominently displaying a central feature of mobile locative media, that is providing mobile urban denizens with an onscreen representation of the people and places around them.[16] The data mentioned in this paper was gathered in the course of an earlier study in which we actually connected to Foursquare in Place Saint-Sulpice to 'see' what a connected Perec of today might 'see' there.

THE 'FAMILIARISATION' AND 'PAROCHIALISATION' OF URBAN PUBLIC PLACES

Perec's opening lines involve a description of what the gaze of the sitter might encounter in Place Saint-Sulpice:

> There are many things in Place Saint-Sulpice; for instance: a district council building, a financial building, a police station, three cafés, one of which sells tobacco and stamps, a movie theater, a church on which Le Vau, Gittard, Oppenord, Servandoni, and Chalgrin have all worked, and which is dedicated to a chaplain of Clotaire II, who was bishop of Bourges from 624 to 644 and whom we celebrate on 17 January, a publisher, a funeral parlor, a travel agency, a bus stop, a tailor, a hotel, a fountain decorated with the statues of four great Christian orators (Bossuet, Fénelon, Fléchier, and Massilion), a newsstand, a seller of pious objects, a parking lot, a beauty parlor, and many other things as well.[17]

The way Perec describes what there is or can be seen on a permanent basis in Saint-Sulpice square frames the relationship between him and his reader and their mutual stance in a very specific way. He describes the buildings and their function in categorical terms that are available and recognisable by any member of the public going there for the first time: a police station, a cafe, a church, etc. The things that he mentions which he probably cannot see as a sitting character (e.g. the fact that one of the cafe also sells stamps) also make sense on the basis of common-sense categorisation. One 'knows' on such a basis that the cafes which sell cigarettes in France (visually recognisable through a sign) usually also sell stamps. Similarly, the historical references which Perec associates with some of these milestones are framed in the style of guidebooks, which are made for a readership of touring strangers. They also point to the *Histoire de France* manuals, which at the time still epitomised the French public primary education system, through references to the kind of famous historical figures which find their way both in such manuals and in the public space in the form of architectural milestones.

Such a description of a Parisian square therefore eliminates all traces of personalisation and possible familiarity with the place. It frames the writer as an onlooker for whom the events in the street are a public spectacle and the place a public space container for such events which are supposed to unfold 'in' it. The square appears as an objectivised vessel for passing strangers who are to remain somehow disconnected from, and potentially unaffected by, the place itself. In that frame, Place Saint-Sulpice, as described by Perec, appears as a juxtaposition of buildings, places and things visually available and reportable in a depersonalised way, which tightly fits the kind of perception that is expected of a readership endowed with the same competencies and experiences as passing strangers. The onlooking writer-stranger thus addresses other urban strangers, who are expected to view the city and understand urban places in, through and as generic descriptions and common-sense or institutional categorical terms. From the start the authorial voice frames itself as being also one of these strangers, albeit one sitting at an outside cafe and with the power to tell and write. The sitting author seems to be watching from a stylised distance which also insulates him from what may be going on. In all these respects, Perec's stance epitomises the nineteenth- and twentieth-century representations and experience of the western metropolis as a place of and for strangers.[18]

'SEEING' PLACES WHICH MIGHT BE 'HERE', BUT NOT THERE

What might a twenty-first century Perec, connected to a location-sensitive mobile social networking (LMSN) application like Foursquare, 'see' sitting on a cafe terrace, which, though ordinary, would still be worthy of a literary inventory? The difference between the actual, unconnected Perec and the connected Perec is that, for the latter, places may not only be available through gaze, but also through the screen of his smartphone. Based on the technology-mediated awareness of the user's location, the Foursquare interface provides a list of the places nearby. These appear on screen in a different way than they do to the sweeping gaze of the onlooker. First, 'places' are available on screen in a pre-organised fashion: they are already presented as an ordered list (as opposed to the list designed and provided by the unconnected Perec), with the 'trendiest' at the top, that is first those which several other users have already checked into, then those which the user has marked as 'favourite' and then the rest ranked by proximity. The connected Perec does not have to select places to create a written list any more, one is provided to him from the start, with which he can elect to align his own written list or which he might decide to resist by elaborating another, distinctive, written list of places. Second, the criterion for the onscreen presence of these places is not that they should be visible to a sitting observer, but that they have been created within the application (either by the designers or the users), and that they are close enough in terms of geolocation. Figures 12.1 and 12.2 show examples of what appeared on screen when one connected to Foursquare at a cafe in Place Saint-Sulpice at the time of our study. While some of the onscreen places are indeed visible from the cafe, others are not, being as they are features located in surrounding streets. The

Figure 12.1 (*left*) **and Figure 12.2** (*right*) These figures are scans from parts of the list of places which became visible on screen in 2013 when one connected to Foursquare from the same cafe terrace used by Perec. The places in Figure 12.1 are in the top part of the list and those in Figure 12.2 appear after some amount of scrolling down. Of note are the locations in nearby streets in both figures, and the highly indexical-relational formulation *soeur* ('sister') in Figure 12.

places which appear on screen to the connected Perec thus 'spill' beyond the immediately visible Saint-Sulpice vista available to the sitting beholder.

Third, and most importantly, surrounding places, whether actually visible or not, appear on screen in a textual and iconographic fashion. They come pre-packaged with descriptions or formulations as well as categorising icons (Figures 12.1 and 12.2). While such formulations may occasionally take the form of the formulations by strangers for strangers used by Perec, some other formulations embed and index the familiarity of their creator with a given locale (such as 'sister' in Figure 12.2 or elsewhere 'Roger's flat', 'home sweet home', etc.), or they may even take the shape of a localised event rather than a place. To capture this distinction, researchers in the Human Computer Interaction (HCI) field have used the distinction between 'geographical' formulations of places (guidebook-like and identifiable by all) and 'relational' formulations of places (indexical, and often only intelligible to a selected few), and have shown that a significant proportion of places 'created' in the application by users had a relational character.[19]

So, the connected Perec beholds onscreen places which he would not be able to see with his naked eyes and which 'spill' beyond the square that presents itself to his gaze as he sits. Some of these places are digitally formulated in non-generic and personalised terms, which would not fit the perspective of a stranger and would not find a place in a traditional tourist guidebook. 'Sister' makes relevant and enacts a separation between those who understand the reference, who know who is being referred to here and whose sister she might be, and those who are strangers, not just in the sense in which pedestrians in the streets may be strangers with respect to one another, but in the sense of being strangers with respect to the social group for which such a formulation is meaningful. Such formulations are relational for they enact an 'in-group' (encompassing all those for whom 'sister' is personally meaningful) and an 'out-group' (all the others). Because of the performative power of such formulations, the gaze of the connected Perec, who reads them on screen, loses the neutrality which characterised the unconnected Perec, gazing at publicly available urban fixtures. If he is unrelated to this particular 'sister', the connected Perec is turned into a member of the out-group with respect to the relational formulations of places which appear on his screen. Should he prolong his gazing, his gaze would now run the risk of turning voyeuristic (the voyeur gazes at intimate scenes that a stranger should not see or not stare at in this way), in a way that the gaze of the sitting and unconnected Perec contemplating strangers on the square could not become.

The public availability of such familiarity- and relation-oriented formulations of places is one aspect of the kind of 'parochialisation' of public places which is performed by mobile locative media,[20] and which makes it difficult to maintain the stance of the Goffmanian stranger gazing at public places perceptible and reportable as generic guidebook-like descriptions. This could even undermine Perec's project in a radical sense, since the latter is founded precisely on the possibility of such a stance, and its intelligibility to a reader who is posited as a stranger and socialised as such to the use of the city. Would a list which ran like, 'Place Paul Claudel, Au Bon Saint-Pourçain 10 rue Servandoni, Sister, etc.', still be a list of the things that are in Place Saint-Sulpice, or even of the things that are near Place Saint-Sulpice? And, for what kind of reader would it be such a list?

'OWNED' PUBLIC PLACES

Goffman remarked that one of the properties constitutive of a 'public' place is that what happens there, and who happens to be there, is always available as a potential spectacle for onlookers.[21] Conversely, an onlooking participative stance, whenever straightforwardly assumed by anyone present, constitutes places and events as 'public' in that sense: the gaze of the onlooker, his/her character as a stranger and what he/she beholds as 'public' are mutually elaborative. Moreover, the onlooker watches from a distance, and he/she is not involved in any other way in the unfolding events (this would mean reframing oneself in another participative status). The onlooker behaves as a disengaged observer, which also allows him/her to separate the place where an event happens from the event itself and to treat the former as a context 'containing' the latter. Perec's effort to provide an 'inventory' of what happens in Place Saint-Sulpice, of what is generally 'not taken note of', is grounded in the possibility of disengaged forms of watching. Such a distance is required to categorise urban occurrences in terms which, as we have started to see, are generic, and tailored to be intelligible to readers-strangers. The disengaged stance of the onlooking, unconnected Perec is central to the way his discursive project functions, and it is already visible in his opening description of the buildings in Place Saint-Sulpice, and the way the very positioning of such a description as a preface turns these buildings and places into a containing context for the entities and events he will describe later.

The experience and participative stance available to the Foursquare-connected Perec would be different. First, the connected Perec would have his smartphone turned on and, as a Foursquare user in urban public places, he would often switch from the stance of an embodied onlooker to some more active form of involvement with the screen. Unlike the places that are available to his disengaged onlooking sight, those which appear and are made active on screen are not just there to be seen, but also to be acted upon: they are actionable, like 'affordances' for clicking. Should he indeed elect to click upon one of these 'places', then he would get another page including comments from other users who have checked into there before, an indication of whether there is a 'mayor' for that particular digital formulation of a locale and who that might be, etc. Foursquare is more than just a social network, it involves some 'gamification',[22] which is manifest in the way the application tries to engage users in competition to become the 'mayor' of its various places: several forms of notifications have been designed to induce such competition. Such notifications are performative.[23] They also project further action and involvement on the part of the user and shape the forms this might take. In that sense, remaining apparently disengaged requires some form of active resistance to their appeal.

Central to such gamification is the possibility for users to claim places which become visible when they check in, and to compete for digital features such as the title of mayor by checking into this digital locale as often as possible, whether it be a cafe or something like *soeur*. Digital locales are thus 'owned', and such ownership can be claimed by disembodied users, visible through nametags and digital profiles, who thus differ from the anonymous and embodied strangers who roam the real metropolis. Even Place Saint-Sulpice's digital namesake had its mayor (Figure 12.3). Such an apparently innocuous form of ownership, designed to make the use of the LMSN more playful, may still interfere with 'real-life claims'. Some inhabitants of private places they had created as 'home' or 'sister' on Foursquare declared to us in interviews that they had felt an unpleasant pinch when it had happened that a complete

Figure 12.3 One 'mayor' of 'Place Saint-Sulpice' at the time of our study, as she appeared when we clicked first on this 'place' on the Foursquare list, and then on the 'mayor' active link.

stranger had claimed mayorship of their virtual 'home', even though such claims had no consequence on their material residence there.

Such an interference shows how local places, which become available to connected Foursquare users, are not just surrounding buildings whose description can be separated from the events which happen in and around them. They are irreducibly entangled with people, whether those who have commented on that locale or those who are competing for mayorship and making claims. They thus appear as multi-layered and multimedia texts combining, names, pictures, profiles, comments, hyperlinks, etc. And, they appear as affordances for action, amid a web of performative events, such as notifications inviting users to get involved further. The expected or default stance of the Foursquare user is therefore an involved one in which it is made easy, relevant and appealing to see surrounding 'places' on screen, to click on them and possibly check in there and claim mayorship of them. Of course, Foursquare users do not have to do any of these things, but then they have to ignore the way the mobile application may appeal to them and project further engagement. Such an experience is radically different from that of the twentieth-century metropolis, where the buildings and surrounding locales seemed to be there just to be beheld by an onlooker, and not to make relevant or project any kind of next action to be done regarding them. The connected Perec is a differently, and more actively, involved figure than his onlooking, unconnected counterpart. For the connected Perec, onscreen features of his surroundings are made available to him as an entanglement of places, particular people and text, designed and presented to be acted upon.

ENCOUNTERS WITH (PSEUDONYMOUS) STRANGERS IN PUBLIC PLACES

Perec's project, as we have seen above, is not just to draw up a list of places. His list of the things which may be seen in Place Saint-Sulpice is framed as an opening tableau, preliminary to the more ambitious project of describing and listing all that visibly passes or happens while he is sitting at his cafe and gazing away at the square. What would the connected Perec, taken as an active user of mobile locative media, have to cope with if he were to tackle a similar project today?

ENCOUNTERS WITH STRANGERS IN PLACE SAINT-SULPICE FROM A STRANGER'S PERSPECTIVE

A typical list runs like this:

> I again saw buses, taxis, cars, tourist buses, trucks and vans, bikes, mopeds, Vespas, motorcycles, a postal delivery tricycle, a motorcycle-school vehicle, a driving-school car, elegant women, aging beaus, old couples, groups of children, people with bags, satchels, suitcases, dogs, pipes, umbrellas, potbellies, old skins, old schmucks, young schmucks, idlers, deliverymen, scowlers, windbags. I also saw Jean-Paul Aron, and the proprietor of the 'Trois canettes' restaurant, whom I had already seen this morning.[24]

Perec's descriptions mix people with related things, as seen from an onlooker's perspective (the things they wear, the things they carry, the things they drive and are transported in). People are literally captured as passing strangers, unknown to the disengaged observer, and they are described according to common-sense categories, visually available to and recognisable by anybody (i.e. any reader socialised to the position of passing stranger in public places, and therefore able to read from such a category-based stance). Perec's perspective is that of the ordinary onlooker, proposing a stranger's perspective on passing strangers in an urban public place to readers-as-passing-strangers themselves. Even the people he knows by name are enunciated in a way which reinforces that particular framework of ordinary urban events. Jean Paul Aron is known by sight and described by name, but as a celebrity the name of which, and perhaps the visual appearance of which, might be known to (almost) anybody. The restaurant owner is someone who is visually recognisable to Perec's onlooking narrator, but he is framed as someone whose name is not relevant, either because the author does not know it, or because the intended reader would not know it. Although he has met him before, he describes him just as a fleeting acquaintance lacking personal details: he appears exactly as one of Stanley Milgram's 'familiar strangers' who do not know one another but share some reason for occasional encounters, which is 'an aspect of urban anonymity'.[25]

Perec's descriptive stance therefore enacts the urban public place as a place where strangers are 'thrown together',[26] and the city as a place of and for strangers.[27] Such strangers appear reportable and accountable under generic and shared categorisation, mostly as anonymous and equivalent bodies (their equivalence being here embedded and enacted in the enumerative form of the text). Some may be pinpointed according to more precise descriptions, but which still point back to recognisable and common-sense participation statuses relevant to the occupation of urban public places as loci for passing strangers, such as children, drivers, policemen or delivery men. There might be the occasional celebrity or 'familiar stranger' but their presence even highlights the description of Place Saint-Sulpice as a place for strangers observed from a stranger's perspective.

Goffman has shown how encounters between strangers in urban public places were expectedly minimal, and based on 'civil inattention'. The participation status of strangers in public places is endowed with a 'right to tranquility',[28] a mutual expectation from strangers that their 'negative face'[29] should be preserved in urban encounters. Such expectations are also foundational to the very possibility of Perec's stance as a narrator: his literary project is completely founded upon, and embedded in, the recognisability and meaningfulness of his posing and behaving as an onlooking and disengaged stranger watching other strangers. In that sense Perec's narrator is on a par with the *flâneur* or Goffman's 'civilly inattentive passerby', as one of the figures who best epitomise the experience of the nineteenth- and twentieth-century metropolis.

Only twice during the course of Perec's enumeration does he see personal acquaintances. These occurrences reveal yet another aspect of urban life. First, someone he seems to know vaguely greets him:

The café is packed
   A distant acquaintance (friend of a friend, friend of a friend of a friend) passed by in the street, came over to say hello, had a coffee.
   A Paris-Vision bus goes by. The tourists have headphones
   The sky is gray. Fleeting sunny spells.[30]

Later on, he happens to see a friend from afar:

Passage of a 63 bus
   Geneviève Serreau passes by in front of the café (too far away for me to get her attention)
   Project: a classification of umbrellas according to their forms, their means of functioning, their color, their material . . .[31]

These two brief occurrences in the course of sustained observations over three days testify to the relative scarcity of such chance encounters with acquaintances in the street. The default expectation for the urban denizen is that he will continuously encounter strangers in the street, so that a chance meeting with an acquaintance may appear as a rare and unexpected treat. Perec's description also points to the normative organisation which governs such encounters with known acquaintances: the 'discovery' of mutual proximity between visual acquaintances makes relevant a meeting, if only a minimal one.[32] This accounts for the apparent ordinariness of the act of Perec's friend going over to see him and greeting him in the first instance, and makes relevant Perec's excuse in the second. Just his mentioning that he saw a friend passing raises the expectation that they should greet each other. An excuse thus becomes relevant to account for why this has not been the case, and the sudden appearance of a first-person justification is highly noticeable in a text which aims primarily at a neutral and disengaged authorial stance in describing taken-for-granted occurrences in the street.

CONNECTED APPEARANCES IN PLACE SAINT-SULPICE

A connected Perec would still have to cope with the same kind of visual occurrences. However, connected users nearby would also become visible to him in a different manner, on screen. A crucial feature of social networking mobile locative media is that it makes users aware of the presence of other connected users nearby, either automatically, through the (passive) use of geolocation technology, or because they have actively 'checked in' their location in the mobile application (as is the case with Foursquare). In this case, their embodied figures may either be visible to the sitting onlooker on Place Saint-Sulpice or remain unavailable to the latter's gaze, because they are inside a building or outside but in a nearby street. As was the case with locations, the sense of the presence of others provided by mobile locative media involves a kind of awareness which extends beyond the boundaries of usual sensory experiences, and particularly sight. Producing a literary inventory of what happens 'in' Place Saint-Sulpice then becomes a completely different kind of endeavour for the connected Perec.

For him, others, whether they be strangers or acquaintances (and the mobile application will provide its own sense of acquaintanceship as well), frequently appear on screen when he is localised by the mobile technology. The way a connected observer engages with the mobile application shapes the form of such an appearance. At the time of our study, when one checked in in Place Saint-Sulpice, one would get a location notification ('you are here'), a list of the 'persons here', taking the form of personal icons (friends declared as such in the application would be highlighted if present) and some recommendations from other users (see Figure 12.4). Should the connected Perec leave it at that, those other 'persons here' he sees on screen would remain strangers to him, although 'here' takes on a different meaning than to the older and unconnected Perec. However, the interface offers the connected author the option of engaging a bit more with these strangers simply by clicking on their icon, in which case he might get something like Figure 12.5, which appears on his smartphone.

This shows that other users are 'clickables', who will unveil more of their digital selves to the more involved user (in the sense that he/she must click on their icon). Their onscreen appearance is endowed with personal information: a name tag, some information on their previous history of use and a list of their friends. Other location-aware sites provide even more detailed profiles. Users who appear on screen are therefore not just anonymous strangers, they are 'known' as singular individuals even though one may never have set eyes

218   CHRISTIAN LICOPPE

Figure 12.4 A typical screen which would appear after checking in in Place Saint-Sulpice.

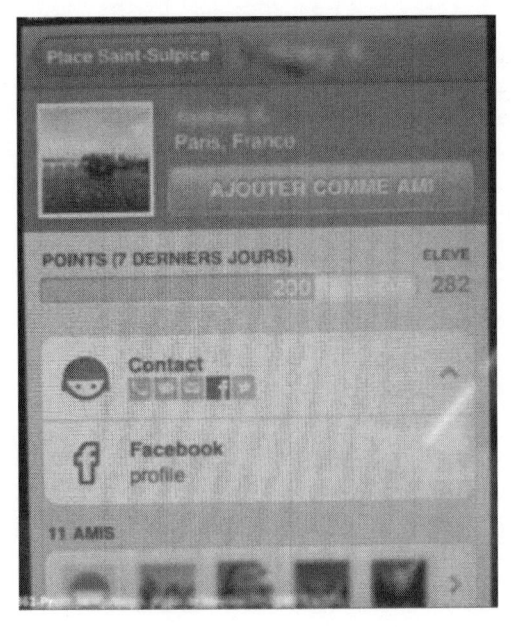

Figure 12.5 Clicking on the icon of one of the users present 'here' unveils further personal information.

on them before and would be unable to recognise them by sight. Therefore the connected Perec would 'encounter' in Place Saint-Sulpice all kinds of individuals, mostly strangers with perhaps a few acquaintances, but who are singularised by the personal knowledge which their onscreen appearance makes available.

The more active the connected Perec is (thereby behaving less as an uninvolved onlooker), the more digital personae from connected strangers nearby will present themselves to him on screen. As such they would deserve a mention in his 'augmented' inventory of what happens in Place Saint-Sulpice, albeit with a literary format yet to be determined. Because those urban denizens nearby who appear digitally do so in a form that is pervaded with personal knowledge, they cannot be accounted for in terms and categories that are generic and meaningful to readers themselves formatted as strangers equipped with similar descriptive and interpretive resources. The descriptions of the connected Perec would have to be shaped in a way that would account for the personal character of their appearance, and that would also engage the readership in a different stance from that of the fictive passive and embodied stranger. Such a literary project has yet to be done, but we can already perceive how it would be completely different from the original one, and would have to build another form of coherence between experience and description.

The tension between appearing as a passing and embodied stranger and appearing on screen as a nearby, disembodied and individualised digital persona is particularly salient in situations in which a passerby appears both on the square and on screen. This gives rise to a specific form of augmented encounter in urban public places, that is 'encounters with pseudonymous strangers', the particulars of which will be discussed below.

'ENCOUNTERS WITH PSEUDONYMOUS STRANGERS' IN PLACE SAINT-SULPICE

The connected Perec may 'see' on screen other users who have checked in nearby. The mobile application also makes such appearances potentially mutual: the nearby user who appears on Perec's screen may reciprocally see the connected Perec on his/her own screen when he/she attends to it. So, users usually know that when they see someone appearing on the screen as a nearby user, they may also be available to the other in a similar way. In that sense, they treat such onscreen appearances which index physical proximities as a kind of encounter. Such an orientation takes a concrete form when they act upon it, initiating greetings and some form of conversation through the mobile chat modules that are usually associated with the location-aware mobile social networking applications.

However, such encounters are different to those between anonymous passing strangers in terms of membership categorisation.[33] When Perec as a sitting onlooker sees a stranger passing by in Place Saint-Sulpice, it opens up the possibility of a mutual gaze and interaction (the unmarked form of which would be Goffman's 'civil inattention', that is just an ostensibly brief exchange of gazes) performed in a way which makes relevant their categorisation as a relational pair of 'anonymous strangers'.[34] When the connected Perec 'sees' another connected Foursquare user nearby, it opens up the possibility of mutual screen-mediated awareness. However, such a particular form of mutual sighting highlights mutual personal knowledge and ensures it will be shared. Both participants in the onscreen encounter are thus construed as a different type of relational categorical pair, something we might describe as a relational pair of 'pseudonymous users' (who know each other as pseudonyms and online profiles, even though they may never have been in one another's presence) to which are bound specific types of conduct (such as a mobile chat exchange acknowledging the onscreen encounter, for instance through greetings).

These differences may develop into specific tensions in the particular case in which the strangers who may be seen on the street might also be a connected stranger visible on screen and vice and versa. Let us suppose for one moment that during one of the connected Perec's days of observation in Place Saint-Sulpice, a gathering of Foursquare users had been planned there. Then, most of the passing strangers on the square would also be connected users who have checked in in the mobile application. The embodied strangers he would see (and who would be able to see him) with their eyes would also be mutually available on screen as pseudonymous Foursquare users. Encounters would then take the very particular form of an 'encounter between pseudonymous strangers' (and not just pseudonymous users).

Such encounters are characterised by several constitutive features. First, connected users who appear on screen have checked in nearby so that they are deictically related to the embodied 'here-and-now' of the observer. The situation is 'folded' and the onscreen avatar indexes the presence of a body nearby. Second, participants may engage in them in two distinctive ways which make relevant different membership categorisation devices ('anonymous strangers' vs 'pseudonymous users', equipped with some amount of personal knowledge), with different category-bound activities, and which involve two different ways of producing mutual awareness (i.e. the gaze vs the screen). Third, encounters with pseudonymous strangers are situations which involve a crucial 'evidential boundary' in which what is done on screen by one participant may not be seen by the other's eyes.

This makes possible some particularly characteristic forms of conduct. Because appearing on screen automatically makes relevant the nearby presence of an associated body, it raises the possibility that such a body might also be visible. Identification and recognition concerns reflect the duality that is inherent in the encounter. A connected Perec seeing other Foursquare users appearing 'here' when he checks into the virtual Place Saint-Sulpice would try to identify them visually, and try to match their physical appearance with the digital information available about them. Glaring mismatches would become noticeable and reportable in his literary account. Moreover, the onscreen 'discovery' that we have personal knowledge digitally available of someone – even a stranger – who is physically close to us, has normative implications regarding a possible face-to-face encounter. We have shown elsewhere that the mutuality of such a discovery projects its acknowledgement and expectations regarding a possible co-present meeting.[35] And, because of the presence of a sharp evidential boundary, different trajectories of encounter become possible. One such possibility is the actual physical greeting of one another. This can be done either while acknowledging onscreen mutual awareness, in which case both channels of awareness become aligned, or without acknowledging such onscreen mutual awareness in the physical world, which then constitutes what I have described elsewhere as a 'timid encounter'.[36] Another option is ignoring one another both physically and on screen. And there are many other possibilities besides, but I cannot develop all of the subtleties of such encounters and all the possible interactional trajectories here for lack of space.

This reflects critically on the translation of Perec's literary project to a more contemporary and connected setting. The connected Perec would have to make many choices which were foreign to the unconnected Perec's public experience, and this would impact the kind of literary inventory he might produce. The connected Perec would thus have to find a way to describe the onscreen appearance of other connected users as he is sitting at the cafe, users who appear with a halo of personal information, which contrasts with the generic way in which one might describe them as passing strangers in a public place. Moreover, he might have to determine whether or not to make his readership aware of the fact that some of the strangers on the square may be identical to some of these onscreen users. And, if he chooses to do so, how then can he combine the two sets of categorisations and descriptions which become available for these 'hybrid' strangers and acquaintances in his written account? If the connected Perec remains faithful to the initial project of an exhaustive account of what is happening 'here', he should also take care to write about what happens on screen. This would threaten the initial project to exhaust a Parisian location in writing, which rested on the remarkable coherence between the onlooking stance and the generic, common-sense categorisations of urban public life, with a radical fragmentation. Moreover, the connected Perec as an author would necessarily be an involved and personalised figure, the explicit agency of which would contrast with the apparent distance and lack of involvement of the sitting Perec as (just) an onlooker of public urban life.

CONCLUSION

I have used here Perec's *An Attempt at Exhausting a Place in Paris* as a starting point for a thought experiment in which I have tried to imagine what would become of such a project if urban denizens were to become active users of mobile locative media (here exemplified by Foursquare). In the light of this imaginary displacement, I have highlighted how the representation of the nineteenth- and twentieth-century western metropolis as a 'city of strangers', which has been so central in urban sociology and anthropology studies, was foundational to the remarkable literary coherence of Perec's *An Attempt*. Perec's original voice was that of the onlooker apprehending people and places as a stranger amid other strangers in a public place. Such a stance was performatively construed by the guidebook-like characterisation of places and common-sense descriptions of people and events which his inventory is made up of and which were meant to be meaningful to any reader reading from a stranger's perspective. Even the format of the list and the inventory itself points to the management of people as identical and depersonalised types and cases, and towards a bureaucratic zeitgeist which bears some kinship to the city as the site of fluxes of anonymous bodies, the circulation of which needs to be bureaucratically disciplined. Perec's observer and the literary project which it underlies are, therefore, as much an epitome of the urban experience as the earlier and better-known *flâneur* and Simmelian *blasé*.

What the modest thought experiment I have tried to conduct here vividly shows is the extent to which such a typically metropolitan onlooking stance is unsustainable for a postmodern Perec reborn as an active user of mobile locative media. First, the sense of what is 'here', 'in' Place Saint-Sulpice, is completely different for this latter Perec. For him, 'here' would no longer merely refer to the location of the people, places and vehicles he may sight from his sitting perspective, but also to all of those nearby enough to appear on the screen of his smartphone, even should a fair number of them not be visible from the cafe in Place Saint-Sulpice. The connected meaning of 'here' spills beyond the boundaries of the sitter's gaze for those locations which become perceptively available through a different socio-material chain of mediation. Second, and most importantly, their presentation on screen involves not only descriptions meaningful to all, but also formulations and references which are designed to be meaningful to a handful of familiar readers. In the case of locations, a significant number of those would thus have been formulated and archived by other users in 'relational terms'. For the connected Perec, Place Saint-Sulpice no longer has the impersonality of the public place, for it now entails some familiarity. Place Saint-Sulpice 2.0 is a layered place, in part a public place, in part a parochial location. Regarding the people 'here', and particularly those who appear on screen, they mostly do so in a disembodied fashion and within a digital halo of personal information (e.g. names, whether real ones or digital tags, profiles, prior history of uses, friends, etc.). As such, they cannot just be looked upon by other strangers, they appear as what I have called 'pseudonymous strangers': they are layered as well, appearing in part as strangers open to the public gaze, and in part as digitally individualised personae. Should the use of mobile locative media become pervasive, the expectation would be that cities would become loci for encountering 'pseudonymous strangers' instead of just strangers. Third, and finally, for pseudonymous strangers to appear on screen, some active engagement is required from the part of the author qua user of mobile locative media. The connected Perec can no longer assume the disengaged stance of the observer, which was both central to the original project and constitutive of the possibility of experiencing the city as a place where one encounters and is expected to encounter strangers and to impersonally manage urban public life as such.

For all these reasons, a future 'attempt at exhausting an (augmented) place in Paris' would take a very different form. It would no longer be able to build on the resources of form (e.g. list and inventory) and of generic, common-sense categorisations to provide for the coherence of urban experience as a reportable public matter: the author as an anonymous urban onlooker, the public character of the places and events he may gaze at, the writer describing publicly accountable anonymous strangers and ordinary events from a stranger's perspective (that of the authorial character qua onlooker) and the reader as a stranger grasping the description of remote events from that perspective. A future *An Attempt* would have to come to terms with the parochialisation of places which their digital formulation may entail and the individualisation of the online personae which appear on screen as 'nearby'. It would have to cope in a literary way with the new duality of passing strangers who would potentially be simultaneously available as anonymous passing bodies and as personalised and individualised digital figures. It is difficult to presume how the original Perec would have handled an attempt to describe a public square experienced as a place of and for pseudonymous strangers, or even if this exercise would have remained meaningful to him. However, one may surmise that any *An Attempt 2.0* would necessarily involve some fragmentation of descriptive categories and character-author-writer-reader participative stances to account for the layered nature of the augmented city.

NOTES

1. Charles Baudelaire (1863), *The Painter of Modern Life*, London: Phaidon Press, p. 12.
2. Lyn Lofland (1973), *A World of Strangers: Order and Action in Urban Public Space*, Prospect Heights, IL: Waveland Press.

3. Doreen Massey (2005), *For Space*, London: Sage.
4. Baudelaire, *The Painter of Modern Life*, p. 9.
5. Chris Jenks (1995), 'Watching Your Step: The History and Practice of the *Flâneur*', in Chris Jenks (ed.), *Visual Culture*, London: Routledge, p. 144.
6. Baudelaire, *The Painter of Modern Life*, p. 11.
7. William H. Whyte (1980), *The Social Life of Small Urban Spaces*, Washington, DC: Conservation Foundation.
8. Erving Goffman (1963), *Behavior in Public Places*, New York: Free Press, p. 84.
9. Erving Goffman (1974), *Frame Analysis. An Essay on the Organization of Experience*, New York: Harper & Row, p. 225.
10. Georges Perec (2010), *An Attempt at Exhausting a Place in Paris*, Cambridge: Wakefield Press, p. 3.
11. Lee Humphreys (2010), 'Mobile Social Networks and Urban Public Space', *New Media & Society*, vol. 12, no. 5, pp. 763–78.
12. In 2014, the social networking, check-in and gaming features of Foursquare were packaged into a new application, Swarm, while the Foursquare brand was kept for a spatial search application derived from the 'Explore' feature introduced in 2011. The study on which this chapter draws was done with the initial version of Foursquare, in which all features were available under a single application.
13. Karen P. Tang, Jialiu Lin, Jason I. Hong, Daniel P. Siewiorek and Norman Sadeh (2010), 'Rethinking Location Sharing: Exploring the Implications of Social-Driven vs. Purpose-Driven Location Sharing', in Khai N. Truong and Paddy Nixon (eds), *Proceedings of the 12th ACM International Conference on Ubiquitous Computing*, New York: ACM Press, pp. 85–94.
14. Henriette Cramer, Mattias Rost and Lars Erik Holmquist (2011), 'Performing a Check-In: Emerging Practices, Norms and "Conflicts" in Location-Sharing Using Foursquare', in Markus Bylund, Oskar Juhlin and Ylva Fernaeus (eds), *Proceedings of the 13th International Conference on Human Computer Interaction with Mobile Devices and Services*, New York: ACM Press, pp. 57–66; Mattias Rost, Louise Barkhuus, Henriette Cramer and Barry Brown (2013), 'Representation and Communication: Challenges in Interpreting Large Social Media Datasets', *Proceedings of the 2013 Conference on Computer Supported Cooperative Work*, New York: ACM Press, pp. 357–62; Jordan Frith (2014), 'Communication Through Location: The Understood Meaning of the Foursquare Check-in', *Journal of Computer-Mediated Communication*, vol. 19, no. 4, pp. 890–905; Christian Licoppe and Marie-Christine Legout (2014), 'Living Inside Mobile Social Information: The Pragmatics of Foursquare Notifications,' in James E. Katz (ed.), *Living Inside Mobile Information*, Dayton, OH: Greyden Press, pp. 109–30.
15. Janne Lindqvist, Justin Cranshaw, Jason Wiese, Jason Hong and John Zimmermann (2011), 'I'm the Mayor of My House: Examining Why People Use Foursquare – A Social-Driven Location Sharing Application', in Desney Tan, Geraldine Fitzpatrick, Carl Gutwin, Bo Begole and Wendy Kellogg (eds), *Proceedings of the SIGCHI Conference on Human Factors in Computing Systems*, New York: ACM Press, pp. 2409–18; Jordan Frith (2013), 'Turning Life into a Game: Foursquare, Gamification, and Personal Mobility,' *Mobile Media and Communication*, vol. 1, no. 2, pp. 248–62.
16. Licoppe and Legout, 'Living Inside Mobile Social Information'.
17. Georges Perec (2010), *An Attempt at Exhausting a Place in Paris*, trans. Marc Lowenthal, Cambridge, MA: Wakefield Press, p. 3.
18. Lofland, *A World of Strangers*.
19. Tang et al., 'Rethinking Location Sharing'.

20. Humphreys, 'Mobile Social Networks'.
21. Goffman, *Frame Analysis*.
22. Frith, 'Turning Life into a Game'.
23. Christian Licoppe (2010), 'The "Crisis of the Summons": A Transformation in the Pragmatics of "Notifications", from Phone Rings to Instant Messaging', *Information Society*, vol. 26, no. 4, pp. 288–302.
24. Perec, *An Attempt at Exhausting a Place in Paris*, p. 18.
25. Stanley Milgram (1992), 'The Familiar Stranger: An Aspect of Urban Anonymity', in John Sabini and Maury Silver (eds), *The Individual in a Social World: Essays and Experiments*, New York: McGraw-Hill, pp. 51–3.
26. Massey, *For Space*.
27. Lofland, *A World of Strangers*.
28. Isaac Joseph (1999), 'Activité située et régimes de disponibilité', *Raisons Pratiques*, vol. 10 (La logique des situations), pp. 157–72.
29. Penelope Brown and Stephen C. Levinson (1987), *Politeness: Some Universals in Language Usage*, Cambridge: Cambridge University Press.
30. Perec, *An Attempt at Exhausting a Place in Paris*, p. 33.
31. Perec, *An Attempt at Exhausting a Place in Paris*, p. 42.
32. Christian Licoppe (2009), 'Recognizing Mutual "Proximity" at a Distance. Weaving Together Mobility, Sociality and Technology', *Journal of Pragmatics*, vol. 41, no. 10, pp. 1924–37.
33. Harvey Sacks (1992), *Lectures on Conversation*, Cambridge: Cambridge University Press.
34. Sacks, *Lectures on Conversation*.
35. Christian Licoppe and Yoriko Inada (2010), 'Locative Media and Cultures of Mediated Proximity: The Case of the Mogi Game Location-aware Community', *Environment and Planning D: Society and Space*, vol. 28, no. 4, pp. 691–709.
36. Christian Licoppe and Yoriko Inada (2015), 'Mobility and Sociality in Proximity-Sensitive Digital Urban Ecologies: "Timid Encounters" and "Seam-Sensitive Walks"', *Mobilities*, Vol. 11, No. 2, pp. 1–20.

CHAPTER 13

The Quick Brown Fox Jumps Over the Lazy Dog: Perec, Description and the Scene of Everyday Computer Use

Rowan Wilken

We don't pay attention to what exactly is in front of our eyes.[1]

The current plethora of conceptual analysis of the present time is matched by a singular lack of phenomenological description.[2]

INTRODUCTION: PEREC AND HCI

As Charles Acland points out, we continue to encounter a relentless techno-boosterist rhetoric that proclaims the supersession of the old by the new. Not only are we told that the desktop personal computer is dead but, if we are to believe Apple CEO Tim Cook, so is the laptop computer as well. And, yet, 'residual media', as Acland terms them, continue to matter,[3] not least because of enduring use and because we still barely understand our 'endotic' or routine modes of engagement with these everyday devices and the familiar settings within which this use occurs. In this chapter, I take up Georges Perec's call to 'question the habitual' and do so in relation to the scene of everyday computer use. My questioning of habituated computer use is framed within a consideration, first, of human–computer interaction (HCI) research on skilled typing and, second, in relation to computer-based typing and everyday computer use. HCI research is an academic field of inquiry that began its rise to prominence during Perec's lifetime, and it shares with him a strong interest in *description* as a means of understanding everyday, habituated processes. And, yet, to the best of my knowledge, HCI research has never engaged directly with Perec's numerous writings and thinking on this issue (or vice versa).[4]

Throughout the 1970s and up to the time of Perec's death in 1982, HCI research was comprised, for the most part, of two overlapping and dominant strands of research – one preoccupied with ergonomics issues (otherwise referred to as human factors research), and the other drawing from human sciences approaches, especially cognitive and experimental psychology.[5] The importance of ergonomics to the study of HCI was identified very early on in the history of computers,[6] while the merit of human sciences approaches to HCI runs even further back, at least to early twentieth-century studies of machine use.[7]

The specific strand of HCI research – broadly conceived – that I wish to concentrate on in the first part of this chapter is the work conducted in the 1970s and 1980s on the acquisition of 'skilled cognitive-motor performance' in 'expert typing', both for typewriters and for computers.

This would have been of interest to Perec. His own personal fascination with typewriting and typewriters is well documented. For instance, David Bellos details the three special typewriters that Perec had throughout his life: an Underwood Four Million, an IBM golf-ball machine and an Olivetti ET 221 used during his time in Australia in 1981. Of these, the first held a special place: 'it had been Perec's friend, companion, and unfailing prop for two decades'.[8] Perec even 'commemorated its eventual demise' by incorporating it into the last of the plays that he wrote for German radio, *Sonate für ältere Schreibmaschine* ('Sonata for an Ageing Typewriter'), stipulating that the composer/performer 'use only an Underwood Four Million model'.[9] Indeed, a picture of Perec's Underwood Four Million is even reproduced by Bellos in his biography *Georges Perec*, where it is included, presumably, as a kind of pictorial biographeme vital to the telling of Perec's (and the machine's) 'life in words'.[10] As for the question of Perec's own skill as a typist, accounts vary considerably: according to Suzanne Tyc-Dymont, Perec's colleague in the Paris neurophysiology research laboratory where he worked performing a variety of administrative duties, Perec typed 'faster and more accurately than a trained typist'; according to another lab colleague, Henry Gautier, he was fast but nonetheless still what they call a hunt-and-peck rather than a touch typist, while, in the opinion of his lab boss, André Hugelin, Perec was a 'hamfisted joker who made countless involuntary keyboard mistakes'.[11]

My immediate interest in this chapter, however, is not in drawing out this connection between HCI typing research and Perec's personal interest in and (contested) skill as a typist. Rather, what interests me is the shared concern for, but differing take-up of, description. It is in this particular subfield of HCI work on skilled typing that fine-grained descriptive accounts of machine use are most strongly in evidence.

In taking up an examination of Perec and HCI in this chapter, the argument I wish to develop is structured in three parts. In the first section, I explore how HCI skilled typing research shares with Perec an interest in using description as a means of understanding – of unlocking – everyday, routinised practices. This takes the form of almost obsessively detailed micro-level descriptive accounts of typists' hand movements. In the second part of the chapter, I jump forward to the early 2000s, a period when computer-based typing had become so thoroughly familiar and 'domesticated' as to almost pass unnoticed, both by everyday users and by academic researchers. Perecian description, I suggest, provides a productive means of shedding light on quotidian computer use. The central argument of this chapter is that *description* offers an innovative method for generating new insights into the material contexts and conditions of media use, especially the everyday conditions of routine human–computer interaction. In building this argument, in the final part of the chapter, I close with a brief reflection on why description matters, not as a means to some critical larger ends, but in and of itself. What happens, in other words, when we move from thinking description through, to *thinking through description*? I begin with an account of HCI research on skilled typing.

'PEOPLE CAN TYPE VERY QUICKLY':[12] MICRO DESCRIPTION IN SKILLED TYPING RESEARCH

Timothy Salthouse provides a valuable account of the state of typing research at that time and the efforts of researchers over the preceding years to understand how skilled typists are able to type as fast as they do.[13] The enduring research question for those working in this field is that of why skilled typists regularly outperformed what laboratory tests predicted they ought to be able to do. For transcription typists:

> The average latency, or delay between the presentation of the stimulus [the written material to be transcription typed] and the pressing of the button, is approximately 250 milliseconds [. . . which] yields a typing rate of 48 words per minutes [. . .] yet speeds of twice that rate are fairly common.[14]

Why is this the case? Salthouse states that one of the long-standing explanations for this in typing research relates to the idea that increased speed was achieved by expanding the size of textual units from single characters to words to perhaps even phrases – that is, the greater the amount of text ('stimuli') that is 'previewed' (otherwise known as the 'detection span' or 'copying span'), the greater the typing speed.[15]

The long-standing explanation for why preview confers an advantage for typists Salthouse refers to as 'chunking theory'. This is the idea that transcription typists can work at speeds greater than 60 gwpm (gross words per minute

– i.e. typing that is not corrected for errors) because, during previewing, 'the material to be typed gets mentally "chunked" into multicharacter units' consisting of familiar textual content such a syllables or common (and generally short) words.[16] For instance, in studying typists keying in 'The quick brown fox jumps over the lazy dog.' – a standard sentence long used in the teaching of typing – Salthouse found that time intervals differed when typing the letter *o* in this sentence: '370 milliseconds in the word *brown*, 160 milliseconds in *fox*, 185 milliseconds in *over* and 130 milliseconds in *dog*'. These 'different latencies in different contexts', he suggests, lends some support to the chunking hypothesis.

However, Salthouse's larger argument is that the skilled typing research conducted in the early 1980s, with its detailed modes of laboratory description, suggests numerous qualifications to this dominant theory. One example is found in the study of typing errors – an enduring area of interest to skilled typing researchers. David Rumelhart and Donald Norman develop a detailed typology of typing errors, which they divide up into various classes, including 'transposition' errors (which → whihc), 'doubling' errors (gibbs → giibs), 'alternation reversal' errors (these → thses), and others such as 'homologous' errors (where the wrong hand is selected), 'capture' errors (efficiency → efficient), 'omission' errors (amount → amont), 'misstrokes' (the → tje) and more. In his own research on typing errors, Salthouse found that a large proportion of them 'are detected immediately, and not at the end of multicharacter groups'. These studies of errors along with other experiments – such as providing expert typists with texts whose familiarity was disrupted (such as by getting them to transcribe a page of standard sentences set out in chunks but in reverse, as in .god yzal eht revo spmuj xof nworb kciuq ehT) – all suggest that high typing speeds cannot be attributable solely to 'a switch from single-character to syllable- or word-length units of analysis'.[17]

The key to explaining typing speed, Salthouse suggests, rests with the idea of an 'overlapping of "processing operations"'[18] – that is, the ability to 'execute more than one operation at a time'.[19] Evidence to support this interpretation has been amassed from a raft of studies that examine the micro-movements of expert typists and, in particular, their corresponding 'latencies' (the time intervals between the stimulation, such as previewing a text/text fragment for typing, and the response, the act of keying in the text/text fragment).[20] While situated within a cognitive sciences framework, many of the findings of these studies emerged through the laboratory-based use of *description* of routine practices.

In the essay 'Approaches to What?', Perec encourages readers to undertake a series of interrogations of the everyday, including by asking: 'How many movements does it take to dial a phone number? Why?'[21] These are the very sorts of questions that HCI researchers have asked of skilled typing.[22] Indeed,

Salthouse identifies and summarises twenty-nine different 'basic phenomena' associated with expert typing and 'for which convincing empirical support is available'. Rumelhart and Norman group these phenomena into three broad categories: those involving errors (as touched on above), those involving the general organisation of the typing process and those involving the timing of keystrokes. Here I restrict discussion to the last of these: work on keystroke timing. From the available research on this issue of keystroke speed, the following findings emerge: that speed depends on 'factors such as the position of the preceding keys and subsequent keys';[23] that 'cross-hand interkeystroke intervals are faster than those from consecutive strokes on the same hand';[24] that typing depends on individual finger movements and strength[25] and on finger combinations; that the frequency of letter combinations is faster for alternative hands than for the same hand; and that frequency of letter combinations, and thus typing speed, is also linguistically determined ('only 104 three-letter sequences (26^3, or 17,576) account for nearly half of the occurrences of three-letter sequences in English').[26]

What is especially striking about this body of research work is the level of detailed *description* – textual and figural – that informs these accounts of typists' hand movements, latency and speed. To illustrate this point, I draw two examples – one pertaining to micro-level temporal description, the other to micro-level spatial description – from the later (mid-1990s) work of computer-interaction researcher, Bonnie John. In her article, 'TYPIST', John divides up the task of typing into three processes: *perceptual operators* (in play when reading the transcription text); *cognitive operators* (in play when mentally processing the transcription task); and *motor operators* (in play when physically typing the transcription text).[27] Drawing from videotaped recordings of expert typists, John makes 'estimates of the motor operator for typists at different speeds' as they transcribe the following example sentence: One reason is quite obvious; you can get in and get out without waiting for the elevator.[28] She does this by deploying 'critical path analysis', a representational approach drawn from engineering project management, which breaks down tasks into various subtasks and the 'operators' necessary to accomplish these, representing each 'as a box with a duration' (see Figure 13.1), concluding that a '60-gwpm-typist would be able to type the 89 characters of the example sentence in 17,800 msec'.[29] Elsewhere in the same article, John draws on Fitts's Law[30] of human movement to explore what Rumelhart and Norman refer to as the 'degrees of freedom problem'[31] concerning individual finger shifts of skilled typists and, specifically, the directions and distances of travel required by the left middle and index fingers when typing on a QWERTY keyboard. John depicts these diagonal, vertical and horizontal movements in detail, measuring each one in decimal inches (see Figure 13.2). These are just two brief examples, drawn from the same article, that are indicative of the extraordinary level of

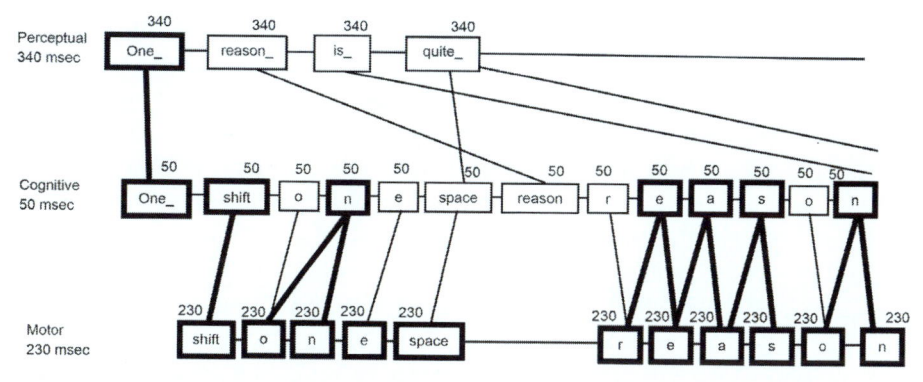

Figure 13.1 Diagram illustrating the use of 'critical path analysis' and which depicts 'a schedule chart and critical path for the example sentence for a 60-gwpm typist with an initial motor operator estimate of 230 msec'.

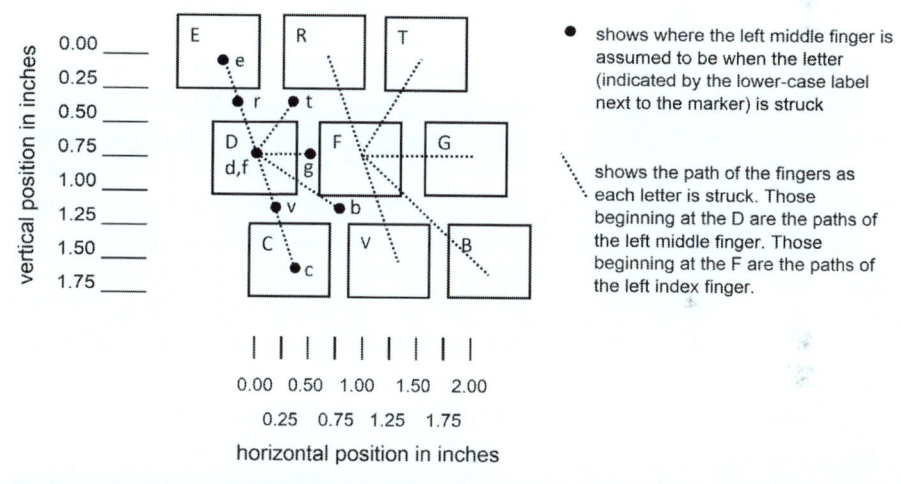

Figure 13.2 Diagram illustrating 'assumed movement of the left, middle, and index fingers when striking keys on a QWERTY keyboard'.

descriptive detail that HCI researchers have brought to bear on analyses of expert typing.

Aspects of expert typing research would likely have appealed to Perec. In addition to his well-known personal fascination with and use of typewriters (as noted earlier), there are obvious affinities between his exploration of Oulipian constraint and expert typing research experimentation with textual inversion, letter coupling and linguistic restrictions. There are also clear similarities between his calls for describing everyday actions and the focused attention within typing research on (micro) description. Indeed, on one level, both Perec and HCI typing researchers appear to share the belief that 'there are unknown things concealed by what is visible, things that are hidden not in the obscure, but in the obvious'.[32]

On another level, however, the aims and goals of HCI skilled typing research interest in description differ markedly from Perec's interest in description. For his part, Perec professed to be motivated by a desire to 'describe the rest instead', to capture 'that which is not noticed, that which has no importance: what happens when nothing happens'.[33] Gilbert Adair refers to this as Perec's attempt to accord 'an eleventh day to a ten day's wonder'.[34] The journal *Cause commune*, which Perec had a close association with, saw its aim as 'to undertake an investigation of everyday life at every level, right down to the recesses and basements that are normally ignored or suppressed'.[35] Or, as Virilio recalls, their aim was 'to be journalists of that which did not seem to interest anybody, to talk about things that were not obvious'.[36] What is especially striking about this approach to description is its non-utilitarian focus – Adair refers to this as its 'neutrality', which is, in his opinion, its 'single most radical feature'.[37]

In the case of skilled typing research, the immediate aim was specifically to understand 'skilled performance' and 'control of skilled motor movements'.[38] The larger goal, however, was twofold. First, to incorporate knowledge gained from this research into research and development efforts in building future human–computer interaction systems.[39] Second, to use this research to feed the development of 'a unified, integrated model of human behavior',[40] a model that would be of value not just to HCI designers, but also to industry and the military (and it is worth noting that at least two key skilled typing studies were funded by the US Office of Naval Research and the Air Force Office of Scientific Research). Thus skilled typing research (and its descriptions of micro-motions) was strongly utilitarian in focus, motivated less by a concern for grasping the fugitive qualities of the quotidian than with the achievement of greater efficiencies in skilled performance. In this respect, skilled typing research can be viewed as a direct descendent of Taylorist 'time-motion' studies and of Frank and Lilian Gilbreth's interest in the disciplining of motion and micro 'mobility as habit'.[41] Indeed, HCI research application of descriptive methods and technological capture of precise measurements is preceded by the Gilbreths' micromotion study of female typists' body positionings and hand actions using what they called a 'cinematograph' – a 'moving picture of people at work against a background divided into regular squares' within a grid.[42] The difference is that, whereas the Gilbreths' aim was 'to mould human movement at the level of habit, below the radar of consciousness',[43] for HCI researchers studying skilled typing, their concern is with understanding human movement at the level of habit in order to then apply (redeploy?) this skill and knowledge elsewhere.

Strong research interest in studying skilled typing persisted into the 1990s. By the early 2000s, however, the HCI research agenda had broadened significantly,[44] and with micro movement studies focusing on 'tasks and on descriptive accounts of physical and mental operations'[45] becoming increasingly less prevalent within the HCI research literature.

Interestingly, this research agenda shift within HCI studies occurred at the precise moment when desktop personal computer (PC) use had become thoroughly normalised and 'domesticated',[46] and where, in a corporate setting at least, the 'image of a grey workstation dominated by a recent model Dell desktop computer running Microsoft Outlook' still prevailed.[47] This is 'a vision of technology', Melissa Gregg suggests, that is 'so ordinary as to be mundane'.[48] 'And yet', she argues, 'it is a vision that so many "new media" [and, I would add, HCI] scholars seem resolutely prepared to ignore.'[49] Through its ubiquity and mundaneness, everyday office PC use has thus come to be regarded as a form of 'residual' media[50] and, because of this, attracts significantly less critical interest from HCI and 'new media' researchers, despite the fact that, precisely because of this ubiquity and familiarity, everyday computer use is increasingly *un*familiar to us and remains poorly understood. The result is that, as users and critics, when it comes to everyday, routinised computer use, 'we don't tend to pay attention to what exactly is in front of our eyes'.[51] But, as I wish to argue below, one especially productive means of paying attention, of 'making the familiar strange' again, is, as Perec has shown us, via the act of describing what is right there, before us.

My contention is that the forms of detailed descriptions of micro-motions employed by HCI researchers are insufficient for capturing what is involved in computer-based typing and human–computer interaction as it occurs within everyday settings.[52] Looking back on HCI skilled typing studies, what is especially striking is the recurrent focus on exceptionally detailed description of micro-level practices (finger movements, time latencies, etc.), but a total absence of any consideration of the wider situational and other contexts of typewriter or keyboard use.[53] The body of published laboratory-based HCI research thus tells us, in finely granulated detail, a great deal about the actions of speed typing, but little (if anything) about the larger contextual settings in which this sort of work regularly occurs (the office, the home, etc.), and the socio-cultural and socio-technical complexities associated with each of these settings. To put this issue somewhat differently, skilled typing research (to borrow Perec's words) provides insight 'from an ergological (physiology, muscular effort)' perspective, yet offers little by way of a 'socio-ecological perspective (its spatio-temporal setting)'.[54] By contrast, attentiveness to immediate context and setting is a characteristic feature of almost all of Perec's uses of description, and is evident, for example, in everything from his novel *Things* and novella *A Man Asleep*, the questions he asks of the act of reading in his essay 'Reading: A Socio-Physiological Sketch', his *Lieux* project and his books *Species of Spaces* and *An Attempt* at *Exhausting a Place in Paris*. In the following section, I want to adopt a Perecian mode of description in order to begin to examine what this might offer for trying to understand computer-based typing and the immediate scene of computer use.

DESCRIPTION AND THE SCENE OF EVERYDAY PERSONAL COMPUTER USE

What might description of computer-based typing involve if we attempt to account for the *scene* of everyday computer use? In exploring these concerns, and to remain consistent with earlier skilled typing research, I take as my starting point the physical act of keying in: The quick brown fox jumps over the lazy dog. How many keystrokes are employed in the typing of this nine-word sentence? As a pangrammatic sentence, one might logically assume the answer to be twenty-six. However, unlike 'Mr Jock, TV Quiz Ph.D, bags few lynx', 'The quick brown fox jumps over the lazy dog.' is an imperfect pangram. This is because it contains an extraneous *the*, as well as three extra letter *o*'s, an *e*, an extra *u* and an extra *r*. Combined with an additional eight spaces between the words, depressing the shift key once in order to begin the sentence and concluding with a full stop, and the total number of keystrokes adds up to forty-five. As a touch-typist, I use all eight fingers, plus my right thumb to hit the space bar, when typing it out. The average time it takes me to unhurriedly key in this sentence is approximately eight seconds (I did not time this in milliseconds). This somewhat generous measure is due to the fact that, while I would call myself a touch typist, I do occasionally need to visually orient my fingers on the keyboard, despite my familiarity with the 'home position', as indicated by the presence of the Braille-like protrusions on the *f* and *j* keys.

This basic account would be strengthened significantly by the insights of HCI skilled typing research. For example, as noted earlier, Salthouse reports that the time intervals in milliseconds when typing the letter *o* differ significantly depending on which word it appears in,[55] and furthermore, that there is a 'lack of systematic correlation between the speeds of keystrokes made in succession by people [such as myself] typing "The quick brown fox . . ."'[56]

This, however, only reveals so much. It tells us little, for instance, about the contextual 'curtilage' that surrounds and shapes the actions involved in keying in this sentence. To borrow Lance Strate's words, 'my composition of this sentence, as I sit in front of my [office] computer and type on the keyboard, is an event.'[57] This is to say that it occurs *in medias res*, within existing, already unfolding situational contexts and spatial settings. Viewed from this perspective, responding to Perec's call to question 'how many *movements*' would involve a dramatically expanded repertoire of actions that need to be accounted for, including not just descriptions of micro-motions such as keystrokes, but description of all that precedes and facilitates and succeeds and occurs around and during these micro-motions which are part and parcel of everyday computer use. To do justice to this 'event' and its full documentation requires, with apologies to Perec, an attempt at exhausting the scene of computer use. Such an 'attempt' might look something like this description of an average work day, as I unlock and enter my university office of a morning:

> I step into the office. I scan the room. I walk to the desk. I place my keys on the desk. I turn from desk to chair. I drop my bag on the chair. I walk to the computer. I press the button to turn on the screen. I press the button to turn on the hard drive. I walk from computer to chair. I begin to unpack my bag: I remove my lunch. From bag to desk: I place it on the desk. From desk to bag: I remove my water bottle. I walk from bag on chair to computer. I place my water bottle on a tile mosaic my daughter made that is to the right of the computer. I walk back to chair. I remove my books from bag. I remove my paperwork. From bag to desk: I place these items on desk. From desk I walk to desk chair. I sit on the desk chair. I begin to prepare for the day's work. I roll my chair from desk to workstation. I position myself at the computer. I look down at the keyboard. I type in my computer password. I look up at the screen. I wait for the system to load. I locate the Word shortcut. I click on the Word shortcut. I glance out the window. I wait for Word to open with a new Word document. I look back at the screen. I look down at the keyboard. I find the 'home position' for my fingers on the keys. I commence typing. The quick brown fox jumps over the lazy dog.[58]

One of the many challenges of description, as Paul Virilio points out, is that 'looking is not self-evident' – 'we look but we do not see' – and, thus, like a set of Russian dolls, the more we *see*, the more there is to describe.[59] Robert Willim, for instance, provides a detailed description of one item nested within the above description: the deceptively simple task of turning on one's computer. In the year 2000, this evidently involved many internal computational processes and a fair amount of elapsed time. Willim's 280 word description reads as follows:

> I push a square button on the front of my computer. Some lights come on. A green light shows that the power supply to the computer is on. A red one indicates that the hard disk is being searched. There is a hiss and a buzz as the hard disk increases in speed. After a few seconds the light

on the front of the floppy disk drive comes on. A rattling sound is heard when the computer checks whether a disk is inserted. Then the start-up process continues, or 'booting up', as people often say. [. . .] I can read on the screen, in white text on a black background, the basic configuration of the computer, the performance of the processor in MHz and so on. The amount of internal memory is counted figure by figure for a few seconds. The larger the memory, the longer the count takes. When the computer's basic functions have been started, the introductory screen showing the logotype of the operating system is shown – Microsoft Windows 98. In the ensuing seconds the Window image of white clouds against a blue sky disappears and white text against a black screen shows technical data. The Windows picture returns and disappears, replaced by a background picture – the desktop. An hourglass is seen in the middle of the screen. After a moment a number of icons pop up. For a further few seconds I can hear the hard disk still working, whizzing away. After a few seconds the sound falls silent and all that is left is the hum of the fan. The computer has started and is ready to use. The whole process took 2 minutes and 34 seconds.[60]

While I don't have the space here to 'exhaust' the descriptive possibilities inherent in this scene, the above examples suffice for drawing out the key point regarding what it is that Perecian-inspired description provides. It offers a productive means for understanding familiar, routinised technology use. Description provides a means of engaging 'the inconspicuous as an object of attention'.[61] Description unsettles the familiar by encouraging us to *see* rather than *look* (to return to Virilio's distinction). In so doing, it also opens us to new ways of seeing. As Jeffrey Kittay points out, the power of description rests in the way that it 'can open to possibilities, explore, include what somehow does not belong, what is inessential, but that accidence is essential, is essence'.[62] Description, then, as Steven Connor puts it, provides 'a way of thinking through things rather than thinking them through', and of making it 'possible to say interesting and precise things about our relation to the many quasi-objects of our intimately, or extimately, technologised world – dashboards, joysticks, screens, wires, keyboards, mouses, say, and what they did to and with hand, eye and skin [. . .]'.[63]

In the final section of this chapter to follow, I wish to offer some short reflections on the issue of what is at stake in *thinking through description* (to adapt Steven Connor's words). I mean this in a double sense: (1) How might we *think description through*, grasping what is important about it? And, (2) how might we *think through description*, asking whether description be understood as constituting a critical approach in its own right?

'RECORDING THE VAGRANT REALITIES OF THE EVERYDAY':[64] THINKING THROUGH DESCRIPTION

A key question asked of description in general, and of Perec's uses of description in particular, is: 'Can it stand by itself?'[65] To the ethnologist Howard Becker, this is a somewhat unsettling question. Becker writes, 'a list without explicit formal analysis of its contents is a potent representational device, used much more by artists than by social scientists'.[66] It is 'potent' because what appears as random, trivial and altogether unimportant ultimately 'adds up': 'the whole is more than the parts'.[67] In other words, what is revealed via this technique only really emerges when the fabric that is woven from the individual strands of description begins to take shape. This whole, however, is 'not easily characterised'. For example, in endeavouring to analyse Perec's *An Attempt at Exhausting a Place in Paris*, Becker confesses:

> As I try to generalize what he has done in this little book, I find myself increasingly stuck for words, as though there was no other way to describe it than just to repeat and list what he has already described.[68]

Becker suggests that

> as you read Perec's descriptions, you increasingly succumb to the feeling [. . .] that this is important, though you can't say how. If we don't have ideas and theories about it, we ought to.[69]

Becker speculates 'whether every kind of social description does not have two aspects: a desire to show and a desire to explain'?[70] As a social scientist, what is of lingering concern to him is that Perec offers description without explanation – to Becker, then, as Fred Lukermann once said of Strabo, 'he was a describer of things, not an analyst.'[71]

Becker's sense is that 'it is the tension between these two [description and analysis] which holds every kind of social analysis in place'.[72] To my mind, this position arguably misses the point of Perec's descriptions. As Samuel Beckett wrote of James Joyce's *Finnegans Wake*, 'Here form is content, content *is* form.' In a similar vein, one might say of Perec's quotidian-focused works, 'here analysis is description, description *is* analysis'.[73] As Blanchot asks:

> Might not [. . .] description be the sole mode of presentation that does not disturb the strange disenchantment of appearances and disappearances in which we exist?[74]

In light of Highmore's suggestion that 'the everyday doesn't have a form of attention that is proper to it',[75] I tend to share Steven Connor's view that, when it comes to understanding the scene of everyday computer use and computer-based typing, we are 'no worse off, in principle, trying to make sense of experience' through description than we are 'in trying to make sense of the evidence of what is done to [and with] experience'.[76]

In this chapter, I have taken up Perec's call to us to 'question the habitual' and explored how human–computer interaction (HCI) research, particularly in the early 1980s, has responded to this question in their studies of skilled typing through the use of detailed descriptions of micro-motions. I then have sought to argue that, by the late 1990s and early 2000s, computer-based typing had become widespread and normalised, and largely ignored by HCI researchers, despite the fact that we still understood very little about these routinised human–computer interactions and their immediate socio-spatial and socio-technical contexts of use. My contention has been that the forms and styles of description developed by Perec (rather than the micro-level description of skilled typing research) would have offered and do offer a productive means of uncovering what is involved in (and at) the scene of everyday computer use, and of 'recording the vagrant realities of the quotidian'.[77] These 'common things', to use Perec's phrase, are precisely what, as HCI and media and communication researchers, we should continue to 'take account of'.

NOTES

1. Georges Perec and Kaye Mortley (2009), 'The Doing of Fiction', *Review of Contemporary Fiction*, no. XXIX: 1, p. 99.
2. Giorgio Agamben (1995), *Idea of Prose*, trans. Michael Sullivan and Sam Whitsitt, Albany, NY: State University of New York Press, p. 89.
3. Charles R. Acland (2007), 'Introduction', in Charles R. Acland (ed.), *Residual Media*, Minneapolis: University of Minnesota Press, pp. xiii–xxvii.
4. In developing the arguments in this chapter, I draw on an extensive (although not exhaustive) review conducted by Suneel Jethani of the HCI literature in the ACM SIGCHI (Association for Computing Machinery Special Interest Group on Computer–Human Interaction) hosted HCI Bibliography. I wish to thank Suneel for his invaluable assistance in gathering this background research material. I would also like to thank Anthony McCosker and Esther Milne for their valuable feedback on an earlier draft of this chapter.
5. Brian R. Gaines (1985–6), 'From Ergonomics to the Fifth Generation: 30 Years of Human–Computer Interaction Studies', *Computer Compacts*, vol. 2, no. 5, pp. 158–61.
6. Brian Schakel (1959), 'Ergonomics for a Computer', *Design*, no. 120, pp. 36–9.
7. Timothy A. Salthouse (1984), 'The Skill of Typing', *Scientific American*, no. 250, p. 129. The importance of the human sciences to HCI has been reasserted at various points in its history. See, for example: Brian Schakel (1969), 'Man–Computer Interaction – The Contribution of the Human Sciences', *Ergonomics*, vol. 12, no. 4, pp. 149–63; Erik Hollnagel (1983), 'What We Do Not Know About Man-machine Systems', *International Journal of Man–Machine Studies*, no. 18, pp. 135–43; John Seely Brown and Susan

E. Newman (1985), 'Issues in Cognitive and Social Ergonomics: From Our House to Bauhaus', *Human–Computer Interaction*, no. 1, pp. 359–91.
8. David Bellos (1999), *Georges Perec: A Life in Words*, London: Harvill, p. 490.
9. Bellos, *Georges Perec*, p. 262.
10. Bellos, *Georges Perec*, photograph 25, between pp. 322 and 323.
11. Bellos, *Georges Perec*, p. 263.
12. David E. Rumelhart and Donald A. Norman (1982), 'Simulating a Skilled Typist: A Study of Skilled Cognitive-Motor Performance', *Cognitive Science*, no. 6, p. 19.
13. Salthouse, 'The Skill of Typing', pp. 128–35.
14. Salthouse, 'The Skill of Typing', p. 128.
15. Salthouse, 'The Skill of Typing', p. 129.
16. Salthouse, 'The Skill of Typing', p. 131.
17. Salthouse, 'The Skill of Typing', p. 133.
18. Salthouse, 'The Skill of Typing', p. 131.
19. Salthouse, 'The Skill of Typing', p. 135.
20. In addition to the Salthouse (1984) and Rumelhart and Norman (1982) references already cited, see: L. H. Shaffer (1975), 'Control Processes in Typing', *Quarterly Journal of Experimental Psychology*, no. 27, pp. 419–32; L. H. Shaffer (1978), 'Timing in the Motor Programming of Typing', *Quarterly Journal of Experimental Psychology*, vol. 30, no. 2, pp. 333–45; Ernst Z. Rothkopf (1980), 'Copying Span as a Measure of the Information Burden in Written Language', *Journal of Verbal Learning and Verbal Behavior*, no. 19, pp. 562–72; Stuart K. Card and Thomas P. Moran (1980), 'The Keystroke-Level Model for User Performance Time with Interactive Systems', *Communication of the ACM*, vol. 23, no. 7, pp. 396–410; Timothy A. Salthouse (1985), 'Anticipatory Processing in Transcription Typing', *Journal of Applied Psychology*, vol. 70, no. 2, pp. 264–71; and, for slightly later research on these same issues, Richard A. Heath and Christopher H. Willcox (1990), 'A Stochastic Model for Inter-keypress Times in a Typing Task', *Acta Psychologica*, no. 75, pp. 13–39.
21. Georges Perec (1999), 'Approaches to What?', in *Species of Spaces and Other Pieces*, ed. and trans. John Sturrock, Harmondsworth: Penguin, p. 211.
22. Maxwell (1953) develops a general typology of hand movements made by typists using a QWERTY keyboard. This typology consists of balanced, inward rolling, and outward rolling hand movements, and repetitious stroking with the same finger on the same key and on different keys. See W. C. Maxwell (1953), 'The Rhythmic Keyboard', *Journal of Business Education*, vol. 27, no. 8, 327–30; Jan Noyes (1983), 'The QWERTY Keyboard: A Review', *International Journal of Man–Machine Studies*, vol. 18, no. 3, pp. 265–81.
23. Salthouse, 'The Skill of Typing', p. 135.
24. Rumelhart and Norman, 'Simulating a Skilled Typist', p. 20; see also Donald R. Gentner (1983), 'The Acquisition of Typewriting Skill', *Acta Psychologica*, no. 54, pp. 233–48.
25. 'Our model of the hand is too simple, neglecting the differences in strengths and speeds of the fingers, and treating each finger independently of the others' – Rumelhart and Norman, 'Simulating a Skilled Typist', p. 35.
26. Salthouse, 'The Skill of Typing', p. 135.
27. Bonnie E. John (1996), 'TYPIST: A Theory of Performance in Skilled Typing', *Human–Computer Interaction*, no. 11, p. 324.
28. John, 'TYPIST', pp. 330–1.
29. John, 'TYPIST', p. 331.
30. Paul M. Fitts (1954), 'The Information Capacity of the Human Motor System in Controlling the Amplitude of Movement', *Journal of Experimental Psychology*, vol. 47, no.

6, pp. 381–91. As MacKenzie (1992) explains, Fitts's Law suggests that 'human movement can be modeled by analogy to the transmission of [bits of] information (p. 91) and, 'if the number of bits is divided by the time to move, then a rate of transmission in "bits per second" can be ascertained' (p. 93). Fitts's Law has had wide application in skilled typing research and wider HCI research, where, as MacKenzie puts it, 'the need for a reliable prediction model of movement time of computer input tasks' (p. 93) is considered a key factor in the designing of systems. In addition to typing, it has been applied to use of devices such as 'the mouse, trackball, joystick, touchpad, helmet-mounted sight, and eye tracker' (p. 94). See: I. Scott MacKenzie (1992), 'Fitts's Law as a Research and Design Tool in Human–Computer Interaction', *Human–Computer Interaction*, no. 7, pp. 91–139.
31. Rumelhart and Norman, 'Simulating a Skilled Typist', p. 15.
32. Paul Virilio, quoted in Enrique Walker (2001), 'Paul Virilio on Georges Perec', *AA Files*, no. 45–6, p. 17.
33. Georges Perec (2010), *An Attempt at Exhausting a Place in Paris*, trans. Marc Lowenthal, Cambridge, MA: Wakefield Press, p. 3.
34. Gilbert Adair (2009), 'The Eleventh Day: Perec and the Infra-ordinary', *Review of Contemporary Fiction*, no. XXIX: 1, p. 183.
35. Cited in Enrique Walker (2001), 'Paul Virilio on Georges Perec', *AA Files*, no. 45–6, p. 15.
36. Paul Virilio, quoted in Enrique Walker (2001), 'Paul Virilio on Georges Perec', *AA Files*, no. 45–6, p. 15.
37. Adair, 'The Eleventh Day', p. 177.
38. Rumelhart and Norman, 'Simulating a Skilled Typist', p. 2.
39. Bonnie John suggests that skilled typing remained a compelling research concern within HCI circles into the mid-1990s for the precise reason that typing was still 'by far the most prevalent form of human-to-computer communication' and examination of it would 'allow consideration of human typing capabilities in the design of many computer systems' (John, 'TYPIST', p. 321).
40. John, 'TYPIST', p. 324.
41. See Tim Cresswell (2006), *On the Move: Mobilities in the Modern Western World*, London: Routledge, p. 106. See also Anson Rabinbach (1992), *The Human Motor: Energy, Fatigue, and Origins of Modernity*, Berkeley: University of California Press.
42. Cresswell, *On the Move*, p. 99, and for an illustration of this particular 'cinematograph', see p. 100.
43. Cresswell, *On the Move*, p. 107.
44. The significant broadening of the HCI research agenda throughout the 2000s is evident, for example, in the following titles: Jenny Preece, Yvonne Rogers and Helen Sharp (2014), *Interaction Design: Beyond Human–Computer Interaction*, 4th edn, Hoboken, NJ: Wiley; Judith S. Olson and Wendy A. Kellogg (eds) (2014), *Ways of Knowing in HCI*, New York: Springer-Verlag.
45. Clayton H. Lewis (1990), 'A Research Agenda for the Nineties in Human–Computer Interaction', *Human–Computer Interaction*, no. 5, p. 136.
46. Elaine Lally (2002), *At Home with Computers*, Oxford: Berg; Thomas Berker, Maren Hartmann, Yves Punie and Katie Ward (eds) (2006), *Domestication of Media and Technology*, Maidenhead: Open University Press.
47. Melissa Gregg (2011), *Work's Intimacy*, Cambridge: Polity Press, p. 16.
48. Gregg, *Work's Intimacy*, p. 16.
49. Gregg, *Work's Intimacy*, p. 16.
50. Acland, 'Introduction'.

51. Perec and Mortley, 'The Doing of Fiction', p. 99.
52. I have written elsewhere on the wider cultural impacts and importance of computers and computer use. See, in particular: Rowan Wilken (2014), 'Peter Carey's Laptop', *Cultural Studies Review*, vol. 20, no. 1, pp. 98–118.
53. Although, it should be noted that other HCI researchers were acutely aware of the importance of accounting for contexts of use around this time. For example, in her landmark 1987 book, Lucy Suchman critiqued the planning model of interaction that was then dominant among artificial intelligence (AI) researchers, arguing that this model was inadequate in that it did not account for the 'situatedness' of most human behaviour. See: Lucy Suchman (1987), *Plans and Situated Actions: The Problem of Human–Machine Communication*, Cambridge: Cambridge University Press, especially pp. 49–67.
54. Georges Perec (2009), 'Reading: A Socio-Physiological Sketch', in *Thoughts of Sorts*, trans. David Bellos, Boston: Verba Mundi, p. 88.
55. Salthouse, 'The Skill of Typing', p. 132.
56. Salthouse, 'The Skill of Typing', p. 133.
57. Lance Strate (1999), 'The Varieties of Cyberspace: Problems in Definition and Delimitation', *Western Journal of Communication*, vol. 63, no. 3, p. 389.
58. In another, more speculative descriptive work of a similar nature, Sophie Cornanguer provides an account of the '4000 actions that a robot would have to carry out to live for one day as the inhabitant of a house'. This list of actions is presented in visually dizzying capitalised sans serif white font on a black background (thus resembling text on an early computer screen). And, like Perec's written account of an employee within a large bureaucracy futilely seeking a raise, Cornanguer's description runs with minimal punctuation (commas and ellipses only, no full stops) over seven-and-a-half pages. The description of the necessary steps required to prepare a morning coffee alone fills a page and a half. See: Sophie Cornanguer (2004), 'I Am a Robot', in Vicente Guallart (ed.), *Media House Project*, Barcelona: Institut d'arquitectura avançada de Catalunya, pp. 80–7. A further, famous example of detailed description of routine human action is found in Samuel Beckett's novel *Watt*, where Beckett, as Mark Byron explains, documents in uninterrupted block text 'all thirty-six possible permutations of to-ing and fro-ing' within a single room by the character Knott 'between any two of the room's objects (door, window, fire, bed)'. See: Mark Byron (2012), '"Change All the Names": Revision and Narrative Structure in Samuel Beckett's *Watt*', *AUMLA: Journal of the Australasian Universities Language and Literature Association*, April, endnote 3, p. 65, available at: http://aulla.com.au/wp-content/uploads/2013/12/AULLA-2011-Proceedings.pdf.
59. Paul Virilio, quoted in Enrique Walker (2001), 'Paul Virilio on Georges Perec', *AA Files*, no. 45–6, p. 17.
60. Robert Willim (2003), 'Claiming the Future: Speed, Business Rhetoric and Computer Practice', in Christina Garsten and Helena Wulff (eds), *New Technologies at Work: People, Screens and Social Virtuality*, Oxford: Berg, p. 126. For a further, albeit much abbreviated, account of this same process, see Deborah Lupton (1995), 'The Embodied Computer/User', *Body and Society*, vol. 1, no. 3–4, p. 97.
61. Stephen Clucas (2000), 'Cultural Phenomenology and the Everyday', *Critical Quarterly*, vol. 42, no. 1, p. 26.
62. Jeffrey Kittay (1981), 'Introduction', *Yale French Studies*, no. 61, p. iv.
63. Steven Connor (2000), 'Making an Issue of Cultural Phenomenology', *Critical Quarterly*, vol. 41, no. 1, pp. 4–5.
64. Stephen Clucas, 'Cultural Phenomenology and the Everyday', p. 25.
65. Kittay, 'Introduction', p. iv.

66. Howard Becker (2001), 'Georges Perec's Experiments in Social Description', *Ethnography*, vol. 2, no. 1, p. 66. For a prime example of the kind of artistic usage to which Becker is referring, see Daniel Spoerri (1995), *An Anecdoted Topography of Chance*, London: Atlas Press.
67. Becker, 'George Perec's Experiments', p. 69.
68. Becker, 'George Perec's Experiments', p. 71.
69. Becker, 'George Perec's Experiments', p. 71.
70. Becker, 'George Perec's Experiments', p. 75.
71. Fred Lukermann (1961), 'The Concept of Location in Classical Geography', *Annals of the Association of American Geographers*, no. 51, p. 206.
72. Becker, 'Georges Perec's Experiments', p. 75.
73. Samuel Beckett (1961), 'Dante . . . Bruno. Vico . . Joyce', in Samuel Beckett, Marcel Brion, Frank Budgen, Stuart Gilbert, Eugene Jolas, Victor Llona, Robert McAlmon, Thomas McGreevy, Elliot Paul, John Rodker, Robert Sage and William Carlos Williams, *Our Exagmination Round His Factification for Incamination of Work in Progress*, London: Faber & Faber, p. 14.
74. Maurice Blanchot (1993), *The Infinite Conversation*, trans. Susan Hanson, Minneapolis: University of Minnesota Press, p. 98.
75. Ben Highmore (2002), *Everyday Life and Cultural Theory: An Introduction*, London: Routledge, p. 161.
76. Connor, 'Making an Issue', p. 4.
77. Stephen Clucas, 'Cultural Phenomenology and the Everyday', p. 25.

Afterword

CHAPTER 14

The Afterlives of a Writer

David Bellos

In the writing business, dying is not a good idea. You lose your chance of a Nobel Prize and you have to give up book tours and television chat shows. You aren't writing anything new, so your publisher has less reason to keep your back titles in print. True, you get your name in the papers for a few days when the obituaries come out, but that is usually the end.[1] Most major authors suffer posthumous occlusion for a couple of decades and only some of them re-emerge after a generation-length gap. This cycle has been observed many times in the history of literature. Although it is not amenable to the kind of measurement applied to economic cycles, the 'generational succession' of literary eminence in roughly thirty-five-year waves is one well-established way of accounting for how the canon gets shaped.[2]

By this yardstick, Georges Perec should be emerging around now, from a period of relative obscurity, to take his place in the literary pantheon. It is true that he is at last scheduled to appear in the most prestigious 'complete works' collection in France, the Bibliothèque de la Pléiade,[3] but the story of his posthumous life is in most other respects quite possibly unique.

When he fell victim to cancer in 1982, Perec was not at the forefront of the literary scene. He had enjoyed two brief moments of prominence – on the publication of *Things*, which won the Renaudot Prize in 1965, and with *Life A User's Manual*, which took the Prix Médicis in 1978. However, none of the fifteen other books he published in his lifetime brought him near the limelight. *What Little Moped with Chrome-plated Handlebars at the Back of the Yard?*,[4] *A Man Asleep*,[5] *La Boutique Obscure*[6] and *W or The Memory of Childhood*[7] were commercial flops and ignored by most critics. Unlike his more visible literary contemporaries, Perec didn't belong to any one publishing house, let alone to the prestigious imprints of Gallimard or Minuit. He wasn't a publisher's editor or a *directeur de collection*.[8] Unlike Philippe Sollers, he didn't run a literary review, and he didn't judge literary prizes, unlike Alain Robbe-Grillet.[9] He'd been on the television book show *Apostrophes* only once, where he didn't make much of an impression,[10] and his radio work, which had mostly been done abroad, was almost a secret in France.[11] As he was barely a reserve in the B team of literary glory, dying ought to have been a terminal event for his work. But it was not. Not only did he acquire more readers after his death than he had ever had before, he rose to a position of national and international eminence that far outshone the celebrities who had overshadowed him during his life.

I would like to believe that he owes his present standing to the intrinsic quality of his work. In fact, I do believe without reservation that he was a writer of genius. I have no patience with the cynical view of Perec's readers and fans as sheep-like consumers of newly-legitimated cultural goods. On the other hand, I'm not happy to fall back on the cliché that's been made of Mallarmé's *tel qu'en lui-même enfin l'éternité le change* and say, just like my mother, that 'genius will out'. Perec was not destined by ineluctable forces to cross the paths of the other contributors to this volume – but those encounters weren't the result of a media conspiracy either. Like all real events in history, the powerful afterlife of Georges Perec is the product of only partly coordinated actions taken by real people in response to motivations of different kinds. Why those actions were taken, and why they had the results that they did, are the questions I want to address.

The story begins with a great sadness. Perec's unforeseen demise was a terrible shock to three core groups: his friends and relations (the former more numerous by far); the active members of the writers' group Oulipo, to which he belonged; and a handful of fans who had begun to collect his scattered writings, many of which had never existed in more than a hundred copies.[12] All three circles (there were of course individuals who belonged to more than one of them) sincerely wanted to keep Georges Perec alive. The circumstances made that a hard thing to do.

Perec was an only child with no offspring and at the time of his death, he had no legal spouse. He did not have an agent and he had made no will so there was no simple answer to the immediate question of who would manage his literary rights. In fact, it took years to locate all his collateral heirs and wind up his estate. However, because Perec was not a high-selling author or a prominent figure on the literary stage, most of the distant cousins who found to their surprise that they were heirs to a writer they'd never met were happy to abdicate their portion in the literary work to a person prepared to devote herself full-time to keeping it alive.

Nothing had prepared Ela Bienenfeld for the role she took on as her cousin's *ayant-droit*. With modesty and good sense she sought help from all three circles of Perec's community of friends – the obsessive bibliographers and literary scholars among his fans, the experienced writers from Oulipo, and the academics from his wider circle of friends who knew some of the ropes of the publishing world. Many of these would also need her permission to publish or quote from his works.

These were the circumstances in which an informal non-profit group, 'Les Amis de Georges Perec', was set up; it was later re-incorporated as a recognised voluntary body under its present name, 'Association Georges-Perec'. It borrowed a tiny room in the library where Perec's former spouse worked to house its donated collection of papers, periodicals and books. In due course, Perec's companion allowed the writer's papers to be transferred from his apartment to the same archive, which became a convivial and productive base for scholarly work. The association also sponsored a residential conference on Georges Perec at Cerisy-la-Salle, the same place where, in 1959, a famous conference on Raymond Queneau had led to the creation of Oulipo.[13] Papers from the 1984 Perec conference were published as the first of the *Cahiers Georges Perec*, which also made available some of the vast hinterland of the writer's work.[14]

The scholarly bent of these initial moves was essential – not so much because academic work can grant cultural legitimacy, but because much of Perec's work consisted of essays, stories, short pieces, poems and exercises published in little-known, limited-circulation and already defunct reviews. How does a writer stay alive in the public domain? By bringing out new books. Finding the rest of Perec's work was the pre-condition for his posthumous life.

The *Nachlass* was not huge, but it was extraordinarily diverse. Perec had said in the one piece that he'd published in a national daily that his ambition was 'to write every kind of thing it was possible for a writer to write nowadays',[15] and the growing collections in the Arsenal Library began to show how close he had come to fulfilling it. The first step in bringing the 'other Perecs' to light was the publication of a miscellany of essays on diverse topics together with some jewels of formal writing. *Thoughts of Sorts* (original title: *Penser/Classer*), which appeared in 1985, displayed Perec's unpretentious wit and his interest in fields as far-flung as the psychology of reading, the art of sorting books, and experimental cookery. It also included Perec's foundational 'Statement of Intent', which gave readers a way of understanding the nature of his literary project – in 800 words. When the editor of the series in which *Thoughts of Sorts* appeared moved from Hachette to Le Seuil, he was able to resume the programme of keeping Perec alive as an author of new books.[16] The second volume of 'lost pieces', *l'infra-ordinaire*,[17] was perhaps even more instrumental in widening our vision of Perec's mind, as it collected most of the pieces in which the writer had investigated the anthropology of everyday life. The subsequent volume, *Je suis né*,[18] opened up previously hidden dimensions of Perec's autobiographical projects, including unpublished manuscript material. *Cantatrix sopranica*[19] disinterred a set of hilarious scientific spoofs, some of which had previously circulated only in photocopied sheets, and *LG*[20] focused attention on Perec's early essays as a theorist of literature. *Le voyage d'hiver*,[21] the slimmest but most pregnant of the series, reissued a brain-teasing Borgesian short story that had virtually disappeared, save for a translation into English.[22] It gave rise to a series of partly parodic sequels by members of Oulipo, initially published in the pamphlets of the *Bibliothèque oulipienne* but now gathered in a fat volume in English translation (the latest contribution features the writer of this essay). The series concluded with *Beaux presents, belles absentes*[23] which made available Perec's most exquisite formal poetry. None of these volumes were bestsellers, but they had a powerful cumulative effect on Perec's place in the world of letters. Like a living writer, he was bringing out a new book a year. The tousle-haired imp whose photograph featured on the paperback reissue of *Life A User's Manual* was turning by stages into the creator of an *oeuvre*.

Three other ventures enriched the 'Perec Galaxy' in the public sphere in those years, and inflected the course of his afterlife quite profoundly. First, Bienenfeld invited Philippe Lejeune, a recognised authority on self-writing, to help her read through the substantial quantity of personal and autobiographical material that had been found among Perec's unpublished manuscripts.[24] These included two large, unfinished projects called 'Places' (*Lieux*), and 'The Tree' (*L'Arbre*), as well as diaries, drafts, letters and essays. It did not prove possible to make publishable books out of the unfinished works, but the study of the manuscripts resulted in a fundamental work on Perec's struggle with memory and forgetting, *La Mémoire et l'Oblique*,[25] which in its turn transformed understanding of *W or The Memory of Childhood*.[26]

In the second place, two of Perec's closest friends in the Oulipo, Harry Mathews and Jacques Roubaud, worked out how to turn the finished chapters and draft fragments of the detective novel Perec was working on at the time of his death into a readable work, *"53 Days"*, despite there being no certainty as to what the solution to the mystery was.

The third event came from outside Perec's circles of friends and colleagues. Sami Frey, a well-known actor, devised a theatrical recitation of the 479 sentences beginning 'I remember', recording trivia from Perec's childhood and youth that had appeared as an almost unnoticed book in 1978. First performed in Geneva, and then at the 1988 Avignon Festival, *Je me souviens* enchanted audiences old and young, and when it transferred to Paris filled the Mogador Theatre every night for months.

Permission has never been granted for film or TV adaptations of any of Perec's work, and his posthumous life has been mediated exclusively through print, radio and live theatre. As this volume shows, Perec's influence can be felt across many of the new media, but it springs exclusively from old media forms.

The cumulative effect of the staged release of Perec's scattered fragments in slim, thematically organised volumes over the period 1985–94, the opening up of the vast autobiographical projects through Lejeune's detailed study, the publication of *"53 Days"* and the popular appeal of the stage version of *I Remember* transformed the very meaning of the name Georges Perec in the decade following his death. As the material available grew ever more diverse, unsuspected connections between its parts were revealed. Almost every new piece in the puzzle illuminated some element in *Life A User's Manual*, and the meticulous, myopic, almost cultish rereading of the novel became an academic trend.[27] But the reciprocal effect outside the academy was just as important. Perec's masterpiece seemed less and less like a one-off marvel designed to keep arithmological textologists in thrall for years, but the visible part of an unpretentious but complex engagement with fundamental issues: the organisation of space and time, the nature of the self and the understanding of modern society.[28]

Apart from the special situation in Germany (see note 18), Perec had had no significant presence outside of France during his lifetime and was entirely unknown in the English-speaking world. His publishers regarded his works as 'untranslatable' and made no effort to sell *W or The Memory of Childhood* or *Life A User's Manual* abroad. The English translation of *Life* that appeared in 1987 was, therefore, not the result of initiatives taken by Perec's estate, by his publishers, by French cultural institutions or by the friends and scholars who gathered in the Arsenal Library and at the newly instituted monthly seminar on the premises of the University of Paris-VII. On the other hand, once I'd put myself forward and disregarded the negative response from Hachette, I found initially wary but increasingly warm support from all those quarters. The estate shared Perec's preparatory notebooks with me; the Association Georges Perec gave me unlimited access to its archive; the master of formal writing, Bernard Magné, as well as many members of Oulipo, answered my questions about the functioning of Perec's constraints; Eugen Helmle went over the precious copy of the novel that Perec had annotated for him in view of its German translation.[29] As my work advanced, the two publishers involved, in the USA and the UK, became as convinced as I was that we were dealing with a masterpiece of universal importance. The initiative was mine, but I didn't complete the crazy task I'd taken on all by myself.

The path that led to the publication of *Life A User's Manual* is not typical. Few books are ever translated into English that have not been acquired by publishers on the basis of reports from scouts, book fair buzz or agents' plugs; one-man campaigns to get a deceased and unknown foreign author taken on by a major house almost always go straight into the waste-paper bin. I would not recommend it to any established translator, and even less to a tyro, which I was at that time. But, history is made of unlikely events; I wouldn't try explaining them all.

Translating is one thing, publishing another, and they work hand in hand. But reception is an entirely different matter. The majority of literary works translated into English reach small audiences and quickly disappear from bookstore shelves (even those by winners of the Nobel Prize). The exceptions to this dismal rule don't have any discernible collective quality: *Dr Zhivago*, *The Name of the Rose*, Schlink's *The Reader* and the Millennium Trilogy are as like as chalk and cheese. This leaves us without a way of explaining why *Life A User's Manual* became a hit, except through the history of how it occurred. Perec's novel benefited, as by the bouncing of rubber bullets, from two unplanned and unforeseen attempts to stop it in its tracks: a vituperative review by a senior English novelist roused to high dudgeon by the suggestion on the publisher's dust-jacket blurb that Perec's novel could be set alongside Joyce's *Ulysses*[30] and a take-down of the translation in the *Times Literary Supplement* (not a newcomer to snobbish disparagement) by an author-academic who might have liked to translate Perec himself.[31] The ensuing brouhaha did more to commend *Life A User's Manual* to young readers fed up with stuffed shirts than any imaginable PR strategy could have done. But, however the ball was made to start rolling, the popularity of Perec's masterpiece in English translation has to be counted an implausible but genuinely cultural phenomenon. English readers recognised (or mistook) the game-playing, puzzle-setting dimension of *Life A User's Manual* as part of the specifically British tradition of the comic novel. The fact that the several extracts from *Tristram Shandy* are more visible in the translation than in the original (because they are in the original, not in translation) may have been a big prompt,[32] but readers brought up on Dickens, Carroll and Waugh generally found it easy to relate to *Life* as a game. Just as striking to British readers was the absence from Perec's novel of the conventional subject matter of routine literary fiction of the period. One writer called me after she'd read the galley proofs. 'It's wonderful!' she exclaimed. 'No sex, no drugs and no violence! So refreshing!' It's not entirely true, of course.[33] What's important is that Perec's shift of focus felt like an escape from the twin rocks of the Hampstead romance and the low-life exposé. A third strong feature of the reception of the novel in English was its appeal to readers far outside the target audience. Letters poured in (and still do, in a dribble) from maths students, computer science graduates, trainee architects, sociologists and all kinds of geeks expressing enthusiasm and asking questions about the construction of the text and about the author himself. *Life A User's Manual* seems to have created its own Anglophone reading public which persists to this day: every week, for the past quarter century at least, fifty people have bought a new copy somewhere in the English-speaking world.

Life impacted Perec's afterlife in three fundamental ways. Its wide sale made Perec's other titles tradeable objects, and the *oeuvre* began to appear in English translation (and from then on in many other languages, too) backwards-way on: in 1988 *W or The Memory of Childhood*, a work of 1975, and in 1990 *Things* and *A Man Asleep*, first published 1965 and 1967 respectively. It's much easier to understand the shape of Perec's work if you start with its culmination than if you read it in chronological order. English Perec thus has a profile quite distinct from its original. All the same, *Life* did not automatically hoist the other works to the forefront and none of them has sold very well in English translation. Restrospectively, it seems likely that Perec would not be what he is today outside of France had he been launched in London and Boston in 1987 with *W or The Memory of Childhood*, or even *A Void*.

As few French novels get translated into English and even fewer of them get reviews, let alone high sales, *Life A User's Manual* reinforced perception of Perec as a major author inside France. It wasn't responsible for the series of talks, readings and shows put on at the 1988 Avignon Festival under the title 'La Galaxie Georges Perec' – but it was featured there, as clear evidence for the international audience of the festival that Perec was now a presence on the world stage.[34]

However, the most dramatic consequence of the publication of *Life A User's Manual* was the idea that dawned in the mind of its London publisher to commission a life of Georges Perec. No such thing was likely to emerge in France. The overlapping circles that came together to make Perec's work available and to promote it shared an unspoken understanding that there would be no prying into the writer's 'private life'. Besides this collective self-silencing compact, the dominant mode of academic inquiry in France was formalist, sometimes rigidly so. Between them, Michel Foucault and Roland Barthes had effectively put interest in the lives of actual writers out of court, and Roland Barthes' later dabbling with 'biographemes' had only served to make conventional life writing seem like old hat.[35] But, quite apart from these personal and intellectual blockages, there was no prospect of a French publisher financing major research of the kind needed for such a task. That is why the definitive biography of Sartre was commissioned in New York, not Paris – and pioneering lives of Camus, Beauvoir and Beckett (to take just three examples) were all written in English.[36] Consequently, properly documented biographies are known in French as 'biographies à l'anglo-saxonne'. It wasn't completely unrealistic for a London publisher to think he could sponsor a life of Perec – but it was a long shot.

The initial idea was for some kind of 'Reader's Guide' to *Life A User's Manual*, with a separate and equally brief narrative of the writer's life. Within a few months of starting work on these projects in 1988, I realised how interlocked they were. Beyond the two stories – of a book and a life – there was a third, and it was the most interesting by far: the story of their interlocking. That's the main reason why *Georges Perec: A Life in Words* is so long!

I had never written a biography, I had never met Perec and didn't belong to any of his circles of friends, and I had no position in French institutional life. The only assets I had were exactly those – together with the goodwill felt by many towards Perec's first English translator. As my research proceeded, I was struck by the affection that everyone I met felt for Georges Perec. Literary theory hasn't ever predicated the lasting impact of a writer on his personal amiability, but in the case of Perec it simply cannot be left out. Living among temperamental Left Bank intellectuals with legendary backbiting skills, Perec had no enemies![37] The original name of the ad hoc group that sought to preserve the writer's work, 'Les Amis de Georges Perec', turned out to be neither a euphemism nor a metaphor, but a literal truth. The founding members were all affectionate friends of a man who had said of himself, when trying to sum up his rather patchy love-life, 'l'amitié aura été ma grande passion'. If the first decade of Perec's afterlife can be presented as a remarkable story of collective action then what powered it along was payback for the many deep friendships that Perec inspired as a man.

Just as noteworthy was the company Perec kept. He collaborated with visual artists and musicians, he knew people in film, he was in touch with architects and sociologists, he cultivated old chums who'd followed academic and professional careers, but he didn't hobnob with literary celebrities – even those he admired like Michel Butor.

Researching the life of a writer among contemporaries who were still in mid-career led perhaps inevitably to unearthing all kinds of forgotten things – hundreds of letters, a few short stories and early novels that had been abandoned, forgotten or simply lost when moving house, book reviews published under pseudonyms and stray articles in forgotten journals, in addition to administrative documents (a baptism certificate, a file in the German War Reparations Office, his military record) and traces of Perec's passage in Brisbane, Belgrade, East Lansing, Warwick, Venice and Saarbrücken. Much of what I found then would have been lost by now, without any doubt. From some points of view it was too early to write a full biography, less than ten years after Perec's death; in practice, however, no biographer would have been able to bring all that material to light had the project been deferred for a decade or two. *Georges Perec: A Life in Words* is structured by chronology, as life stories conventionally are; its merits and defects are also dependent on the thread of time.

The French version of that book, prepared in parallel with the English original and published a few weeks later, was selected by the Goncourt Academy for an award in 1994. In his presentation speech, the president, Michel Tournier, made it clear that the prize was to be taken as an apology by the Goncourt panel for having 'missed' *Life A User's Manual* on its launch in 1978. That's an amazing turn of the tables in the space of fifteen years. The most prestigious legitimating instance on the French literary scene had come to *need* Perec more than Perec ever needed the Goncourt prize.

Just as significant was the publication in *l'infini* of a short piece by Perec's biographer on his own work.[38] *L'infini* is the journal of Philippe Sollers, the only person who could reasonably be called an enemy of Georges Perec.[39] By 1995, with almost his entire *oeuvre* made accessible in print, with his work translated into English and many other languages besides, and with his life-story available in a prize-winning book, Perec was a superstar in the literary firmament. Quite right, too: but, as I hope to have shown, it didn't happen by magic but through a long, mostly serendipitous, string of collective and individual acts.

Georges Perec is the same age as Ismail Kadare, and his friends and first readers are long past three score years and ten. The devotion of Bienenfeld and the efforts of scholars created the illusion over many years that Perec's career carried on throughout his natural span. As that now approaches its end, it's possible that his work will fall into the trough that typically comes after a writer's death, confirming the conventional view of the effect of generation change on cultural canons. But, I don't think that will happen. With a thousand dissertations on *W or The Memory of Childhood* in university repositories already, with his works available in translation throughout the world (even his biography has been translated into Japanese and Hebrew), with his papers now the property of the Bibliothèque nationale and Oulipo going from strength to strength as it combines complex literary experiment with accessible public entertainment – with all these vectors of cultural and popular support, Perec's position is now too deeply entrenched to shift very far any time soon.

What's more, Perec's afterlife has hardly begun. His first completed novel, *Le Condottière*, long believed lost, was published in French in 2012 and in English, as *Portrait of A Man*, in 2014. And there are more early works to come.

Beyond these sturdy circumstantial props, my confidence in the perennial appeal of Perec's writing is based on something else. Perec's writing is not inimitable, by design. I don't mean anyone can be a genius and beat Perec at his own game. I mean that the forms of writing that he uses are inherently learnable through imitation. This applies to simple Oulipian exploits like the lipogram and to mind-bending alphabetical manipulations like *belles absentes*. His non-Oulipian exercises in style – a whole chapter in the conditional tense (in *Things*), a whole novel in the second person (*A Man Asleep*), a story whose single hero has a hundred different names (how about that for the unknown soldier?) (*What Little Moped . . .?*), a stage play consisting of the iteration of the steps determined by a mock algorithm for approaching your boss for a raise

(*L'Augmentation*), or a 'kick-starter' formula such as 'I remember . . .', 'I've forgotten . . .', 'Please don't tell me . . .' – all these forms of play with words provoke active responses and prompt readers (especially young ones) to try their own hand.

There are many reasons for Perec's presence as a ferment and provocation in visual art, music and social thought but his basic appeal is ever more apparent in an age of interactive media. Perec's work is a pedagogy of writing. It made a translator and biographer out of me. I expect it will go on making writers out of many other readers he is sure to have.

NOTES

1. Sour grapes alone can account for the claims I have heard other writers make that Perec's premature death was his best-ever advertising stunt.
2. Henri Peyre (1948), *Les Générations littéraires,* Paris: Boivin, is the classic exposition; Robert Escarpit (1965), *Sociology of Literature,* trans. Ernest Pick, Painesville, OH: Lake Erie College Press, gives a bite-sized version.
3. Edited by Christelle Reggiani and Jean-Luc Joly, the one-volume 'Pléiade Perec', due out in December 2016, will not in fact contain all of Perec's writing, but with all his narrative prose texts together with some of his essayistic works and a selection of poetry, it will be a very substantial collection.
4. Georges Perec (1966), *What Little Moped with Chrome-plated Handlebars at the Back of the Yard?,* Paris: Les Lettres Nouvelles.
5. Georges Perec (1967), *A Man Asleep,* Paris: Éditions Denoël.
6. Georges Perec (2013), *La Boutique Obscure: 124 Dreams,* trans. Daniel Levin Becker, New York: Melville House.
7. Georges Perec (1987), *W or The Memory of Childhood,* trans. David Bellos, Boston: Godine.
8. The publisher of *Life A User's Manual* did in fact give Perec a retainer as a 'literary adviser' after the writer left his job at the CNRS, but Perec preferred to give his opinions on manuscripts over the telephone and never actually wrote a reader report. He didn't spot any budding geniuses; it wasn't a job he liked very much. (Information from Paul Otchakovsky-Laurens.)
9. Sollers founded *Tel Quel* in 1960 and remains the editor of its successor journal, *l'infini;* Robbe-Grillet was a member of the Médicis prize jury.
10. On 8 December 1978, alongside Alain Robbe-Grillet, who, with his stentorian voice and easy manner, stole the show.
11. Full details can be found in Ariane Steiner, *Georges Perec und Deutschland,* Würzburg: Königshausen & Neumann, 2001; in English, see David Bellos, 'Radio Perec'.
12. Every year Perec produced around one hundred cyclostyled booklets of 'thematic puns' as his New Year's gift to friends. These *Vœux* have always been collectors' items, as are first editions of *Ulcérations* in the Bibliothèque oulipenne pamphlet series, and of *La Clôture,* with photographs of Rue Vilin by Christine Lipinska, of which exactly 100 copies were made. Copies of *Métaux,* poems written to accompany large-format *graphisculptures* by Paolo Boni, are even rarer.
13. The conference was titled *Une nouvelle défense et illustration de la langue française* and it

was held to honour the author of *Zazie dans le métro* (1959) and publication of *Cent Mille Milliards de poèmes* (1960). Conversations among participants led to the idea of monthly meetings in Paris to pursue the study of mathematics and literature; after some hesitation the name Oulipo was adopted in the spring of 1961. Hervé Le Tellier (2006), *Esthétique de l'Oulipo*, Bordeaux: Le Castor Astral, pp. 7–8.

14. Twelve issues of the *Cahiers Georges Perec* have appeared to date. The first eleven are all available for download from the website of the Association Georges-Perec. With the exception of Volume 7, all contain useful and often invaluable material.
15. David Bellos (1993), *Georges Perec: A Life in Words*, London: Harvill, pp. 649–51. As 'Statement of Intent', in Georges Perec (2009), *Thoughts of Sorts*, trans. David Bellos, Boston: Godine, pp. 3–5. Also as 'Notes on What I am Looking For', in Georges Perec (1997), *Species of Spaces and Other Pieces*, trans. John Sturrock, London: Penguin, pp. 141–3.
16. Less arbitrarily, Maurice Olender's *Librairie du XXe siècle* series also changed its name and is now the *Librairie du XXIe siècle*.
17. Georges Perec (1989), *L'Infra-ordinaire*, Paris: Seuil, Librairie du XXIe siècle.
18. Georges Perec (1990), *Je suis né*, Paris: Seuil, Librairie du XXIe siècle.
19. Georges Perec (1991), *Cantatrix Sopranica L. et autres écrits scientifiques*, Paris: Seuil, La Librairie du XXIe siècle.
20. Georges Perec (1992), *LG: Une aventure des années soixante*, Paris: Seuil.
21. Georges Perec (1985), *Le Voyage d'hiver*; as *The Winter Journey*, trans. David Bellos, Greensboro, PA: Post-Industrial Press.
22. First written for *Saisons*, an internal publication of the Hachette publishing house distributed to staff as a New Year's gift, *Le Voyage d'hiver* was reprinted in *Le Magazine littéraire* in 1983. I first came across it at the Cerisy conference and translated it straightaway, as a try-out. It appeared in the UK in *Encounter* in July 1985 and was picked up by *Conjunctions* in the USA (issue 12 (1988), pp. 81–6). It was also published as a hand-made art book by Post-Industrial Press of Greensboro, PA, in 1990. A barely variant translation by John Sturrock was later published in *Species of Spaces*, pp. 277–85.
23. Georges Perec (1994), *Beaux Présents, Belles Absentes*, Paris: Seuil, Librairie du XXIe siècle.
24. The combination of formalism and reception aesthetics in Philippe Lejeune (1988), *On Autobiography*, trans. Katherine Leary, Minneapolis: University of Minnesota Press (French edition, 1975), succeeded in giving autobiography a new respectability in literary scholarship.
25. Philippe Lejeune (1991), *La Mémoire et l'Oblique*, Paris: POL.
26. The second year of the Georges Perec Seminar at the University of Paris-VII in 1988–9 was tellingly titled '*W ou le souvenir d'enfance*: une fiction'. The prejudice against 'anecdotalism' was first seriously dented by Lejeune's contribution to the seminar. A selection of papers from it was published as the second of the *Cahiers Georges Perec*, with a give-away amendment to the title, '*W ou le souvenir d'enfance*: une fiction?'
27. The formal approach was dominated by Bernard Magné, whose *Perecollages 1981–1993* collects most of the papers he produced. Other notable analysts of Perec's textual microstructures are Dominique Bertelli and Mireille Ribière. The infuriatingly microscopic style of their work led to many remarkable discoveries.
28. Claude Burgelin (1989), *Georges Perec*, Paris: Le Seuil, was a pioneering attempt to balance the different sides of Perec's achievement. There still is no better short book on the writer.
29. Perec established friendly relations with the (West) German translator of *Things* from 1966. Eugen Helmle went on to translate all of Perec's books in prose, out of fidelity and

interest, for small houses outside the mainstream of German publishing. *Das Leben Gebrauchsanweisung* (Zweitausendeins, 1980), for example, is a collectors' marvel, with two-colour printing, and comes in a hand-made black box with a silk ribbon to tie it closed, in imitation of the boxes made by Madame Hourcade for Bartlebooth's puzzles (*Life*, p. 46). The box also contains a 100-piece jigsaw of the Bertall engraving used for the cover of the French paperback edition of *La Vie mode d'emploi*. It appears that each copy of this irregular, hand-cut puzzle has a different piece missing. A reassembly of the jigsaw in the copy I acquired serves as the cover design of the UK paperback edition, published by Harvill in 1988.

30. Anthony Burgess (1987), '*Life A User's Manual*' [review], *The Independent*, 16 September.
31. Gabriel Josipovici (1987), '*Life A User's Manual*' [review], *Times Literary Supplement*, 30 October.
32. *Life A User's Manual*, p. 329, lines 4–10 is the most visible among them; there are eight or nine others.
33. Sex can be found on pp. 119 and 152, and seven or eight other pages, and the story of Sven Ericcsson on pp. 156–73 is a violent one. Only drugs are entirely absent from *Life A User's Manual*.
34. Events at this huge festival of mostly dramatic art included a 'spatialised reading' of *Life A User's Manual* involving the simultaneous recitation of different chapters in different rooms of a multi-storey town house; a stage reading of *W ou le souvenir d'enfance*; and an exhibition of first editions and photographs of Georges Perec.
35. See Michel Foucault (1969), 'Qu'est-ce qu'un auteur?', *Bulletin de la Société française de Philosophie*, vol. 63, no. 3, pp. 75–104, and Roland Barthes (1977), 'The Death of the Author', in *Image Music Text*, trans. Stephen Heath, London: Fontana, for the rejection of literary biography; see Roland Barthes (1981), *Camera Lucida*, trans. Richard Howard, New York: Wang & Hill, for the concept of 'biographeme', which, despite its initial impact, has been left to lie in peace.
36. See Deirdre Bair (1990), *Simone de Beauvoir: A Biography*, New York: Summit; James Knowlson (1996), *Damned to Fame: The Life of Samuel Beckett*, London: Bloomsbury; and Herbert Lottman (1979), *Albert Camus: A Biography*, New York: Doubleday. There were many fine French exponents of literary biography in earlier periods (André Maurois, for example), and there are many well-documented, research-based biographies produced in Paris in the twenty-first century, too (Anissimov's *Romain Gary*, for example). The antibiographical stance of the Parisian intellectual establishment was principally a phenomenon of the period 1960–90.
37. Correction: just one. See note 28.
38. David Bellos (1994), 'Mes années Perec', *l'infini*, no. 47, pp. 38–48.
39. Philippe Sollers's 'Je me souviens des années 80' is, despite its brevity, one of the nastiest posthumous put-downs I have had the displeasure to read.

Index

Page numbers in *italics* indicate illustrations.

9SG design puzzle, 182–3
'*53 Days*', 5, 248, 249

AA Files, 173–4
Aballí, Ignasi, 36–7
Abstract Paintings (Reinhardt), 25
Acéphale, 166
Acland, Charles, 226
action, 140
actuality, 10–11, 12, 58, 99, 105
Adair, Gilbert, 145, 175, 232
address labels, 70–1
Admassu, Emanuel, *180*
aesthetics, 161, 163
afterdeaths, 16
afterlife, 8–10, 32–40
afterlives, 5, 6–7, 11, 58–60
algorithms, 12, 13, 85, 86, 87–8
   Art and Craft of Approaching Your Head of Department to Submit a Request for a Raise, The, 193
   banality, 136
   Game Studies, 189, 191
   Life A User's Manual, 93–8, 195
   lists, 129
   poetry, 59–60
   social media, 124
Alphabets, 4
ambient intimacy, 139–40
Anomalous, 59
Antelme, Robert, 126, 130
anthropology, 142–3
anticipatory plagiarism, 38–40, 165

anti-computational turn, 124
applications, 15–16, 208; *see also* location-sensitive mobile social networking (LMSN)
'Approaches to What?', 229
Aragon, Louis, 161
arbitrariness, 49–50, 51, 128, 133
arbitrary naturalism, 107–8, 116
architectural design and compositional constraints, 177–85
Architectural Uncanny, The (Vidler), 183
architecture, 30
   infatuation with philosophers and writers, 171–3
   Perec's posthumous grand debut in, 173–5
Architecture Association, 173
architext, 176
Archiv (Schmid), 39
Areopagitica (Milton), 9–10
Aristotle, 54
Armantrout, Rae, 59
Art and Craft of Approaching Your Head of Department to Submit a Request for a Raise, The, 12, 87, 92–3, 121, 193
artificial intelligence (AI), 59–60
artworks, 8–9
Association Georges Perec, 7, 247, 249; *see also* 'Friends of Georges Perec, The'
Attempt at a Description of Things Seen at Mabillon Junction on 19 March 1978, 39

INDEX

'Attempt at an Inventory of the Liquid and Foodstuffs Ingurgitated by Me in the Course of the Year Nineteen Hundred and Seventy-Four', 141
Attempt at Exhausting a Place in Paris, An (*Tentative d'épuisement d'un lieu parisien*), 3, 206–7, 208–9
   description, 237
   encounters with pseudonymous strangers, 219–21
   encounters with strangers, 214–17
   everyday, 126
   exhaustion, 105–7
   location-sensitive mobile social networking (LMSN), 15, 209–14, 217–23
   observation, 212
   visual arts, 36
attention, moral economy of, 132–3
Audin, Michèle, 166
Auschwitz, 2, 56, 123
Auster, Paul, 38
autobiographemes, 159, 164
autobiographical writing, 121
automatic machine, 88
automatic production, 89–90
automation, 123, 124
automatism, 120–1
avant-garde, 10, 28, 161

backgammon, 94, 95
Badiou, Alain, 49, 146
Ball, Lucille, 69
banality, 13, 136–7, 147
   and the everyday, 137–8, 149
   Memorial to the Murdered Jews of Europe (Eisenman), 183
   Pillow Book, The (Shōnagon), 143–6
   Twitter, 138–41
   see also everyday
Barraclough, Simon, 59
Barthes, Roland, 26, 106, 171
Barthesian methods, 146–7
Bataille, Georges, 166
Baudelaire, Charles, 15, 205–6
Beaux presents, belles absentes, 57, 248
Becker, Howard, 147, 237
Beckett, Samuel, 71, 237
Bedient, Calvin, 168n
Bellos, David, 4–5, 6, 55, 65n, 121, 189
Bénabou, Marcel, 7, 12, 54, 73, 157, 189
   on Marcel Duchamp, 28
   PALF, 89–90
   potential, 54
Benjamin, Walter, 9
Berge, Claude, 161
Bibliothèque oulipienne, 166, 248
Bienenfeld, Ela, 17, 246, 248, 253

big data, 124, 141, 145, 149
Bilder von der Straße ['Images of the Street'] (Schmid), 39
biographical data, 38
biography, 17, 189, 251–3
biological coding, 177
biopolitics, 7, 10
Bjarnason, Baldur, 140
Black Paintings (Stella), 25
Blanchot, Maurice, 137–8
Blast Theory, 81–2
Bogost, Ian, 129
Bök, Christian, 59, 160
Boltanski, Christian, 37–8, 132
books, 9–10
boredom, 106, 117
Borges, Jorge Luis, 165–6
Bourdieu, Pierre, 148
Braffort, Paul, 86, 87
Breakwell, Ian, 79
Breeze, Mary-Anne (Mez), 60, 81
Breton, André, 27
brevity, 13
'Brief Notes on the Fine Art of Arranging One's Books', 37
Brown, Michael, 59
Buck, Laura, *181*
Burgelin, Claude, 24
Bus Reflections (Estes), 30

Cache, Bernard, 171
Cage, John, 78
'Cahier des charges de *La Vie mode d'emploi*', 36
Cahiers Georges Perec, 7, 32, 247, 255n
CalArts, 160
Calle, Sophie, 38, 44n
Calvino, Italo, 12, 61, 69, 72, 120, 172–3
Candy Store, The (Estes), 30
Cantatrix sopranica, 248
capitalism, 8, 109, 111
Casanovas Blanco, Lluis Alexander, *179*, *180*
Castle, The (Kafka), 172
Castle of Crossed Destinies, The (Calvino), 173
categorisation, 4–5, 29
Cause commune (*Common Cause*), 3, 165, 174, 232
Cent mille milliards de poèmes (Queneau), 27, 53–5, 85–6, 98, 129–30
Centre national de la recherche scientifique (CNRS), 92
chance/anti-chance, 128
Chesterton, G. K., 69
Chouliaraki, Lilie, 123, 132
Chromatic Diet (Calle), 38
chunking theory, 228–9
cinema, 79–81

INDEX 259

cinematography, 36–7
cities, 175, 176; *see also Attempt at Exhausting a Place in Paris, An*; metropolis
city space, 15
class culture, 111–14
clinamen, 57–8, 86–7, 90, 98, 99, 184
CNRS Laboratoire Associé 38 (LA 38), 3, 5
codework, 81
combinatorics, 66n
committed literature, 24, 109
Common Cause (*Cause commune*), 3, 165, 174, 232
community and constraint, 163–5
compositional constraints, 177–85
computation, 12, 87–9, 121–2, 124–5, 129–30
  Art and Craft of Approaching Your Head of Department to Submit a Request for a Raise, The, 92–3
  and ethical writing, 131–3
  Machine, The, 90–2
  see also algorithms
computer database software, 5
computer games *see* Games Studies
computer languages, 59–60
computer programming, 60, 89
computer use
  everyday personal computer use, 233, 234–6, 238
  human-computer interaction (HCI), 226–34
computer-assisted text, 87
concentration camps, 2, 56, 123, 126–7
conceptual art, 85
conceptual poetry, 59
conceptual writing, 12, 85, 87
Connor, Steven, 236, 237–8
consciousness, 8
Consenstein, Peter, 163
consonantia, 76
constraint, 45–7, 194
  and architecture, 176–85
  and community, 163–5
  and discontinuities, 128
  and language, 161–2
  in *Life A User's Manual*, 195
  mathematics, 52
  mechanical, 93–4
  Memorial to the Murdered Jews of Europe, 183
  morality of, 49–51
  natural science, 52
  and poetry, 53–4, 57–60, 92
  politics of, 14, 159, 164
  and potentiality, 98–9
  programmatic, 93–4
  programmed, 133
  Sophie Calle, 38

  as substructure, 47–8
  Twitter, 142
  see also limitations
'Constructing the Architext: George Perec's *Life A User's Manual*' (Mitchell), 176
consumer culture, 29, 111–15
consumption, 146
Cornanguer, Sophie, 241n
Cosmicomics (Calvino), 72
Crewe, Louise, 145
critical path analysis, 230, *231*
critical realism, 107–8
Critique of Everyday Life (Lefebvre), 7–8, 109–10
cross-references, 76–7
cultural rituals, 115–16
'Cybernetics and Ghosts' (Calvino), 61

Das Leben Gebrauchsanweisung, 256n; *see also Life A User's Manual*
data *see* big data
database logic, 85
databases, 193–4
Days Under the Sign of B, C, & W (Calle), 38
day-to-day *see* everyday
de Certeau, Michael, 122, 137
de Paula, Daniel, 32, *33*, 36
Dean, Jodi, 140
'Défense de Klee', 25–6
Degraël, Vincent, 165
Deguelle, Anne, 35–6
Deleuze, Gilles, 184
democracy, 14
Derrida, Jacques, 171, 173
Desaparició (Aballí), 37
description, 237–8, 241n
  micro description, 228–34
  and the scene of everyday personal computer use, 234–6
design game, 182
design puzzle, 182–3
désoeuvrement (inoperativity), 54–5
diary writing, 144
'Dictionary of Received Ideas, The' (Walker), 177–8, *179–81*
Die Maschine (*The Machine*), 12, 55–6, 87, 90–2
digital aesthetics, 81–2
digital games *see* Games Studies
dispossession, 131
'Distinguishing Features: NIL' ('Signe particulier: NÉANT'), 37
Dites-le avec des fleurs, 37
Dorsey, Jack, 139–40
Double Game (Calle), 38
doxa, 106
Drabble, Margaret, 69

Duchamp, Marcel, 28
Duras, Marguerite, 69
Durie, Robin, 50
Durkheim, Émile, 137
Duvignaud, Jean, 3
Dworkin, Craig, 12, 85

École des hautes études en sciences sociales, 26
'Écriture et mass media', 26–7
Eisenman, Peter, 183, 184–5
Eisenstein, Sergei, 24
Elkin, Laura, 49–50, 159, 160
Elson, Rebecca, 59
Embracing the Ordinary (Foley), 138
end of history, 53, 54
End of Oulipo? The (Esposito, Elkin), 159, 160–1
endotic anthropology, 128–9
Entscheidungsproblem (halting problem), 88, 97, 99
epigrams, 69–70
Espèces d'espaces (*Species of Spaces*), 3, 30–1, 32, 122, 126, 173
esperance, 46–7, 62n
Esposito, Scott, 159, 160
Estes, Richard, 30
ethical writing, 123–5, 131–3
ethnography, 142–3
Eunoia (Bök), 59
everyday, 7–8, 12–13, 120, 122–3, 147
  and banality, 137–8, 149
  description, 237–8
  ethical writing, 132
  Henri Lefebvre, 109–10
  infra-ordinary, 125–7
  Paul Rabinow, 115–16
  technology, 124–5
  see also banality; infra-ordinary
everyday personal computer use, 233, 234–6, 238
Exeter Text, The (*Les Revenentes*), 3, 157
exhaustion, 16, 106–7
exhaustiveness, 207
experience, 46–7, 62n
'experimental', 51–2
experimental writing, 52
expert typing *see* skilled typing research
exteriorisation, 123
exteriority, 128, 129–30
external memory, 129

falsification, 52
fashion, 145, 146, 148–9
feminism, 59
field theory, 182
filing system *see* Peekaboo

film, 4, 24, 36–7, 79–81
Finnegans Wake (Joyce), 25, 71, 237
Firebrace, William, 173
Fitts Law of human movement, 230, 240n
Flambo, 193
flâneur, 15, 205–6
Foley, Michael, 138
'For a Realist Literature', 108
Foucault, Michael, 7
Foulipo, 59
Foursquare, 15, 208, 209, *210*, 212–14, 217, 220–1, 224n
fragile overlapping, 124
Frey, Sami, 17, 248
'Friends of Georges Perec, The', 17; *see also* Association Georges Perec
Front national, 163
Frosh, Paul, 132
'Funambulist Pamphlets', 172
functionality, 182

Gallery Portrait, A (*Un Cabinet d'amateur*), 5
Galloway, Alexander, 191, 197
games, 14–15, 192–3
  design game, 182
  see also play
Games Studies, 189, 190–2, 196–8
gamification, 213–14
Gaming: Essays on Algorithmic Culture (Galloway), 191
Garréta, Anne, 7, 49, 157, 163, 164
Gautier, Henry, 227
general and particular, 108–9, 110, 111
General Line (*La Ligne générale*), 24–6, 165, 174
General Line, The (Eisenstein), 24
geographical formulations of places, 211
George Perec: A Life in Words (Bellos), 17, 189, 251–3
Getzler, Pierre, 174, 175
Gilbreth, Frank, 232
Go, 192–3
Goethe, J. W. von, 55, 90, 91
Goffman, Erving, 206, 212, 216
Going, Ralph, 29–30
Goldsmith, Kenneth, 12, 59, 67n, 85, 160
Goncourt Academy, 252–3
Google Street View, 14, 185–6
'Great Palindrome', 56–7, 65n
Gregg, Melissa, 233
grids, 130–1, 176–7, 183–4
Guardian, 136
Gupta, Suboh, 37

halting problem (*Entscheidungsproblem*), 88, 97, 99
Hanley, Miles, 77

Harkin, James, 141
Hausmann, Georges-Eugène, 177
Hegel, G. W. F., 53–4
Hejduk, John, 182–3
Helmlé, Eugen, 12, 90, 249, 255–6n
Henry IV (Shakespeare), 46
Hilbert, David, 88
Hirst, Paul, 173
history, 162, 164
    end of, 53, 54
History of the Lipogram, 28, 162
Hodges, Andrew, 88–9
Hölderlin, Friedrich, 58
Holocaust, 2, 49, 121, 123, 130–1, 159, 175
Holocaust Memorial (Eisenman), 183
Hörspiel, 55–6
Howe, Sarah, 59
Hughes, Francesca, 177
human interest novels, 24
human-computer interaction (HCI), 16–17, 226–8
    skilled typing research, 228–34
Humanities Computing Centre, 92, 193
Humphreys, Lee, 142
hyperrealism, 29–30, 42n
hypertext, 81, 82n

I Remember see Je me souviens
identity, 146
identity politics, 59
indexes, 75–7
indexing, 193
information technology, 190–1; *see also* technology
information-storage-and-retrieval system, 5–6, 193
infra-ordinary, 125–7, 129–30, 136, 145
    ethical writing, 123, 131, 132
    L'infraordinaire, 3, 247
    new anthropology, 146–50
    see also everyday
inoperativity, 54–5
insignificant, 106, 110, 114, 116–17; *see also* infra-ordinary
interaction order, 206
interiority, 113, 128, 129; *see also* infra-ordinary
internet, 59
intertwingled, 71, 82n
intimacy, 139–40
Introduction card of M. Gaspard Winckler, 70
Introduction to Reading Hegel (Queneau), 53
intuition, 89, 97–8
Invisible Cities (Calvino), 172

James, Alison, 86, 122, 133
Jameson, Fredric, 171

Je me souviens (*I Remember*), 3, 17, 36, 158
    Christian Boltanski, 37
    Joachim Schmid, 39
    theatre performances, 248, 249
Je suis né, 247–8
jigsaw puzzles, 35, 77–8, 94, 95–7, 195–7
John, Bonnie, 230
Jones, William, 182
Jouet, Jacques, 157
Joyce, James, 25, 76, 108, 237
Judaism, 56

Kadare, Ismail, 253
Kafka, Franz, 172
'Kafka and His Precursors' (Borges), 165–6
Kalyva, Eve, 79
Kant, Immanuel, 63n
Kaufmann, Vincent, 163
Kenner, Hugh, 76
Kim, Myung Shin, *181*
King Lear (Shakespeare), 45, 46, 48, 61–2, 62n
Kittay, Jeffrey, 236
Klee, Paul, 10, 25–6
'Knight's Tour, The' (*La Polygraphie du cavalier*, Lidl), 33–5, *34*
Kojève, Alexandre, 53–4, 54–5
Kristeva, Julia, 64n

La Boutique obscure, 3, 4, 245
La Clôture, 4, 57
La Disparition (*A Void*), 3, 35, 36–7, 56, 162
    constraint, 142, 157, 159, 194
    Holocaust, 49–50
La Ligne générale (*General Line*), 24–6, 165, 174
La Mémoire et l'Oblique, 248
La Poche Parmentier, 4
La Polygraphie du cavalier [The Knight's Tour] (Lidl), 33–5, *34*
La Vérité sur 'Le Voyage d'hier' (Audin), 166
La Vie mode d'emploi see Life A User's Manual
Lambert, Leopold, 172
language, 25
    computer languages, 59–60
    as data, 85
    and poetry, 55–6, 161–2
language studies, 26
Lanier, Jared, 140
L'Arbre (*The Tree*), 248
L'Attentat de Sarajevo, 2–3, 5
Le Condottière (*Portrait of a Man*), 3, 5, 253
Le Lionnais, François, 3, 27, 85, 170n
Le Lionnais pole, 160
Le Monde, 197
Le Voyage d'hier (*Yesterday's Journey*, Roubaud), 166

Le Voyage d'hiver (*The Winter Journey*), 158, 165, 248, 255n
Le Voyage Obscure (*The Obscure Journey*, Levin Becker), 166
Leak, Andrew, 176
Lederer, Jacques, 25
Lefebvre, Henri, 7–8, 109–10, 120, 137
Leggett, Mike, 79, 80
Leiris, Michael, 121
Lejeune, Philippe, 17, 248
Les Amis de Georges Perec, 252; *see also* Association Georges Perec
Les Choses see Things
Les Lieux, 31, 38, 173, 174–6, 248
Les Lieux d'une fugue, 37
Les Revenentes (*The Exeter Text*), 3, 157
Les Voyages d'hiver & ses suites (*Winter Journeys*), 165–7
L'Espace critique, 174
letters, 61
Leviathan (Auster), 38
Levin Becker, Daniel, 48, 161, 163, 166, 167
LG, 248
Lidl, Christl, 33–5, *34*
life, 8
Life A User's Manual (*La Vie mode d'emploi*), 3, 5, 17, 70, 159, 248, 249
  algorithms, 94, 95, 193–4
  architecture, 176–7
  Calvino on, 172–3
  constraints, 87, 93–8
  English publication, 173
  Games Studies, 190, 191, 195–8
  Go, 192–3
  hyperrealism, 29
  Joachim Schmid, 39
  and *La Polygraphie du cavalier*, 33, 35
  playfulness, 189
  Prix Médicis, 245
  relationship between reader and writer, 26
  Rue Simon-Crubellier, 11–12
  Sophie Calle, 38
  translations, 249–51, 256n
  see also Searching for Rue Simon-Crubellier
lifestyle magazines, 112–13
limitations, 116–17; *see also* constraint
l'infini (Sollers), 253
L'Infraordinaire, 3, 247
lipogram, 159, 162
lists, 129–30, 136–7, 144, 145–6, 147–8, 237
location-sensitive mobile social networking (LMSN), 209–14, *210*, *213*, 217–21, *218*
London Review of Books, 49–50
looped architecture, 177
Lucretius, 86
Lukács, Georg, 107–8, 109, 110, 116, 125

Mabillon Junction, 39
Machine, The (*Die Maschine*), 12, 55–6, 87, 90–2
magazine industry, 112–13
Magné, Bernard, 87, 159, 249
Malaby, Thomas, 191
Mallarmé, Stéphane, 58, 66n, 246
Man Asleep, A (*Un Homme qui dort*), 3, 5, 37, 245, 251, 253
Manovich, Lev, 85
Many Subtle Channels (Levin Becker), 161
market research, 112, 113
Mars-Jones, Adam, 49, 63n
mass media, 26–7, 29–30
materiality, 113–15
mathematical intuition, 89
mathematics, 52, 54, 88
Mathews, Harry, 57, 86, 248
Meaning of Contemporary Realism, The (Lucács), 107–8
mechanical constraints, 93–4
media, 126
  mass media, 26–7, 29–30
  mixed media, 26–7
  new media, 15–16
  residual media, 16, 226, 233
  see also social media
media art, 81–2
media ethics, 123, 131–2
mediation, 132
Memorial to the Murdered Jews of Europe (Eisenman), 183
memory, 129
Meschonnic, Henri, 159
Metaux, 56
metropolis, 205
mezangelle, 60
micro description, 228–34
microblogging, 151n
micro-scale, 124
Milner, Jean-Claude, 66n
Milton, John, 9–10
Miranda, Maria, 11–12, 71–4
Missouri Breaks, The (Penn), 82n
Mitchell, David, 131
Mitchell, Peta, 176
mixed media, 26–7
modality, 48
modernism, 10, 24–6, 28, 116
modernist literature, 109
Moment oulipiens, 157
Monument à Georges Perec – la disparition (Deguelle), 35–6
moral economy of attention, 132–3
morality of constraint, 49–51
Morley, David, 128
Morocco, 115–16

Morris, Kate, 175, 176
Morris, Simon, 42n
Motte, Warren, 65–6n
Mythologies (Barthes), 26

Naor, Idan, *180*
national poetry, 161
natural science, 52, 59
naturalism, 25, 107–8, 109
Netsch, Walter, 178, 182
Neumark, Norie, 11–12, 71–4; see also
 Searching for Rue Simon-Crubellier
neurophysiological research unit, 3, 5, 193
neutrality, 232
New American Picture (Rickard), 185–6
new anthropology, 136–7, 146–50
new media, 15–16; see also location-sensitive mobile social networking (LMSN); social media
New Scientist, 59
Nikki Bangaku tradition, 144
Norman, Donald, 229, 230
nostalgia, 67n
Nouveau Roman, 24, 25, 109
novels, 24, 25

objects, 112, 128–30
Obscure Journey, The (*Le Voyage Obscure*, Levin Becker), 166
Oiseau (Bök), 59
Oracle Machine, 12, 88–9, 97
ordinary affects, 149
ordinary life, 127; see also everyday life
Ørum, Tania, 77
Oulipian author, 158, 160
Oulipian politics, 163–4
Oulipo, 3, 5, 14, 17, 27–8, 64n, 120
 afterlife, 58
 anticipatory plagiarism, 11
 and the avant-garde, 161
 chance/anti-chance, 128
 clinamen, 184
 computation, 122
 constraint, 48, 49, 51, 52, 85–6, 142, 163–5, 194
 creation, 247, 254–5n
 critics, 160, 168n
 ideals, *57*
 impact, 7
 Perec's influence on, 157–9
 potentiality, 10, 98
 programmed constraint, 133
Oupeinpo (Ouvroir de peinture potentielle), 50
Out-of-Sync, 11, 71, 74
Ouvroir de Littératur Potentielle see Oulipo

Pädagogisches Skizzenbuch (Klee), 26
PALF, 87–8, 89–90, 92
palindrome, 56–7, 65n
Parc de la Vilette, 171, 184
particular and general, 108–9, 110, 111
Partisans, 5
Pas un jour (Garréta), 49
Pear Analytics, 139
Peekaboo, 5–6, 193
Penn, Arthur, 83n
Penser/Classer ('Thoughts of Sorts'), 3, 145, 247
Perec, Cyrla Szulewicz, 2
Perec, Georges
 biography, 17, 189, 251–3
 life, 2–4
 Nachlass, 247–53
 oeuvre, 4–7; see also individual titles
Perec, Icek Judko, 2
'Perec's Alternative Topography' (Morris), 176
Perloff, Marjorie, 85
personal computers (PCs), 233, 234–6
personal essays, 144
Phenomenology of Spirit (Hegel), 53
Physics (Aristotle), 54
Picasso, Pablo, 10
Pieces and Other Species of Spaces (de Paula), 32, *33*, 36
'Pierre Menard, Author of the Quixote' (Borges), 166
'Pigeon Reader' (Morris), 42n
Pillow Book, The (Shōnagon), 13, 136–7, 143–6, 148–50
pity, politics of, 132
Place Saint-Sulpice see *Attempt at Exhausting a Place in Paris, An*
places, 209–14; see also *Attempt at Exhausting a Place in Paris, An*; spaces
plagiarism by anticipation, 38–40, 165
play, 192–3, 194–5
playfulness, 193
plays, 227; see also theatre
Poe, Edgar Allan, 58
poetry, 4, 11, 55–62
 and computation, 90–2
 and language, 161–2
 Raymond Queneau, 53–5
Poetry, Etcetera: Cleaning the House (Roubaud), 161–2
politics of aesthetics, 163
politics of constraint, 14, 159, 164
politics of pity, 132
politics of recognition, 14
Popper, Karl, 52
Portrait of a Man (*Le Condottière*), 3, 5, 253
postmodernism, 10, 28

potential, 54–5
potential literature, 53, 74
'Potential Literature' (Queneau), 58
potentiality, 98–9
prelives and afterlives of constraint, 58–60
prepotential literature, 58
Priest, Graham, 54
Printing Out the Internet project (Goldsmith), 59
programmatic constraints, 93–4
programmed constraint, 133
programming, 60, 89
proper distance, 123, 131–2
prose, 53, 54
pseudonymous strangers, 219–21, 223
pseudonymous users, 220
psychological naturalism, 107–8, 109
psychosociologues (psychosociologists), 111–12
public places, 212–14
public spaces, 15, 206, 207
  encounters with strangers, 214–17
Puschman, Cornelius, 136
puzzles, design puzzle, 182–3; *see also* jigsaw puzzles

Quel petit vélo...? (Which Moped...?), 3, 245, 253
Queneau, Raymond, 3, 51, 120
  anti-chance, 161
  Cent mille milliards de poèmes, 27, 53–5, 85–6, 98, 129–30
  creation of Oulipo, 247
  Introduction to Reading Hegel, 53
  mathematics, 52
  'Potential Literature', 58
  'Story as You Like It, A', 92
  Sunday of Life, 54
Queneau pole, 159–60

Rabinow, Paul, 115–16
radio plays, 12, 21, 55–6, 87, 90–2, 227
Rancière, Jacques, 163
Rappolt, Mark, 173, 186–7n
'Raven, The' (Poe), 58
realism, 12, 13, 25–6, 105, 106, 107–8, 109; *see also* hyperrealism
reality, 106
recognition, politics of, 14
Rega Calvos, Eduardo, *180*
Reggiani, Christelle, 23, 52, 86, 164
Reichelt, Leisa, 139
Reig, Christophe, 163, 164
Reinhardt, Ad, 25
relational formulations of places, 211
remembrance, 37
residual media, 16, 226, 233
Retallack, Joan, 59

Review of Contemporary Fiction, The, 5
Rickard, Doug, 185–6
Risam, Roopika, 60
rituals, 115–16
Robbe-Grillet, Alain, 24
'Robert Antelme or the Truth of Literature', 130
Rogers, Richard, 139, 141
Ross, Kristin, 111, 113
Roubaud, Jacques, 3, 7, 98
  53 Days, 248
  history of Oulipo, 158
  Le Voyage d'hier, 166
  Poetry, Etcetera: Cleaning the House, 161–2
  potential, 54
  'Queneau pole' versus 'Le Lionnais pole', 159–60
Rowe, Beverly Charles, 53
Rue Simon-Crubellier, 11, 70
  Searching for Rue Simon-Crubellier, 71–9, 81
Rumelhart, David, 229, 230

Saarländischer Rundfunk, 90
safety, 123, 132
Salthouse, Timothy, 228–9, 230, 234
Salzani, Carlos, 54–5
Sartrian 'committed literature', 24, 109
Schmid, Joachim, 39–40
Schwartz, Oscar, 59–60
Schwartz, Paul, 2, 3
science, 52, 59
Science of Logic (Hegel), 54
Searching for Rue Simon-Crubellier, 71–9, 81
'Second Manifesto' (Le Lionnais), 170n
Second World War, 2, 121, 123, 126–7, 159
self, 128
semiology, 115
Shakespeare, William, 11, 45, 46–7, 61, 69
Sheringham, Michael, 7, 121, 125, 133, 137, 146–7
Sherman, Cindy, 38
Shōnagon, Sei, 13, 136–7, 143–6, 148–50
'Signe particulier: NÉANT' ('Distinguishing Features: NIL'), 37
significant, 106, 116–17; *see also* insignificant
Silverstone, Roger, 123, 132
skilled typing research, 227–34
Sloterdijk, Peter, 171
Smith, Brian Reffin, 50
Smith, Terry, 174
social change, 109, 111
social media, 13, 136–7, 138, 149
  banality of, 138–41
  form, 141–3
  lists, 145

social networking, 208; *see also* location-sensitive mobile social networking (LMSN)
Sollers, Philippe, 253
SOM, 178, 182
Sonate für ältere Schreibmaschine ('Sonata for an Ageing Typewriter'), 227
Sorkin, Michael, 183
space, 30–1, 206
spaces, 14, 15–16, 175–6, 206, 207; *see also* places; UnSightly/UnSitely
Spahr, Juliana, 59, 67n
Species of Spaces (*Espèces d'espaces*), 3, 30–1, 32, 122, 126, 173
Sphinx (Garréta), 164
Spoerri, Daniel, 30
'Statement of Intent', 4, 28–9, 165
Stein, Alejandro, *181*
Stella, Frank, 25
Stewart, Kathleen, 149
Stoic Comedians, The (Kenner), 76
'Story as You Like It, A' (Queneau), 92
strangers in public places, 214–17
  pseudonymous strangers, 219–21, 223
substructure, constraint as, 47–8
Sunday of Life (Queneau), 54
surrealism, 27, 161
symbolism, 115
systematic versatility, 98, 121

tableux-pièges, 30
Tarde, Gabrielle, 137
Taussig, Michael, 142–3
technology, 15–16, 87, 208
  and ethical writing, 124–5
  Google Street View, 185–6
  location-sensitive mobile social networking (LMSN), 209–14, *210*, *213*, 217–21, *218*
  see also human-computer interaction (HCI); new media; residual media; social media
Tel Quel collective, 64n
television, 4
Tentative d'épuisement d'un lieu parisien see Attempt at Exhausting a Place in Paris, An
Tentative d'épuisement I/II (Aballí), 36
theatre, 4, 17, 79–81, 248, 249
Théâtre I, 4
theatre of the Absurd, 24
Things (*Les Choses*), 3, 5, 17, 26, 37, 111–15, 126, 129
  capitalism, 8
  language, 26
  lists, 129, 146
  Renaudot Prize, 245
  style, 253
  translations, 251, 255n
'Things That Should Be Short' (Shōnagon), 144
'Thinkers for Architects', 172
Thomas, Jean-Jacques, 86
'Thoughts of Sorts' (*Penser/Classer*), 3, 145, 247
timid encounters, 221
'Tlön, Uqbar, Orbis Tertius' (Borges), 166
total book, 165
'Towards a Semiology of Paragrams' (Kristeva), 64n
town planning, 30
transcription typists, 228
translations, 249–51, 253, 255–6n
trap pictures, 30
Tree, The (*L'Arbre*), 248
trends, 148–9
Troilus and Cressida (Shakespeare), 46
trompe d'oeil, 30
Tschumi, Bernard, 171, 184–5
Turing, Alan, 12, 87–9, 90, 91, 99
Turing machine, 88
Turing Test, 59–60
'Twelve Sidelong Glances', 143, 146, 148
Twitter, 13, 136–7, 148, 149
  banality of, 138–41
  form, 141–3
  lists, 145
Tyc-Dymont, Suzanne, 227
typewriters, 227
typing *see* skilled typing research
typing errors, 229
'TYPIST' (John), 230

Ulcérations, 57
Ulysses (Joyce), 76, 77
Un Cabinet d'amateur (*A Gallery Portrait*), 5
Un Homme qui dort (*A Man Asleep*), 3, 5, 37, 245, 251, 253
uncreative writing, 59, 85
uncreativity, 160
'Under Constraint' (Walker), 177, 178
Universal Dictionary of Letters, 162
universal machine, 88, 90, 91, 99
unoriginal genius, 85
UnSearching, 71–4, 78–9
UnSightly/UnSitely, 74–9, 83n
Unsitely Aesthetics (Miranda), 74
UNWORD (Breakwell), 79, *80*
urban landscapes, 30
urban sociology, 206, 207
urban spaces, 14; *see also Attempt at Exhausting a Place in Paris, An*
Urban Studies, 206

US, 25
US 4651993 Design game and modules for use therein (Netsch), 182

Vernier, Hugo, 165
'Verse in the Universe: The Scientific Power of Poetry' (Firth), 59
video games *see* Games Studies
Vidler, Anthony, 183
Virilio, Paul, 3–4, 174, 232, 235
Voeux, 57
Void, A see La Disparition

W or The Memory of Childhood (*W ou le souvenire d'enfance*), 3, 4, 245, 248
    Christian Boltanski, 37
    constraint, 159, 198
    English translation, 251
    everyday, 126–7
    Games Studies, 190
    Joachim Schmid, 39
    play, 192, 196
Walker, Enrique, 173, 177–8
Wandrers Nachtlied (Goethe), 55, 90, 91
Wang, Rui, *181*
Wark, McKenzie, 190

What They Remember (Boltanski), 37
Which Moped...? (*Quel petit vélo...?*), 3, 245, 253
Whyte, William H., 206
Willim, Robert, 235
Winter Journey, The (*Le Voyage d'hiver*), 158, 165, 248, 255n
Winter Journey, The (Vernier), 165
Winter Journeys (*Le Voyage d'hiver & ses suites*), 165–7
Wittkower, Rudolf, 183
Woolf, Virginia, 108
Word Index to Ulysses (Hanley), 77
'Work of Memory, The', 122
working memory, 129

Xenotext Experiment, The (Bök), 59

Yesterday's Journey (*Le Voyage d'hier*, Roubaud), 166
You Are Not a Gadget (Lanier), 140
Young, Stephanie, 59, 67n

Zaera-Polo, Alejandro, 185
Zappavigna, Michele, 151n
Zuihitsu genre, 144